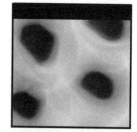

Strategies for
Web Hosting and
Managed Services

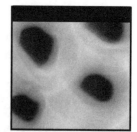

Strategies for
Web Hosting and
Managed Services

Doug Kaye

Wiley Computer Publishing

John Wiley & Sons, Inc.

NEW YORK · CHICHESTER · WEINHEIM · BRISBANE · SINGAPORE · TORONTO

Publisher: Robert Ipsen
Editor: Cary Sullivan
Managing Editor: Gerry Fahey
Text Design & Composition: Carlisle Communications

Designations used by companies to distinguish their products are often claimed as trademarks. In all instances where John Wiley & Sons, Inc., is aware of a claim, the product names appear in initial capital or ALL CAPITAL LETTERS. Readers, however, should contact the appropriate companies for more complete information regarding trademarks and registration.

This book is printed on acid-free paper. ∞

Published by John Wiley & Sons, Inc., New York

Published simultaneously in Canada.

This publication is designed to provide accurate and authoritative information in regard to the subject matter covered. It is sold with the understanding that the publisher is not engaged in professional services. If professional advice or other expert assistance is required, the services of a competent professional person should be sought.

Printed in the United States of America.

10 9 8 7 6 5 4 3 2 1

*To Cessna, my wife and partner, who makes
so many great things possible.*

Contents

Acknowledgments

To the extent that this book is valuable, I owe much gratitude to a team of superb reviewers. This isn't just a frivolous thanks. If you'd seen the manuscript before these folks got their red pens out, you'd know exactly what I meant.

First, thanks go to my wife, Cessna, for agonizing over every word in every chapter, finding ways for me to more clearly express what's important, and to call my bluff on the things that weren't. Thank goodness no one else, not even the reviewers, had to endure the first draft.

I owe a very special thanks to a core team of four extraordinary technical reviewers who pushed me on every point: Paul Guth (Wired Digital), Tim McNerney (Truis), Jason Monberg (Carbon Five), and Lloyd Taylor (Keynote Systems). Also part of my "A" team, I owe thanks to Nancy Kieffer for her persistent (and fast) copyediting.

The reviewers who provided specific feedback on one or more chapters were Ken Beames (JPMorgan Chase & Co.), Cliff Bernstein (Internet Health Resources), Bob Hammond (Mirror Image Internet), Steve Page (Matrix Logic), Mike Palmer, Patrick Rogers (Scale Eight), Hal Speed (epicRealm), Chris Tacy, Jen Wang, and Jon Zeeff (SolidSpeed Networks).

As source material I interviewed more than 40 industry and technology experts (some of whom provided additional feedback) including Rolyn Acosta and Tim Wilson (Digital Island), Rachel Albert and Alan Thompson (SiteSmith), Dave Asprey and John Pecoraro (Exodus), Dan Berkowitz, Matt Parks, Jason Pfannenstiel, Roger Hayes, David Talovic, and Lloyd Taylor (Keynote Systems), Cliff Bernstein (Internet Health Resources), Brian Bershad (Appliant), Pierre Bouchard and Mark Law (Navisite), Dave Donohue and Patrick Rogers (Scale Eight), Kevin Epstein, (Inktomi), Jeff Fisher, Josh Krasnegor, and Eric Wilson (FusionStorm), Amy Forbus, and Richard Yoo (Rackspace), Bob Hammond (Mirror Image Internet), Warren Hart (IBM), George Kurtz (Foundstone), Asa Lanum (Fortel), Robin Lawson (the ASP Consortium), Larry Lenhart (CAT Technology), Keith Lowry and Phil Simmonds (Pilot Networks), Tim McNerney (Truis), Sharmilla Mulligan (Totality), Michael Pusateri (ithought.com), John Quarterman (Matrix), Marina Rosales (Activa), Doug Schneider (Verio), Bruce Schneier (Counterpane), Cliff Skolnick (Steam Tunnel Operations), Gordon Smith (Speedera Networks), Hal Speed (epicRealm), and Jon Zeeff (SolidSpeed Networks).

Thanks to Bruce Schneier for his New York City car alarm analogy and for his excellent books on security; to Lloyd Taylor for the Sun Tzu quotation; to Cliff Skolnick for being the person I can (and do) always call on for pragmatic help on the most technical issues, and for naming the web-hosting idiot savant concept; and to Randy Hawkins, for bailing me out on Memorial Day weekend when I managed to cast adrift my own domain registration in an attempt to fix it.

For their help navigating the twisty passages of the publishing maze, thanks to my agent, Neil Salkind, the rest of the Studio B gang, and the entire editorial and production team at John Wiley & Sons. And finally, a very special thanks to Cary Sullivan, my editor at John Wiley & Sons, not only for her personal help with the manuscript, but for being the one editor, more than any other, who understood the need for this book and had the courage to fight for it.

Preface

In my day job as a strategic technology consultant, I help my clients develop and execute their web-hosting strategies. One day, a client casually suggested, "You ought to write a book." Little did he—or I—know that I'd take his suggestion seriously.

I fully expected that a trip to the local bookstore would dissuade me from this fantasy by convincing me such a book wasn't necessary. Certainly, I assumed, there must already be dozens of books on web hosting among the hundreds of Internet- and web-related titles. Web hosting is a multibillion dollar industry, after all. Yet, a search on the shelves and online for "web hosting" yielded remarkably little. Likewise, when I polled a few CIOs, CTOs, and webmasters as to what was on their personal bookshelves, they read me the usual assortment of titles addressing specific technologies, but not a single book about web hosting per se, and certainly none about the strategies for outsourcing it.

With so many books available about other aspects of the Internet and the World Wide Web, why are there so few on web hosting? The web is still a new platform, and we're still learning how to use it. Even with the shakeout of the dot-coms, the web remains exciting and glamorous, just as television was in its early days. Also, like TV, most of the excitement, glamour, and helpful books on the subject are focused on the *development of content,* in this case, building cool, or killer, web sites.

By comparison, the day-to-day *operation* of web sites is considered mundane. Everyone wants to build a web site. No one wants the headaches of keeping one running. Operations are seen as neither exciting nor glamorous, and they get very little attention except from those who have operational responsibility as part of their job descriptions. As unglamorous as running a web site may be, however, it's the very place where organizations quietly spend most of their time and money on the Internet, and where decisions have the greatest impact on a company's bottom line.

Strategies for Web Hosting and Managed Services is written with this strategic (i.e., business-driven) perspective toward technology. One early manuscript reviewer described it as, "addressing strategic issues for business-challenged sysadmins (system administrators)." It's my hope that the book will be equally as effective at explaining web-hosting infrastructure issues to technically challenged web-site owners, managers, and executives.

Those in the web-hosting industry have a way to go before they can say they're doing a good job. And throughout this book I've tried to set a high bar. By that I mean that, in addition to describing vendor offerings as they are today, I often describe vendor offerings as I think they ought to be. In most instances, you'll be able to find at least one vendor that follows a recommendation, but you won't find any vendor that follows them all. In a few instances, particularly regarding service level agreements (SLAs), you probably won't find any vendors that do what I think they should. Perhaps, a few years from now, SLAs with real teeth in them will be common, and maybe someone will point to this book as one of the catalysts responsible for that change. That would be very satisfying. In the meantime, I've got to admit that setting the bar high is easy. Being a writer/consultant, I'm not the one who has to jump over it.

Doug Kaye
doug@rds.com
July 2001

Introduction

The phone rang. I squinted at the clock radio. 2:12 A.M.

"Doug, the site is down again, and the board meeting is at 8:00 A.M. Fix it."

It was my boss, our CEO, and it was the third night in a row he'd called to deliver the same news. Bad enough that the site was down—again—but even worse because the CEO knew about the outage before I did. Embarrassing, to say the least.

Keeping the web site up and running was my job. At least as long as I *had* a job. I was the one who had selected our web-hosting service, and it was letting me down. As I stumbled over to my computer to see what I could do to solve the problem from home, I had already made up my mind: I needed to move our site to a new web-hosting service.

This scene is repeated hundreds of times, every night, with a cast of system administrators, CTOs, and CIOs who are responsible for the successful operation of web sites. *Strategies for Web Hosting and Managed Services* is for those sysadmins and their managers. May it help them sleep more soundly.

A Book to the Rescue

Strategies for Web Hosting and Managed Services won't help you restart a web server at 2:12 in the morning. It will, however, make it less likely that you'll have to. Likewise, it's not one of the hundreds of books that will help you build or develop a web site. Rather it will help you *manage* a site that's already been built.

There are two groups of people who need this book: (1) those who've already made bad web-hosting decisions and (2) those who will. Those of you in group one know who you are. Everyone else falls into group two.

Perhaps in five or ten years, selecting a web-hosting vendor will be as easy as picking a long-distance telephone company. Okay—maybe it's not all that easy to pick a long-distance telephone company, but at least the risk of picking the wrong one is low, and it's easy to change vendors if you discover you've made a mistake. But if you've ever had to switch web-hosting services (i.e., you're in group one), you know how very painful and expensive it can be. It hurts much more than you ever imagined. Those of you in group two will get a good idea of what to expect from the rest of this book.

This book was written with three types of people in mind:

Techies. For hands-on system administrators and their managers who have the responsibility for selecting and working with web-hosting services, this book will help you relate your technical knowledge and experience to the business perspective of web-site operations. By the time you finish this book, you'll be able to incorporate sound business methodologies in your planning and decision-making processes, and be able to explain and justify your decisions to nontechnical managers. If you're in this group, read the whole book.

Nontechies. This book is also written for those of you who are looking at web-hosting from the opposite point of view. Whether you have the responsibility of making web-hosting decisions, or just want to know that your IT staff is making them correctly, this book will add a technical perspective to your business-oriented approach. After reading this book, not only will you know much more about the technological issues surrounding web hosting, but you'll also be well protected against someone trying to fool you with technobabble or geek-speak. If you're in this group, make sure you read everything through Part Three, "Strategies." Venture further only if you feel up to it.

Small-site owners. Many (but by no means all) of the issues and examples in this book come from the world of large-scale web-site hosting. But fear not. Chapter 4, "Shared and Dedicated Servers," is written just for you. Furthermore, you'll learn some very important strategies and tactics from reading about all the things that can go wrong for the big guys.

How This Book Is Organized

This book follows a logical process that will enable you to make informed web-hosting decisions and to successfully manage your relationships with web-hosting services and MSPs.

In Part One, "Perspectives," we'll look at the web-hosting marketplace and the categories of web-hosting services. We'll also discuss the pros and cons of outsourcing, then look at the relationships of the individual components of web-site operations, and consider which of them should be outsourced.

In Part Two, "The Vendors, we'll dig deeper into each of the four categories of web-hosting vendors (shared servers, dedicated servers, colocation, and MSPs) and examine the services offered by the vendors in each category.

Part Three, "Strategies," addresses a number of issues surrounding the selection and ongoing management of a web-hosting service. We'll start with the problems and fears of outsourcing, including the risks of lock-in and loss of control. Next we'll consider strategies for successful outsourcing, followed by a formal risk-management process. That will take us into a discussion of service level agreements (SLAs) and some additional strategies, such as how to leverage resources shared with other customers; whether it's better to buy, lease, or rent hardware; and how to manage applications and content. This part concludes with the development of web-site traffic models and a discussion of how to use them.

Part Four, "Technologies," explores the technical issues, beginning with web-site architectures. Next we'll examine caching and content delivery networks (CDNs) and the issues surrounding Internet connectivity practices. This part concludes with in-depth studies of storage, backup and recovery, and security technologies and strategies.

Part Five, "Tools," includes tips on diagnosing connectivity problems, web-site monitoring, a *net detective* toolkit for researching vendors and, registering and managing domain names and the Domain Name Service (DNS), and references to additional on- and offline resources.

TIP **Throughout this book you'll see tips such as this one. Each relates to the context in which it appears. For example, if you're within a chapter on shared-server vendors, the recommendations in that chapter will be specific to selecting such a vendor.**

The Companion Web Site

Outsourcing web-site operations is the right decision for most web-site owners, but it's not a low-risk undertaking. During the months I spent writing *Strategies for Web Hosting and Managed Services*, some of the vendors I interviewed or used as examples changed their offerings in fundamental ways, were acquired, or filed for bankruptcy. Between the time I'm writing this and the time you're reading it, all vendor-specific bets are off. I'm certain some of the few companies I've mentioned by name will be gone. I just don't know which ones. Therefore, although I can't recommend specific vendors in these pages, I've given you the tools to select your own and to protect yourself as much as possible from the volatility in the web-hosting marketplace.

I mention very few vendors by name in this book, and when I do, they serve only as examples. Neither do I name web-hosting vendors because of the remarkable volatility in this still-nascent industry. The Appendix, "Resources," is particularly vulnerable, so check the official web site that accompanies this book at www.wiley.com/compbooks/kaye for updates. There you'll find the following important resources:

- Downloadable copies of all of the spreadsheet files presented in this book
- A chapter-by-chapter recap of the tips
- An updated bibliography
- Links to other online web-hosting resources

You can also find these and other features at my own web site, www.rds.com. I also invite your feedback via email to doug@rds.com.

Perspectives

You've built a great web site. Now you just need someone to keep it running. How hard could that be? Certainly not as hard as it was building it in the first place, right? You could do this yourself, but the vast majority of web sites are turning to a whole new industry of web-hosting services to outsource some or all aspects of their ongoing web site operations.

Not long ago there was no World Wide Web at all, so who could imagine there would be an entire industry dedicated to housing and operating Internet data centers. Today that industry includes more than 15,000 web-hosting services that range from Bobby's Servers-in-a-Closet to large, publicly traded companies with market capitalizations in the tens of billions of dollars.

Navigating through this maze of web-hosting and managed service providers can be a nightmare, and, I can say from my own experience and that of many others, there's almost no way to make the right decisions the first time without help. Even people who are trying to select a hosting service for their second or third time tell me it's still difficult.

Unlike other decisions one has to make in the course of getting and keeping a business online, the selection of a hosting or management vendor is very high risk. In particular, the cost of making the *wrong* decision can be great. For many new-economy businesses, their web sites *are* their businesses. If the site is down, so are they. Over time, even traditional bricks-and-mortar businesses have come to depend on their web sites being up and available to their customers.

Selecting the wrong vendor and suffering frequent or lengthy outages of your web site are bad enough, but you won't really feel the pain until you need to relocate your site to another hosting service. The *switching costs*—the impact of changing hosting services—are extraordinary. As an old saying goes, the only thing worse than a fire is a move. So true is this that you'll tend to stick with a weak provider far longer than you should, and at that point you'll be stuck with managing a dysfunctional vendor relationship on an ongoing, day-to-day basis. Ugh.

The premise of *Strategies for Web Hosting and Managed Services* is that you can select the right vendors the first time, and manage those vendors more effectively through good strategic planning. We'll begin our exploration of this concept in Part One, "Perspectives," by laying the foundation for the in-depth sections that follow.

In Chapter 1, "Web-Hosting Options," we'll look at your web-hosting needs relative to those of others, and we'll introduce the classifications by which we'll segregate the various web-hosting service vendors. We'll then discuss the benefits of outsourcing web-site operations and consider when it makes more sense to keep them in house.

In Chapter 2, "The Components of Web Hosting," we'll present another perspective that's helpful in breaking down the offerings of various vendors. The *service component pyramid* will provide structure to our discussions by showing how the various components of web hosting are segregated, how they relate to one another, and which of them are typically provided by vendors in each of the categories.

Web-Hosting Options

Why do so many web-hosting decisions seem to go wrong?

Handing over the responsibility for web-site operations to a web-hosting service or *managed service provider* (MSP) is a form of *outsourcing*. Information technology (IT) departments have been outsourcing for decades, but as the web is relatively new, outsourcing the operation of a web site is still a nascent process. The oldest vendors have been in the web-hosting business only since 1995, and most for far less time than that. Likewise, few web-hosting customers have had experience with more than one vendor, and certainly not for more than a few years.

It's not that web-hosting vendors aren't trying and doing the best they can. But they're being asked to build and manage computer and networking systems to handle unpredictable and, in some cases, overwhelming demand. Many pre-Internet processes and tools simply don't work in this new environment. For these reasons—the lack of experience of both customers and vendors, compounded by the lack of standards in the web-hosting business—selecting a web-hosting service is a difficult task.

Web-hosting services (like web sites) come in all shapes and sizes. Some are large and some are small. Some are expensive and some are cheap. And of course, some are good while others are. . . not so good. You can get a perspective on the range of web-hosting services just by flipping to the back of almost any Internet trade magazine. There you'll see page after page of advertisements for web-hosting services offering what appear to be terrific bargains: $29.95 per month, $9.95 per month, and even free web hosting. Then turn to the editorial section of the same magazine, and you'll likely

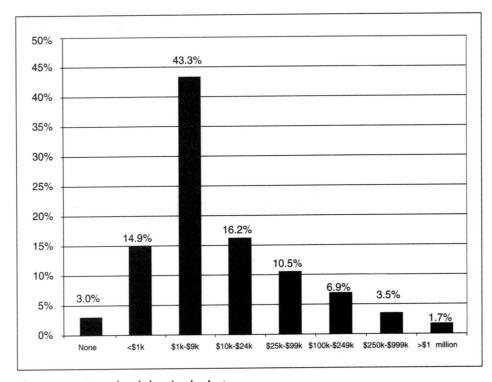

Figure 1.1   Annual web-hosting budgets.

ActivMedia Research (www.activmediaresearch.com)

find an article about a company that is spending hundreds of thousands of dollars per month for its web hosting.

Ten dollars to $100,000 per month? That's a 10,000:1 ratio—quite a range for a single group of products or services. So before we get into the details, it's probably worthwhile to find out where you fit into this huge arena we generically call web hosting.

The chart in Figure 1.1 shows the distribution of annual web-hosting budgets for U.S. businesses. The average budget is on the order of $1,200 to $1,800 per year ($100 to $150 per month), but note that more than 10 percent of all businesses surveyed spend more than $100,000 per year.

Because of such a tremendous range of offerings, one might think that the services at one end of the spectrum are very different from those at the other end. In fact, these services are far more alike than they are different. For example, all web sites, no matter how small or how large, require web servers, domain name services, backup and recovery, and (of course) connections to the Internet. But it would be nearly impossible to analyze as a single group this wide range of offerings that fall under the web-hosting umbrella. In order to keep our analysis more manageable, and to keep the results more relevant to specific readers, we'll begin by segregating the vendors into categories, then study each category in detail.

The Categories

After a few years of confusion over the various types of web hosting available, the vendors have settled into four distinct service categories. Nearly everyone in the web-hosting industry and the trade press has universally accepted these categories. As a result, the categories are now consistent and helpful in distinguishing the many vendors.

In the least expensive, or low-end, category are *shared servers*. As their name implies, these are computer systems that are shared by more than one web site, and hence are appropriate for small, simple, low-traffic sites.

Next on the list are *dedicated servers*. These are nearly identical to shared servers with the obvious exception that they're not shared but rather dedicated to a single web site or to multiple web sites owned and controlled by the same business entity. As compared to shared servers, dedicated servers offer more capacity, flexibility, and better security, but at a higher price.

The next category is a substantial step away from the previous categories, but in some ways it's a step backward. Instead of offering more support than is available from shared- and dedicated-server web-hosting services, *colocation* is a rather bare-bones service that merely houses servers in a data center and connects those servers to the Internet. It doesn't include the server hardware or any of the software and services that are necessary to operate a web site. Colocation by itself is aimed at customers who want to supply and manage their own web-site hardware and software, but who don't want to provide their own physical facilities and may not want to manage their links to the Internet.

In the early days of the web, any organization that was building a web site large enough to be located at a colocation service was also large enough to hire its own staff to manage that web site around the clock. Such companies had little choice, since there were no vendors offering management services for large-scale sites, and the only way these companies could obtain the expertise necessary to run such a web site was to hire the system administrators, database administrators, and network engineers that knew how to do it.

Over time, two changes occurred. First, those system administrators, database administrators (DBAs), and network engineers who knew how to run large web sites became harder and harder to find and more and more expensive when they could be found. Second, a new subgroup called *managed service providers* (MSPs)—our fourth and final category—appeared in 1997 to address the huge gap between the bare-bones offerings of colocation services and the needs of owners of major web sites. Colocation services and MSPs have developed truly symbiotic relationships in which one could not succeed without the other, and the combination of these two services is often the best choice for high-end web sites.

Application Service Providers

You may be wondering why we haven't mentioned *application service providers* (ASPs). While this book could contain an entire section on ASPs, it would be notably out of place, because ASPs, for the most part, aren't infrastructure providers. In fact, many

ASPs are themselves customers of web-hosting services, and many MSPs view ASPs as prospective customers.

Application service providers (no surprise) provide *application* services. For example, an ASP might offer hosting of *enterprise resource planning* (ERP) applications such as manufacturing, order entry, warehousing, accounting, and human resources developed by software vendors such as PeopleSoft, SAP, and Oracle. In these cases, the hosting isn't for the public World Wide Web, but rather for corporate intranets.

The distinction between web-hosting services, MSPs, and ASPs isn't simply a matter of experience with public Internet versus corporate intranets, but rather the additional skills that web-hosting services and MSPs have that go far beyond application packages. Some ASPs offer hosting of web-based applications, but the expertise of these companies tends to be in applications such as specific third-party e-commerce packages, not in supporting technologies such as Internet connectivity, DNS, security, firewalls, web servers, and operating systems. For help with these supporting technologies, most ASPs—like most web-site owners—turn to web-hosting vendors and MSPs.

Outsourcing

All four categories of web-hosting services fall into the practice called outsourcing—an arrangement in which one company provides services to another company, where such services typically have been provided in-house. Outsourcing is a trend that's becoming more common in information technology and other industries for services that have previously been regarded as intrinsic to managing a business. In some cases, the entire IT management of a company is outsourced. Outsourcing agreements can range from large contracts—in which a company like EDS manages IT services for a company like General Motors—to the practice of hiring contractors and temporary office workers on an individual basis.

Benefits of Outsourcing

Primarily, this book answers the question of *how* to outsource, but it would be a huge mistake to skip over the obvious first question of *why* to outsource. Understanding the why behind outsourcing lays the foundation for the how decisions you'll eventually need to make.

Why would you want to outsource your web hosting? What do you hope to achieve? The following five criteria will help you evaluate the benefits.

Focus. Is configuring routers or making DNS changes a good use of your time or that of your staff? Is it your area of expertise? Probably not. The classic argument for outsourcing is that it allows you to focus on your strengths and what's unique about your business.

Cost. Ask yourself, "Do I have the budget to build a data center with multiple diesel generators, biometric controls for physical access, security cameras, and alarms? Can I afford an on-site 24/7 staff of system administrators, hardware technicians, and database administrators?" Probably not.

A web-hosting service, on the other hand, can amortize these costs over many customers and web sites. This not only saves money (some of which is hopefully passed on to you), but it also allows the hosting service to provide services and facilities that would never be practical for a single web site to provide on its own.

You should expect to save money by outsourcing, although it's sometimes difficult to determine whether in fact you're saving anything since in-house and outsourced services can be so different. For example, let's say you're currently hosting your own web site, and your 24/7 support staff consists of just one guy with a pager. You can't directly compare the services you're currently receiving to those you'd expect from hosting at a data center fully staffed by on-site 24/7 technicians. While the latter is true 24/7 support, the former works only so long as the guy with a pager remains available and motivated. What happens when he's out sick or on vacation?

Speed. Even if you could afford it, you probably couldn't build a team and assemble the components of in-house hosting on your own in anywhere near the time frame that the outsourced hosting service team can. Since your vendor will already have such a team in place, you should expect them to help you get your web site up and running more quickly than your existing, less robust staff. Of course, if your site is being hosted at a facility that charges $19.95 per month, you've got to be realistic about what services you're going to get for that price.

Quality. You should expect that outsourcing will result in a higher quality of operations than if the same tasks were performed in-house. (If not, why would you outsource?) In Chapter 10, "Service Level Agreements," we'll examine how SLAs can help you and your vendor agree on the standards by which you'll measure the quality of the services you receive.

Confidence. Confidence is the inverse of risk. There are many things that can go wrong with a web site, and your outsourcing provider has likely encountered most of them already. We'll discuss how you can increase your confidence, and that of your senior management, by reducing many of the risks associated with outsourced web hosting.

The In-House Hosting Option

As compelling as the advantages of outsourcing may be, some organizations still choose to host their web sites in-house. Organizations that have valid reasons for hosting in-house typically share one or more characteristics:

- They have existing IT staffs that already handle 24/7 support.
- They have midsized web sites. (Companies with small, low-traffic web sites typically outsource because they can't justify the cost of staff. Those with large, high-traffic web sites, on the other hand, tend toward outsourcing because they can't provide adequate data center facilities or Internet connectivity at their own locations.)
- They are Internet-based enterprises for which web technologies are a must-have core competency.
- Their businesses and back-end systems are tightly integrated with the web.

Perhaps you do have the option of hosting your web site in-house, and maybe you could manage it using your own staff, but the vast majority of managers and web-site owners faced with this decision are electing to outsource some or all aspects of their on-going web-site operations. Today there are simply too many compelling reasons to outsource web hosting, the most important of which will be presented in this book.

So many people have made the decision to outsource that it has created a fast-growing web-hosting industry that didn't exist a few years ago. That industry now includes more than 15,000 web-hosting vendors. Some industry analysts expect the annual revenues from web hosting to exceed $20 billion by 2005.

Clearly, you can choose *not* to outsource your web hosting. Just consider that you will, in effect, be going into the web-hosting business, but with only one customer: your own organization. You'll have to hire, develop, and maintain a staff with all of the required expertise, whereas those who outsource hosting can focus their resources in areas that more effectively leverage their companies' core competencies.

In fact, you may decide to outsource some aspects of your web hosting but not others. In the next chapter, "The Components of Web Hosting," we'll break down web hosting into the logical pieces that we'll use throughout the remainder of this book and according to which you should make your outsourcing decisions.

The Components
of Web Hosting

In Part Two of this book, "Vendors," we'll explore in depth the four categories of web hosting: shared, dedicated, colocation, and managed services. But before we do, we need to understand the actual *service components* that make up the product offerings of the vendors in each class.

Service components don't exist in isolation. Each component depends on others. So even before we discuss the service components one by one, it's important to understand how they relate to one another and how the components logically fall into groups.

The Service Component Pyramid

The *service component pyramid* in Figure 2.1 clearly illustrates the relationships of the separate components of web hosting. Each layer generally supports the layers above it, and likewise depends on the layers below it. For example, operating-system software provides an environment for application servers yet requires hardware on which to run.

The dependencies in the service component pyramid are not particularly strict. For example, load balancing does not require generic monitoring in order to function. Generally speaking, however, those services toward the top of the pyramid are referred to as being relatively higher level as compared to those below them, which are described as relatively lower level. Higher-level components tend to depend on lower-level ones, whereas the opposite is not true.

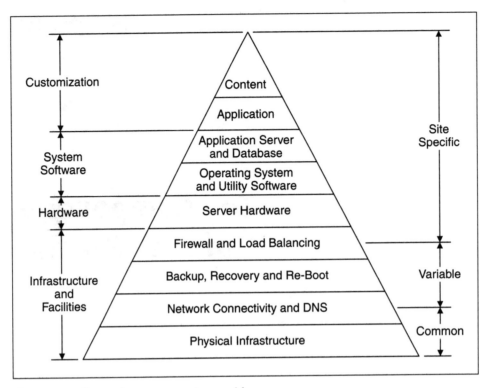

Figure 2.1   The service component pyramid.

The notations on the left side of the service component pyramid divide the services into four groups for convenient reference. Along the right side, another set of notations indicates which services are typically common (sharable) across multiple web sites operated by a hosting service, and which are more likely to be dedicated to each individual site. The group in between—labeled "variable"—contains services that can be either shared or dedicated.

Which Services Should Be Outsourced?

The service component pyramid doesn't contain every component or service of web hosting, but it does include all the major ones. In general, the farther down a component is in the pyramid, the better the argument for outsourcing it. For instance, no matter where you host your web site, you're not likely to generate your own electricity, which is part of physical infrastructure at the bottom of the pyramid. You may, however, want to control your own content or write your own applications (shown near the top of Figure 2.1).

When evaluating which services to outsource and which to keep in-house, start at the bottom of the pyramid and work your way up. At some point, you'll likely identify the first (lowest-level) service to be kept in-house. You'll probably want to keep in-house all of the services above it as well.

In some cases, such as when working with a managed service provider (MSP), you'll outsource the lowest-level services to one company (a colocation service), outsource a middle tier of services to an MSP, and keep in-house the top-tier services.

It may even make sense to outsource all the components in the pyramid. In some cases, the same people who design the web site will also take responsibility for its operation. But if yours is an e-commerce site (i.e., orders are accepted online) then your organization will likely have no choice but to be involved in its operation. On the other hand, if your web site contains only marketing content (sometimes referred to as *brochureware*) and doesn't allow visitors to place orders online, you can outsource all aspects of design and operation, just as your company may already be doing for advertising or other services.

Even for a web site containing only marketing content, however, the designers would typically further outsource to third parties all services except the application and content at the very peak of the pyramid. The skills that go into designing a site—even a site that is very technical in nature—are not the same as those required to keep that site running 24 hours a day.

In this first part, we've taken a brief look at the components of web hosting (as illustrated by the service component pyramid), we've answered the question of whether or not to outsource, and—for those who elect to outsource—we've addressed some of the considerations to help determine which services to outsource and which to keep in-house. We'll use the service component pyramid again in the next section, Part Two, "Vendors," as we consider the service offerings of the vendors in each category of web hosting. We'll continue our discussion of the philosophy of outsourcing in Part Three, "Strategies."

PART Two

The Vendors

We'll begin our in-depth study of web-hosting and managed services with a look at the vendors and the services they offer. In this section we'll answer the following questions:

What's available? Chapter 3, "Comparing Vendor Categories," sets the stage by looking at areas in which web-hosting services differ: services, capacity, and cost.

What do I need to know about each of the specific categories? The next chapters explore the categories of web-hosting services in depth:

- Chapter 4, "Shared and Dedicated Services," explores the vendors that offer these low-cost solutions for generally simple web sites.

- Chapter 5, "Colocation," examines this no-frills web-hosting services that's typically used by web-site owners who prefer to manage their own servers.

- Chapter 6, "Managed Services," looks at the newest breed of vendors that provide a high level of service and support in conjunction with colocation.

By the end of this section you should know which category of vendor is right for you, and be ready to begin your vendor selection process.

Comparing Vendor Categories

We've divided the universe of web hosting services into four categories: shared servers, dedicated servers, colocation, and managed services. These are the generally accepted categories within the web-hosting industry; but to understand them more completely— enough to know which category is the best for your web site—we're going to examine their similarities and differences from three different perspectives:

Service components. First we'll go back to the *service component pyramid* to explore how the service categories differ according to the specific components they offer.

Traffic. Next we'll compare the number of *hits, page views,* or *bytes* of web traffic each category of service is intended to accommodate.

Cost. Finally, we'll look at the typical budgets of the web sites that use the web-hosting services in each category.

Service Components

The most important differences between the categories of web-hosting vendors are the services they provide. To highlight these differences we'll again make use of the service component pyramid introduced in Chapter 2, "The Components of Web Hosting." The pyramid is the same, but in Figure 3.1 there's a new scale along the right-hand side that shows the services offered by the vendors in each category.

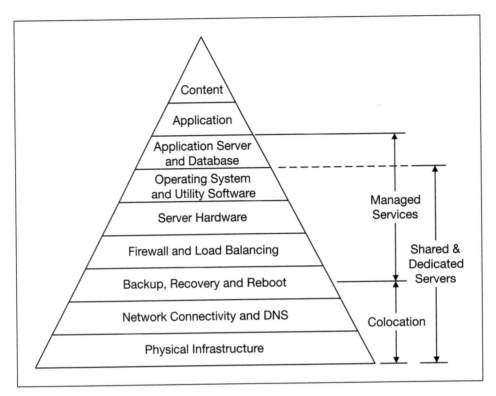

Figure 3.1   Services by vendor category.

Note the following:

- The service components available from shared- and dedicated-server web-hosting services are essentially the same and have, therefore, been combined into a single group.

- Colocation, on the other hand, includes very few service components—just those at the lowest levels of the pyramid. When colocation is combined with managed services, however, the service components actually exceed those available with shared and dedicated servers.

- The incremental difference between the shared/dedicated and colocation/managed service provider (MSP) combinations is the MSPs' support of application servers and databases. This is because the web sites outsourced to MSPs are typically those that are the largest and most complex. They're often based upon application servers that, in turn, depend on high-end databases packages such as Oracle or Microsoft's SQL Server.

Web-Site Traffic

The second criterion we'll use to segregate the four classes of web-hosting services is the amount of Internet traffic their customers' web sites generate. If you know how

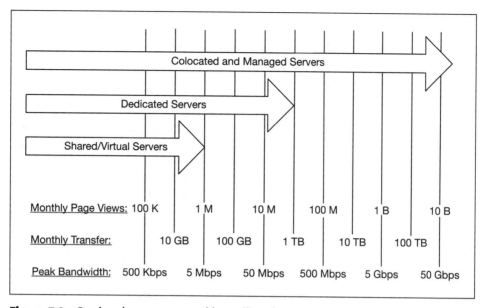

Figure 3.2 Service classes compared by traffic volume.

much traffic your site will generate, you can use that as one basis for determining the best web-hosting solution for your site.

TIP If you don't already know the volume of traffic your web site generates (or will generate), develop a *traffic model* using an Excel spreadsheet as explained in Chapter 11,"Traffic Models."

The typical ranges of traffic for each category are illustrated in Figure 3.2.

Figure 3.2 allows you to pinpoint your web site according to its traffic volume. This will give you an idea of where your bandwidth requirements match up with the capacities supported by the vendors in each category. For instance, if your site will deliver approximately 5 million page views per month, shared servers will be unsuitable. You should instead consider dedicated servers or colocation (with or without managed services).

If your site will deliver only 100,000 page views per month, shared servers will likely be your best alternative so long as you can accept the other limitations of shared-server hosting, as discussed in Chapter 4, "Shared and Dedicated Servers."

The arrows for colocated, managed, and dedicated servers extend all the way to the right to illustrate that all options are available for small sites.

All three of the traffic measurements (page views, transfer, and peak bandwidth) are related to one another (see the sidebar *Measuring Web-Site Traffic and Bandwidth*), but the relationships aren't all that simple. If the monthly page views increase, for example, so will the volume of data transfer and the demand for peak bandwidth. But the ratios of these measurements (or *metrics*) to one another aren't constant. For instance, two web sites may each deliver 1 million page views per month, but if the pages on one site are twice the size of the pages on the other, the former site's data transfer will be twice that of the latter site.

It's also important to note that the analysis presented here is based solely on the delivery of web pages. Other content types such as file downloads, streaming audio, video, and real-time data have different traffic characteristics, and must, therefore, be considered and modeled independently.

Likewise, *caching*, most of which is beyond your control, and which we'll explain in detail in Chapter 13, "Caching and Content Delivery Networks," can substantially affect the traffic to your web site. At the very least, caching by your visitors' browsers may make a huge difference between what visitors see and the number of hits to your servers.

For these reasons, any web-site traffic forecasts should, if possible, be based on analysis and extrapolations of your *current* traffic according to your servers' log files.

Cost

We've looked at the web-hosting service categories from two perspectives: the traffic volumes they can handle and the service components they offer. The final comparison we'll make is according to their costs, as illustrated in Figure 3.3.

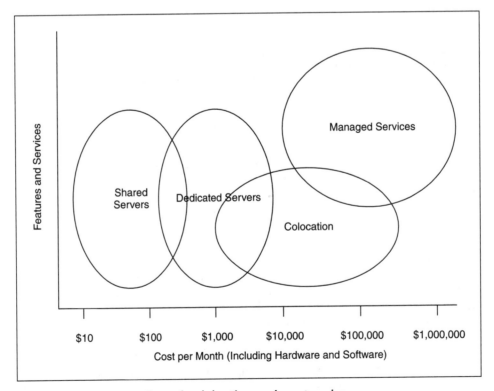

Figure 3.3 Cost comparison of web-hosting service categories.

MEASURING WEB-SITE TRAFFIC AND BANDWIDTH

The measurements shown in Figure 3.2 are the three most commonly used in analyzing web-site traffic volume.

Page views. The number of web pages delivered to users. This metric is used most in Internet advertising, since page views or *impressions* of banner ads are one way by which ad campaigns are planned and measured. The most popular sites, such as Yahoo!, deliver on the order of 5 billion (5 B) page views each month.

Monthly transfer. The metric most commonly used by shared- and dedicated-server web-hosting services. It's a count of all the data (measured in bytes) that a web site's servers transfer to or from the Internet. If you know the average size of your web site's pages, you can directly compute the monthly transfer as the number of page views multiplied by the average page size. For example, if your site's average page size is 40 K bytes, and the site delivers 1 million pages each month, it will transfer 40 billion bytes (40 gigabytes or 40 GB) per month. (Note that you may need to adjust the average page size according to the frequency of delivery of pages, since some sites deliver large pages more frequently than small pages, or vice versa.)

Peak bandwidth. Used by colocation and managed service providers. If you think of a web site's connection to the Internet as being like a pipe, *bandwidth* (the capacity of the pipe) is a measurement of the diameter of the pipe that's required to handle your site's traffic, while page views and monthly transfer are measurements of the actual amount of data that flows through the pipe.

Think of the electrical service that enters your home or office: If you open the service panel, you may see a circuit breaker labeled "200 amps." This is the maximum amount of electricity you can use at one time. This is like bandwidth. And the bill you get each month from your utility company for the amount of electricity you actually used is comparable to monthly transfer.

Just because a colocation service or MSP charges by bandwidth as opposed to transfer doesn't mean you'll pay more using this method of measurement. In fact, since sites hosted at colocation facilities or by MSPs tend to be larger and busier than those hosted by shared- or dedicated-server vendors, their actual cost of connectivity to the Internet is typically less due to volume discounting.

Most colocation vendors and MSPs use something called the *95th Percentile Rule,* which is explained in detail in Chapter 11, "Traffic Models." The most important factor to understand for now is that under the 95th Percentile Rule bandwidth is not billed according to the absolute peak, or *burst,* but rather according to the greatest usage that's sustained over certain units of time. Using the electricity comparison again, the 200-amp circuit breaker won't trip just because of the very short spikes that occur when, say, an air conditioner is turned on. Rather, the current must exceed 200 amps for a certain period of time.

The computation of peak bandwidth from monthly page views is not as exact as the computation of monthly transfer since one web site may deliver its page views evenly over a 24-hour period, whereas another may tend to be visited mostly during a narrower period of time during the day. An approximation of 1 Mbps (one megabit per second) of bandwidth for 200,000 page views per month is a good rule of thumb.

The x-axis of Figure 3.3 indicates the total cost per month for hardware and software of an operational web site. Note that the scale is logarithmic! The costs range from less than $10 to over $1 million per month.

In order to make an apples-to-apples comparison, Figure 3.3 includes the monthly cost of hardware and software it takes to run a web site. Shared- and dedicated-server vendors (and in some cases, MSPs) own the server hardware and most of the software licenses. They rent or lease those components to their customers, hence the inclusion of these costs in the comparison. In the case of pure colocation, however (i.e., without the addition of third-party managed services), the customer must either own the hardware and software or lease these components through third parties. For colocation, therefore, the budgets shown include either the monthly leasing costs of these components or the equivalent depreciation or amortization.

The y-axis scale has no values or calibration points. Instead it's a relative scale of features and services. Higher on the scale implies more features or a greater level of service.

> **TIP** If you already know the category of service vendor you'll need, use the chart to get some idea of the range of prices you'll pay and how those prices compare to what others already spend. If you have a fixed budget, use the chart to more accurately refine your choice of hosting solutions.

We've now looked at the four categories of web-hosting vendors from three perspectives: We've seen how they vary according to the services they offer, by the amount of web-site traffic they are each intended to handle, and by cost. In the next three chapters, we'll examine each category in detail. In the next chapter, we'll consider shared- and dedicated-server web hosting. In Chapter 5, "Colocation," we'll look at this bare-bones service category, aimed at larger and more complex web sites. Finally, in Chapter 6, "Managed Services," we'll see what the newest category of web-hosting service has to offer for sites with complex requirements and large budgets.

4

Shared and Dedicated Servers

A *shared server* (also referred to as a virtual server) is a single computer system on which a web-hosting service runs multiple small web sites owned by separate customers. The software for each web site runs in a *virtual operating environment* that protects it from other web sites running on the same physical server, and vice versa. Figure 4.1 illustrates a shared-server operating environment.

Shared servers are used for the vast majority of all web sites. Because these web sites require relatively low levels of computer resources, multiple sites—sometimes thousands—can be run on a single server. This means, in turn, that a shared-server hosting provider can offer web hosting for as little as $19.95 per month and still make money. Low-cost shared-server hosting can be an excellent choice for simple, brochureware sites (i.e., those that contain only marketing and promotional content and don't support complex e-commerce). Major web-hosting services that specialize in shared servers typically build large *server farms*—Internet data centers with rows upon rows of racks filled with shared servers—which is how these vendors achieve the economies of scale necessary to offer shared-server hosting at low monthly prices. But because prices are low, and profit margins are therefore slim, shared-server hosting includes very little in the way of hand-holding services such as help troubleshooting or configuring of a customer's web site.

Shared-server hosting is sold in packages that typically range in cost from $20 to $100 per month, although at one extreme some vendors offer free hosting (discussed in the upcoming section titled *Free Web Hosting*); and at the other extreme some shared

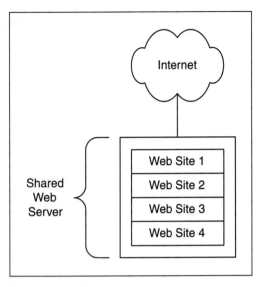

Figure 4.1 Shared server.

hosting costs as much as $500 per month. Most vendors offer more than one package, and allow customers to migrate or upgrade to a larger or more expensive package, as the customers' needs increase.

> **TIP** Make sure that your shared-server hosting service provides room to grow by offering higher-level packages. Be sure you aren't starting with its largest and most expensive package. You should also have the option of upgrading to a dedicated server should you require it.

Although the details of shared-server packages can vary greatly, the standard means by which vendors define their packages are:

- Monthly fee (recurring)
- Setup fee (one-time or nonrecurring)
- Monthly data transfer cap (maximum)
- Maximum disk storage
- Number of email accounts (such as info@yourdomain.com)

Table 4.1 lists these parameters for three sample shared-server packages.

Typically, these packages are designed so that if you exceed the limit of any one of the measurements (data transfer, disk storage, or number of email accounts), you're expected to move up to a more expensive package. Using the sample packages in Table 4.1, for example, if your site requires 100 MB of disk storage but will only transfer 2 GB of traffic per month onto the Internet, you'd be forced to buy the midrange package rather than the low-end one.

Table 4.1   Typical Shared-Server Packages

	LOW END	MIDRANGE	HIGH END
Monthly Fee	$20	$75	$500
Setup Fee	$25	$75	$250
Monthly Data Transfer	5 GB	20 GB	50 GB
Disk Storage	50 MB	200 MB	1 GB
Email Accounts	5	10	50

Some sites present particular challenges because they require an inordinate amount of one service component relative to the others. For example, a site that expects a large number of file downloads (such as a site that offers MP3 music files) might find that the data transfer volume is very high, while the disk requirements and number of email accounts is very low. Similarly, a site that includes a large number of photographic images (JPEG files) but that doesn't anticipate much traffic might require far more disk space relative to data transfer.

There are two solutions to this problem. First, shop around. Some vendors' packages offer more bandwidth (data transfer) relative to disk storage than others, and vice versa. Second, many of the shared-server hosting vendors offer upgrades of individual components within the package. For instance, a vendor of the midrange package shown in Table 4.1 (20 GB data transfer for $75 per month) might offer additional data transfer à la carte for $5 per GB per month. Other upgrades for disk storage or email accounts may likewise be available.

TIP Find a vendor that offers a package (based on an upgrade or otherwise) that meets your specific balance of capabilities and capacities in order to avoid paying for services you don't need.

Volume and Standardization

The computer hardware on which shared web sites run varies greatly. Some shared-server vendors use a small number of large servers, each of which can host thousands of sites on a single computer system. Increasingly, however, shared-server vendors are turning to a larger number of less powerful, compact servers that are physically only 1U in height. (A "U" or *rack unit* is 1½ inch.)

TIP In case you're wondering why shared-server vendors are motivated to offer standardized services on such a large scale, consider the economics. A single 7-foot-high equipment rack—the standard for Internet data centers—can hold more than 40 such servers (leaving adequate space for cooling, cables, and supporting devices) and can support more than 5,000 small web sites. A typical data center is at least 50,000 square feet—enough to support more than 500 such racks. If a 50,000-square-foot data center were filled to capacity with high-density shared servers, it could operate 2.5 *million* web sites. At the low end of only $20 per month per site, a single such data center could generate $600 million per year in web-hosting revenues. Not too shabby for one data center.

In order to support such a large number of sites at such a low price, shared-server hosting is necessarily based on a very high degree of standardization. All components of shared-server hosting are treated as though they were part of an assembly line.

Shared-server hosting vendors typically offer menus of features and components from which a customer can select when building a web site. Fortunately, due to intense competition in the shared-server hosting business, these menus include a large number of features, and it's relatively easy to compare vendors' offerings to one another.

The following is a typical menu of shared-server hosting features:

- Daily backup to tape
- Off-site tape storage
- Email accounts (mailboxes)
- Outbound email relaying
- Email redirectors
- Email autoresponders (for automated responses to info@yoursite.com, etc.)
- Microsoft FrontPage extensions
- Discussion forum software
- Anonymous FTP
- Administrative access via telnet or secure shell (SSH)
- Electronic shopping cart software
- Secure Socket Layer (SSL) for secure web pages and forms
- Credit card merchant accounts and transaction processing
- Log file processing and analysis tools
- Support for scripting languages such as Perl and PHP
- Web-based control panels or access to configuration files for managing web sites
- Simple database software such as MySQL
- Firewall protection of the web server
- Streaming media servers (optional, at additional cost)

In addition to providing these site components, a shared-server hosting vendor maintains all of the hardware and software.

Competing for Resources

The economics of shared servers (like those of shared bandwidth) are such that a hosting service tries to optimize the load on the system by balancing two concepts: profit and customer satisfaction. On one hand, the vendor wants to run as many web sites on each server as possible in order to minimize the costs of hardware, power, real estate, and air conditioning for each web site. On the other hand, if the vendor runs too many sites on each server, the performance of those sites will deteriorate to the point that the owners of the sites become dissatisfied. It's a balancing act that unfortunately doesn't align the vendor's objectives with the customer's needs.

Shared servers are designed to protect one web site from another by ensuring that no single site can monopolize shared resources such as CPU time, disk input/output, or access to the Internet. But if your site is a busy one—where many requests arrive in rapid succession—you may find the protection software inhibits the processor from servicing your site's requests promptly.

TIP Ask prospective shared-server vendors what they do to ensure that all sites on a shared server get their fair share of system resources, and that no single web site can monopolize a server.

Shared-Server Security

At best, any web server is only moderately secure. After all, it's designed to be accessed from anywhere in the world, so the door to hackers is already cracked open. Many configurations include a firewall between the web server and the outside world. These firewalls permit the types of access that the web server is intended to support, and block all other types of access.

In the case of a shared server, however, there is certainly no firewall between your site and the other sites on the same server. As good as virtual server software may be, it's still moderately susceptible to attacks or programming errors by other sites on the same system. If you share a server with 100 other sites, and just one of them is hacked by an intruder, your site will be compromised. One could say you've increased your chance of attack a hundredfold.

Security issues on shared servers are not limited to attacks by hackers. Sharing a server with other web sites is inherently less stable than running on a server of your own. No degree of application testing can guarantee that the code of another web site won't affect your site.

TIP If you store confidential data about your customers, your suppliers, or your own business, don't use a shared server.

Chapter 17, "Security," offers detailed coverage of security issues.

Planning for Growth

The traffic volume of most web sites—hopefully including yours—will increase over time. While this is great for your business, it also means that over the same period of time more and more of your web server's resources will be consumed. As each of the sites on a shared server receives more traffic, the server (and hence each site it hosts) becomes slower and slower.

A shared-server vendor has three solutions to this inevitable problem. First, the vendor can migrate (i.e., move) some web sites from the overloaded server to another. This can usually be accomplished without shutting down any web sites so long as the sites are simple and have no transactional databases, and the vendor knows what its doing and has done it many times before.

TIP Ask prospective shared-server vendors to explain how they handle upgrades and the migration of web sites from one server to another.

The second solution is to move your site to a dedicated server, as we'll discuss later in this chapter in the section entitled *Dedicated Servers.*The third solution—one that is increasingly popular—is the use of *clustered shared servers,* which are discussed in detail in Chapter 12, "Web-Site Architectures." In this configuration, each web site is replicated, and runs on at least two servers. If one server goes down, the site can continue to operate from one of the other servers.

Later, in Part Four, "Tools," we'll explore ways to determine the response times of web sites hosted on shared servers in order to evaluate the extent to which a hosting service may be overloading its servers.

TIP Ask vendors not just *if* they monitor shared-server CPU load, network throughput, and server response-time, but *how* they do so. Also ask them what limits they have established for these values, which, if exceeded, will cause them to offload sites to other servers in order to guarantee a level of service to your site.

Shared-Server Bandwidth

The typical shared-server account is limited to 5 GB to 10 GB per month of data transfer. How much is that? Let's do a little arithmetic. If we assume an average web page size of 40-K bytes (a reasonable assumption), 10 GB is equal to 250,000 page views per month. If each visitor views an average of 10 pages per visit, that's 25,000 visits per month, or an average of about 835 visits per day.

TIP If you expect your web site to receive more than 1,000 to 2,500 visitors per day (depending on the number of page views per visit and average page size), you shouldn't be considering a shared server. Step up to a dedicated or colocated solution.

The Self-Serve Model

The most important thing to keep in mind if you decide to host your web site on a shared server is the level of service you should expect to receive. Be realistic. At $19.95

per month, for example, a hosting service can't afford to spend more than about 10 minutes a month helping you. So if you think you'll need more than just a few minutes of support each month, you should expect to pay more. There are three ways in which you can get additional support services from a shared-server vendor:

Consulting services often can be purchased directly from a shared-server vendor at additional cost. The advantages of going this route are that you still get low-cost hosting and you don't have to deal with additional vendors. You must be sure, however, that the vendor can actually deliver the services you require. Many shared-server vendors have staff with limited expertise.

Resellers of shared web hosting often provide additional value-added services above and beyond those offered by the shared-server providers themselves. By going through a reseller, you still get low-cost hosting, and a more service-oriented party is there to help you. Resellers are discussed in more detail later in this chapter.

Managed service providers (MSPs) provide high-touch (and high-cost) services. This is a much more expensive option, but if you need the highest levels of service, MSPs are your only choice unless you hire your own staff. MSPs are discussed further in Chapter 6, "Managed Services."

TIP Have a plan for the additional professional services you'll need. Discuss options for professional services with the vendor *before* you sign a contract. If the vendor is in any way hesitant to provide the services you need (even for an additional charge), consider using another vendor or perhaps going through a reseller.

Free Web Hosting

You may have seen offers for free hosting, and as you might imagine, there's a catch. Most so-called free hosting services make money by requiring their customers to reserve space on their web pages for banner ads. The vendor then sells those ads to third parties and pockets the revenues. There are all sorts of problems with this business model, and it's a situation to avoid unless you can't afford even a $10 per month service.

Most obviously, if your site is hosted by such a service, you have no control over the selection of ads that appear on your web site. That could at the very least prove embarrassing. It also robs you of a potential revenue stream that could be valuable at some time in the future.

On the other hand, the effectiveness of banner ads on the Internet has steadily declined as the novelty has worn off (just consider how often, if ever, you click on a banner ad). Therefore, the rates vendors are able to charge for banner ads have dropped sharply. If a vendor that depends on advertising revenues hosts your web site, your site's at risk. As the vendor's profit margins continue to erode, the quality of their services is likely to deteriorate. Ultimately, such a business may well have to shut its doors, and since going out of business is rarely done in an orderly manner, it could catch you by surprise and without sufficient time to find another web-hosting solution or to plan an orderly migration of your site.

Another concern is that many free web-hosting services will create a strong lock-in (described in Chapter 7, "The Dark Side of Outsourcing") since they host sites only under their own domain names. This means your web-site address with such a vendor would likely look like this:

```
www.vendor.com/yourcompany
```

instead of the preferred:

```
www.yourcompany.com
```

In the latter case, your web address or uniform resource locator (URL) is portable. As long as the address was properly registered (see Chapter 21, "Domain Names and DNS") you can move your site to another web-hosting service and take the address with you.

Finally, remember that you get what you pay for. Expect very strict standardization and very low levels of service from any free web-hosting service.

TIP Avoid free hosting for any web sites other than those that truly have no budget and that can afford the risks of being shut down and effectively lost on the Internet.

Three Tiers of Shared-Server Vendors

The ranks of shared-server vendors are actually divided into three different *tiers* (or subcategories), and each tier offers advantages in certain situations.

Facility-owner vendors. Vendors that own their servers and also operate their own data centers.

Tenant vendors. Vendors that own their servers, but rent space within colocation facilities.

Resellers. These vendors don't even own the hardware, but rather act as agents of facility-owner or tenant vendors.

You might think "larger is better" and that facility-owner vendors are better than tenants, who are in turn better than resellers. But this isn't necessarily the case. There are, in fact, three very different skill sets required, and to some extent each tier specializes in one of those skill sets.

Facility-Owner Vendors

Today, the state of the art for data centers is quite high, and very few vendors (shared-server or otherwise) have the capitalization or borrowing power required to build and operate such facilities. On the other hand, these first-class facilities do exist, and there's no reason why your web site—no matter how small it may be—shouldn't reap the benefits of being located in one. The small number of shared-server web-hosting companies that are large and wealthy enough to build their own first-class data centers should certainly be considered as potential vendors.

Most of the owners of first-class data centers, however, don't directly offer shared-server hosting, since they're more likely to offer services at the high end of the hosting spectrum. The vendors that own large data centers are more experienced in dealing with customers who have web-hosting budgets on the order of $10,000 per month or more.

If you can't find an appropriate shared-server vendor that operates its own first-class data center, you can host your web site with a tenant vendor or reseller and take advantage of the fact that its servers are located within the facilities of a third party's first-class facility.

Tenant Vendors

Many smaller web-hosting services came to realize over time that their second-class infrastructure was not only insufficient, but was also causing them to lose customers to competitors who had better Internet connectivity, power, air conditioning, and physical security. The smart ones—those who realized they would otherwise be at a competitive disadvantage—adopted an "if-you-can't-beat-'em-join-'em" attitude, and opted out of providing any of the physical aspects of web-site hosting. They themselves are customers (or *tenants*) of colocation facilities, but since they, in turn, offer shared-server hosting, they are *tenant vendors*.

If you can find a good one (isn't that always the gotcha?), a tenant vendor can be an excellent alternative for a shared-server customer. You get the advantages of a first-class data center and of having someone who is focused entirely on the operation of the shared-server systems. (In Chapter 20, "The Net Detective Toolkit," we'll look at techniques for determining whether a web-hosting service is, in fact, using the facilities of another.)

Of course, it's not always that simple. For example, a tenant vendor may be a very small outfit, and there is no guarantee, no matter what the vendor's size, that the quality of its services will be sufficient. You still need to do your homework to learn which vendors are good, and which may be out of business a few months down the road.

Resellers

Resellers are the third tier of shared-server vendors. A reseller bundles shared-server web hosting from a third party with the reseller's own value-added services.

At first, the practice of reselling was considered deceptive, and today there are still some resellers who attempt to hide what they're doing from their customers. The better resellers, however, recognize that both they and the parent web-hosting service are providing value to the end customer, and these resellers understand that it makes more sense for the customer to be aware of exactly what's happening. (You should ask any shared-server vendors whether or not they operate their own data centers. You'll learn how to find out if they're telling the truth in Chapter 20.)

From one perspective, resellers are simply salespeople who sign up customers and collect money. But there are some resellers who actually provide a substantial level of service above and beyond the services provided by the parent vendors for whom they resell. For example, some resellers (like some tenant vendors) provide the site design, setup, and maintenance services that a high-volume shared-server vendor doesn't offer.

Likewise, some resellers and tenant vendors have particular *vertical-application expertise* that may be of substantial value and importance. Vertical-application expertise means experience with shared-server hosting to specific industry groups. There might be a reseller or tenant vendor, for instance, that offers shared-server hosting for realtors.

Such a vendor might include a number of services that are unique to getting a real estate brokerage site online.

When selecting a vendor that offers such services, there are two things to watch out for. First, just because a vendor specializes in your industry doesn't guarantee that it's capable of keeping your web site running 24/7. Don't stop once you're satisfied the vendor knows your industry. You still need to evaluate it as a web-hosting service. Second, by signing up with a vendor that supplies specialized web-site components or vertical expertise, you're a target for lock-in, a risk that you'll be committed to the services provided by a single vendor and, therefore, won't have the choice of changing web-hosting services. Lock-in is described in detail in Chapter 7.

TIP If a shared-server vendor claims to own and/or operate its own data center, make sure that it really does, and the facility is truly first-class.

See Chapter 20 for tips on how to check out who owns the data center, and Chapter 5, "Colocation," for what to look for in a data center.

The primary advantage of obtaining your web-hosting services from a reseller is that (if you select your reseller carefully) you can receive a higher level of service than you would if you were to purchase directly from the larger web-hosting service. You'll likely have to pay extra for that service—it isn't free—but you can often get services that simply aren't available from the larger companies, which are necessarily more focused on the volume and scale of their operations.

TIP It's better to use a tenant vendor or a reseller that in turn uses the facilities of a first-class colocation facility (so long as it's up-front and honest about this relationship) than it is to use an owned-facility vendor whose data center is substandard.

Dedicated Servers

Dedicated servers are essentially the same as shared servers (i.e., they're owned by the hosting service and come with a standard suite of software and tools), but each web site gets its own server, and doesn't have to share it with other sites. In fact, the same companies that offer shared-server web hosting typically offer dedicated servers as well, and some treat the two categories as virtually identical.

As compared to shared servers, dedicated servers offer the following advantages:

Increased capacity. Dedicated servers can handle substantially more of everything than a shared server can. Some dedicated servers can handle up to the following limits:

- 100 GB disk space
- 1 TB (a terabyte, or 1,000 gigabytes) monthly data transfer
- Peak data transfer rates approaching 100 Mbps

Improved security. Dedicated servers eliminate the risks associated with sharing the hardware with other web sites.

Table 4.2 Typical Dedicated-Server Packages

	LOW END	MIDRANGE	HIGH END
Monthly Fee	$200	$2,000	$20,000
Setup Fee	$750	$2,500	$18,000
Server Hardware	(1) 1-CPU server	(2) 2-CPU servers	(3) 1-CPU servers
			(1) 2-CPU servers
Software	Linux, Apache	NT, IIS	Solaris, Apache
Monthly Data Transfer	100 GB	300 GB	1,000 GB
Disk Storage	36 MB	100 GB	100 GB RAID

Improved reliability. As with security, a dedicated server is less subject to outages and slowdowns caused by interactions with other web sites.

Additional configurations. Some web-hosting services allow customers to build sites using multiple dedicated servers that can be configured in a variety of ways to increase reliability, capacity, functionality, or all three, as discussed in detail in Chapter 12.

The cost of dedicated-server hosting ranges from $200 to $20,000 per month, and like shared-server hosting, it's sold in packages. Table 4.2 lists some typical examples.

Two Tiers of Dedicated-Server Vendors

Unlike the shared-server business, where such relationships are common, few resellers or tenant vendors are in the dedicated hosting business. There are, however, two distinct types of dedicated-server vendors.

Shared/dedicated vendors. Vendors that offer both services. In most cases, their dedicated-server business grew out of their shared-server business. As their shared-server customers' requirements increase, these vendors move those customers to dedicated hardware.

Dedicated-only vendors. Vendors that are part of a somewhat newer breed. They don't offer any shared-server hosting.

Shared/dedicated vendors tend to treat both categories of customers (shared or dedicated) alike. Since these vendors evolved from the shared model, that's how they tend to view all web sites. Many of the issues regarding shared servers earlier in this chapter also apply to this tier of dedicated-server vendors. For example, shared/dedicated vendors are committed to standardization and the self-service model.

Since dedicated-only vendors are relatively new, they began with a fresh start. These vendors tend to offer somewhat higher levels of customization and professional services than are available from the shared/dedicated vendors, and, no surprise, they tend to do so for a higher price.

Shared and shared/dedicated vendors generally offer their support services in a de-personalized manner. You'll most likely communicate with them via email; and when you do need to speak to someone on the phone, you're not likely to speak to the same person on any regular basis. Typically, shared and shared/dedicated vendors build call centers into which all email messages, calls, and alerts are funneled through a single queue, with the one possible exception of segregating NT and Unix/Linux issues since the skill sets necessary to support web sites based on these two families of operating systems are so different.

Because the average revenues per customer are substantially higher for dedicated-only vendors, these vendors tend to incorporate at least some level of personalized service into their offerings. Depending upon the complexity of your site and your monthly fees, you may, for example, be assigned a technical account manager (TAM), or perhaps an account team that deals with your site and perhaps as many as 50 to 100 others.

TIP If the only reason you need a dedicated server is because a shared server won't meet your traffic requirements, start your search by looking for a shared/dedicated vendor. But if one of the reasons for selecting dedicated-server web hosting over shared-server hosting is to obtain a higher level of service, start your search by looking for a dedicated-only vendor.

Although you'll likely get more service from a dedicated-only vendor (and pay more for it), it's also likely you'll find that the vendor has higher expectations of you as a customer. Shared- and shared/dedicated-server vendors expect to be working with small sites, and with customers who have little technical expertise. Dedicated-only vendors, however, expect customers to be more knowledgeable. The advantage of this (if you *are* a somewhat more knowledgeable customer) is that you'll receive the services and respect you deserve. If you have little technical knowledge or expertise, you'll find a dedicated-only vendor's support staff not to be quite the right fit.

When selecting between the two tiers, the most important factor is to make sure your needs and expectations match the capabilities of the vendors in the tier. (A more detailed discussion of matched expectations is provided in Chapter 8, "Getting It Right.") The dedicated-only vendors are clearly aimed at a more technically sophisticated customer than are the shared/dedicated providers.

TIP If your configuration is in any way complex (e.g., you have both NT and Unix/Linux servers, you're running any significant software beyond what's provided by the hosting service), you're technically sophisticated, or you'll need a moderate level of service, begin your search with the dedicated-only vendors.

Although shared- and dedicated-server web-hosting vendors represent the low end of the web-hosting market, they offer by far the greatest value. In the following chapter, "Colocation," we'll look at the next step up from shared and dedicated hosting, but as you'll see, it's only a solution that's appropriate for those who can't get by with a simpler and less expensive web-hosting solution.

Colocation

Now that we've covered shared and dedicated hosting, let's look at *colocation* (or *colo*). This is the oldest and most basic of the four web-hosting services, and unlike shared or dedicated hosting, it's aimed at high-budget, sophisticated customers. Colocation vendors supply the fundamental services that are sometimes referred to as "power, pipe and ping," a catchy phrase that includes, at the bare minimum, the following services:

- "Real estate" (equipment racks, cabinets, or cages)
- Electrical power (including battery and/or generator backup)
- Air conditioning
- Physical security
- Fire suppression
- Connectivity to the Internet

Some colocation vendors provide the following ancillary services:

- Domain Name Service (DNS)
- "Remote hands" to reboot servers or to cycle them off/on
- Basic web-site monitoring and alert notification (pagers, phone calls)
- Swapping of backup tapes (i.e., the customer manages the backup, but the colocation service removes and replaces tapes from the drives)

- Hardware installation services
- Spares management (i.e., management of spare parts made available to hardware repair technicians)

Internet Data Centers

A physical Internet data center (IDC) is the most fundamental component provided by any web-hosting service, yet it's the one component that few web-site owners understand. Years ago, only high-end web sites were hosted in first-class facilities, but since the migration of even the smallest web-hosting vendors into the colocation vendor's facilities, every web site now has the opportunity to be hosted in a top-tier IDC.

If you have the opportunity to visit a prospective vendor's facilities, take advantage of it. If you don't have a chance to see the facility where your site will be hosted—or even another facility owned by the same vendor—try to take a tour of *any* state-of-the-art web-hosting facility. You'll find it very educational. In this section we'll discuss some of the important things to look for when you take such a tour or when you listen to a vendor's sales pitch.

Oooh! Ahhh!

Every new data center that's built (at least in major metropolitan areas) has to be bigger and better than the ones that came before it. Through 1999, the unprecedented opportunities in the colocation business caused the vendors to embark on very aggressive IDC construction plans. Even so, as long as demand exceeded supply, some customers had no choice but to locate their servers in second- and third-class facilities. However, in 2000 and 2001, the pendulum swung the other way as the IDC construction boom, coupled with the demise of many dot-com companies, created an excess of capacity. The oversupply of colo space increased competition, which, in turn, raised the bar for the quality of IDC facilities.

Many of these newest data centers are very impressive. When you visit one you'll have to restrain yourself from saying "Oooh!" and "Aahhh!" Truthfully, much of what you'll probably be shown on a tour is more to impress you than to really make a difference in your web hosting. For example, you may come across data centers that are secured by vaultlike doors and biometric palm-scanning authentication devices. But in more than one such facility you can enter the data center by merely crawling under the raised floor from an adjoining unsecured office. So much for security!

Remember that the physical facility—while absolutely critical—represents only a very small portion of a complete web-hosting service, so don't give the facility more weight than other service components. (For more on this topic, refer to the discussion of the *hosting idiot savant syndrome* in Chapter 7, "The Dark Side of Outsourcing.")

TIP Be careful not to be overly impressed by the gee-whiz aspects of an Internet data center. A beautiful facility doesn't guarantee that, for example, it's staffed by qualified personnel or that the vendor can provide any of the other services you need.

Back-Hoe Protection

Web sites and hosting services are vulnerable to outages caused by many things, from hardware failures to Internet routing problems. But one of the nastiest causes of major Internet failures is the dreaded construction-site back-hoe. Try as we might to keep track of the location of underground cables and pipes, and to communicate that information to construction crews, these two-headed monsters are masters at finding new ways to thwart our efforts. Ask the manager of any data center what strikes fear in his heart, and he'll likely tell you it's a back-hoe cutting a major fiber-optic line.

A point of entry (POE) is the back-hoe's invisible target: a location at the perimeter of an Internet data center where services such as electricity, natural gas, and telecommunications connections enter the building. As a defense against back-hoes, a first-class data center has multiple POEs for each of these services, preferably on opposite sides of the building.

Good facilities have multiple POEs not only for fiber-optic entry, but for utilities as well; and if they have exterior diesel generators, the outputs of those generators should each have a separate entrance to the building. It may seem like overkill, but the very best facilities have three separate POEs for each service. Some data centers even put their generators inside the building.

Electrical and natural gas POEs are relatively straightforward, but they must be fed by entirely independent sources as well, because if two POEs connect to the same main service, and *that* service is cut by a back-hoe, then *both* services to the data center will be shut down. The redundant services that pass through separate POEs should never rejoin into conduits or pipes in the same underground trench.

Electrical and gas services are commodities: There's no practical difference between the electrons or molecules entering through one wall versus those entering through another. The same isn't true for fiber-optic connections, however. If a data center has two fiber POEs, for example, it may be that the web-hosting service connects to some major ISPs through one fiber bundle at the first POE, and to other major ISPs through another fiber bundle at the second POE. The challenge is this: If the first fiber is cut, will all of the routers—those of the web-hosting service and the ISPs—automatically reconfigure their routing tables so that your web site can be reached by the disconnected ISP's customers via the second (still directly connected) ISP? Many data centers brag about their multiple POEs, but they haven't, in fact, configured their routers and fiber connections to utilize the redundancy. It doesn't do any good to have two holes in the wall if you don't take advantage of them.

TIP Ask prospective vendors (a) if they have multiple points of entry (POEs) for all services, (b) whether they connect externally to separate facilities, and (c) whether your web site would be reachable from all locations on the Internet if the connections through a single POE were cut.

Air Conditioning

The computers used in web-hosting data centers put out a tremendous amount of heat. As CPUs get faster and faster, and servers are loaded with more and faster RAM, the number of BTUs (a measure of heat) per square foot continues to rise. All of the electricity used to run servers ends up as heat inside the building and requires air conditioning to move it to the exterior.

Without air conditioning, the servers and routers in a data center would fail in a matter of a few minutes. High-end servers and routers have internal thermostats, and they'll shut themselves off before they become hot enough to damage themselves. For this reason, all good data centers must have redundant air conditioning, just as they have redundant power and Internet connectivity.

Small data centers simply install two air conditioning systems and operate them each at 50 percent of capacity. Larger centers, however, employ an $n+2$ (n plus two) or $n+3$ model in which they install two or three more air conditioning systems than they need to handle the current cooling requirements. The $n+2$ designation means the IDC can maintain the desired air temperature if as many as two of the air conditioners are down. An $n+1$ model isn't satisfactory, since it's common to have one unit offline at a time for scheduled maintenance, and a failure of any other unit during a maintenance period would result in inadequate cooling capacity. The $n+2$ model is the minimum requirement for a first-class facility, and $n+3$ is typical for larger sites.

TIP Ask prospective vendors if they have at least *n+2* redundancy for air conditioners.

Power

Electricity used to be just another commodity service that every colocation vendor took for granted. It was plentiful and inexpensive, and a large, battery-supplied uninterruptible power supply (UPS) and one diesel generator could cover the few hours a year that an Internet data center was without power. A four- or eight-hour supply of diesel fuel was usually considered adequate.

Then three events converged to create a crisis. First, some western states, particularly California, stopped constructing the power-generation plants necessary to keep up with their growth in population and industry during the 1990s. That was compounded by an inept deregulation of California's power industry that forced the state's major utilities to buy electricity on the volatile spot market, and sell it for substantially less than the purchase price. (That's not meant to imply that the utilities weren't entirely blameless.)

The final straw was the remarkable increase in the demand for electricity to feed the Internet and the World Wide Web. According to Pacific Gas and Electric—the utility company that supplies power to northern California—at the end of the year 2000, more than 25 percent of all electricity used in Silicon Valley was consumed by web-hosting colocation services. These are businesses that didn't even exist five years before. Web hosting in Silicon Valley alone required 1,200 megawatts of power at that time, enough for the residents of a city of 1.2 million people, nearly twice the number of people that live in the city of San Francisco. By some estimates, by the year 2011, the Internet and other technology services will consume 30 percent of all of the power used in the United States.

Beyond the Grid

As you evaluate colocation vendors, you'll likely encounter many different solutions to the problems of power supply and reliability, including the use of multiple grids, off-grid power generation, and standby generators.

The standard method of providing backup power is through dedicated generators. Small IDCs may use propane or natural-gas powered generators, but most facilities use larger generators powered by diesel fuel. There are three issues you should be aware of when evaluating an IDC's backup generation plan:

Redundancy. As with air conditioning systems, generators themselves will fail from time to time. They certainly may be down for maintenance on occasion, although not nearly as frequently as air conditioning systems. A first-class IDC should have at least an $n+1$ diesel-generator capability. In other words, it should have enough generators so that if one were to be down or fail, the other(s) could handle the entire load. Truly superior IDCs use an $n+2$ generator configuration.

Capacity. Some IDCs skimp on generator capacity by planning only to run the servers on generators, and not the lighting or air conditioning systems. This is based on their assumption that power outages will be short enough that the temperature will not rise substantially, and that any work in progress can be suspended or continued via flashlights. Such logic won't work in California, for example, where *rolling blackouts* cause outages of one to two hours at a time.

Fuel. Another consideration is the amount of diesel fuel on hand. Enough fuel to run a data center for four to eight hours might be sufficient for most outages, but what happens when a natural disaster or other major catastrophe (even a heavy snowfall) makes it impossible for delivery trucks to refill the tanks on time? Some vendors claim to have high-priority contracts with their diesel suppliers, but when push comes to shove, a contract is only as valuable as the paper it's printed on. It can't actually guarantee that the trucks will be able to fill up and make it to the IDC. Most conservative designs for IDCs will provide enough on-site fuel to run the generators at full load for at least 48 hours.

TIP When evaluating a vendor's backup generator provisions, look for at least an $n+1$ configuration, adequate electrical capacity to power lighting and air conditioning in addition to the servers, and 48 hours worth of diesel fuel storage capacity.

Because of the increase in extended power outages, and forecasts that the situation will continue to get worse throughout the United States, many colocation vendors are looking at alternatives to backup generators. One such alternative is to use their generators not for backup, but as the primary source of power. Their belief is that they can control their own power generation and use the grid as a backup or co-generation source. Some IDCs are building their own high-capacity, power-generation plants that use generators even larger than the trailer-sized 1 to 2 megawatt units most often used for backup.

In some areas of the United States it's even possible to purchase power from two or more entirely independent providers. This is a good option that tends to be more commonly available around military facilities, making those locations attractive for Internet data centers.

Real Estate

Real estate has become a term commonly used to describe physical space for housing servers, routers, and other web-site hardware components. There are three types of real estate available from colocation services: open racks, cabinets, and cages. The variations in pricing for colocation real estate are primarily based upon the type of space provided.

Open Racks

Open racks are best for sites that don't have enough servers to fill an entire rack or cabinet. Originally called "relay racks" because they held mechanical telephone relays before the advent of semiconductors, these come in standard 19- and 24-inch widths, and are typically 6 or 7 feet tall. If you only have one or two servers, renting space in a shared, open rack is probably your best solution unless you're willing to rent an entire cabinet and leave most of it empty. (Some vendors offer half-height locked cabinets, which may be a good compromise.)

The problem with keeping your servers in open racks is that they'll be in a relatively vulnerable high-traffic area because colocation vendors use open racks to house a large number of small customers. This means there will be constant changes to hardware and cabling as customers come and go and swap out one server for another. It's not uncommon for a technician working on the server above or below yours to accidentally hit one of the cables attached to your server and not even be aware that he or she has done so. It's even possible for a technician or another customer to unplug your server and start to walk away with it. (He or she shouldn't be able to make it past the security guards, but there have been such cases of mistaken-server identity.) Still, open racks are the standard for colocation of most small web sites.

The charges are based on the percentage of the rack used, or the number of inches or *rack units*. For example, some vendors charge for each half or quarter rack, while others charge by the inch, foot, or "U." (One U or *rack unit* is equal to 1.25 inches. A server or other piece of rack-mountable equipment that's 6U in height, for instance, requires 7.5 inches of vertical rack space.)

Table 5.1 shows typical pricing for a site that has four small servers occupying one half of a single open rack. Note that in this example, the vendor will be rotating backup tapes and providing a *Remote Hands* service that's described in the next chapter.

TIP Use open racks only if you need less than three feet of rack space and can tolerate the potential risks of sharing space with other web-site owners.

Table 5.1   Sample Partial-Rack Colocation Pricing

SERVICE	QTY	ONE-TIME (SETUP) EACH	TOTAL	MONTHLY EACH	TOTAL
Half Open Rack	1	$1,000	$1,000	$ 500	$ 500
Minimum Bandwidth (1 Mbps)	1		$ -	$1,000	$1,000
Remote Hands Service (Per Server)	4		$ -	$ 50	$ 200
Daily Tape Rotation (Per Tape)	1		$ -	$ 500	$ 500
Totals			**$1,000**		**$2,200**

Table 5.2   Sample Locked-Cabinet Colocation Pricing

SERVICE	QTY	ONE-TIME (SETUP) EACH	TOTAL	MONTHLY EACH	TOTAL
Cabinet Rental (Per Cabinet)	2	$1,200	$2,400	$700	$1,400
Minimum Bandwidth (1 Mbps)	2		$ -	$750	$1,500
Additional Bandwidth (Per 1 Mbps)	3		$ -	$750	$2,250
Daily Tape Rotation (Per Tape)	2		$ -	$500	$1,000
Totals			**$2,400**		**$6,150**

Locked Cabinets

If you have enough servers, *locked cabinets* are an excellent choice. Not only do they reduce the number of problems that occur as a result of maintenance to neighboring systems, they also improve security. In addition, a locked cabinet is a great place to keep
tools and spare parts—something you can't do with open racks.

Charges for locked cabinets are per-cabinet. The example in Table 5.2 is for a site using two locked cabinets and a total of 5 Mbps of bandwidth.

TIP Use locked cabinets unless you can't afford one or need more than five
or six.

Cages

Finally, *cages* can be used to create small, private data centers. Data center cages look
very much like those in a zoo. They're typically made from a material that resembles

Table 5.3 Sample Cage Colocation Pricing

SERVICE	QTY	ONE-TIME (SETUP) EACH	ONE-TIME (SETUP) TOTAL	MONTHLY EACH	MONTHLY TOTAL
Cage Rental (10'x10" with 4 Racks)	1	$5,000	$5,000	$6,500	$ 6,500
Minimum Bandwidth (1 Mbps Per Rack)	4		$ -	$ 750	$ 3,000
Additional Bandwidth (Per 1 Mbps)	6		$ -	$ 750	$ 4,500
Remote Hands Service (Per Server)	14		$ -	$ 50	$ 700
Daily Tape Rotation (Per Tape)	4		$ -	$ 500	$ 2,000
Totals			**$5,000**		**$16,700**

Cyclone fencing, but that's much tougher. They're fully enclosed (i.e., they go all the way to the ceiling) and have doors with padlocks. The smallest cages are approximately 7 feet by 10 feet and can hold three or four open racks. Larger cages can hold hundreds of racks. (Open racks aren't a problem when they're used inside a private cage. In fact, it's much easier to cable and maintain servers installed in open racks than when they're installed inside enclosed cabinets.)

Most web-site owners find that cages are particularly attractive if they need more than five or six racks or cabinets and expect to manage their own servers or use an MSP independent from the colocation vendor. A cage gives you the ultimate in isolation from other customers. And because you have floor space in addition to the rack space, you can store even more tools, spare parts, and servers than you can store in cabinets.

The charges for cages may be based on the size of the cage, the number of racks within the cage, or both. Table 5.3 is a sample of cage colocation pricing.

TIP Use cages if you need more than six cabinets or if you want to be as isolated as possible from the colocation vendor and other customers.

Bandwidth Costs

Nearly all colocation vendors charge for connectivity to the Internet using the 95th Percentile Rule in which the 5 percent of busiest bandwidth measurements, taken every five minutes, are discarded, and the next-highest measurement is the one used for billing purposes. The 95th Percentile Rule is discussed in detail in Chapter 11, "Traffic Models." The retail cost of bandwidth at relatively low volumes begins at a maximum cost of about $1,000 per Mbps per month. For example, a site that delivers 1 million page views per month might use a 95th percentile peak bandwidth of 5 Mbps. The cost (before any quantity discounting) would be $5,000 per month.

Colocation services make more money from their bandwidth than they do from renting their real estate, so there's typically a minimum usage of 1 to 2 Mbps per cabinet or rack. If you have three cabinets, for instance, you may be asked to pay for a minimum of 3 to 6 Mbps bandwidth even if you don't use that much.

Colocation Trends

A number of changes are taking place in the colocation category, many of which will affect not only colocation vendors' direct customers, but also customers whose sites are hosted at shared- and dedicated-server facilities operated within colocation facilities by tenant vendors and resellers. Some of these changes and their effects on customers are described in the following subsections.

Shortage of Financing

Of all of the categories of web-hosting services, colocation has by far the greatest requirement for long-term financing of fixed assets. Colocation facilities are expensive to build, and therefore need tremendous amounts of capital or debt financing. Data center construction costs run from $500 to $1,200 per square foot, if you include the costs of fire-suppression equipment, security systems, air conditioning, and so on. At that rate, a typical 50,000-square-foot facility requires $25 million to $60 million of long-term financing.

By comparison, the shared- and dedicated-server vendors, particularly those that are tenants of colocation facilities, only need to finance their servers, which tend to (a) scale with their current customer demand (it's easy to add more servers), and (b) depreciate over relatively short periods (e.g., 36 months). Likewise, MSPs—at least those that don't own their data centers—have relatively low requirements for facilities.

As the financial markets swing back and forth, occasionally some of the colocation vendors (including the long-distance telephone companies, or *telcos*) find it difficult or impossible to finance their expansion. Telcos have the added problem of simultaneously trying to finance the deployment of new fiber and switching equipment, and their occasionally low bond ratings have made it virtually impossible for them to raise the required cash from time to time. When money is tight, the only companies that don't seem to have trouble building new data centers are those that already have huge cash resources on hand.

Focus on Revenue per Cabinet

Because some colocation vendors are having a difficult time raising the money from lenders and capital markets to fund their expansions, they're looking for other ways to expand their businesses. Many of them are focusing on increasing the revenues generated from their existing facilities. Their hope is to expand their businesses faster than they can expand their physical infrastructure.

To accomplish this, these vendors are trying to increase their *revenue per cabinet* or *revenue per square foot,* and they're doing so by pursuing customers that will use more bandwidth per cabinet, and by moving into the managed services business.

Due to the constantly increasing density and quantity of servers, a third choice—raising prices—isn't really an option for these vendors. And that will remain true at least as long as there isn't a shortage of data center space. (There *are* some shortages of data center space, but they tend to be only in certain locations such as downtown San Francisco, Silicon Valley, or New York City.)

Vendors will always try to sell to customers with large and ever-growing budgets and to those who will purchase more bandwidth. After all, bandwidth and real estate are what the colocation vendors have to sell.

The risk to you as a customer is that over time you might cease to be within the range of your vendor's ideal target customer, and that you may no longer be in its *sweet spot*. In other words, as the vendor's hypothetical ideal customer evolves to be one with a higher budget and the need for more bandwidth, if your budget and requirements don't likewise increase over time, you'll run the risk of becoming a customer that's less profitable for the vendor, and you may therefore not receive the treatment you expect. It may not be fair, but it's a fact of life in the web-hosting business (see Chapter 8, "Getting it Right," for more information about the vendor's sweet spot).

The Shift to Managed Services

The other opportunity colocation vendors have for increasing revenues is also a risk to customers. The vendors have noticed that MSPs get far more money per cabinet or per square foot and do it without having to actually build much of anything. The colocation services have observed MSPs and resellers leasing colocation space for x, adding services, and selling that same space for $10x$ or more. Some of the colocation vendors want a piece of that action, so they're adding managed service offerings of their own.

When a colocation vendor refocuses on customers with larger budgets, pure colocation customers may suddenly discover they're no longer wanted. After all, why would a vendor want to keep a customer paying x, when the vendor could fill the same cabinets or racks with another customer paying $10x$? If you're caught in this scenario—and it's happening regularly—you're in an even worse position than just slipping out of the sweet spot; you're at risk of being *dumped*. Dumping is a practice by which some vendors purposely reduce the quality of the services they deliver to their old customers, hoping the customers will leave and can then be replaced with new, more profitable customers. (See Chapter 8 for more information about dumping.)

> **TIP** If you want pure colocation, find a vendor that has a long-term commitment to support that model and that isn't likely to want to replace you with a customer to which it can sell more services.

The CDN Threat

Content delivery networks (CDNs) are an increasingly popular method of transmitting data from a web site to its customers. CDNs maintain copies of images and streaming data—typically a site's largest files—on *caches* or *edge servers*, which are similar to your web servers except that they're located closer to the visitor's web browser. (See Chapter 13, "Caching and Content Delivery Networks," for more information on CDNs.)

This can do wonders for a web site's performance, reliability, and scalability. Because these large files are no longer transmitted directly from the web site, however, the use of a CDN deprives the web-hosting vendor of one of its two sources of revenue: bandwidth. It's entirely possible for some sites to reduce their colocation bandwidth requirements by 90 percent or more by instead paying a CDN to deliver those files. As a solution, some colocation vendors are looking into offering CDN services themselves.

As a customer, it's important to realize that changes like these are occurring, and that web hosting is a constantly evolving business with some complex economics.

Two Tiers of Colocation Vendors

Some colocation providers *are* committed to a strategy of pure colocation. The problem is that many of them only lease their facilities on a wholesale basis, sometimes without even providing connections to the Internet. In this way they reduce their cost of construction to as little as $200 per square foot. Like builders of shopping centers, they tend to secure their *anchor tenants* before construction even begins in order to make their data centers easier to finance.

These data center *landlords*—those committed to colocation—can be hard to identify and even harder to find. Such vendors certainly won't offer partial-rack colocation. In fact, they may offer nothing smaller than cages, and fairly larger ones at that. Their space tends to be entirely divided into these large cages, each leased by an MSP, application service provider (ASP), or tenant shared- or dedicated-server vendor.

Unfortunately, wholesale colocation vendors are not a good choice for most web sites because the quality of the vendors' Internet connectivity tends to be poor. Remember, such vendors are trying to keep their costs low, and many tenants bring in their own private links to the major ISPs. This class of colocation vendor can provide excellent power, but doesn't offer much in the way of pipe and ping.

TIP Unless you intend to supply and manage your own connectivity, avoid hosting services that focus on wholesale pure colocation.

With or Without an MSP?

If you want to own and manage your servers, you want pure colocation. But you can also use colocation and separately outsource the management of your servers to (and possibly lease the servers from) an MSP, as discussed in the next chapter.

Pure Colocation: Do-It-Yourself Management

In the case of pure colocation, the vendor supplies the physical space, power, air conditioning, and so forth, as well as a connection to the Internet, but virtually nothing else. Your staff will have the primary responsibility for installation, configuration, management, and maintenance of your servers. In this case, you'll need to select a colocation facility that's in close proximity to your staff.

If your site is small and your servers will be located in racks shared with other sites, the colocation vendor will likely handle the physical installation of your servers. This makes sense, since the vendor needs to protect the other servers from anything you may do, such as knocking out network or power connectors.

On the other hand, if you have dedicated racks or cabinets, or if your site is located in a private cage, plan to handle the installation of the servers yourself. The staff of colocation vendors is not typically equipped to do this for you.

TIP If you're using pure colocation, select a facility that's close to your staff, and plan to have your staff install, configure, manage, and maintain the servers. Don't depend on the colocation vendor's staff for any hands-on services.

Colocation and Managed Services

As an alternative to do-it-yourself management, you can use a colocation vendor for the low-level service it provides, and outsource the more sophisticated care and feeding of your servers to an MSP. This combination is becoming increasingly popular, and we'll look at it in more detail in Chapter 6, "Managed Services."

You need to be aware that most colocation vendors and MSPs have a love/hate relationship with one another. On one hand, the colocation vendors appreciate the MSPs because the MSPs bring in customers. On the other hand, the colocation vendors hate the fact that the MSPs make more money from those customers than do the colocation vendors themselves. The colocation vendors also know that the customer's loyalty is to the MSP first (because of the higher-value relationship the customer has with the MSP), and only coincidentally to the colocation vendor.

Some colocation vendors intend to expand into the MSP business as soon as possible, and it's only a matter of time before they effectively sever their relationships with the MSPs that are currently their partners.

TIP Investigate carefully the relationship between the colo and the MSP, as it's very possible that those that are partners today will become competitors tomorrow. You're going to be stuck with the MSP, and if their new customers are at a different facility than their old ones (including you), you'll become a second-class customer, or be forced to move your site.

Colocation is a must-have for any site that's large and complex enough that it can't be run on dedicated servers. The big question, which we'll address in the next chapter, is whether to go with pure colocation or to employ the services of managed service providers, the newest breed of web-hosting services.

6

Managed Services

As you move up the web-hosting ladder from shared to dedicated web-hosting services, you'll encounter increased levels of vendor service and support. But when you take the next step—to colocation—you'll discover you're on your own when it comes to building and managing your web site.

It's like moving from renting an apartment to owning your own home. In the apartment days, maintenance was someone else's problem. But now that you've got the freedom to do whatever you want, you've also got more responsibilities. In some ways it almost seems like a step backward.

But if you host your web site at a colocation service, you don't need to go it alone. If you're not a manage-it-yourself kind of company, you can turn to a managed service provider (MSP) who will configure and manage your colocated web site for you.

The Birth of MSPs

For many years, if you opted for colocation, you had no choice but to manage your colocated servers yourself. Over time, more and more web-site owners found themselves in this position. Because those owners tended to have the largest budgets, a new market opportunity appeared for someone who was willing and able to come in and manage the high-end web sites housed at colocation facilities.

To exploit this opportunity, a new web-hosting service category, managed service providers, was born. Managed services are specifically designed to work in conjunction with colocation and to provide those services that are not addressed by colocation vendors themselves.

Why don't the colocation vendors offer managed services? In fact, many *do* offer them now, but only recently, in reaction to the success of the MSPs (some of which were acquired by the colocation vendors) as a way to enter the MSP business. But for years, although customers screamed that they needed such help, colocation vendors simply couldn't provide managed services themselves. The reason comes back to a recurring issue: The skills that are required to provide good power, pipe, and ping (colocation) are very different from those required to support and manage servers and applications. Even the cultures of such organizations are very different. (Just imagine calling your phone company's service center for help with a database performance problem, and you'll understand the difference.)

MSP Segmentation

In the previous chapters, where we covered shared, dedicated, and colocation web hosting, we were able to further break down those classifications into subcategories. But because of the relative newness of the managed service business, the breakdown of vendors and the definitions of services are not as precise or as widely accepted as with shared, dedicated, and colocation hosting. The jargon has not yet stabilized, and there's an extraordinarily wide range of companies that now call themselves MSPs.

So rather than create categories that aren't already in use by the MSP industry, our approach in this chapter will be to identify the raw criteria that distinguish one MSP from another. Once you understand these differences, you'll be able to determine which MSPs are right for you, even if you can't instantly identify the appropriate vendors with a single label. The criteria we'll explore in this chapter include:

Flexibility. Some MSPs support a very limited (rigid) set of software and hardware products, while others are quite flexible in this regard. But as we'll see, flexibility isn't necessarily a good thing.

Facility neutrality. Some MSPs own their own data centers, while others are *portable* or data-center independent.

Staffing models. MSPs organize their personnel that support your site in different ways.

Service levels and pricing models. MSPs offer different levels of service and use pricing models that range from time-and-materials to flat-rate (component) pricing.

In the pages that follow, we'll examine in more detail each of these criteria and discuss how to select an MSP.

Vendor Flexibility

The first MSPs approached the task of managing web sites in much the same way as the classical IT staff outsourcers. They simply provided a staff that was skilled in web operations on a professional services basis, and billed by the hour. Such MSPs still ex-

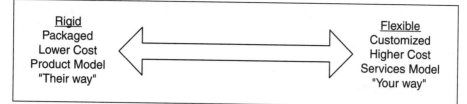

Figure 6.1   Rigid versus flexible MSPs.

ist and are referred to in this book as *flexible* MSPs, for reasons that will become clear shortly.

Other MSPs recognized, however, that they could achieve certain economies of scale, and perhaps even offer services of superior quality, by standardizing on a specific, limited set of hardware and software products and repeatable processes and procedures to support those products. These are referred to as *rigid* MSPs ("rigid" isn't a derogatory term, and it's the best word to describe this class of vendors). There are advantages and disadvantages to both the rigid and flexible models, and there are MSPs at all points in between, as illustrated in Figure 6.1.

The Flexible Model

At one end of the spectrum, fully flexible MSPs are essentially contract-staffing organizations that will support any technologies, hardware, platforms, and applications. They're in the professional services business, providing system administrators, database administrators, and others on either a full-time (dedicated) basis or on an on-call basis and shared with other clients.

Most flexible MSPs add more value in two ways. First, they tend to specialize in certain technologies, either companywide or by employing individuals with specialized skills and experience. Second, these MSPs implement a variety of processes and systems that are shared by all of their customers. These systems include those for monitoring a web site's uptime and performance, as well as customer resource management (CRM) components such as call-center and incident-tracking systems.

The general approach of a flexible MSP is to provide services *your way,* and to try and function as an extension of your own in-house staff. The primary advantage of working with a flexible MSP is that you can build your web site using any hardware and software. If you want to use an application developed by ABC running on servers made by XYZ, no problem. If it's a combination the MSP has never encountered before, it will ramp up on it, and do whatever's necessary to make it work.

But the real benefit of using a flexible MSP shows up later, when you decide to enhance your site by adding new features and systems that you couldn't have anticipated at the time you selected your MSP and designed your initial configuration. If you or your organization tends to live on the cutting edge of web and Internet technologies, you might do well to work with an MSP that can commit to this type of flexibility.

Of course, flexibility doesn't come without a downside. As we'll see, more rigid MSPs can sometimes achieve higher levels of efficiency and reliability due to their focus on repeatability and scalability. While a flexible MSP can and will do whatever you need, it may cost you more in dollars, time, and reliability.

TIP Favor flexible MSPs to the extent that you believe you're an early adopter of technology and that there's a chance you'll want to utilize leading-edge web-site components in the future.

The Rigid Model

"Do one thing—but do it better than anyone else," could be the mantra for the more rigid MSPs. By limiting the number of hardware and software technologies they support, they can do a better job than if they had to spread their resources across a broader range. This is not marketing fluff. It's a very real advantage of this model. By doing the same things day in and day out, and creating economies of scale, a rigid MSP can simultaneously improve quality and keep costs down.

By working with a rigid MSP that's committed to a predefined and limited set of products, you not only share staff with other customers (that's the case with flexible MSPs as well, of course), you also share the cost of training that staff since you and other customers are all using the same technology. Furthermore, when a new problem occurs with a given component or combination, there's a good chance that another customer will have experienced the problem first, giving you the benefit of a preventive fix, before the problem shows up on your web site.

The rigid model isn't perfect, either, of course. The obvious disadvantage is that you often can't have things entirely your way. If an MSP supports only Oracle databases, for instance, but you want to use Sybase, you'll have to go to another vendor or manage the database yourself.

But the greatest risk of using a rigid MSP occurs not at the time you select the MSP, but later, when you see how that MSP responds when you decide to add features and functionality to your site. If your MSP is entirely rigid (i.e., it has no policy for exceptions), you may find that you simply can't deploy your new features unless you switch to another MSP. This is an example of the risk of *lock-in*, as discussed in Chapter 7, "The Dark Side of Outsourcing."

TIP Favor rigid MSPs that have track records with the products on which your web site is based. Leverage the experience an MSP gains from supporting identical components for multiple customers.

Exceptions

Most MSPs are neither strictly rigid nor entirely flexible, but fall somewhere in between those extremes. Nearly all have *some* limits as to what they can and will do, even if they aren't willing to admit it.

A good way to uncover the sometimes subtle differences between otherwise similar MSPs is to investigate how they handle exceptions to their standard list of supported technologies. The best way to begin that investigation is to ask them.

In response to, "Suppose I want to use a different technology?" you should hear something like, "We have a formal process for handling exceptions." Of course, you should investigate the process, but at least you know it exists. Be concerned if you hear, "We don't do that," (too rigid), or, "No problem," (too flexible—it will cost too much). And don't ask the salesperson (you *know* what he or she will say). Instead ask the executive or manager in charge of operations—the person who's responsible for keeping things running.

You may find a rigid vendor that supports exactly the technologies your web site requires, and no others. That's okay, as long as you're certain your needs won't change over time. But when you can't find that perfect match, or you think your needs may change, the chances are you'll need an MSP that offers at least some degree of flexibility.

TIP Ask MSPs in advance how exceptions will be handled, even if you don't anticipate having any. Get sample pricing for the support of nonstandard products.

Co-Management

When you're trying to decide whether a flexible or rigid MSP is right for you, consider the extent to which you want to co-manage or share responsibility with your MSP for the management of your web site. One clue can be found by looking at your own staff.

Do you have system administrators and DBAs on staff that you expect to be involved with your web site, if only during the development phase? If so, it's likely that they'll also continue to have some involvement once the site is launched. In this case, you'd do well to avoid extremely rigid MSPs, since the extent of your staff's involvement might have the potential to put them at odds with a very rigid MSP.

If you have skills in some areas but not others (for example, sysadmins but no DBAs), consider a more flexible MSP that specializes in the areas in which you and your staff are weak. An MSP that specializes in database tuning and maintenance, for example, can complement your in-house system administrators.

On the other hand, if you have no operational staff, or if you do have such staff but are absolutely certain they won't be involved with operation of the live site, then by all means consider a rigid MSP.

Co-managing can be tricky, and it makes it virtually impossible (and therefore unreasonable) to ask for strong service level agreements in the areas in which you'll share responsibility with your vendor.

It's easier to go one way or the other. Either give the MSP 100 percent of the responsibility, and keep your staff away from the servers, or consider the MSP to be a professional services firm that takes its direction from you.

TIP Use your current staff as an indicator of whether you'll end up co-managing your web site with an MSP. Either you'll co-manage or you won't. There's no gray area.

If you do share responsibility with your MSP, make sure the areas of responsibility are clearly defined.

The Rev-Lock Problem

The large web sites typically managed by MSPs tend to be complex, and are generally built using hardware and software components from many different vendors. The application program interfaces (APIs) and other interactions between these components are complex. And since these APIs and interactions change over time (as hardware and software vendors release new versions of their products), they tend to be weak links in the chain of website stability and reliability.

One advantage often claimed by the rigid MSPs is that they have extensive experience with the interactions of specific versions of various software and hardware products. If an MSP supports, say, Sun's Solaris operating system and Oracle's database, it has likely deployed and supported this combination for multiple customers. If those are your choices for an operating system and a database, you'll receive the benefit of the MSP's past experience, and share with other customers the cost (both in dollars and headaches) of past and future learning.

A rigid MSP doesn't take risks with new, untested releases. As a benefit to both itself and its customers, such an MSP will test and certify that specific revisions of each are compatible with one another before deploying them on any customer's systems. For example, an MSP may support Oracle 9.1 with Solaris 8.2, but not with other versions of each. While this compatibility testing is valuable, there's a corresponding disadvantage: *revision locking* or *rev-lock*.

Suppose that Oracle releases version 9.2, which has some new features that are particularly valuable to your web site and application. Perhaps you'd like to take advantage of this new version, possibly as a prerelease or beta-test user.

This puts you at odds with the fundamental philosophy of a rigid MSP whose model is based on repeating the tried and true. Such an MSP offers lower costs (certainly for the same level of reliability) than an MSP that's entirely flexible, but it does so by limiting your options.

If a rigid MSP were to install Oracle 9.2 on your system only (i.e., not on the systems of its other Oracle customers), it would be working against its own model of fixed versions and combinations. If an MSP were to support a dozen software packages, and each one has three near-current revisions, the total number of combinations would be 3^{12} or over a half a million. It clearly isn't practical to test and certify all those combinations.

Therefore, rigid MSPs certify only specific combinations, and new combinations are not certified frequently or quickly. If you want, for instance, Oracle 9.2, you may have to wait until the MSP certifies a new version of Solaris as well. The MSP's certification for Oracle 9.1 is therefore rev-locked to Solaris 8.2. You can't upgrade one without the other. That may take time, and may have other disadvantages.

TIP If you expect to be an early adopter or want to mix and match revisions, use an MSP that's more flexible and that supports more than rev-locked combinations of products.

Facility Neutrality

The primary value of an MSP is its ability to manage web sites and keep them running. The physical infrastructure of the data center—the air conditioning, power, and security— is not the forte of most MSPs. Yet these things are still required. You can't run a web site without them, and each MSP, therefore, has a way to provide such infrastructure for its

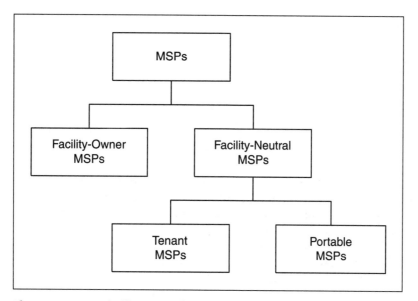

Figure 6.2 MSP facility ownership.

customers. How they do so, however, varies greatly, and this is another important crite-rion for your evaluation of MSPs.

Figure 6.2 is a "family tree" of MSPs, illustrating how they can be further divided into groups according to their relationships to data center facilities.

The first group—which we'll refer to as *facility-owner MSPs*—comprise those that own their data centers. In addition to being MSPs, these vendors are also in the colocation business, and they manage web sites and servers that are located in their own facilities.

The other MSPs all belong to the *facility-neutral* group. MSPs in this category don't own data centers. Instead, they provide management services for sites and servers that are colocated at third-party facilities.

The facility-neutral group is further split into two subgroups according to whether the MSPs work only with specific colocation vendors or they're entirely independent of the hosting location. The first subgroup (we'll call them *tenant MSPs*) rent dedicated space within the data centers of one or more colocation vendors, and require that their customers' sites be housed at a data center operated by one of those partners. Tenant MSPs have these special relationships with one or a small number of colocation vendors.

Portable MSPs, members of the other subgroup of facility-neutral MSPs, are *entirely* neutral, and will manage sites located anywhere in the world, even in their customers' own corporate facilities. MSPs in this group neither own nor rent data center space.

Which group of MSPs is better? As you'll see in the next few sections, life with a facility-owner MSP can be a whole lot simpler than if you try to combine a colocation vendor and a facility-neutral MSP. However, this simplicity alone isn't enough to suggest that facility-owner MSPs are always the right solution. There are, of course, many more issues.

Partnerships

In the following sections we'll look at four issues that are unique to the relationships between facility-neutral MSPs and colocation vendors:

- The politics between them
- The MSP's physical proximity to the hardware
- Remote-hands services from colocation vendors
- Control over the connectivity

Facility-neutral MSPs have one advantage during the vendor-selection phase: their relative objectivity. Many facility-neutral MSPs work with more than one colocation vendor. They know the colocation vendors better than the web-site owners do because they work so closely with those vendors. Based on previous experience with the colos, they know with which one they (and hence their customers) will be more successful.

But some MSPs won't give recommendations for colos unless they're pushed hard to do so. They may be afraid of offending their other colocation partners; and in a few instances, there may be subjective aspects of an MSP's relationship with a colo (such as kickbacks from the colo to the MSP's salesperson or other incentives that affect the MSP's bottom line). But most commonly, what's good for the MSP is also good for you. By comparison, there's no point in asking a facility-owner MSP to recommend a colocation vendor; they're one and the same.

However, not all facility-neutral MSPs work with multiple colocation vendors. Some (particularly tenant MSPs) work with only one. These MSPs are obviously as lacking in objectivity as those that own their own facilities. Likewise, if you've been referred to a facility-neutral MSP by a colocation vendor—a somewhat backward strategy—don't expect the MSP to be objective in its recommendation for colocation. You've started with the answer instead of the question.

MSP/Colo Politics

As you should be starting to see, the relationships between colocation vendors and facility-neutral MSPs are complex and even strained at times. If you're considering facility-neutral MSPs, you need to be aware of what's going on between these two groups and between individual MSPs and colos, because these relationships, particularly as they change over time, will greatly affect you. Let's look at some of the issues between these vendors.

Most of the early MSPs began as facility-neutral vendors. They were created to fill the need for outsourced management that the colocation vendors at the time were unable to fill. As discussed in Chapter 5, "Colocation," the colocation vendors (who generally failed at their early in-house attempts to enter the MSP business) then began to acquire the independent, facility-neutral MSPs. In doing so, of course, they converted the neutral MSPs into nonneutral, *facility-specific* MSPs.

Although more and more web-site owners are learning to begin their search with the MSPs, not the colos, the MSPs still need colocation vendors as a source of leads. Many of the MSPs are small companies, with very little customer brand awareness of their own. The colocation vendors, by comparison, tend to be relatively large, well-known companies.

On the other hand, colocation-only vendors *need* facility-neutral MSPs for two reasons. First, the MSPs bring them business. Second, without MSP partners to whom the colos can refer business, the colos will lose any web-hosting customers that require managed services.

Colocation vendors prefer to partner with MSPs that recommend them exclusively. But the facility-neutral MSPs are free to recommend any of their colocation partners. For these reasons, there's a constant push-shove relationship between these symbiotic classes of vendors, and it's aggravated by the fact that the colocation vendors are always on the verge of diving into the MSP business themselves. It's *coopetition:* cooperating partners today, competitors tomorrow.

The colocation vendors are also envious of the MSPs because the MSP can derive as much as five times the revenues that the colo can from the same web site. The colos hate the fact that the MSPs get the lion's share of the revenues as well as the customers' loyalty. This envy can lead to some tense relationships between MSPs and their colocation partners.

Colocation vendors are also envious of the cost side of MSP economics. As compared to the cost of building data centers, it takes relatively little cash to start an MSP business, and many MSPs are therefore small and poorly funded. But the colocation vendors have considerable financial problems of their own, since they need to increase their margins in order to repay the debt used to build their expensive facilities. The colocation vendors see a strategy of acquiring MSPs as a way to rapidly increase their revenues per square foot of data center space. That's why, although perhaps poorly funded, MSPs have high valuations, and continue to be acquisition targets for colocation-only vendors.

Looking ahead, the colocation vendors don't want to continue to help the MSPs become too successful, since doing so will merely increase the price that the colos have to pay to acquire them at some time in the future.

If you select a facility-owner MSP, you won't need to worry about these issues. But if you opt for a facility-neutral MSP, be aware that these issues exist and that there's a lot of jockeying for position going on behind the scenes.

Proximity and Remote Management

Another issue to consider, if you go with an MSP that doesn't own its data centers, is the proximity of the MSP's staff to your servers. As we discussed in the context of colocation, it's not important that your staff be close to the hardware, but certainly someone must be. Proactive, scheduled tasks such as adding or upgrading servers don't require that technicians be located particularly close to the data center. But what happens when there's a hardware failure?

As we'll discuss in greater detail in Chapter 8, "Getting It Right," some MSPs rely on the hardware vendors or third parties for maintenance. Once they've determined (remotely) that a problem is due to a hardware failure, these MSPs take on the role of dispatcher. They contact whoever's responsible for repairing the hardware and monitor that third party's efforts to resolve the problem.

This isn't a great solution. Such an MSP must perform its problem determination remotely, and hardware problems are especially difficult to diagnose in this manner. If a failure is in one redundant component (such as a single drive in a RAID array), the fix is fairly straightforward. But if, for instance, a server has a RAM or CPU failure, the entire box may become unresponsive, at which point the MSP can only throw up its hands and call the maintenance vendor, who must then come on-site to ultimately diagnose the problem. In many cases the technician will have to make a second trip to fetch replacement parts once the defective part is identified.

An MSP shouldn't rely on a third-party technician to correct an error on his or her own. Suppose a technician replaces a failed disk drive, but while messing about in your cabinet, he or she manages to dislodge a network connection. The tech may have never seen your servers before, and certainly isn't likely to be able to diagnose a cabling problem on his or her own. If an incident is critical enough to call out the third-party hardware technicians, an MSP employee who knows your configuration should be there, too.

An MSP should have someone on-site or very nearby so that the initial diagnosis is more accurate and complete. For example, it's far better to call a third-party maintenance company and tell them you've lost a CPU, than to report, "We don't know what the problem is. The box just doesn't respond." Some MSPs even stock spare parts and can perform repairs on the spot without the need to call (and wait for) third parties.

Facility-owner MSPs always have on-site staff in their data centers so there's no problem with them. Some facility-neutral MSPs also have staff close by their customer's servers, but others do not. MSPs in the tenant subgroup often have staff on site in their data centers on a 24/7 basis because, like the facility-owner MSPs, they have a large number of customers in one location.

But portable MSPs may not have any staff nearby; their closest employees could be thousands of miles away. Using such an MSP will only work if your own staff will handle all on-site tasks (i.e., you're close to the data center or you're using a portable MSP to manage your web site within your own facilities).

TIP If an MSP doesn't have on-site staff, it should at least have technicians that are very close by (less than 30 minutes away) and on call on a true 24/7 basis.

Remote Hands

You'll probably encounter at least one colocation vendor and facility-independent MSP partner that mentions *remote hands.* This is a service in which the colo's employees will perform certain functions such as power-cycling or rebooting a server for you or the MSP.

While remote-hands service comes in handy once in a while, it's not a reasonable replacement for on-site or nearby MSP staff. Sure, your MSP can ask someone to cycle the power on a server rather than waiting 15 or 20 minutes for the MSP's employee to get to the site, but that's about all this service is good for.

TIP Don't accept a colocation vendor's remote-hands service in lieu of having an MSP employee on site or nearby at all times.

Who Controls the Connectivity?

Just as someone needs to take responsibility for on-site support, so must the responsibility for connectivity be clear and unambiguous. This suggests one disadvantage of using a colocation vendor and a separate, facility-neutral MSP: the potential for finger pointing when it comes time to resolve connectivity problems.

TIP Up front, make sure you understand who controls the bandwidth and connectivity. Don't accept a service level agreement (SLA) for connectivity from an MSP that has no control over it.

If you do choose a facility-neutral MSP, there are two possible scenarios. In the first, the MSP acts as a one-stop shop. It buys connectivity from the colocation vendor and resells it to you. The advantage of this arrangement is that the MSP is on the hook to resolve any problems that occur, even if the colocation vendor is at fault. The MSP *should* have more clout than you do, since the MSP has multiple customers hosted with the colocation vendor and can potentially bring in even more business.

The second scenario is a trap. If you bypass the MSP and buy connectivity directly from the colocation vendor, you'll get caught in the middle. One of the responsibilities of your MSP should be to manage the colocation vendor relationship on your behalf. The ability of the MSP to do so is based on the strength of its relationship with the colo. In bypassing the MSP you weaken that relationship.

TIP If you choose a facility-neutral MSP, buy your colocation and connectivity services through that vendor in order to minimize finger pointing between the MSP and the colocation vendor.

Sometimes even the strongest MSP/colo relationships can't solve a connectivity problem. One way to avoid such problems is to use an MSP that purchases some portion of its bandwidth independently—not from the colocation vendor, but directly from ISPs. Tenant MSPs and portable MSPs that normally rely on colocation vendors to supply connectivity sometimes find that the quality of that connectivity deteriorates because the colocation vendor simply doesn't continue to make needed upgrades. Many MSPs have been faced with this dilemma and have had to purchase connectivity directly from major ISPs, bypassing the connectivity provided by the landlord colocation vendor.

TIP Make sure the agreement between your MSP and the colocation vendor permits the MSP to bring in third-party connectivity. Ask your MSP if it has ever had to buy connectivity directly from ISPs to work around poor connectivity from the colocation vendor.

Hopefully, your MSP has already dealt with this problem on behalf of other customers. You don't want to be part of its first experience.

Staffing Models

Over time, many of your MSP's employees will work on your web site. Some will come in, solve a problem, then move on to the next customer's problem. Others may get to know you and your web site over an extended period.

The Private Knowledge Syndrome

If you're supported by a small team of people, they'll be tempted to share information through shortcuts such as voicemail and Post-It notes. Even though the MSP may have processes in place for documenting all activities, the convenience of informality is compelling. People get sloppy. Two people may discuss an issue but fail to tell the other members of the team. This is a case of the *private knowledge syndrome* in which some members of the team have knowledge of certain data and others do not.

The result is that some issues, problems, and solutions don't get documented, which—on a day-to-day basis—can cause tremendous confusion. Additionally, when a person leaves the team and is replaced by another, the new person doesn't have access to the accumulated knowledge of the group. This can lead to the new person's repeating tasks that have already been completed or making changes that are detrimental to the integrity of the site.

The smaller the team, the more likely it is for this problem to occur. A small group can easily communicate verbally, and hence lose valuable information. Larger teams, on the other hand, are forced to use tools such as email, which, if retained, provides some level of documentation to which the team members can refer.

> **TIP** Ask your MSP if it has implemented a formal *knowledge management* system to avoid the private knowledge syndrome. Ideally, it should include a web-based customer gateway.

A knowledge management system is one that tries to improve the efficiency and utilization of human knowledge within an organization. Anything that helps groups of people record and share information is generally considered part of knowledge management.

Dedicated Staff

Each MSP has an organizational model for how it allocates staff for its customers, and the model your MSP selects can have substantial impact on how well your site is maintained. A range of MSP staffing models is illustrated in Figure 6.3.

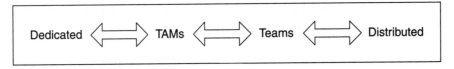

Figure 6.3 MSP staffing models.

If your site is large and complex, and if your budget for managed services is more than $50,000 per month, you may be assigned a dedicated staff that's responsible only for your web site. This is the classical IT outsourcing model.

The major advantage of having a dedicated staff of MSP employees is that they sink or swim based on how well your web site's service levels are met. With this model, dedicated staff can also draw upon the expertise of nondedicated specialists elsewhere within the MSP's organization. For example, your dedicated team may not have full-time security analysts or DBAs, but the team may have access to such people on an as-needed basis. This availability of specialists is one reason why IT outsourcing makes sense. It's a good model for customers who need it and can afford it.

Another advantage of a dedicated team is the sense of ownership shared by its members. People with long-term responsibility for a web site are going to invest in doing things right, not just making quick fixes that may cause even greater problems at a later time. Other staffing models that give people long-term responsibility for your site share this advantage.

Distributed Responsibility

At the opposite end from dedicated staffing on the staffing model spectrum we find the *fully distributed* model, in which no individuals are assigned to specific customers. Any MSP staff member may work on any customer's web site. This is the staffing model used by major utilities, telcos, and cable television companies. It can also be found among the lower-end services such as dedicated- and shared-hosting services.

The obvious advantages of distributed responsibility are that it eliminates dependence on any single individual and precludes the private knowledge syndrome. In theory, everything is either standardized or documented. There can be no exceptions, since there's no expectation that the person who solves a problem or makes a change will be the next person to work on that web site or even be available for consultation. Furthermore, if there *is* a private-knowledge problem in a fully distributed staffing environment, the communications system will break down immediately, and therefore receive prompt management attention.

To see the disadvantages of this model, you need look no further than your own experience with your local telephone or long-distance company. Not only do you deal with a different person for each new incident, but when you try to solve a complex problem over an extended period of time, each person you talk to has to ramp-up on the history of the incident. If incidents are short and simple (such as the need to recover a file from tape backup), then this model works well. But when an incident becomes more complex (such as tracking down a nasty performance problem), it's crucial that it be escalated to specialists who will take ownership of the incident through its resolution. We've all experienced the problem of dealing with a phone company and been frustrated by how long it takes to get to someone who both knows what to do and will stick with the problem until it's solved, without passing the buck.

TIP Avoid MSPs that use a fully distributed staffing model. It's only appropriate for shared and dedicated web-hosting services.

Technical Account Managers

To address the weaknesses of the distributed staffing model, to provide some consistency, and to guarantee that customers don't have to go through a lengthy escalation process each time there's a problem, some MSPs use a staffing model based on the use of technical account managers (TAMs). The ideal TAM is a three-way hybrid between a sales account manager, a project manager, and a system administrator.

In some cases, the TAM replaces the sales account manager once the contract is signed. In others, the salesperson continues to be assigned to the account in addition to the TAM, and can provide a valuable escalation path in case the TAM drops the ball.

The technical account manager serves as a single point of contact for all issues related to a web site. If a problem is detected by the MSP's monitoring systems or operational staff, and can't be corrected immediately, the TAM becomes the first escalation contact. Likewise, if the customer first detects a problem, or if the customer has a proactive change request, the customer calls the TAM. In either case, the TAM then draws upon the appropriate expertise within the MSP's support staff, escalating the incident as necessary.

The TAM model is designed for customers whose sites (or budgets) are too small for dedicated staff and who require some flexibility. Such sites can't be served well by a fully distributed staffing model that depends on extremely strict procedures.

One challenge for an MSP is matching TAMs with customers. Often, TAMs will be assigned based upon areas of expertise. For instance, an MSP may support both Unix and Windows/NT hosting, in which case it may have TAMs that specialize in one platform or the other. But this suggests the first weakness in the TAM model: TAMs need to be superheroes, hence are very difficult to hire and retain.

For example, many sites today include *both* Unix and Windows/NT servers, and therefore require a TAM who's well versed in both technologies. Even sites that use only one of these operating systems, still may use a wide variety of technologies from many vendors, and therefore require a TAM that understands them all.

Remember, too, that TAMs aren't permanent. At some MSPs they're notoriously temporary. The chances are good that even if you like the TAM assigned to your account, someone less satisfactory may soon replace him or her.

The Fire Department Analogy

TAMs enhance customer communications, to be sure, and are particularly helpful for managing proactive, nonurgent issues. But when things go seriously wrong with a live web site, you (the customer) will want a response that's more like that of a fire department. Just imagine your local fire department organized around the TAM model, and what might happen when the TAM assigned to your home comes knocking on your door to introduce himself. It might go something like this:

"Hi, I'm Bob, your local fireman, and I've been assigned to your house. I've made myself familiar with every aspect of your home and your neighborhood, and I want you to know that anytime you have a fire, you can call me directly. Here are my pager and cell phone numbers. Call me day or night.

"By the way if you can't reach me because I'm sick, on vacation, or fighting another fire, there's always someone there to cover for me. But since we each have our own territories, he may not know exactly how to get here, and it may take him a while to find the fire hydrant. While he may not be familiar with some of the materials used in the construction of your home, don't worry—you'll be well taken care of."

Luckily, as opposed to Bob, your local fire department is a good example of the distributed-responsibility staffing model. TAMs don't do well in this situation, and likewise they're not a great solution in web hosting when real problems occur.

> **TIP** Avoid MSPs that use the TAM staffing model. It's only a stop-gap solution to the problems of the fully distributed model. The team model (described next) is almost always superior.

On the other hand, some web-site owners love their TAMs. There's a chance you may get a good one, too, but don't count on it. They're few and far between.

Teams

MSPs that truly understand the staffing issues use a *team* model that falls somewhere between TAMs and the fully distributed model. Each team (sometimes called a *pod*) consists of 8 to 15 people who always work together and are assigned (as a consistent team) to multiple accounts. In some cases, a team may handle only two or three accounts. In others they may be responsible for as many as 40, depending on the size and complexity of their customers' sites.

Many web-site owners have found the team approach to be an ideal model. It addresses the problems of the other models in the following ways:

A team is large enough that it can handle reasonable staff turnover. It's not as difficult to bring one or two new people into a group of 10 as it is to replace one or two in a group of three. Such a team is also large enough to minimize the private-knowledge syndrome, discussed earlier in this chapter. It's also unlikely that a team will decide to quit en masse in the instance of some dispute between the team and senior management.

Unlike the fully distributed and TAM staffing models, with a team of 8 to 15 people there's always someone available who knows your web site. When you reach that person on your team, you can be confident he or she will know who you are and be familiar with your site and its history. Furthermore, a team of such size can be almost entirely self-contained, with its own expertise in most aspects of your site.

> **TIP** Look for MSPs that use a team staffing model. It's a better model for managing most web sites than the dedicated, fully distributed, or TAM models.

The Staff Bait-and-Switch

Whether you opt for an MSP that uses the TAM staffing model or one that's based on teams, you should be aware of two *bait-and-switch* practices that may catch you by surprise. In most cases, there's no deceit or deception intended on the part of the MSP, so bait-and-switch may be an unfair way to characterize these practices. But whether the MSP's intentions are honorable or not, the effect on you will be the same.

The first practice is the use of TAMs or teams during presales that are different from those that actually manage web sites after the contract is signed. Some TAMs, for instance, are such good communicators that their employers use them in a sales-support role to help close accounts. It's very possible—even likely—that the TAMs you meet before you select your MSP will not be the same as those who will be on your account after you sign a contract.

TIP Make sure the TAM or the team you meet during an MSP's sales process is the one that will stay with you through implementation, launch, and beyond.

The second bait-and-switch scenario is the use of *implementation TAMs* or *implementation teams*. In this version, an MSP uses one TAM or team during the so-called implementation phase. But once your web site is up, running, and stable, the MSP switches to a *maintenance TAM* or team. No surprise: The maintenance staff isn't as skilled as the implementation gurus.

There are two fundamental flaws with this practice of segregating implementation and operational staff. First, at the time when your site is handed off to a new TAM or team, all sorts of things get dropped or go wrong. Second, because the transfer of knowledge from the old TAM or team to the new one is usually incomplete, you and your own staff will likely have to put in extra hours to correct any errors that do occur, and (at the very least) educate the new TAM or team in how to work with your organization.

Beyond that, consider what maintenance really means on the web. In the offline world, maintenance mode usually means a state of very few changes. But it's different on the web, where things are always changing in substantial ways.

Just because your site has been running steadily for one month, does that mean it won't change? In fact, you'll probably want to start making substantial changes as soon as your site does become stable. You'll particularly want to add to the site those features that were postponed during development in order to make your launch date.

This will take you into new territory. You're going to make the first substantial changes to your live site. During initial development, you may have had the luxury of working on a system that wasn't yet online, and wasn't, therefore, required to be up 24 hours a day 7 days a week. Now, when the changes you make cause the site to go down, you and your staff will have to react quickly and at all times of the day and night. This isn't a good time to switch to a maintenance team and thereby lose the experience of those who suffered through the implementation.

TIP Avoid MSPs that switch from implementation staff to maintenance-mode TAMs or teams. It's better to have the continuity of people who stay with you all the way.

Service Levels and Pricing Models

The range of services offered by vendors that call themselves managed service providers, and the range of fees paid by their customers, have a big spread. As a group,

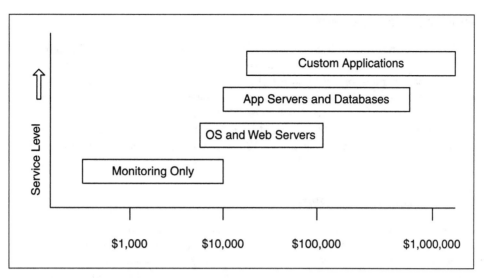

Figure 6.4 MSP monthly pricing ranges.

MSPs are generally aimed toward the high end of the overall web-hosting marketplace, with contracts starting at $1,000 per month. But some managed service contracts exceed $1 million per month—a 1000:1 range.

Service Levels

The range of services and the associated monthly prices are illustrated in Figure 6.4. The monthly fees shown are in addition to the capital expenses of hardware and software.

Monitoring

Note that at the very low end, starting at about $500 per month, MSPs provide only monitoring services. This means that for the established price (up through as much as $10,000), they'll monitor your site, and notify you or specified third parties in case of outages.

If all you need is basic monitoring and notification, you'd do better to avoid MSPs altogether, and get your monitoring from a vendor that specializes in just that. You don't really need an MSP.

The only reason MSPs offer such a basic service is to provide an entry point for customers that they hope will upgrade to higher-cost services. The difference between monitoring for $500 per month and $10,000 per month depends on the number of the servers monitored and the complexity of the web site.

TIP If you need only monitoring, use a dedicated monitoring service vendor. An MSP would be overkill.

We'll look at monitoring in detail in Chapter 19, "Monitoring."

Platform Management

Basic monitoring doesn't include any services to diagnose or resolve problems. The first level of service at which MSPs take responsibility and agree to meet service levels is in the management of the *platform*. At this level, an MSP will take responsibility for infrastructure, server hardware, the operating system software, other highly generic components (such as web-server software), and backup and recovery.

Platform management starts at about $5,000 per month. The high end ($100,000 per month) represents a site that includes 10 cabinets, at a higher ($10,000 per cabinet) price point.

Application Management

Managing applications (databases and application servers) is the goal for most MSPs, and for this, they hope to generate $10,000 or more per cabinet per month in revenues. The chart in Figure 6.4 includes a low end at this price with a single-cabinet customer. A four-cabinet customer paying $15,000 per cabinet will spend $60,000 per month.

Pricing Models

Although the preceding discussions are based on revenues per cabinet, that measurement is not typically used as the basis for charging customers. Rather, it's a way that vendors (particularly those that own the data centers or the cabinets) cross-check their pricing with other aspects of their business models.

MSPs use three pricing models: time-and-materials (T&M), retainers, and component pricing.

Time-and-Materials Pricing

T&M billing has always been the fundamental pricing model for professional services, and you'll find T&M billing in use by MSPs that are organized like professional services companies. In particular, you'll find that MSPs at the flexible end of the flexible/rigid scale tend to be those that use T&M pricing.

If you need the ultimate in flexibility, or a pay-as-you-go arrangement, T&M pricing can work. Recognize, however, that vendors on a T&M basis maximize their revenues and profits by increasing the number of hours they spend on your behalf. Professional services companies that bill on a T&M basis are like lawyers that do the same. They aren't particularly motivated to find efficiencies in their processes in order to reduce your costs. (Some vendors claim that they do try to "find efficiencies as a means of improving the utilization of their resources," but that's just another way of saying that they don't have enough qualified people.)

TIP In general, you'll pay more with a pure time-and-materials pricing model than with the others. Accept this model only if it's not possible to predict or standardize the services you require.

Retainers

As you move away from the flexible end of the flexible/rigid scale, you'll encounter MSPs that organize their services into packages with a monthly retainer—a minimum T&M fee. The retainer covers certain predictable services (such as monitoring and backup), and includes a minimum number of hours of ad hoc professional services. For example, an MSP's midlevel package might include a minimum of 40 hours per month in professional services that are covered by the monthly retainer. The pitch MSPs make to justify the retainer model is that it guarantees a certain level of availability of staff to respond to your problems.

But customers tend not to be any happier with the retainer model than they are with the T&M model. This is because a retainer sets a minimum amount they'll pay each month, whereas anyone who manages a budget needs maximums or *caps.*

Another flaw of the retainer model is that eventually a site is expected to become more stable and require fewer maintenance hours per month. Hence, the retainer (which, if unspent, can't be applied to services in other months) may be wasted.

For these reasons, the retainer model, as well as the T&M model, continue to lose favor among customers and hence among the vendors. These models make sense for web-site development, but not for ongoing operations.

TIP Avoid the retainer pricing model unless it's used only for ad hoc tasks and is combined with component pricing for standardized services.

Component Pricing

Most MSPs have shifted away from pure T&M and retainer-based pricing and toward a model of flat-rate fees for individual components. Many vendors continue to use T&M pricing (often based on a retainer) for some aspect of their services, but by and large they've shifted most of their charges into component-based pricing.

Here are some of the components that are often priced individually on a flat-fee basis:

- A monthly charge for each cabinet
- A monthly charge for each physical server (varying according to the software running on it) that covers management of the operating system and supported applications
- A monthly charge for tape backup based on the number of servers and the amount of data being backed up
- Separate monthly charges for load-balancing and firewall services if they're provided
- Monthly rental fees for hardware and software provided by the MSP

Table 6.1 shows a typical quotation from an MSP for a midsize (by MSP standards) web site.

Table 6.1   Sample MSP Pricing

SERVICE	QTY	ONE-TIME (SETUP) EACH	ONE-TIME (SETUP) TOTAL	MONTHLY EACH	MONTHLY TOTAL
Cabinet Rental (per cabinet)	2	$1,200	$ 2,400	$ 700	$1,400
Web Server SLA	4	$1,500	$ 6,000	$ 500	$2,000
Application Server SLA	2	$2,500	$ 5,000	$1,500	$3,000
Database Server SLA	1	$5,000	$ 5,000	$2,500	$2,500
Bandwidth (per Mbps)	5		$ –	$ 750	$3,750
Monitoring (per server)	7		$ –	$ 300	$2,100
Firewall Service (per public server)	4	$1,000	$ 4,000	$1,200	$4,800
Load Balancing (per public server)	4	$1,000	$ 4,000	$ 800	$3,200
Security Services (per server)	7	$1,500	$10,500	$ 350	$2,450
Tape Backup/Restore (per server)	7	$ 750	$ 5,250	$ 50	$ 350
Tape Backup/Restore (per GB)	50		$ -	$ 50	$2,500
Professional Services Retainer (per hour)	20		$ -	$175	$3,500
Totals			**$42,150**		**$31,550**

Some interesting points in this example include the following:

■ Most components include an initial/setup, nonrecurring expense (NRE) and a monthly recurring expense. The total NRE is $42,150 and the total monthly charge will be $31,550.

■ This MSP uses a retainer model for pricing professional services in addition to the component-based pricing. The customer pays for a minimum of 20 hours each month at a rate of $175 per hour. That amount is due whether or not the hours are actually used during the month. Additional hours are charged at the same hourly rate.

Unfortunately, managed service providers don't post their pricing on the Internet, so comparison shopping for price requires that you get a quotation from each prospective vendor.

TIP Component-based pricing models help you cap costs, but they're complex and require that you study them in detail.

Other MSP Issues

This section is a bit of a catch-all for a number of independent issues regarding managed service providers. We'll look at MSPs that specialize in certain technologies, such as databases, then two MSP practices: root access privileges and their use of *run books* to manage a web site. Next we'll consider three add-on MSP services: staging and content replication, procurement, and rapid provisioning. Finally, we'll explore the differences between MSPs that offer true risk transfer as opposed to simple risk management.

Specialty MSPs

Many MSPs evolved or were spun out from professional services firms, and therefore inherited certain specific skill sets from their former niches. For example, some MSPs are particularly adept at designing, tuning, and maintaining databases. Others may specialize in the use of particular application servers. These specialty MSPs often round out their offerings to include the other standard aspects of web-site operations, such as operating system and web-server expertise, but they continue to acquire new customers based on a good fit with their specialty.

You should consider whether a general or specialty MSP is right for you. If you're outsourcing *everything*—all aspects of the operation of your web site—you'll need expertise in all areas, hence a specialty MSP probably wouldn't be appropriate.

Conversely, if you plan to outsource only a portion of your web-site operations—that is, if you plan to share (co-manage) responsibility for the management of your site with your MSP, as discussed earlier in this chapter—a specialty MSP may be ideal. Suppose for example, you have a staff qualified to handle your customized application and the application servers on which it runs, but you'd like to outsource everything else. An MSP that specializes in databases might be a good choice. This would allow you and your staff to focus on what's unique about your business (the code, data, and customizations), and outsource the more generic components such as the database, web servers, operating systems, and hardware maintenance.

TIP If you plan to manage some aspects of your web-site operations, look for MSPs that specialize in the areas in which your own staff is weak.

Areas in which you may find MSP specialization include:

- Databases
- Streaming content
- Security
- High availability (high uptime)
- Specific application packages

Root Access

Root access is a specific privilege in Unix-based systems, but the concept applies to Windows/NT systems as well. Someone with full root access to a server has the ability to change any aspect of that server's software and configuration. Anyone with the ultimate responsibility for maintaining a server needs unrestricted ability to log in as the *root* or *admin* user.

Customers who want or need root access to their web servers present a particular challenge to an MSP. If the MSP is to assume full responsibility for the operation of your servers, it doesn't want you or your staff snooping around inside those servers, making changes, and potentially causing trouble that the MSP then must resolve. Even if your intentions are honorable, you have all of the required skills, and you're extremely careful, your MSP may have different ways of doing things. What's standard operating procedure to you may not be to the MSP.

MSPs handle requests for root access in five ways:

No root access, ever. Some simply don't permit it. The logic (and it really can't be faulted) is that if you want the MSP to take responsibility for a server, the MSP must have full and exclusive control over that server.

Root access with a reduced SLA. Many MSPs will grant you root access to the servers, but they'll insist on reducing their obligation and responsibility to determine and resolve problems associated with those servers. This is a common, although rather Draconian solution.

Unrestricted root access. Other MSPs (particularly those that don't offer rigorous SLAs) will allow you and your staff to have full root access to your servers. You should be realistic (even if your MSP isn't) and remember that sharing root access fundamentally increases the likelihood that problems will occur.

Restricted root access. Programs such as *Sudo (superuser do)* for Unix systems allow someone with unrestricted root access to grant specific individuals or group certain subsets of root privileges.

Root access as a service. A few progressive MSPs not only recognize that some customers need root access to their own servers but also that there's *value* associated with sharing root access. These MSPs offer root access as an add-on service under an extended SLA. The MSP's level of responsibility doesn't decrease, but there's an additional charge to the customer to cover the MSP's increased risk and liability.

TIP Don't ask for root access unless you need it; but if you do, make sure it doesn't reduce your service level or the responsibility of your vendor.

The security aspects of root access are discussed further in Chapter 17, "Security."

Run Books

Your MSP will create and maintain a *run book* for your web site. A run book documents a site's unique procedures for otherwise common tasks, such as starting and stopping servers, performing backups and recoveries, uploading new content, transferring and deleting log files, and so on. Any site that's complex enough to require colocation and managed services must have a run book.

TIP Ask prospective MSPs to let you see copies of run books (perhaps ones that have been sanitized or anonymized) for existing customers' web sites that most closely resemble yours.

Here are the types of information to look for:

Is it kept up to date? A run book should be updated every time a configuration change is made. Some MSPs only take *snapshots*—complete copies of everything once in a while. But since data and procedures change in between the snapshots, their run books are not always current.

Is the run book managed by a version control system? Some MSPs maintain their customers' run books in printed form. There's nothing wrong with that, so long as the MSP manages your site from a single location. This even has the advantage that when all else fails, there's still a binder with instructions for how to restart the servers. Most MSPs, however, use a database or specialized software to maintain run books. One advantage of such systems is that they can be linked to an incident-tracking or CRM system. In either case, whether run books are electronic or hard copy, it's critical that they be subject to the same change-management procedures as are used for other components of the web site.

Does the entire support team use it? Some run books only document procedures for the MSP's *network operations center* (NOC). Others are used to document everything associated with your web site, such as the contents of configuration files, contact information, and even contracts. The run book is an important mechanism for enabling communications among your MSP's employees and for minimizing the private knowledge syndrome discussed earlier in this chapter.

Staging and Content Replication Services

Developing and managing a complex web site usually requires at least three separate *instances* of the site, as illustrated in Figure 6.5.

The *live* or *production* site consists of the servers located at the colocation facility that deliver content to visitors. Depending on the application platform, there may be one centralized *development* server, or each programmer and interface designer may have his or her own instance of the environment. In some cases, there may be a centralized development server *and* instances for each developer.

Figure 6.5 Content replication.

In order to test new content and applications before they go live, major sites use a *staging site,* which is as identical as possible to the live/production site, except that it's not as large in terms of the number of physical servers or CPUs in each. A separate staging site represents a substantial investment, especially when you consider not only the hardware, but also the cost of software licenses. Some software vendors offer discounts for staging licenses; others do not.

Small sites may be able to implement a staging environment as merely additional instances of the various components such as a web server, application server, and database server, all on the same hardware used for the development site.

Some MSPs, particularly those that are more rigid and specialize in particular application platforms, offer staging as a service. Staging is less expensive when done this way as compared to purchasing the hardware and software outright. In addition, as your web site evolves, and hardware and software are added and removed, you can avoid having to abandon components that were used for only a short period of time.

TIP Use an MSP's staging services instead of purchasing or leasing your own staging hardware and software.

Procurement

Another way in which an MSP can reduce your cost of hardware and software is through its procurement (purchasing) services. Many MSPs aggregate the purchases of their customers' hardware and software, and by availing yourself of such services, you'll receive the following benefits:

Cost. Not only is it likely that the MSP can get better prices due to its volume, this further reduces your costs by minimizing the time that you or your staff spend placing and tracking orders.

Single-vendor responsibility. It's not uncommon for hardware to be shipped improperly configured, or for the wrong version of a software package to be ordered or delivered. Since the MSP has the ultimate responsibility for configuring and installing these systems, why not also give it the responsibility for ordering them correctly in the first place, and for resolving any discrepancies that may occur?

TIP Utilize your MSP's procurement services.

Rapid Provisioning

A number of MSPs, particularly those on the more rigid end of the flexibility scale, have built proprietary systems and processes for provisioning and deploying servers and even complete web sites in remarkably short times. Some MSPs, for example, can get a web server up and running in four hours, or a complete database server in fewer than 24. The key, of course, is a high degree of standardization, both in configurations and processes.

While a rapid-provisioning capability is valuable during the prelaunch phase of your web site, it's even more valuable when it comes time to replace a server that's failed.

TIP If an MSP offers quick-start server provisioning, ask whether that process is also used (and tested) for replacement of existing servers, including the restoration of your customized content, data, and code from backup media.

As valuable as rapid provisioning may be, keep it in perspective. The fact that a vendor can deploy a system quickly doesn't guarantee that it has the skills to keep that system running, a service that's far more important.

Risk Management versus Risk Transfer

Yet another way in which MSPs differ from one another is in how far they go to assume financial responsibility for outages and other web-site failures. Most MSPs provide a class of services that's called *risk management.* In other words, while such MSPs make "best efforts" to find, identify, and resolve problems, ultimately they're not assuming the financial risks associated with those problems.

Some MSPs go further and offer *risk transfer,* whereby they actually share or assume the financial risk of any problems or outages with their customers—sometimes with third-party insurance companies.

Chapter 9, "Risk Management," is devoted to examining risk management—an important concept that isn't unique to managed services.

Choosing an MSP

In addition to the recommendations made earlier in this section, here are some points to consider when evaluating MSPs: (1) start by finding an MSP that knows the applications upon which your web site will be built; (2) select your MSP before you consider colocation vendors; (3) always check references; and (4) research, research, research. We'll discuss each of these recommendations in the following subsections.

Start with the Application

Before you even begin building your list of prospective MSPs, create a list of your requirements. At the very least, begin with the applications and other third-party components upon which your site will depend. For example, you may already know your site will run on Sun hardware and will use Solaris, Oracle, and a particular application server package. Experience in all of these systems should then be an absolute prerequisite for any MSP you put on your list.

TIP Determine your requirements for applications before you begin searching for an MSP. For that matter, do this before you decide whether MSPs in general are required for hosting your web site.

Select the MSP before the Colocation Vendor

If you want to use a facility-neutral MSP, don't make the mistake of first selecting a colocation facility (perhaps because a particular one is physically close to you) and then asking that vendor to recommend an MSP. The response you get will be self-serving. Colocation vendors will only recommend MSPs that use their facilities; hence, you'll only be exposed to a subset of the potential MSPs.

Also, by getting a referral to an MSP in this manner, you'll effectively eliminate the MSP's objectivity when it comes time to select a colocation facility. Few MSPs will take a referral from a colocation vendor, then turn around and suggest that you locate your site somewhere else. An MSP only gets to do that once or twice before the colocation vendor gets the idea that its referral network isn't working too well, and starts recommending a different MSP.

TIP If you plan to use a facility-neutral MSP, select it before you select the colocation service. Give the MSP latitude to recommend the colocation service(s) it works with best.

References

Since MSPs are the new kids on the block in the web-hosting services neighborhood, there are few independent sources of formal comparative data. Therefore, the best sources of information are real-world customers. Ask all prospective MSPs for references, and interview those references at length. Then go beyond the references supplied by the MSP and get in touch with customers *not* referred by the vendor.

Use *Netcraft* (see Chapter 20, "The Net Detective Toolkit") and other tools to track down additional customers of your prospective MSPs, and contact them directly.

Research

In addition to getting customer references, you should do extensive research on the MSPs on your shortlist. Areas in which you should focus your research include senior management, technical staff, the NOC, staff compensation, and contracts and SLAs.

Senior Management

Investigate the credentials of the MSP's executives. Did they come from backgrounds of large-scale IT outsourcing? From telcos or colocation? From professional services? The background of the senior team, particularly the CEO, will tell you a lot about the attitude you can expect from the MSP's staff.

Find out whether the senior team members are also the founders of the company or if they are perhaps recent replacements. If the latter, you can expect the company to change to more closely reflect the backgrounds of the new executives.

TIP Use the backgrounds of current and founding senior management as indicators of what to expect from an MSP.

Technical Staff

Actually interview the technical staff. If you're to be assigned a TAM, take him or her out to lunch. If you're to be supported by a team, get together with as many of the team members as possible in a conference room. Ask them (not the salesperson) to explain what they do, how they do it, and why they think they're the best people to manage your web site. Face-to-face contact is invaluable.

TIP Have a face-to-face meeting with the individuals who will be managing your web site.

The NOC

Once you've met the TAM or the team, ask them for the name of one of the other accounts they handle. The next day, call the MSP's NOC, pretending you're an employee (a manager) of that reference account, and report a problem with the web site. Ask to speak with your TAM or team.

This is a bit sneaky, so use some simple ploy that won't cause trouble. For example, tell the person who answers the phone that you've had complaints that the web site appears slow. (That's a classically vague problem.) See how your call is dispatched and how long it takes to reach your TAM or team. Once you're connected to the right person, admit your ruse, and explain that you were merely trying to see how quickly and easily you could reach him or her.

TIP Pretending to be one of their existing customers, call each prospective MSP to see how quickly you can reach those customers' support teams.

Staff Compensation

Ask the salesperson how your TAM or team is compensated. Don't suggest an answer; wait to hear what he or she says. Ideally, those who support you are compensated at least in part (through bonuses) according to customer satisfaction and the extent to which contracted service levels are achieved or exceeded.

TIP Find out how an MSP's staff is compensated. This should include incentives for customer satisfaction and fulfillment of SLAs.

Contracts and SLAs

Read them! MSP relationships are complex, so expect complex contracts. Don't base anything on verbal understandings; get everything in writing. Unlike shared or dedicated web hosting, MSP contracts are far from standardized. Be prepared to negotiate until you get an agreement that reflects your understanding of the services to be provided.

> **TIP** Read managed-service contracts carefully, and don't be afraid to negotiate. Better now than after the fact.

That wraps up our exploration of the four categories of web-hosting services: shared- and dedicated-server vendors, colocation, and MSPs. By now you should have a very clear idea of which category is right for you, as well as a sense of some of the things you need to do in order to evaluate vendors in that category.

In Part Three, "Strategies," we'll look at the nontechnical issues that will further help you select the best vendor, as well as manage your relationship with that vendor after the contract is signed.

PART

Three

Strategies

Whether you outsource your web hosting or not, running your company's web site can be a high-risk endeavor. If your web site is slow or unreliable, your customers and potential customers will rapidly lose confidence in your company. Your web site is as much a reflection of your business as are your products or services. In fact, some would say that your web site should be treated as though it *were* a product or service of your company. Furthermore, because visitors are viewing your web site unattended—without you or a salesperson to add a personal touch—those visitors form their entire opinion about you based on their on-line experiences. For these reasons, it's critical that your web site be reliable, perform well, and be reachable by your customers, potential customers, suppliers, employees, investors, and other partners.

If you decide to outsource your web operations, your choice of a web-hosting service or MSP can have a substantial impact on the reliability, performance, and accessibility of your web site. In other words, selecting a web-hosting service or MSP is risky because the cost of making a wrong decision can be substantial.

The premise of this part is that, yes, you'll face some very real risks and challenges in outsourcing your web-site operations, but they can be overcome by research and effective planning. In particular, if you take the time to learn from the experiences of others, you may be able to avoid making the same mistakes yourself.

Even if it's the right choice, outsourcing should be approached with skepticism. If you're an optimist by nature, try wearing a different hat for this process. Pessimism and skepticism can come in handy, especially when listening to vendor pitches. Don't assume that just because a vendor knows more than you do that it can deliver on its promises.

We'll begin our investigations of web-hosting strategies in Chapter 7, "The Dark Side of Outsourcing." We'll explore the common fears of outsourcing—justified or not—including loss of control and becoming locked-in to a vendor.

Next, we'll look at how to select the best web-hosting service. Chapter 8, "Getting It Right," explains how to know whether or not you'll be in a prospective vendor's *sweet spot*, where life as a customer is good. We'll also look at strategies to get the most out of an outsourced web-hosting relationship.

Failures are a fact of life in web hosting, and you can either wait until they occur and then decide what to do or you can take extraordinary measures to try to avoid them. But in Chapter 9, "Risk Management," we'll look at a more reasonable approach that balances the cost of avoiding risks with the benefits of doing so.

Chapter 10, "Service Level Agreements," describes the sorry state of this much-touted concept, and shows you how you can improve the quality of SLAs for your benefit and for the web-hosting industry as a whole.

The last component of web-hosting strategies, Chapter 11, "Traffic Models," supplies the transition from the worlds of business and commerce to the technologies necessary to support them. We'll build increasingly complex Excel spreadsheets (the files for which are available on-line) that allow you to forecast your hardware and software requirements and keep them in sync with your company's business plan.

The Dark Side of Outsourcing

Giving up control of your web site to a third party can be a frightening experience, not unlike handing over your car keys to your just-licensed teenage son or daughter. You've thought it through, and you're convinced it's the right thing to do, but you know things can still go horribly wrong. You only hope that after weighing all the plusses and minuses, you'll have made the right decision.

In this chapter we'll open the door to the dark side of outsourcing, to face the most common fears and anxieties. At the top of the list is the most fundamental fear: loss of control. You'll learn in this chapter how good management on your part can at least minimize this risk. Two other fears, lock-in and high switching costs, are very real threats to successful outsourcing, and we'll determine how to minimize these risks as well.

Today, you may have direct control over the staff that manages your web site, but you'll give that up when you outsource, so we'll look at ways to deal with *vendor staff loyalty*. Finally, we'll consider how to detect the hosting idiot savant syndrome—whereby a vendor can excel in one aspect of web hosting and fail miserably at others.

Loss of Control

If your web servers are located in-house, you can exert control over them in two ways: by managing physical access to these systems, and by managing the staff that supports them. If something happens to your in-house servers, you can walk over to them, see them, touch them, and generally take care of them. Likewise, it's your staff, not someone else's, that's responsible for the care and feeding of your in-house servers.

Most people are used to having their computer systems nearby, even on their desktops. There's something about that proximity that makes us feel more secure. But it's often a false sense of security. Hosting a web site thousands of miles away from its owners may provide more control and security than running that site at a nearby location.

If you outsource *all* of the services associated with your web site, proximity to your servers generally will not be an issue no matter how far away they may be, as your outsourcing vendor will take on all of the responsibilities. But if you're outsourcing only *some* aspects of your web-site operations, you may still feel the need to have the hardware close by. Even so, as we'll see when we explore content distribution in Chapter 13, "Caching and Content Delivery Networks," it's sometimes far more important that your servers be located as close as possible to your *customers* and other web-site visitors than it is to have them close to you or to your web-site developers.

It's also true that you're only as close as your on-site staff. It doesn't do much good to have your servers close to your place of business unless you have someone nearby at all times to deal with problems. If a server located near your office fails on a weekend, for example, and there's no one in the office or on-call and nearby, then that proximity has bought you almost nothing.

The fear of loss of control caused by not having your servers under your own roof (real or perceived) hopefully will be more than offset by the benefits of outsourcing. Your servers should be in a better "home" with at least better basic facilities such as power, air conditioning, physical security, and certainly better Internet connectivity than if they were hosted in-house.

Proactive Control

There are actually two types of control. The most common—*reactive control*—is when you get to call the shots and tell people what to do when you need to accomplish a task or solve a problem. An indication that you're already a practitioner of reactive control is that you spend most of your time solving problems or even putting out fires rather than making plans to avoid them.

If you're going to outsource your web-site hosting successfully, you'll have to learn to practice the second type of control—*proactive control*—when you plan and negotiate service level agreements (SLAs) *in advance of the delivery of the services that you're specifying.* (We'll look at the use of SLAs to proactively define services such as Internet connectivity in Chapter 10, "Service Level Agreements.") The difference is subtle yet profound. Someone who practices reactive control will often say, "I feel like I've lost control of the situation," or, "I can't control my own web site." In some extreme cases, a manager who practices only reactive control treats every situation as if it were an emergency.

A manager who practices proactive control will spend time planning for situations that may occur. He or she will exercise control *before* signing contracts and SLAs—when he or she has the *most* control over the relationship—and is more likely to say, "I feel on top of my web site because I know exactly what my web-hosting service will and won't do for me."

To the extent that all of the services and SLAs are carefully defined in advance, such a manager will enter into the outsourcing relationship without fearing loss of control.

TIP Use the strategies in this book—particularly service level agreements—to create the proactive controls you want now, rather than at the time you need to exercise them—that is, when problems occur.

Lock-In and High Switching Costs

At least loss of control is something you can foresee. But with *lock-in,* another risk of outsourcing, by the time you feel it, it's probably too late. Lock-in means you're trapped. It occurs when you feel the need to switch web-hosting services, but you can't leave your current vendor for various reasons. You may become locked-in because:

- You've signed a long-term contract for hosting without adequate options for termination.

- The quality of service you're receiving is inadequate but you don't have the SLAs that would allow you to insist that your vendor meet your expectations.

- You're leasing servers or other equipment from your vendor, and you can't take those servers with you to a new hosting service or get out of the leases.

- You own your servers, but you can't afford to have your web site go down during the time it'll take to move them to a new facility.

- You're using a commercial application that you can't support in-house, and you can't find another vendor who can manage it.

- You've developed your web-site using proprietary software provided by your vendor, and you can't take it with you if you move your web site. Or you depend on a skill that's only available from one vendor.

- You're using a web-site URL that includes your vendor's domain, such as www.vendor.com/yourcompany, so if you change hosting services you can't take your web-site address with you.

None of these problems seems serious until you need to move. At that point you'll become painfully aware of how serious they are.

If you're already in the planning stages of moving your web site from one hosting service to another, you may have some idea of how difficult the process can be. Most people find, however, it's far more difficult than they expect. Like them, you're about to experience the high *switching costs* of web-site hosting, and you'll soon learn how locked-in you are to your current vendor.

Switching costs are the costs you'll incur if you change web-hosting services. Obviously, higher switching costs are bad for you (the customer) but they're good for the hosting service because hosted customers are *sticky.* As an analogy, cell phones are sticky (i.e., they have a high switching cost) because if you change from one vendor to another, you have to change your phone number (at least in the United States), and then somehow communicate this change to everyone who knows your old phone number. Long-distance services, however, are easily interchangeable. You can switch from one to another with little more than a phone call, and no one else will know the difference. Long-distance service isn't sticky and has low switching costs.

Many hosting services boast of their very low customer turnover or attrition rates. What they don't realize (or they choose to ignore) is that many of their customers might be dissatisfied but consider keeping their web site where it is to be the lesser of two evils. Because these customers are sticky, some web-hosting services count on the fact that their customers won't leave, even if those customers aren't happy. The vendors believe the cost to the customer of switching vendors is high. Unfortunately for you, they're right.

Make no mistake about it, high switching costs and the risks of lock-in are a real downside to outsourcing web hosting. How can you mitigate these risks? There are two things you should do. First, try to pick the right hosting solution the first time around so you don't have to make a change down the road. Second, always have an *exit strategy* or a *Plan B* that allows you to relocate your site with a minimum of disruption in case things do go wrong. We'll cover this subject in detail in Chapter 21, "Domain Names and DNS."

TIP To avoid lock-in and reduce switching costs, always have an *exit strategy*—a plan for how you'll switch vendors if necessary.

Avoiding Proprietary Tools and Utilities

With the exception of colocation services (which provide few services to begin with), many web-hosting services try to make their offerings more competitive by including access to tools or utilities that they've developed in-house. For example, most shared- and dedicated-server vendors offer libraries of Perl scripts that one may use to implement simple features such as email autoresponders or HTML form handling.

As attractive as such tools and utilities may be, and as much as they may simplify the tasks of implementing the associated features, try to avoid using them. Once you make use of these proprietary tools or utilities, you'll have instantly created a non-portable, locked-in element of your web site.

The only exception to this rule is if you're given access to the source code for these tools and utilities and you receive—up front—a license that allows you to use them on your web site in the future even if your site is no longer hosted with this vendor.

TIP If you need tools and utilities, try to find them independently, and include them in your site in a manner that's, therefore, portable.

This recommendation doesn't apply only to hosting. Try to avoid proprietary solutions in all phases of your web-site development and operation.

Leveraging Third-Party Outsourcing

As you evaluate vendors, you'll find, of course, that not all of them are perfect. But some may be very close. An otherwise perfect vendor may have just one or two weaknesses or deficiencies, and you may find that the only vendor that has a checkmark in *every* box is one that's much more expensive than the vendor that falls just short. Rather than abandoning that less-expensive but not-quite-perfect vendor, consider placing it on par with the more-expensive vendor by using third parties to fill in the gaps in the less-expensive vendor's services.

TIP Don't be afraid to use a mix-and-match approach to fulfilling your requirements.

For example, suppose you need sophisticated log-file processing and analysis, yet your first-choice (less-expensive) vendor only offers a rudimentary system. Instead of jumping to a more-expensive vendor whose only advantage is a better log-file package, consider further outsourcing that single component to yet another vendor—a third party. In this particular example (log-file processing) there are a number of independent companies that are in the business of generating detailed reports and analyses based on your log files. You'll have to pay them a fee in addition to what you already pay your web-hosting service, but the incremental cost to have a third-party generate your log reports could still yield the best overall solution.

The following are areas in which it may be attractive to use third-party outsourcing rather than get such services from your web-hosting service:

- Traffic (log-file) analysis and reporting
- Content distribution and caching (see Chapter 13, "Caching and Content Delivery Networks")
- Load testing
- Monitoring (see Chapter 19, "Monitoring")
- Hardware leasing and rental (see Chapter 8, "Getting It Right")
- Credit card processing
- Domain Name Service (DNS)

Third-party outsourcing of selected components further reduces the risk of lock-in to your primary vendor because you can take third-party relationships with you when you leave.

If you switch from web-hosting vendor A to web-hosting vendor B, and both of them make use of different log-file analysis packages, for example, you may find that you can't import the statistics of A's package into that of B's. If this happens (and it does, all the time), you'll find that you can't generate continuous traffic reports that span the period of time during which you changed web-hosting vendors. Your graphs and analyses will start from scratch as of the time you switched. On the other hand, if you outsource log-file analysis to a third party, you'll likely have continuous reports and analyses that span the transition. (Of course, your log-file analysis vendor could go out of business, and many of them have. You've got to be just as diligent when selecting third-party vendors as you are with your primary web-hosting vendor.)

A similar strategy can be used for other component services. By retaining consistent third-party services during such a transition, you can compare the services of the old and new vendors. Does traffic increase? Are errors reduced? Are the servers faster? You shouldn't change your measurement technologies at the same time you change that which you are measuring.

TIP Use selective third-party outsourcing that can transcend and outlast the relationship with a specific web-hosting service or MSP to minimize your lock-in to that vendor.

Owning and Controlling Your Domain

One of the most unpleasant surprises for web-site owners comes when they try to move their web sites, only to discover—at the last minute—that they don't own or control their Internet domains. If the relationship between the web-hosting service and a site owner has deteriorated, many vendors will drag their feet when it comes time to co-operate with this aspect of the transition to the new service.

Be aware that there are *domain pirates* out there who may try to steal control of your domain name. If this happens, you may not know it for quite some time. Don't make it easy for them; register your domain properly and check it periodically to make sure the registration data hasn't been changed. How do you do that? The best protection you have is to register your domain name yourself.

Chapter 21, "Domain Names and DNS," explains the right way to register domain names, and how to check to make sure they're still registered correctly.

TIP Register your domain name yourself and check it regularly to ensure that neither your vendor nor anyone else has hijacked it.

Vendor Staff Loyalty

If you have your own web operations (WebOps) staff, you can rest assured they'll be dedicated to supporting your site. Sure, system administrators and other employees take vacations. They can be temperamental. They're hard to hire and retain. But you can expect that if there's a problem, they'll jump through hoops to solve it. They're loyal because their jobs depend on keeping your web site working. On the other hand, if you outsource these services, you can assume the vendor will be managing hundreds of other web sites in addition to yours. At the end of the day the vendor's staff members get their paychecks from the vendor, not from you, so you can count on only a small percentage of their loyalty.

When there's a problem with a web site, someone must be responsible for the solution. That person must react quickly and take it seriously. If he or she works only for you, he or she will stop whatever else he or she is doing (assuming it's less important) to attend to your web site. If, on the other hand, that person works for a hosting service and is responsible for hundreds of web sites, your site's problems are competing for his or her attention with the problems of those other sites.

Your problems are also competing with your vendor's need to complete other, non-critical or routine tasks such as the installation of new servers. The person you're counting on may have to stop working on your vendor's (internal) tasks in order to solve your (external) problem. One would like to think that all hosting services would instill in their staff the idea that "the customer comes first" and that internal tasks and meetings should always take a back seat to customers' problems. But we all know from experiences in our own companies that this isn't always the case. And even if your vendor's staff is customer-oriented, that doesn't mean "the *customer* comes first" attitude translates into "*you* come first." You'll still be competing with other customers for resources and attention.

One way to determine a vendor's commitment to customers is to find out whether customer satisfaction plays a role in employee review and compensation.

TIP **Ask prospective vendors how they evaluate and reward their employees. Is everyone's compensation—even the hands-on engineers'—based at least in part on customer satisfaction? On *your* satisfaction? Also ask about their rates of employee turnover.**

The Hosting Idiot Savant Syndrome

The American Heritage Dictionary defines an idiot savant as, "a mentally retarded person who exhibits genius in a highly specialized area, such as mathematics or music." It may be a harsh comparison, but anyone who has ever had reason to abandon a web-hosting service can tell you how a single vendor can be absolutely brilliant in one area, and yet incompetent in another.

It takes many different skill sets to create and operate a web site, just as it does to make a motion picture. I marvel at the number of different and obscure job titles there are in the credits of a major feature film. The more technologically complex a film, the longer the credits. The same is true in hosting, where a database administrator is no more likely to be able to reconfigure a router than a makeup artist can operate a camera.

In considering the categories of web-hosting vendors, and in evaluating the vendors themselves, keep in mind that it's hard enough to be good at just one thing. It's far more difficult to be good at many things, and nearly impossible to be good at everything.

Vendors will show you what they're particularly good at. Your job is to look deeper, at what vendors *don't* show you. If one wants to show you its data center, ask about its SLAs. If another is particularly proud of its SLAs, ask to see how a cabinet is wired. If the wires are a mess and not secured with cable ties, how likely is the vendor to meet the terms of its SLA?

One due-diligence technique you should use is to refer to the service component pyramid introduced in Chapter 2, "The Components of Web Hosting." In your mind and in your checklists, separate the service components by the layers in the pyramid, and evaluate each layer independently. If you're impressed with a vendor's offering in one layer, reset your impressions to zero for the next layer and again for the next.

Perhaps the biggest trap web-site owners fall into is being dazzled by a vendor's data center or network operations center (NOC), then believing the vendor can do no wrong. Vendors know their data centers and NOCs have this kind of effect on people (particularly techies), and they invest heavily in the showcase aspects of their facilities, particularly in NASA-like control rooms with large projection-TV monitors. They look cool, but they're primarily designed to impress prospective customers.

TIP Remember: A vendor that's good at one thing isn't necessarily good at all things or even one other thing. Evaluate each of the service components independently. Quality and value in one are not guarantees of quality or value in others.

It's rare that one vendor can do everything well, even at a high price. In fact, a high price for a given service component is often a clue that the vendor doesn't supply the service on a regular basis. Sometimes a vendor will set an unusually high price on a service in order to claim that it offers the service, but at the same time discourage customers from using it. For whatever reason, a high price is usually an indication of a problem.

TIP Beware of service components with unusually high prices. These may be components that the vendor rarely provides.

Don't be surprised if, after reading this chapter, you find yourself rethinking your decision to outsource your web hosting. There are certainly many things that can go wrong. But somehow, thousands of web-site owners have managed to succeed in spite of the evil forces of the dark side of outsourcing. In the next chapter, "Getting It Right," you'll see how to do just that.

Getting It Right

Having survived our encounter with the dark side of web hosting and managed services, let's now turn to the task of picking the right vendor and establishing a successful relationship. The first step is to understand how a vendor will perceive you as a customer. Are you the kind of customer it's looking for? Will you spend enough money? How about a few years down the road—will you still be in your vendor's *sweet spot* (as described in the next section) or will the vendor have outgrown you?

Once you've come to grips with these realities, you can fine-tune your strategies. For example, we'll consider when it makes sense to share resources with other customers in order to get better service from your vendor. We'll itemize the relative strengths and weaknesses of renting, leasing, and buying your hardware. Finally, we'll uncover one of the dirty little secrets of outsourced web hosting: that you'll probably still have to take responsibility for managing your own applications and content. You can't get off the hook entirely.

Finding the Sweet Spot

As much as we all would like our vendors to be customer-centric, we also know we can't mandate loyalty. Therefore, the only way to ensure we'll receive the attention we want is through clear communications of our expectations with our vendors.

Many of the problems that occur with outsourced web hosting are due to a mismatch of expectations between the customer and the web-hosting service. In general (and perhaps unsurprisingly), the customer usually expects more than the vendor provides. Mismatched expectations occur for three reasons:

- Inadequate communication between the parties as to exactly what services are to be provided leads each to create its own independent vision.

- Lack of common sense on the part of the customer, and the vendor's unwillingness (or inability) to point this out to the customer, is often a contributing factor.

- Being an unusual customer, such as one with a budget that's much larger or smaller than is typical of your vendor's other customers, is a recipe for disaster.

As we mentioned in the previous chapter, the best way to solve the inadequate communications problem is through SLAs, discussed in detail in Chapter 10, "Service Level Agreements." Lack of common sense is addressed under *Getting Real,* later in this chapter.

As far as making sure you're not an unusual customer, the first step is to determine whether you're in a vendor's *sweet spot*. Every web-hosting vendor has such a spot; it's reserved for its ideal customers in terms of requirements and budget. When you're in your vendor's sweet spot, everything is great. When you need something, it's just what the vendor wants to provide. You're the ideal customer, and you get the attention of your vendor's best people. You may even be included in your vendor's presentations and sales pitches as an example of a happy, typical customer.

In this section we'll look at ways to identify a web-hosting service's sweet spot, and determine how close you are to its center. Unfortunately, the web-hosting industry is changing very rapidly, and a web-hosting service's sweet spot is a moving target. Even if you find a vendor for whom you're an ideal customer today, there's no guarantee you'll be so tomorrow. Therefore, we'll also address how to predict how such a vendor's sweet spot may move over time, and how you should take this into consideration as you go through your vendor-selection process.

Defining the Sweet Spot

Let's start by quantifying the sweet spot. It can be defined both in terms of what's within the sweet spot and what isn't.

Budget. Vendors know how much their target customers will spend each month. Customers who spend too little won't get attention. Those who spend too much—while certainly popular with their vendor—won't benefit from the vendor's scalability and will likely pay for the vendor's educational and experimentation budgets.

Features. Customers in the sweet spot need the same set of services the vendor wants to provide. Make sure what you want is on the pricelist. You don't want to be the unusual customer with special needs who requires extensive professional services.

Balance. Ideally, you'll be typical of your vendor's customers. You don't want your web-hosting service to be proud that you're the largest user of one specific service component.

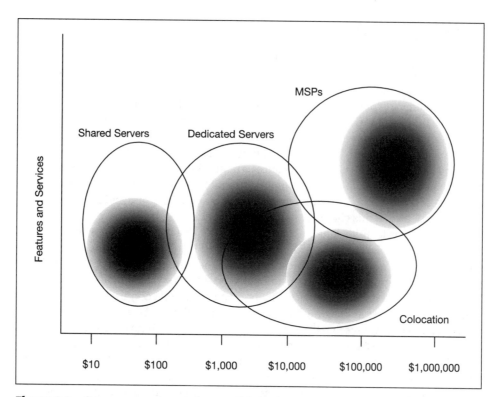

Figure 8.1   Category sweet spots by monthly budget.

Perhaps the most objective way to identify a vendor's sweet spot is by the monthly invoices that vendor sends to its customers. Within each category—shared, dedicated, colocation, and MSP—there will certainly be variations, but the chart in Figure 8.1 gives a general view of the vendor's revenue sweet spots in each category.

Figure 8.1 suggests a few things. For dedicated-server vendors, colocation vendors, and MSPs, the sweet spot tends to be toward the high-budget side of their overall ranges. This is no surprise, since vendors tend to like those customers who spend the most money.

On the other hand, the shared-server sweet spot leans slightly toward the lower-budget side of that category's range. This is because of the low level of services available from shared-server vendors. Higher-end shared-server customers are in some ways getting less for their money than those who have lower budgets, since both groups tend to receive the same services no matter how much they pay each month.

The sweet spots are not entirely at the high-end budgets for any category. While the customer who spends the most money each month may be a marquee account, and loved by the vendor, it's typically an inefficient place to be, because the customer is then paying an inordinate share of the vendor's costs of education and experimentation. Let vendors learn at someone else's expense. You want the benefit of their experience, not to be the source of it.

TIP   Make sure you're in the sweet spot of any vendor you select.

Sweet-Spot Drift

Another aspect of sweet spots not shown in Figure 8.1 is their tendency to move over time. In most cases, they tend to move up and to the right as vendors change their target customers and aim for those with ever-increasing requirements and budgets. There's a tendency for companies to buy services from other companies of similar size, so as a web-hosting service grows, so does the size of its typical customer.

If your hosting requirements move at the same rate as your vendor's sweet spot, you may be okay, but in reality many web-hosting services and MSPs are among the fastest growing of all businesses, and the chances are good that their sweet spots will move faster than changes in your requirements or budget. In the worst-case scenario, a vendor's sweet spot may move so quickly and so far that the vendor decides to dump you, as described later in this chapter.

The solution is to aim slightly ahead of the center of a vendor's sweet spot. That is, you should try to find a vendor for which you will be a major customer, but not the most important. This might buy you some time. If the vendor's sweet spot moves faster than your needs grow, you may still be somewhere in its sweet spot after a few years. If you start behind its sweet spot, it's likely the vendor will soon pass you by, leaving you at the low end of its customer range. Not a good place to be.

The customers that receive the best service from their web-hosting vendor or MSP are those that are just above the vendor's sweet spot, in the area where the vendor is investing in new features and services. If you're willing to take a risk, and are able to beta-test or co-develop a service with your vendor, you'll find that you receive abundant attention and excellent support. The downside to this tactic is that once the vendor *productizes* the service you've jointly developed, you'll no longer receive that special treatment. It's even possible that the vendor will drop the service altogether, leaving you stranded, dependent on an orphaned service.

TIP Aim to be on the leading edge (i.e., higher-budget side) of your vendor's sweet spot.

Note that it's not only the vendors' sweet spots that will drift over time. Yours will, too. Keep that in mind, particularly if you expect rapid growth or changes in your requirements.

Sweet-Spot Stretch

One way to determine a vendor's sweet spot is to ask. But before you tell the vendor's salesperson your budget, ask him or her how much typical customers spend each month. Likewise, rather than starting by submitting a Request for Proposal (RFP), first find out what services the vendor offers.

Every good salesperson has in mind the attributes of his or her target customer: What are customers' budgets? How large and complex are their web sites? How much attention will they require? But for all the reasons that make them effective salespeople, there are times when even the best of them will throw caution to the wind and attempt to close a sale with a customer who's outside of the company's sweet spot. In many such cases, the salesperson may not even be aware that he or she is doing this.

As a potential customer, therefore, you must take on a somewhat skeptical or even adversarial role in order to get at the truth. It may seem obvious, but you can't trust the salesperson to determine the customer/vendor fit. Many mismatched-expectations problems can be traced back to the earliest stages of the sales cycle, when neither the salesperson nor the customer admitted that the fit was like trying to put a square peg into a round hole.

TIP To avoid biasing vendors' sales pitches, always find out what they're selling *before* you tell them what you're buying. Of course, they'll try to do the opposite, so start by asking questions rather than by answering them.

Don't Be a Square Peg

There are two clues that hint you may be a square peg:

The hesitation. The first clue comes after you ask whether the vendor offers some service; the salesperson hesitates—usually just for a moment. For example, you ask, "Do you have an arrangement to store backup tapes off-site?" This is a simple yes-or-no question. If there's any hesitancy before getting an answer, there's a problem. Perhaps the salesperson is just new, but it might mean that the vendor offers such a service, but it's not common or mainstream.

The "professional services" answer. Likewise, you might ask, "Do you provide database tuning services?" Again, the answer should be a quick yes or no; but often the answer you'll hear is, "Certainly. I'll have our Professional Services group get in touch with you." This is a clear indication that these skills are not part of the vendor's everyday practice. In turn, this means you're likely to pay for your vendor's on-the-job learning.

An indication that you're a good fit for your vendor is when the services you're asking for are published in the vendor's literature. Having a published price attached to the individual service component is even better. This isn't a guarantee—plenty of vendors publish descriptions and prices for things they've never done—but at least it means the company has given it some thought.

TIP A service that's described in a vendor's literature *and* has a standard price listed is often preferable to one that's custom, or delivered via "professional services." If there's any doubt, ask for reference customers who have been using the service in question for some period of time; then contact those customers yourself.

One golden rule is to *never* ask your web-hosting service to take responsibility for something it has never done before. You might ask, "We're going to use the new software from software vendor XYZ. Can you support that?" The typical answer is, "No problem. We call that an 'exception,' and we'll send our staff members for training as soon as you sign the contract."

Forget it! In this case the vendor adds no value. You'll be better off either training your own staff or contracting support directly to XYZ. In fact, if XYZ's product is so unusual that the vendor doesn't already support it, you should stop and ask yourself whether you can do without it. If you truly need it, don't pay your MSP to ramp up on it. That would be a very expensive solution, and your support will then depend on the specific individuals who receive that training. No sooner will you pay for them to learn all about XYZ's software than the MSP will send them off for training on something else—that is, unless it turns out that they aren't very good at anything else, in which case you probably wouldn't want them managing your XYZ system in the first place.

> **TIP** Don't ask a vendor to support hardware or software beyond what's contained in its published list. Doing so is both expensive and risky. If you really need that component, find another vendor who can support it. (If you can't find one, consider it an omen.) Otherwise, depend on the manufacturer, a third party, or plan to support it yourself.

Getting Real

When something goes wrong in the course of a web-hosting marriage, it's not always the vendor who's at fault. Frequently, it's the customer (with unrealistic expectations or the inability to fulfill its own obligations to the partnership) who's to blame for the collapse of the relationship.

The most common examples of this are at the low end, with hosting services that offer "free hosting with unlimited bandwidth." Common sense should tell you that if it's truly free and without some hitch, the vendor won't be able to make money, and hence eventually will go out of business. Come on! No vendor can afford to give away, or even sell at a fixed price, unlimited *anything*. Bandwidth, like any commodity, has real costs. If it were economical to supply unlimited bandwidth for nothing, wouldn't Yahoo! be hosted there?

Your vendor needs to make a reasonable profit on the services it provides. If it doesn't make a profit, it's only a matter of time before something backfires. Don't push the limit of what your vendor can provide, and don't go overboard the other way. In other words, don't select a vendor that normally provides a far *greater* level of service than what you need. Don't pay too much and don't pay too little.

Coincident Objectives

The best way to ensure you'll get what you need from a vendor is to select one that's financially motivated and has something at risk. As one CTO called it, "Make sure they have some skin in the game."

Two important inferences can be drawn from the "skin in the game" metaphor:

Vendor upside. Make sure the vendor will profit from having you as a customer. If you think you're going to need a few days of help every month managing your web site, don't use a hosting service that charges $19.95 per month. If you expect to get that much help for such a low monthly fee, you, the vendor, or both of you are going to be disappointed. Every service that has a value should have a matching price tag. Do your homework, not only to ensure that the vendor is asking a fair price for the service, but that the service isn't a *loss leader,* that is, one provided below the vendor's cost in order to get your business. Otherwise, you'll probably get what you pay for.

Vendor downside. Make sure the vendor's profits are tied to your success and satisfaction. This is best done via clear SLAs, as discussed at length in Chapter 10.

TIP Make sure your vendor will profit from a successful relationship with you, and will likewise incur a loss if there are problems caused by inadequate vendor services. Rather than adopt this logic globally, apply it to each service component individually.

Customer Dumping

No matter how far ahead of your vendor's sweet spot you are when you start, eventually you may find that your vendor has passed you by. What then? It's an ugly and unspoken truth, but because these companies are growing so fast, and they're trying to increase their revenues per square foot of data center space so aggressively, they sometimes dump customers in order to bring in new ones with larger budgets.

The most dramatic example (described in Chapter 5, "Colocation") is when a colocation vendor decides that it wants to become an MSP. When that happens, the vendor looks at its customers paying $1,000 to $2,500 per cabinet and sees that the same cabinets could bring in $20,000 or more each month. Suddenly, those customers who have been steadily paying for colocation start to look to the vendor like a problem it wishes would go away. The problem is aggravated by the increased demand for quality services and shortages of talent and funding for data center expansion.

By far the worst case is when you happen (perhaps unknowingly) to be snared by a vendor that's offering a loss leader to attract new business. At some point, reality sets in, and the vendor admits that it can't offer services at the price it promised. "But we have a contract!" you might yell. Remember, all contracts expire, and as long as there's a greater demand for higher-profit services, there may be motivation for your vendor not to renew the agreement when the time comes. You might get around this by making the contract renewable exclusively at your option, but that does nothing to guarantee that you'll continue to be in the vendor's sweet spot. If you're no longer in it, you may be better off not renewing the agreement anyway.

How do vendors dump customers before contract expiration? They sometimes do it by simply reducing the quality of service they deliver. In some cases, this can be an intentional process. I've observed vendors telling their employees to reduce the level of service to a class of customers to the point where they're just barely meeting the levels called for in the SLAs. Is this legal? Yes. Is it ethical? That's a tougher call. The customers are still getting the services for which they contracted, but the vendor has chosen to leave them in the dust. It's certainly ugly.

More commonly, as a vendor seeks to move its sweet spot toward higher-paying customers, the old ones are simply ignored. The experienced staff that managed the old customers' servers suddenly get *repurposed,* and moved into the new activities and accounts that will bring in more money. When the team supporting your account is swapped out for a new, less-experienced team, take it as a hint.

The best solution to this problem is to avoid it, and the best way to do that is to plan ahead, and try to select a vendor whose sweet spot won't pass you by. You never want dumping you to be a reasonable option for your vendor.

The second solution—not quite as effective—is to focus on SLAs that at least offer some degree of protection against reduced services.

> **TIP** Protect against being dumped by a vendor by constantly reviewing your value to that vendor. Put yourself in its shoes.

Do It Their Way

Finally, when you find a vendor that knows how to do something, can do it well, and does it every day, don't interfere. There are many different ways to do the things that need to be done in the operation of a web site, but one thing is certain: A process that works is (almost) always better than one that doesn't.

For example, consider backup and recovery. Although we present some specific ideas about backup and recovery in Chapter 16, "Backup and Recovery," your first-choice vendor may have a very different approach. Stop. Ask yourself whether the improvement you'll gain from switching to a better way is worth the cost and the risks that the vendor won't be able to manage it properly.

If you ask vendors to do something out of the ordinary (their ordinary), you're asking for trouble. If your backup process is "just a little bit different" from that used for the rest of the customers, you may find your backups don't occur quite as regularly as they should. And when it comes time to recover files or a complete server, you may find that your vendor's staff have to develop part of their recovery plan on the fly, as opposed to doing it the same way they do it for everyone else.

> **TIP** Don't ask vendors to do things your way (even if your way is better) unless you consider the additional cost and risks.

In summary, it's important that you select a hosting partner whose expectations of its customers match your expectations of a vendor. You don't want to be its largest or most difficult customer, nor do you want to be its smallest and simplest. You want to be as typical a customer as possible. You want your problems to be the kind of problems it solves every day, and for many customers.

Leveraging Shared Resources

Some of the risks of outsourcing web hosting, such as loss of control and loyalty issues, may at first appear to be disadvantages. However, through some clever management you can finesse these risks to your advantage. The key is to make sure your problems and your hosting service's problems are one and the same.

Consider what happens when your web site has a problem, but it's a problem unique to your site. You'll essentially be fighting for your vendor's attention, competing with other problems that need to be solved or routine tasks that need to be performed.

Compare that to what happens when a web-hosting service has a problem that affects *all* of its customers. That really gets attention. When it happens, you can be confident you'll have its very best people working on *your* problem because it's now the vendor's problem, too.

I think of it this way: When the power goes off at my house, one of the first things I want to know is whether my neighbors' power is also off. At one extreme, if the entire state of California is without power, I know I'm looking at a long outage. At the other extreme, if it's just my house, I become concerned that I may not be important enough to get the attention of the utility company. My best chance of getting power back quickly is when my entire neighborhood has lost its electricity. I want the utility company to have enough pain (i.e., unhappy customers) that it will take the problem seriously, yet not so much pain that the problem is beyond the scope of its typical skills. I want to be in the situation where my problems are those that my vendor handles routinely, such as the failure of a small, local power transformer.

To use the same strategy with outsourced web hosting, you must identify which services are appropriate to share with other customers. For example, all of a web-hosting service's customers use the same fiber to connect their servers to the Internet. If that fiber is cut by a construction site back-hoe (unquestionably the Internet's single worst enemy), all of those servers may go offline. As unpleasant a prospect as this may be, you can expect that the web-hosting service will use whatever resources are available to work around, and eventually solve, the problem.

Some web-site managers think they're better off using colocation with their own, independent connection to the Internet; but if you go that route, you won't be leveraging the skills and attention a web-hosting service could apply to solving a problem that affects all of its customers. (A well-designed data center will have multiple fiber runs entering the building through multiple points of entry so that a single fiber cut can't take the entire building offline. We looked at this in detail in Chapter 5.)

Some service components that may be improved through sharing among multiple web sites include:

- Facilities (power, air conditioning, fire suppression)
- Connectivity
- Monitoring (all types)
- Domain Name Service (DNS)
- Load balancing
- Outbound SMTP (email) services
- Applications (threaded discussions, chat, etc.)
- Dedicated image servers
- Streaming media servers
- Staging services
- Content delivery services
- Load-testing services

TIP Use shared resources and services where appropriate as a way of creating a greater urgency for the vendor in case of failure.

Hardware: Buy, Lease, or Rent?

It's natural to feel that owning your own servers somehow gives you more control. But have you ever bought a desktop or laptop computer, for example, only to wish soon thereafter that you'd waited for the newer model? The psychology of owning your server hardware and software works in a similar way.

You have three choices:

- You can *purchase* your hardware and software outright.
- You can *lease* it from a third-party financial institution.
- You can *rent* it from your web-hosting service or MSP.

Most large companies that are well capitalized tend to purchase their hardware outright. But many companies, large and small, are looking beyond the basic dollars-and-cents issues and are finding that leasing is often preferable. And some web-site owners increasingly see the advantages of the third option: renting from the hosting services themselves. Some of the advantages of renting are obvious (such as the lack of a long-term commitment), but some of the most important ones are not so easy to see.

Renting

Although leasing, as discussed in the next section, is the most obvious and common alternative to outright purchase, renting from your web-hosting service or MSP may be even more attractive. While you'll certainly pay more in rent than you would for leasing, the total cost of rental *with* the associated services may actually be less than leasing and purchasing the same services separately. For example, you may be able to rent a given server with maintenance, basic software, updates, patches, and monitoring for $1,000 per month. By comparison, you may also have the choice of leasing the same server hardware directly from a leasing company for only $750 per month; but the additional services—provided by an MSP—might run you another $500 per month, for a total of $1,250.

Maintenance and Spares

When you purchase or lease, you're responsible for contracting with hardware and software vendors for support and maintenance. If a power supply fails, for example, your MSP may contact the hardware supplier for service on your behalf, but the MSP has no commitment or motivation to get your hardware repaired quickly. Again, it's a matter of having skin in the game. The vendor's service level is probably based on how quickly it contacts the hardware supplier and coordinates the response. The MSP doesn't have responsibility for resolution of the problem (that belongs to the hardware vendor), only for responding to the outage and getting the ball rolling. If the hardware maintenance vendor, in turn, is slow to respond, it's not the colocation vendor's or MSP's problem.

Colocation vendors and MSPs that rent hardware try to do so as profitably as possible, and that objective can actually provide you with better service. When the vendor (not you) is on the hook for the cost of maintenance, it will tend to use its own on-site—or at least on-call—staff for repairs. That staff can often respond to a problem more quickly than a third-party hardware service company that doesn't necessarily have its staff close by.

Likewise, a web-hosting vendor that rents hardware will find it economical to invest in spare parts and even complete spare servers. Again, this can mean a quicker resolution to outages. Without such spares, the vendor would have no choice but to rely on the hardware manufacturers' service agreements. The best option—both for you and your web-hosting vendor—may be to use the hardware supplier to back up the web-hosting vendor's own staff rather than the other way around.

Because the vendor owns the servers, it once again has more skin in the game. When a server fails, it's the vendor's server. It's not just a matter of how reliable the hardware may be; now the colocation vendor or MSP has its own reputation and service level agreement at stake. All other things being equal, you'll get more attention this way.

TIP Consider renting servers if the vendor has both 24/7 on-site maintenance staff and on-site spares.

Upgrades

If you purchase or lease your hardware, you typically don't have the option of upgrading your servers at will. They're yours, and you're stuck with them for the term of the lease or until you sell them. Your only choice is to buy or lease new servers and to find uses for the old ones.

If you're renting, however, you may have the ability to upgrade. As long as it's properly stated in your rental agreement, you should have the option to swap out one server for another larger and more powerful one. Because of the number of its customers, your web-hosting vendor can always find a valuable use for the old server. The vendor will also be glad to get the increased rental and service revenues from the upgrade.

If you own or lease your servers, the upgrade process can be as awkward as a game of musical chairs. For example, suppose you need a larger database server. You may install a new database server, redeploy the old database server as an application server, and finally move the replaced application server into the role of an additional web server. An upgrade like this could be quite costly, since your site (or at least one of your servers) could be offline each time you shut down a server to replace it.

If the hardware is rented from your service provider, your upgrades can be accomplished efficiently. The vendor can provision, configure, test, and install replacement servers in a far more orderly fashion, possibly by creating an entirely new configuration using all-new servers that can be tested as a complete and integrated system.

TIP Favor renting if you anticipate early or frequent upgrades.

Exit Strategy

Finally, the biggest payoff from renting hardware and software from your colocation vendor or MSP is to mitigate lock-in and to reduce switching costs. We examined both of these problems in Chapter 7, "The Dark Side of Outsourcing."

The payoff shows up if, or when, you need to switch to another vendor. In this case, there are two advantages to renting. First, when making such a move, you may decide that you want a different hardware configuration at your new hosting service, or under the control of a new MSP. You probably learned quite a lot about your web site—and about your hosting service or MSP—and you may want to do things a little differently the second or third time around.

If you own or lease the hardware, moving your web site starts to look like a covert spy operation. You'll be planning after-midnight outages with teams of system administrators and others shutting down servers, unplugging them, throwing them into the trunks of their cars, driving to the new location, and reversing the process. And it *never* goes smoothly. Even a small site will be down for hours. A large one can be down for days. There's nothing riskier than moving a site.

Even more valuable when moving your web site—and here's your secret weapon—by renting your hardware and software, you have the option of operating your site simultaneously at both its old and new locations. If you rent hardware at your first location, you can deploy all-new hardware at your new colocation facility. You can have your new configuration installed, tested, and running for days or even weeks before you have to shut down the old one. No quick shuffles of computers in the dark of night. If you have to do this just once, you'll save yourself more trouble than you can imagine.

If you need to move your site, probably it's not due to hardware problems. Typically, it will be because something else has gone wrong with the relationship with your current vendor. Some rental agreements, however, are only cancelable if there's a problem with the hardware, so you must make sure (before you sign, right?) that if you cancel your web-hosting agreement because of a failure of the vendor in some other service, you also have the right to cancel your rental agreement at the same time.

TIP Use renting as part of your exit strategy by mitigating lock-in and reducing your switching costs. Renting gives you the option of operating your web site simultaneously at old and new locations without the need to purchase duplicate hardware.

Study the Rental Charges

When you first see them, the rental fees from a colocation vendor or MSP will look like extortion. You may find, for example, that it costs $1,000 per month to rent a server that you know you could *buy* for only $10,000. (Most web-hosting services and MSPs price their rentals to recover their purchase price within 12 months.) Leasing the same server, on the other hand, might cost only $300 per month with the option of purchasing it at the end of the lease for one dollar or fair-market value, depending on the lease.

There are a few things to take into consideration in order to fairly evaluate the deal you're being offered by the vendor:

Maintenance. This is typically worth 12 to 15 percent per year over the hardware purchase price. It may be worth even more to you if your MSP guarantees faster response and resolution times than the hardware vendor does.

On-site spares. Access to *depot* spares (spare parts located at the service company's offices, rather than at the hosting facility) is included in typical maintenance agreements. Because on-site spares are available more quickly, they may be more valuable to you than depot spares.

Upgrade and cancelation options. As described earlier in this chapter, having the option to upgrade your hardware or to cancel a rental agreement (as opposed to being stuck with long-term leases) is a valuable feature of some rental deals.

Single point of responsibility. If you rent from your colocation service or MSP, the vendor is on the hook to get a failed server up and running quickly and within the timeframes established in its SLAs.

All of these represent values that make up the *total cost of ownership,* or *TCO.* If you perform a *TCO analysis,* you may discover that renting will cost you less. In some cases, however, a vendor's rates for rental still may appear exorbitant, even after a TCO analysis. If that's the case, don't hesitate to bargain with the vendor. If it's serious about renting servers to its customers, it will want to be able to make the TCO case to the next guy. If you can show the vendor that it's losing the TCO argument, it may well consider revising its pricing. Even the largest of the vendors will consider custom pricing if it makes sense to them. Just make sure, as always, that it's a good deal for the vendor as well as for you. You've got to allow the vendor to make a profit.

TIP If rental is your first choice, be prepared to negotiate for a fair price. Consider the total cost of ownership (including the value of spares, upgrade flexibility, and mitigation of lock-in and switching costs) in your evaluation.

Leasing

If, for whatever reason, renting isn't right for you, at least go to a bank or leasing company to finance your hardware and software. On a purely financial basis this option is superior to purchasing hardware and software with cash, but it shares one significant disadvantage in common with purchasing: Whether you purchase or lease, you're locked into the hardware.

Given all of the advantages of renting, why would anyone lease their equipment from a third party? There are three reasons:

■ First, if you're temporarily short of cash, leasing will offer you the lowest *initial* out-of-pocket cost. Some businesses are confident they'll have substantially more cash tomorrow than they have today, and prefer to risk spending more money later for the benefits of spending less today.

■ Second, if your configuration is large—let's say a dozen servers or more—some of the issues that make renting attractive tend to be diluted. The ability to upgrade becomes less valuable because any server that's replaced by a larger one usually can be put to work doing something else within your own configuration.

For example, if you need to replace an application server with one that's more powerful, the old application server hardware can likely be used as a front-end web server. It's also likely that a configuration with this many servers will be built using a three-tier architecture and will therefore grow via the addition of servers, not by the replacement of the existing servers with ones that are more powerful.

■ The third reason that leasing may make more sense—or may be your only choice—is if you require hardware or software that isn't supported or available from your web-hosting service. If your site requires something out of the ordinary, you'll have to buy or lease it.

TIP Use leasing (a) when preservation of short-term cash is your primary concern, (b) if you have a large configuration, or (c) when you require nonstandard components.

Purchasing

The one situation in which it's financially preferable to purchase your hardware and software outright is when your company has plenty of cash but you want to minimize monthly expenses and hence maximize your earnings before interest, taxes, depreciation, and amortization (EBITDA). The monthly depreciation for the hardware and software you purchase will be less than the monthly cash payments you'd make to rent or lease the same components. Therefore, from an accountant's perspective, purchasing is cheaper than renting or leasing. Never mind that you've got to actually pay for it all up front.

If you decide to purchase your hardware and software, consider doing so through your web-hosting vendor. Many vendors (particularly MSPs) offer procurement services, where (for a modest markup) they'll obtain hardware and software on your behalf.

Unless yours is a Fortune 500 company, your web-hosting vendor is probably buying hardware and software in larger quantities (and hence receiving better discounts) than you could get on your own. By combining your purchases with its own and with those of its other customers, it can negotiate even greater discounts.

The advantages of using procurement services go beyond price. For instance, if a server is damaged in shipping, a web-hosting vendor may be able to swap it for another while awaiting delivery of the replacement. Likewise, if your web-hosting vendor will be handling the configuration and installation of the hardware, you can eliminate the finger pointing that could occur between the web-hosting and hardware vendors should some problem occur.

TIP Make use of your web-hosting vendor's procurement services when buying hardware and software.

Managing Applications and Content

The final part of "getting it right" is taking a realistic look at who will have the responsibility for maintaining your custom applications and content—the proprietary and unique aspects of your web site. Will a third-party web-site developer, your web-hosting vendor, or your in-house staff handle this? It's not an easy question to answer.

A web-hosting service's business model—its economic reality—is based on standardization and an assembly-line approach to managing web sites. To the extent that all of a web-hosting service's customers are alike and use the same hardware and software, the vendor stands a better chance of both delivering quality services and making a profit.

Web-hosting services are like telephone companies where every customer has the same kind of telephone and all phone numbers have the same number of digits. It's not just the economics, but also the mind-set of the staff. In order to be good at what they do, the staff of a web-hosting service is encouraged to do things the same way for every customer.

By comparison, web-site development isn't at all like web hosting. The customizations that go into development and make your web site unique (the application code and your content) are anathema to a web-hosting service. No matter what a prospective vendor promises, these are components of a web site its staff is not prepared to maintain.

This is an important issue because so many web-hosting customers enter into outsourcing relationships believing they've completely washed their hands of *all* the problems that will occur with their web sites. This usually isn't the case, and those customers get a rude awakening.

The 80/20 Rule of Web-Site Management

When you outsource to a web-hosting service or MSP, you're giving them only the simplest 80 percent of the tasks associated with managing your web site. The difficult 20 percent of the tasks are still your responsibility.

Why, then, would you bother? Why not just do it all yourself? Even if you did have all of the required skills in-house (and you probably don't), by outsourcing the simplest 80 percent, you allow yourself to concentrate on the 20 percent that differentiates your business from that of your competitors. You should depend on your web-hosting service or MSP to handle everything that's generic and common to all web sites, while you focus on what's unique about yours.

If a web site is properly architected (e.g., there's adequate redundancy so that no single hardware failure can bring down the site), and if the web site is located at a good data center and managed by a good team, the most common causes of problems will then be errors in content or application code. It only takes one typo in Java or Perl or even some malformed JavaScript to make at least part of a web site unusable.

Someone familiar with the customizations of the site can usually correct these errors rather quickly, while a web-hosting service or MSP that wasn't involved with the site's development can waste hours trying to find even the simplest problems.

Furthermore, whenever someone unfamiliar with a web site's application code makes a change to that code, it's very likely there'll be side effects that may cause even more serious problems in the future. When a web-hosting service corrects an application code error in a site it didn't build, the fix tends to be "quick and dirty" rather than carefully considered.

How, then, does one properly manage content and applications? Ideally, whoever develops or owns a web site should take responsibility for maintaining its application code and content. Since failures in these areas can occur at any time of day, the responsible party will always have *some* 24/7 responsibility that can't be successfully outsourced to the web-hosting service or MSP.

If your web site was built in-house, it's your staff that must continue to take responsibility for what it created, as well as any changes that are forthcoming. There's simply no economical way around it.

If third-party developers built your web site, they're the ones who *should* assume the responsibility for support unless or until they've undertaken an extensive and successful *knowledge transfer* to your in-house staff. Unfortunately, the realities of third-party web-site development are that these vendors often are unable to provide the follow-up maintenance and enhancement services you need. Many of them were high fliers through 2000, only to file for bankruptcy or otherwise disappear the following year. Even those that still exist suffer from incredible employee turnover and downsizing, so it's highly unlikely that whoever developed your web site in the first place will be around to maintain it going forward. If you used such a third-party development team, you'll probably have to bring the maintenance work in-house.

TIP Assume that no matter who developed the customized applications and content for your web site, you'll have to take responsibility for its maintenance, including if necessary, 24/7 support.

The more complex a component, the more important it is to follow this recommendation. Specifically, whoever develops your server-side code, such as Java or COM programs, should be the one to fix any problems that turn up there. In the case of client-side code, such as HTML or JavaScript, this recommendation comes with somewhat less emphasis, as it's far easier for someone new to the code to find and correct errors in client-side code than it is in server-side code. Furthermore, problems in HTML and JavaScript tend to affect individual pages, whereas problems in server-side Java or COM can more easily bring down an entire site.

If you ask your web-hosting service or MSP to dig into your code, you'll likely pay an exorbitant fee for one or more people to ramp up on your customizations. And if you require that help again, you might have to pay yet another person or two, since there's no guarantee that whoever solved your problems the first time will be available the next time there's trouble.

The dark side of outsourcing that we explored in the previous chapter usually only presents itself when you ask a vendor to do something that's too far from the center of its sweet spot. By developing a realistic understanding of what vendors can and can't do (which often isn't what they say they can and can't do) you can avoid many of the potential pitfalls of outsourcing your web hosting.

But you'll never be able to eliminate all risks. Hardware and software will fail, and vendors will let you down. In the next chapter, "Risk Management," we'll continue the development of strategies that take such failures into account so that even when they occur, you'll still consider your outsourcing decision to be a successful one.

Risk Management

So far in this book we've focused on what you can do—particularly during the vendor-selection phase—to successfully outsource the operation of your web site. Success includes many things, but clearly one aspect is a web site that stays up 24 hours a day, 7 days each week, 365 days a year. Given all of the potential problems we've already examined (and there are many more to come), it should be obvious that you can't expect 100 percent availability and perfect performance day in and day out from any web site. Things will go wrong. Decades from now we'll probably look back at this period and wonder how we ever managed to keep e-commerce web sites running at all. Eventually, it'll get easier, but until it does, managing a web site remains a difficult road, filled with potholes.

In this chapter, we're going to assume that things *will* go wrong, and that your web site will go down in spite of all your prelaunch preparations. This is a realistic approach, of course, since no amount of effort spent during planning can eliminate all risks. You won't suffer every problem discussed in this book, but you'll certainly encounter some of them. Unfortunately, there's no way to determine ahead of time which problems you'll experience, so you've got to try to anticipate them all.

Given the inevitable, then, let's examine the approaches you can take. First, the ostrich approach. Let's say you just stick your head in the sand, and decide that since you don't know which problems will occur, your best bet is just to charge ahead and deal with them as they come up. This is the way many web sites are run. It's a variation of the if-it-ain't-broke-don't-fix-it philosophy, and believe it or not, it often makes more sense than trying to solve problems in advance when you haven't developed a good plan. The disadvantage of this reactive approach is that it's essentially unmanaged. Not only won't you have any idea of which problems might occur, you also won't have a sense of how they'll affect your business. It would be tantamount to walking into a room filled with coughing, sneezing people in the middle of flu season with a weakened immune system. Because you aren't prepared for anything, even the slightest bug could put you out of business.

An alternative approach is to attempt to identify all possible failures and to eliminate their causes. The futility and extraordinary expense of this approach should be obvious, yet some managers continue to spend more time and money attempting to eliminate potential problems than their businesses would lose if the problems were to occur.

Both of these approaches are extreme. You can't simply ignore the risks, nor can you plan for every possible eventuality. Either strategy could lead to disaster. So what should you do? You might, for example, decide you're going to adopt a reasonable approach to dealing with potential problems. But that raises the question, what's reasonable? Other than your own gut instincts developed from years of experience (you've done all this before, haven't you?), how will you prepare for problems before they occur? The solution proposed in this chapter is *risk management.*

Risk is defined as *the possibility of suffering harm or loss.* Risk management is the process of planning for such eventualities. The goal of risk management isn't to eliminate all risks, but rather to find the right balance between risk reduction and preparing the organization for losses. Our risk-management strategy will be broken down into the following steps:

1. *Risk analysis.* This step can be broken into three substeps: First, identify the types of losses that may occur; next, determine the risks (the causes and the likelihood that a loss will occur); third, calculate the resulting cost to the organization.

2. *Risk reduction.* This process, too, has three parts: One, identify actions to reduce or eliminate the likelihood of occurrence of each risk; two, determine the cost of those actions; three, calculate the benefit of taking each action (i.e., compare the cost of each loss to the cost of preventing it).

3. *Risk mitigation.* The final step addresses the losses that still may occur, in spite of risk reduction, and transfers them, as appropriate, to vendors or insurers.

Risk management isn't a new discipline. Written records dating back to before 2000 B.C. show that it was quite commonly practiced in military circles. The great Chinese general, Sun Tzu, wrote in his treatise, *The Art of War:*

> *If you know the enemy and know yourself, you need not fear the result of a hundred battles. If you know yourself but not the enemy, for every victory gained you will also suffer a defeat. If you know neither the enemy nor yourself, you will succumb in every battle. [3.18]*

Keep in mind "knowing yourself" (your web site and all its components and frailties) and "knowing your enemy" (the causes of downtime) as you read this chapter.

Risk Analysis

The purpose of this first phase of the risk-management process is to get your arms around the losses and risks themselves. First of all, what *are* the potential losses and the risks that might cause them? We'll identify the big ones and categorize them. Then we'll find a way to estimate the likelihood that losses will occur due to these risks, and determine the cost to the business when they do.

Risk and Loss Categories

Losses come from actually losing something, such as revenues, profits, goodwill, intellectual property, and fixed assets (e.g., equipment). A risk is the likelihood that an event in a particular category will trigger those losses. Risks include failures of connectivity, hardware, and software, as well as security breaches and disasters such as fires and floods. Table 9.1 is a matrix illustrating the relationship of various categories of risks associated with web-site operations and the losses that can result from events in each category.

Most web-site owners must address five categories of risks shown in this table:

Fixed-asset losses. Fixed assets for a web site generally include the hardware and software that are used in the development and operation of the site. Although the risk of loss of these assets due to failure, fire, theft, and so on, is very real, it's also very easy to mitigate through warranties, service contracts, and third-party property insurance. These losses don't make for a particularly interesting analysis, so we won't discuss them further. But make sure you do address them with your web-hosting service or insurance carrier.

Table 9.1   Risks and Losses

RISKS	LOSSES FIXED ASSETS	THIRD-PARTY DAMAGES	INTELLECTUAL PROPERTY	GOODWILL	REVENUES AND PROFITS
Connectivity Failures				X	X
Hardware and Failures	X		X	X	X
Bug and Software Failures		X		X	X
Disasters	X			X	X
Security Breaches		X	X	X	X

Losses due to damages to third parties. A web site may be exposed to certain third-party liabilities. These include the accidental disclosure, publication, or loss of personal data that can be caused by security breaches or bugs. Other similar liabilities may exist, depending on the nature of the business and the type of customers, vendors, or partners. We'll discuss security breaches in Chapter 17, "Security." Third-party damages due to bugs are best covered by business insurance, as discussed later in this chapter.

Loss of intellectual property. If your content, data, or application code are lost, you could be in bad shape. We're not going to analyze this one, however, since you have no excuse for not adequately backing up these assets. If you lose them, shame on you! (Refer to Chapter 16, "Backup and Recovery, " for more information on backup and recovery.)

Loss of goodwill. If a visitor tries to access your site and finds it down or slow, he or she may never return. While losses from such causes are difficult to quantify, they are very real, and may be caused by events in any risk category. Losses of goodwill will be included in our analysis.

Losses of revenues and profits. The risk that keeps most web-site owners up all night is the potential loss of sales and the effect of such losses on their bottom lines. As with loss of goodwill, these losses can be caused by essentially any event. Losses of revenues and profits will be the cornerstone of our sample risk analysis.

The Likelihood of Failures

How often *will* a web site go down and thereby cause losses of revenues, profits, and goodwill? If you're running a very large web site, it's not too difficult to estimate failure rates for certain individual components. For instance, if your site has 200 web servers, you can plan quite accurately for the frequency with which you must replace those systems, particularly if the servers have been in operation for some time.

As the operator of an average web site—one that doesn't have hundreds of web servers—you have no way to predict the rate at which your hardware or software will fail, and you certainly have no way to predict how often an employee of your web-hosting service or MSP will make some operational error and bring down your web site. Predictions of this sort are particularly difficult during the planning stages, when you've had no empirical experience with the hardware, software, or services provided by your vendor.

Luckily, there *is* a source of information regarding failure rates: your web-hosting service or MSP. Your vendor should have more than enough experience with web sites like yours, and it should have been collecting failure rate data for many years.

Your web-hosting vendor or MSP should be able to give you two numbers. One is the uptime it's willing to guarantee. The other is the actual average uptime its customers have experienced over the previous 12 months. (If a vendor doesn't have the latter number, how can it promise the former?) The actual average uptime value should be slightly better than that to which the vendor is willing to commit, although some vendors try to snare customers by promising uptimes that are greater than they're confident they can deliver.

TIP Ask each vendor for the average actual uptime percentage its customers have achieved for the past 12 months. Use the range between this value and the uptime promised by the vendor's SLA as the basis of your risk analysis.

The Cost of Downtime

We've identified the potential losses (revenues, profits, and goodwill) in our risk analysis process, and we've found a way to estimate the likelihood that your organization will incur such losses (via your vendor's historical failure-rate data). The final step is to estimate the cost to your organization of such failures.

NOTE The examples in this section assume a fairly typical retail e-commerce web site. If you're in a different business, you can use the same principles to develop your own downtime cost model.

We'll start by determining the cost (as a percentage of annual revenues) of a one-hour outage. The benefit of working with a percentage is that it can be used to determine the cost of one hour of downtime for *any* company, large or small, by multiplying the company's annual revenues by the percentage. We can then determine the total cost of any outage by further multiplying that result by the length of the outage in hours.

There are 8,760 hours in a 365-day year, so one hour represents 0.014 percent of a year. This means, for instance, that an online business that generates $100 million in revenues per year would lose $14,000 in revenues during a one-hour outage.

Here's the formula for calculating the direct losses in revenues caused by a web-site failure:

$$\text{revenue loss} = \text{annual revenues} \times \text{length of outage (in hours)} \times 0.014\%$$

While mathematically accurate, this base rate of 0.014 percent is overly simplified. In reality there are many factors that will cause the actual rate (and hence the actual revenue losses) to be higher or lower. For example, most web sites' revenues tend to vary over the course of each day as well as day-to-day and seasonally. Web sites that cater to local visitors can go down for a few hours in the middle of the night without substantial consequence. But if, for example, Amazon goes offline for an hour during the weeks leading up to Christmas, the impact would be huge.

In order to come up with a percentage that can more accurately estimate losses, we need to determine the value of a *multiplier* that adjusts the base rate for reality. We'll find that multiplier by looking at the losses (as calculated by industry analysts) caused by some well-publicized outages at public companies. Starting with those loss estimates, we'll work backward to find the value of the multiplier.

eBay

In June 1999, eBay suffered a complete failure and was down for 22 hours. The company reported a revenue loss of between $3 million and $5 million attributed to the outage. But we need additional data in order to find our multiplier.

By looking at its quarterly reports, we find that eBay had $48.5 million in revenues for the quarter in which the outage occurred. That's $194 million annualized, so a loss in the range of $3 million to $5 million represents 1.5 to 2.5 percent of annual revenues. Per hour, that's a range of 0.0703 to 0.117 percent; so in this instance, the multiplier we're looking for is in the range of 6 to 10.

What would account for the 6 to 10 times increase in eBay's estimate over the base rate of 0.014 percent per hour? One explanation is that eBay had to void or extend all of the auctions that were underway at the time of the failure. Because eBay's auctions can run as long as 10 days, it was hit with *cascading losses,* losses that occur over a period greater than the duration of the outage. eBay also may have factored in the impact of lost goodwill due to the outage when estimating its losses.

AOL

When AOL went down for 24 hours in June 1996, the company was forced to credit its customers $3 million. It reported $992 million in revenues for the year in 1996, so that $3 million represented 0.302 percent for the 24-hour period, or 0.0126 percent of annual revenues per hour of downtime. That's about 0.9 times our base rate of 0.014 percent.

But AOL didn't just lose $3 million in *revenues;* it was $3 million AOL had to take off of its bottom line. The loss showed up as a $3 million reduction in *profits* for the year, not just revenues. Assuming a 15 percent pretax profit, a $3 million expense is the equivalent of losing $20 million in revenues. Doing our math again, that comes out to 0.084 percent per hour, for a multiplier of 6 times the 0.014 percent rate.

Robertson Stephens

In a report published in May 2000, a team from Robertson Stephens (an investment banking firm) wrote:

> We estimate that the cost of just 15 hours of downtime (representing less than 0.5% of total available hours) could be as high as $1.3 million for an organization with 1,000 employees that averages approximately $25 million per month in Internet revenue. (Source: Richard A. Juarez et al., "Virtual Bricks II: Virtual Econ 101 Update, A Comprehensive Guide for Understanding ecommerce Infrastructure Evolution and Convergence—CSPs, ASPs, IUPs and IPPs"(Robertson Stephens, May 2000)

Let's do the math using the firm's numbers: $1.3 million is 0.433 percent of the hypothetical company's annual revenues (12 × $25 million, or $300 million per year). That's 0.0289 percent per hour, or approximately 2 times our 0.014 percent figure. Most likely the analysts at Robertson Stephens didn't take into account much loss of goodwill.

Loss Multiplier

In these three analyses we've seen multipliers in the range of 2 to 10 times applied to the hour-to-year ratio (base rate) of 0.014 percent when computing lost revenues due to outages. When you calculate the cost to your own business of an hour of downtime, consider using a multiplier in this range.

The updated loss calculation formula is:

revenue loss = annual revenues × length of outage (in hours) × 0.014% × multiplier

When selecting a multiplier, the following suggestions may help:

- Use 2× (0.028 percent) if an outage will not cause indirect (goodwill) or cascading losses.

- Use 4× to 6× (0.056 to 0.084 percent) if you want to include the cost of goodwill.

- Use up to 10× (0.14 percent) if the impact of an outage will be felt for an extended period of time, beyond the period of the outage itself (i.e., cascading losses).

Remember that these multipliers will give you the effect of outages on *revenues*. When comparing the losses from anticipated outages to the cost of reducing those losses, you should also consider your organization's pretax *profits*.

Figure 9.1 is a spreadsheet that calculates loss per hour and total losses (for a given number of hours of downtime) of both revenues and profits. This hypothetical example assumes a 15 percent profit, and approximates the numbers from the Robertson Stephens estimate. (A live version of this spreadsheet can be found on the web site that accompanies this book at www.rds.com/books/hosting/models/OutageLoss.xls.)

TIP Confer with your company's financial management to determine (a) which loss multiplier should be used for estimating your losses, and (b) whether to model losses and risk-reduction costs relative to the *top line* (revenues) or the *bottom line* (profits).

	A	B
1	Multiplier	2
2	Hour/Year Ratio	0.014%
3	Resulting Rate	0.028%
4	Annual Revenues	$300,000,000
5	Revenue Loss per Hour	$84,000
6	Profitability	15%
7	Profit Loss per Hour	$12,600
8	Downtime (hours)	15
9	Total Revenue Loss	$1,260,000
10	Total Profit Loss	$189,000

Figure 9.1   OutageLoss.xls.

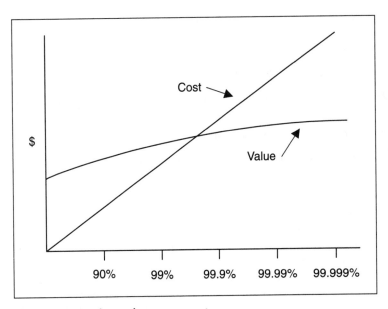

Figure 9.2 Uptime value versus cost.

The Game of Nines

Uptime guarantees are usually expressed as a percentage, such as 99 percent, 99.9 percent, or 99.95 percent, but as we'll see when we explore SLAs in the next chapter, there are many different ways to interpret these percentages. For the purpose of our analysis, we'll assume that they're applied uniformly across all units of time. For example, we'll assume that 99 percent uptime implies 1 percent downtime whether measured over a day, a month, or a year.

Figure 9.2 compares the value received from increased uptime to the cost of the increase. For example, increasing uptime from 99 percent to 99.9 percent results in an additional 80 hours per year. Taking the next step—increasing uptime from 99.9 percent to 99.99 percent—yields only another 8 hours, yet the cost of taking this step may be as great as the one before. Clearly, the returns diminish as one approaches 100 percent uptime.

The graph in Figure 9.2 illustrates that it makes sense to increase the uptime only so long as the cost of doing so is less than the increased value. Beyond some point (indicated by the intersecting curves) any additional investment to increase uptime will not yield a positive return.

Note that the graph in Figure 9.2 isn't to scale, and the point at which the curves intersect isn't the same as where it might be for your web site. Your goal, therefore, should be to determine where these two curves intersect for your web site and your web-hosting vendor's SLAs.

The spreadsheet reproduced in Figure 9.3 helps you accomplish this by comparing the projected losses in revenues and profits based on three different uptime levels. Here are some conclusions we can draw from this example of a company with $50 million in revenues and a 15 percent pretax net profit.

	A	B	C	D	E	F	G	H
1		Starting Point	Upgrade to	Upgrade to				
2	Uptime	99.00%	99.90%	99.99%				
3	Downtime (hours per year)	87.60	8.76	0.876				
4	Total Revenue Loss	$2,452,800	$245,280	$24,528				
5	Total Profit Loss	$367,920	$36,792	$3,679				
6	Incremental Uptime (hours per year)		78.84	7.88				
7	Savings (annual revenues)		$2,207,520	$220,752				
8	Savings (annual profits)		$331,128	$33,113				
9	Savings (monthly revenues)		$183,960	$18,396				
10	Savings (monthly profits)		$27,594	$2,759				
11								
12	**Assumptions**							
13	Profitability	15%						
14	Multiplier	4						
15	Hour/Year Ratio	0.014%						
16	Resulting Rate	0.056%						
17	Annual Revenues	$50,000,000						
18	Revenue Loss per Hour	$28,000						
19	Profit Loss per Hour	$4,200						

Figure 9.3 UptimeROI.xls.

Upgrading from 99 percent to 99.9 percent uptime will increase revenues by $183,960 per month and profits by $27,594. If the cost of such an upgrade is less than $27,594 per month, it would clearly be worthwhile. Depending on the company's business objectives (the relative importance of revenue and profit goals), the upgrade may still be worthwhile even if it costs as much as $183,960 per month, the equivalent of the savings in monthly revenues.

An upgrade from 99.9 percent to 99.99 percent uptime (another 1 percent increase) is a very different story. The increases in monthly revenues and profits would be only $18,396 and $2,759, respectively. Clearly, this upgrade would only be worthwhile if it cost less than these amounts, again depending upon the business objectives.

You now have the tools to make the following four determinations:

■ You can estimate the cost to your organization of any specific outage.

■ You can estimate the likelihood of outages, using your vendors' SLAs as a guideline, and therefore estimate your uptime.

■ By combining the first two options, you can determine the total exposure your organization faces for losses due to outages.

■ You can compare uptime guarantees from one or more vendors to determine which will give your organization the best return on its investment.

TIP Use formal modeling to estimate the cost of downtime and to determine which increases in uptime guarantees will save more than they cost.

Force Majeure

We can't leave the topic of risk analysis without considering another class of events that includes lightning strikes, fires, floods, earthquakes, theft, vandalism, labor strikes, backup power failures, and fiber cuts by the infamous back-hoe. Risk of loss from these events is very real and must be addressed in any risk management plan.

Read the boilerplate of many web-site hosting agreements, and you're likely to find paragraphs labeled *force majeure*, which is defined as *an unexpected or uncontrollable event*. If you find such a paragraph, it probably states that the vendor shall not be held liable for losses caused by events *beyond its control*.

But wait! Isn't protection for your web site against such risks one of the reasons you selected your vendor? What about the beautiful data center that can supposedly withstand a nuclear attack, the triple power grids, the overkill N+3 generators, and the fancy FM-200 fire suppression system? What good is a vendor's claim that its facilities protect you from risks if it won't support that claim in the contract? That's a good question to ask prospective vendors.

In any case, you'll probably find it difficult to get web-hosting vendors to take responsibility for force majeure. Their insurance underwriters usually require that limitations of such liabilities be in all contracts. But you should carefully review what's considered force majeure. What's beyond the vendor's control and what isn't? If, for instance, you're hosting your site in redundant, geographically diverse facilities owned and operated by a single vendor, you should get at least some level of contractual protection against losses due to force majeure.

Remember, any risk not assumed by the vendor remains yours. You'll have to either cover such risks with an insurance policy of your own or assume the risk yourself.

> **TIP** Review web-hosting contract provisions for force majeure more carefully than you would when considering a typical business contract.

Risk Reduction

Having analyzed the causes, likelihood, and impact of web-site failures, the next question is obvious: What can we do about them? This takes us into the realm of *risk reduction*, where the objective is to reduce risks to the extent that the costs of doing so are less than the anticipated losses.

Breaking the Chain of Events

A failure may have only a single direct cause, but there's usually a chain of events that leads up to it. In most cases we can break a single link in this chain of events and thereby keep the failure from occurring. For example, think of the chain of events leading up to a hypothetical car accident injury:

1. You made a new friend in college.
2. Your friend called you on your cell phone while you were driving.

3. The cell phone distracted you, causing you to run a red light.

4. Because you ran the light, you hit another car.

5. Your airbag was defective, so you hit the steering wheel and broke your nose.

Breaking this chain of events at any stage would have eliminated your injuries from this particular accident. For example, any of the following actions could have eliminated your injury:

- If your airbag was functional, you wouldn't have broken your nose.

- If you hadn't hit the other car, you wouldn't have needed an airbag.

- If you hadn't been talking on your cell phone, you wouldn't have run the red light and hit the other car.

- If your friend hadn't called, you wouldn't have been on your cell phone.

- If you hadn't gone to college, you never would have met your friend.

None of these actions can eliminate *all* such injuries, however. For example, you could meet someone at work rather than in college. Or you could be distracted by tuning your car radio rather than by talking on your cell phone. So while breaking a link in the chain may eliminate certain *individual* accidents, it only *reduces the risk* that *all* such injuries will occur.

By banning the use of cell phones in automobiles, we can reduce the *likelihood* that injuries will occur, and we can even reduce the *total number* of automobile-accident injuries, but we can't *eliminate* all injuries in this way.

To substantially reduce the risk of injuries, we must identify and *weaken* the links on the chains of events leading up to the largest number of injuries. This will increase the likelihood that one of the links will break, which, in turn, reduces the statistical likelihood (i.e., risk) that injuries will occur.

The effects of risk reduction can be multiplicative. For example, if each action we take reduces the likelihood by 90 percent and there are four such actions, we may be able to reduce the total risk from 100 percent to 0.01 percent.

The Risk-Reduction Waterfall

To explore this idea further, let's switch from automobile accidents to web-site outages. Figure 9.4 illustrates a risk-reduction methodology that's based on weakening the major links in the chain of events that lead to web-site failures.

Rather than the link-and-chain metaphor, think of this strategy as a series of waterfalls in which only 10 percent of the water arriving at each level spills over to the next. In other words, each risk-reduction action reduces the risk by 90 percent. We start in the upper left corner with a risk of 100 percent. After four steps—each one filtering 90 percent of the risk it inherits—we have reduced the risk to 0.01 percent. The final step (risk mitigation) deals with the residue: that percentage of risk that cannot cost-effectively be eliminated through reduction.

Specific risk-reduction actions in each of the categories shown in Figure 9.4 are discussed throughout this book. Here are some examples.

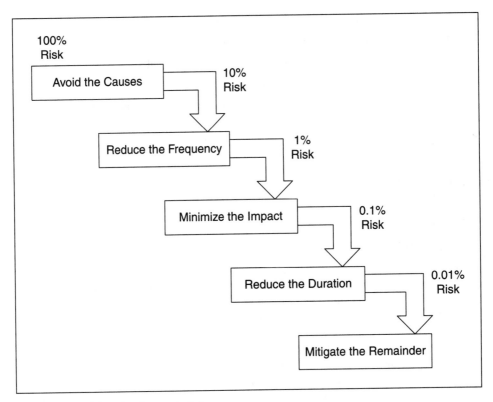

Figure 9.4 Risk-reduction waterfall.

Avoid the causes. If you can avoid taking a risk in the first place, you'll never have to deal with it. Specifically, avoid *technology risks* by sticking with the tried and true whenever possible. Don't use the latest-and-greatest leading-edge (i.e., high-risk) technologies unless they give you a substantial competitive advantage.

Reduce the frequency. Reducing how often a particular problem will occur is another way to effectively reduce risk. For example, some operating systems (even specific versions) are more reliable than others. The same is true for hardware and application software. With a little research (mostly by asking other web-site owners) you can find out what's reliable and what isn't. When selecting components, don't just think of performance and features; also consider reliability and your risk-management strategy.

Minimize the impact. You won't be able to reduce the frequency of all failures to zero, but you can minimize the impact of *single points of failure.* For example, you can design your configuration to use redundant servers such that if one fails, another can perform the same function. Servers that can't be duplicated, such as certain databases, can be purchased with internally redundant components. For example, if you have only one web server, and that web server has only one power supply, a failure in that power supply will bring down the server and hence your entire web site. Either a redundant power supply *or* a second web server will reduce the impact of such a failure from a critical event to one that is of relatively low severity. (Using both would be redundantly redundant—an unnecessary expense. Refer to Chapter 12, "Web Site Architectures," for a more detailed discussion of redundancy in web-site architectures.)

Reduce the duration. The faster you can recover from failures, the less they'll financially affect your organization. Having on-site hardware spares, on-site staff, and using disks for backups instead of tape are three examples of strategies for reducing failure duration. See Chapter 16, "Backup and Recovery," for more information on these strategies.

Mitigate the remainder. Even after applying all reasonable risk-reduction techniques, some failures will slip through the cracks. *Mitigation* (to reduce the *business impact* of incidents) is discussed in the next section.

TIP Your risk management plan should include specific risk-reduction strategies to avoid and reduce the frequency, impact, and duration of failures.

Risk Mitigation

There's always some chance that a problem will make its way through all of the previously named risk reductions, and significantly affect your business. You can't cost-effectively eliminate all risks, so your risk-management strategy should include a plan for *risk mitigation* to deal with those losses that slip through the cracks.

To *mitigate* means *to moderate, relieve, or alleviate.* In the context of web hosting and managed services, there are two components of risk mitigation:

Risk transfer. The process by which your web-hosting vendor or MSP assumes some or all of the financial liability for certain failures.

Insurance. From traditional and other sources, insurance is the ultimate fallback to cover risks that cannot be cost-effectively reduced or transferred to a vendor.

Risk Transfer

All web-hosting vendors claim that their services will minimize outages, but what will those vendors do to *compensate* you in case such events do occur? Will they assume the risks or at least share the losses with you?

If your web site goes down, your losses will likely far exceed the pro-rata fees you pay to your web-hosting service during the outage. For instance, a 24-hour outage will probably cost you more in lost revenues and goodwill than one day's worth (one-thirtieth pro-rata share) of your monthly web-hosting budget. Therefore, even if your web-hosting vendor issues you a refund or credit, it will be insufficient compensation for the loss you will have endured.

Consider an analogy of film-processing vendors. These photo-finishers make reasonable attempts at risk reduction. They have ticket and labeling systems to keep track of each roll of film, and they maintain their equipment and chemicals properly in order to minimize the chance that customers' film will be damaged.

Suppose you photograph a special event such as a wedding, and you take your film in for developing and prints. What happens if the photo-finisher loses or damages your film? Typically, the vendor's liability is limited to replacing that roll of film with a new, unexposed one, but that hardly addresses your loss.

Thus, your risk has been reduced, but it hasn't been eliminated. The risk is still there, and it's yours. The photo-finishing vendor hasn't assumed it. The wedding photos are gone; no one can do anything about that. But if you decide to reshoot the bride and groom and the rest of the wedding party, you'll have to pay whatever it takes to get them together, in the same location, and to rent those tuxedos again, among other things.

Of greater value (and at greater cost to you) would be *risk transfer*, in which the photo-finisher actually assumes the risks associated with the damage to, or loss of, that film. Imagine if, at the time you dropped off your film for processing, the photo-finisher had offered to take financial responsibility for your potential losses in case of a processing error in exchange for a higher price for its services. In the motion picture business this is called *negative insurance*, and it covers the cost of reshooting scenes from a movie if the original film negative is unusable due to problems with the camera, processing, and so forth.

Like photo-finishers, web-hosting vendors that offer risk management will, at most, credit or refund fees you've paid as mitigation for losses you may incur. Those vendors that offer risk transfer, on the other hand, will reimburse you amounts that more closely match your actual losses. Of course, you'll usually pay more for risk transfer, so you need to determine whether you'll get a positive return on that investment. Vendor-supplied risk transfer is a great thing, but it's not always worthwhile.

Deciding whether a vendor that offers risk transfer is right for you is a matter of risk analysis. Your prospective vendors or their insurance partners should be able to help you with this task. Consider the cost of each type of problem that you could encounter, the likelihood that it will occur, and the cost (insurance fees) of transferring the risk to a third party.

TIP Vendors that offer risk transfer are more expensive, but the additional cost may be justified. Use risk analysis to determine whether the services of such a vendor are worthwhile.

Insurance

Most web-hosting vendors that offer true risk transfer do so through one or more insurance company partners. In order to increase their own profits, and to offer competitive premiums, insurance companies work with web-hosting vendors to reduce risks to web-site owners. For example, an insurance company may request a third-party audit of a vendor's security practices as a condition to insuring the vendor's customers. The better the security practices, the lower the risk that a customer will suffer a loss due to a security breach. The lower the risk, the lower the premium that the insurance company must charge. Everybody wins. By implementing the earlier risk-reduction strategies, you'll also reduce the risk to your insurers, and perhaps be entitled to lower insurance premiums.

The losses that vendors and their insurance company partners typically assume are due to some of the following risks:

- Security breaches
- Revenue and profit loss
- Data loss
- Fixed-asset damage
- Goodwill losses (business impact)

TIP If you intend to purchase insurance to cover losses due to web-site outages and other failures, consider using a web-hosting vendor that already has a relationship with an insurance company.

Why Sites Fail

Before we leave the subject of risk management, let's take a look at the actual causes of web-site failures. Figure 9.5 illustrates the findings of a study by the Gartner Group of the causes of unplanned downtime.

The Gartner Group found that, "Unplanned application downtime causes havoc and great expense. Conventional vendor wisdom focuses on redundancy to improve availability. Redundancy, however, solves just 20 percent of the problem."

Based on extensive feedback from its clients, the Gartner Group estimated that, on average, "...unplanned application downtime is caused: *20 percent* of the time by hardware

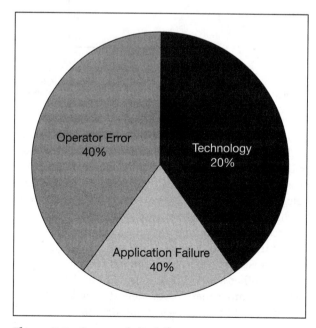

Figure 9.5 Causes of site failure.

Source: D. Scott, *Making Smart Investments to Reduce Unplanned Downtime* (Gartner Group, 1999)

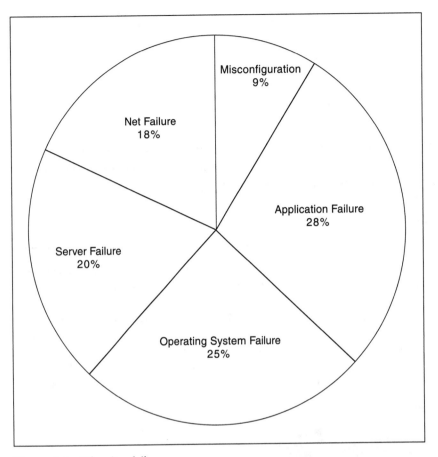

Figure 9.6 Why sites fail.

Source: Richard A. Juarez et al., "Virtual Bricks II: Virtual Econ 101 Update, A Comprehensive Guide for Understanding ecommerce Infrastructure Evolution and Convergence—CSPs, ASPs, IUPs and IPPs" (Robertson Stephens, May 2000)

(e.g., server and network), OSs, environmental factors (e.g., heating, cooling and power failures) and disasters; *40 percent* of the time by application failures including 'bugs,' performance issues or changes to applications that cause problems (including the application code itself of layered software on which the application is dependent); and *40 percent* of the time by operator errors, including not performing a required operations task or performing a task incorrectly (e.g., changes made to the infrastructure components that result in problems and incur unexpected downtime).

"Thus, approximately 80 percent of unplanned downtime is caused by people and process issues, while the remainder is caused by technology failures and disasters."

Figure 9.6 illustrates the results of another study, this one by IDC and Robertson Stephens. They broke the causes into five rather than three categories, and except for *misconfiguration* errors, they didn't segregate human causes of failures from others. But the data is equally as interesting.

At first it would appear that these two studies have drawn contradictory conclusions. But the studies approached the problem from entirely different directions.

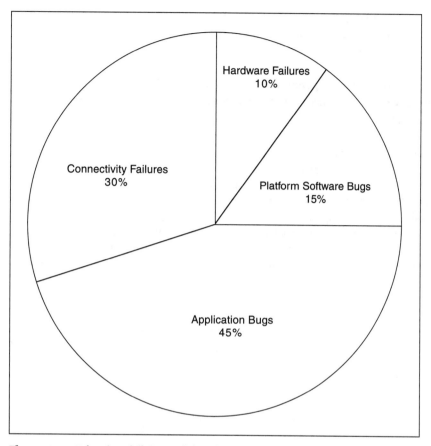

Figure 9.7 Why sites fail (consolidated).

Specifically, the IDC/Robertson Stephens team didn't segregate problems caused by people and processes from those caused by nonhuman failures. While their Misconfiguration category is clearly associated with people, in all likelihood the other categories in the IDC/Robertson Stephens study include human errors as well.

If we try to put these two studies together, and throw in a pinch of practical experience, we might get the breakdown shown in Figure 9.7.

In my experience, decent hardware rarely fails unless it gets some help, such as from a data center technician. Likewise, most of the platform software products we use, such as operating systems, web servers, and databases, are relatively reliable, and they don't typically fail on their own. That's not to say there aren't some real lemons out there, but so long as you select the right packages, and don't insist on living on the bleeding edge, the platform won't be your greatest problem.

At 30 percent, connectivity failures are one of the most significant causes of web-site failures. Of those, the majority (certainly more than the 9 percent reported by IDC/Robertson Stephens) are misconfigurations of routers, switches, or DNS.

But by far the single greatest causes of web-site failures (45 percent as a reasonable guess) are errors in custom web-site applications. This category includes both bad design and outright bugs. If you include this category, the Gartner Group is probably correct that approximately 80 percent of unplanned downtime is caused by people and process issues.

TIP Since they cause 80 percent of unplanned downtime, due diligence of vendors' staff and processes should be included in your risk-reduction strategy plan.

By adopting a formal management approach—just as you might do for software development or project management—to risk analysis, risk reduction, and risk mitigation based on the concepts presented in this chapter, you'll discover that the risks of losses from failures, disasters, and security breaches can be managed like any other aspect of operating a web site. The next chapter, "Service Level Agreements," will show you how SLAs can become the cornerstone to your risk management plan, by putting into writing exactly the services your vendors will provide, and what will happen when things go wrong. SLAs will allow you to anticipate failures rather than deal with them in panic mode.

Service Level Agreements

Service Level Agreements (SLAs) are everywhere. At least they seem to be if you believe the buzz. Customers want them. Vendors claim to offer them. The Internet trade press talk about SLAs as though they were as ubiquitous as air.

In fact, most web-hosting contracts *don't* have real service level agreements—documents that specify *exactly* what services the vendor will provide, how much the customer will pay, and what will happen when things go wrong.

State of the Art In SLAs

By and large, the web-hosting industry has made great strides during its very brief history. But when it comes to service level agreements—although there are a few exceptions—most web-hosting vendors have done a remarkably poor job. Most of the few SLAs that do exist don't come close to describing the levels of service that vendors say they can deliver and that they (verbally) lead their customers to expect.

But it's not only the vendors that are at fault. Web-hosting customers are equally to blame for signing contracts that specify levels of service that are well below what they actually consider acceptable. Would you be satisfied if your web site went down for a full eight-hour business day nearly every month? Would you say, "My web-hosting service does just what I expected it to do?" If you're using a vendor that offers a 99 percent uptime SLA, that's what you've agreed to. If your site goes down that often, don't be surprised when your vendor thinks everything is just fine. You'll be on record for having said that's good enough for you. Which one of you is responsible for creating mismatched expectations? You both signed the same contract.

Vendors say that they actually deliver higher service levels than what they put into their SLAs, but that they must be conservative. Why is that? We don't do that in our other contracts and warranties. We put into writing exactly what will and won't happen in case something goes wrong.

If you buy a new car, you get something like a 36-month warranty. Everyone knows what that means. Once you're past the 36th month, you're on your own. There are no surprises and no mismatched expectations. No one expects a car manufacturer to repair a car for free beyond the warranty period, and no car salesperson would suggest that his or her company would do so. So why should we expect web-hosting vendors to deliver levels of service that are higher than what's in their SLAs? It seems to be something unique about the web-hosting industry. Too much of it's built on unwritten expectations.

Make web-hosting vendors compete for your business—not with glossy brochures and verbal promises, but through specific, written commitments to deliver the services they claim they can provide. It's only in reaction to customer demand and the pressures of competition that SLAs will become the valuable documents they deserve to be.

In this chapter we'll examine service level agreements—not from the perspective of what's out there (although we'll look at one real-world example), but rather with a vision for how things ought to be. Our examples of *good* SLAs don't exist in the real world, and if you walk into a web-hosting service or MSP waving copies of them, you'll probably be greeted with (at best) a polite chuckle. But don't let that stop you; do it anyway.

Our explorations will begin with a look at the purposes of service level agreements. We'll then separate SLAs into three types—performance, reactive, and proactive—and analyze an example of each. Along the way, we'll look at the criteria for categorizing incidents by severity. We'll wrap up this chapter with a look at some of the legal/contractual issues surrounding SLAs, including why you may be better off with no SLA at all. As important as they are, some real-world SLAs can do more harm than good.

The SLA Context

Service level agreements were born along with the trend toward outsourcing—not just the outsourcing of web hosting or even IT services, but the outsourcing of any service. SLAs are just what their name implies: *agreements* between the customer and the vendor as to the *services* to be provided by the vendor, and the measurable *levels* of those services that the vendor is expected to achieve.

Think of how an SLA might be written for a commercial janitorial service, a service that is commonly outsourced. It might contain a description of what will be cleaned (the service) and how frequently, and during what hours (the service level). It might contain many other sections as well, such as how much the customer will pay for the service, and what credits or refunds the vendor will issue if the service level isn't achieved.

A tenant in a large office building might have many similar services such as security, elevator, air conditioning, and others. When multiple services are to be provided, they can be described in individual SLAs, or in a single consolidated agreement.

Physically, SLAs are not typically standalone contracts, but rather tend to be exhibits or attachments to a more general agreement that contains boilerplate and other terms and conditions. As attachments, they're as legally binding as the rest of the contract.

Like the web-hosting and managed services contracts to which they are attached, SLAs are not standardized across the industry. Every vendor's SLAs are unique, and if you're working with an MSP or you're a large-budget colocation customer, your SLAs will likely be negotiated and customized along with the rest of your contract.

A good SLA will describe a web-hosting vendor or MSP's services in great detail by answering the following questions:

- What *exactly* is the service to be provided?
- What are the responsibilities of both the vendor and the customer with regard to this service?
- How will the quality of the service be measured?
- Based on those measurements, what are the *service levels* the vendor is expected to achieve?
- How will the vendor's performance be reported to the customer?
- What corrective actions will the vendor take if the service levels are not achieved?
- What fees will the customer pay for the service?
- What financial remedies will be used to compensate the customer when the service levels are not achieved?

Why SLAs?

Ask customers what they expect from their web-hosting vendors, and you'll generally hear something like, "To keep the web site up and running and, if it does go down, to get it back up again as quickly as possible." Remarkably, some web-hosting contracts don't go into much more detail than this, and many customers naively enter into such agreements thinking that everything will be fine.

One reason for such passivity and ignorance is that at the time that most customers are signing web-hosting agreements, they're usually overwhelmed by the immediate task of getting their new (and usually behind-schedule) web sites up and running. The pricing may get their attention, but instead of thinking ahead to the realities of keeping the site up 24/7/365, some customers just say, "I'm sure we can work out the details later."

Many of these customers find that soon after the launch they begin to question their vendor's ideas of what's considered "running" and "as quickly as possible." Once past the panic of getting the site up, these customers realize that what the vendor considers business as usual is not at all what they had in mind. (Remember the soapbox example of 99 percent uptime.) Eliminating this mismatch of expectations is the primary purpose of service level agreements.

Communications

Most customers and vendors agree that the greatest cause of disputes is the gap in understanding between what the web-hosting service or MSP intends to provide and the results expected by the customer. A service level agreement will help align these expectations by clearly expressing, up front, the intended levels of services to be provided.

The extent to which the two parties can develop mismatched expectations when there's no SLA is amazing. In some cases the disparity is caused by an over-zealous salesperson who makes everything sound better than it really is. But most of the time the root cause is something more benign—simply a matter of each party's operating from its own perspective and not bothering to communicate its understanding to the other party. Ignorance is bliss until things go wrong.

Guarantees and Due Diligence

Does the existence of an SLA guarantee you'll get the service it describes? Not really, no more than a new car's guarantee can prevent it from breaking down. The guarantee merely specifies what will happen if something does go wrong.

While an SLA should give you some degree of confidence, the document itself can't perform the service. It's just a piece of paper. You still need the vendor's staff and facilities. An SLA is also not a substitute for your due diligence during vendor selection. You shouldn't, for example, select a vendor solely on the basis of which one has the best SLA any more than you would select application software packages by first reading their license agreements. You need to evaluate which vendor is most likely to be able to *achieve* the service levels you need, and at a fair price.

For example, some vendors advertise 100 percent uptime. Sounds good, doesn't it? Better than 99.9 percent or 99.999 percent for sure. But, as common sense will tell you, 100 percent just isn't realistic, and as you might expect, vendors that make this claim rarely achieve it except within the caveats of the fine print in their contracts. When you compare apples to apples, you may find that a vendor offering 99 percent uptime has a better track record than one offering 100 percent.

An SLA can't make a good web-hosting vendor out of a bad one. It's one thing to have a clear expression of mutual expectations. It's another to have confidence that the vendor you select can actually deliver on its commitments. Don't begin your search for a web-hosting service by reading SLAs, and don't impart too much significance to SLAs during the vendor evaluation process. Like any other contract, an SLA should be addressed somewhat later.

TIP Don't rely on SLAs in lieu of actual due diligence. It's more important to research a web-hosting vendor to determine whether it can actually achieve the service levels to which it commits.

SLA Categories

For the purpose of our examples and analysis, we've divided SLAs into three categories: performance SLAs, reactive SLAs, and proactive SLAs. The SLAs in each category are designed to answer one of the following questions:

- *Performance SLAs.* What are the expectations for the normal operation of the site in terms of uptime and connectivity?
- *Reactive SLAs.* How quickly will the web-hosting service or MSP respond when a problem occurs, and how quickly will the problem be fixed?
- *Proactive SLAs.* What will the vendor do in terms of preventive maintenance to avoid problems and minimize their impact?

Following are some examples of services that can be covered by each type of SLA:

Performance SLAs

- Server and web-site uptime and performance
- Internet connectivity
- Content delivery and caching

Reactive SLAs

- Call center and network operations center (NOC) response times
- Resolution of hardware failures
- Resolution of facility failures (power, air conditioning, fire suppression)
- File and database recoveries from backups and archives
- Responses to security threats

Proactive SLAs

- Monitoring
- Backup
- Audits of security and error logs
- Installation of patches and upgrades to operating systems, utilities, and applications
- Log-file processing and cleanup
- Domain Name Service (DNS) changes
- Database and application performance analysis and tuning
- Capacity analysis and planning

We'll look at each of these types of SLAs in the sections that follow.

Performance SLAs

Performance SLAs are those that address ongoing services such as connectivity and up-time. These SLAs set expectations for the *quality* of these services based on objective measurements and a baseline of values that establish acceptable service levels.

All web-hosting services supply connectivity to the Internet in one manner or another, so no matter what the size of the vendor (or the customer, for that matter), all web-hosting services should have a formal SLA for connectivity.

Beyond Its Control

One issue that must be dealt with in any performance SLA is control. This usually causes vendors to draw a proverbial line in the sand over which they won't cross. From a vendor's point of view this is a no-brainer. How can it possibly take responsibility for anything under the control of someone else? For example, a vendor *can* control how well it delivers packets to ISPs based on peering relationships, but it may steadfastly refuse to take responsibility for what happens to those packets from there on. This makes sense if you're a vendor, but as a customer it doesn't address your requirements. You need to get those packets delivered to a web-site visitor, and you need to have some confidence they'll get there.

This is a case in which more progressive (and aggressive) vendors step up to the plate. While a vendor can't actually control the handling of individual packets once they leave its network, the vendor does have some control over the business and technology relationships with the ISP partners with whom it connects. Some vendors do a better job of managing these relationships than do others, and it's the *results* of good relationship management (as measured by its effect on connectivity) that you should be looking for in an SLA. You can't hold a vendor accountable for a particular set of numbers for packet loss or latency on each and every connection, but you can and should expect that the vendor will manage its infrastructure and peering relationships so that the connectivity you receive (when measured abstractly and objectively) is at least as good as, let's say, the industry average.

Specifically, you can measure your web-hosting vendor's connectivity *as perceived by visitors to your web site,* and compare it to an average of such measurements from a statistically significant number of similar vendors. The philosophy of this approach is that a vendor can be held accountable for the *overall effectiveness* of its peering and other relationships relative to the effectiveness of other vendors. The best way to do this is via an independent, objective third-party measurement service. Refer to Chapter 19, "Monitoring," for more information on such services and measurements.

> **TIP** Require vendors to assume responsibility for things beyond their control to the extent that these things can be measured by an objective third party and compared to industry averages.

Connectivity

In the subsections that follow we'll look at two examples of connectivity SLAs. The first is taken from the real world; it's a connectivity SLA from a major web-hosting service. We'll review some of its weaknesses in detail. (There aren't really any strengths.) After that we'll look at an SLA that is based on some of the concepts put forth in this book and that addresses the weaknesses found in the real-world example.

A Real-World Connectivity SLA

This example connectivity SLA is organized by the vendor into three sections: one that covers availability, another for packet loss, and the third for latency. We'll start by looking at the Availability section.

XYZHost Network Availability Service Level Guarantee

XYZHost's Network Availability Service Level Guarantee ("Guarantee") is that the XYZHost Network will be available 99% of the time. The XYZHost Network is the combination of XYZHost-operated equipment, servers, circuits, and other data transmission facilities comprising XYZHost's TCP/IP wide-area network. XYZHost's Network Guarantee will be measured based on the number of minutes that the XYZHost Network was not available as determined by XYZHost based on the following conditions ("Unavailability").

Each month's network performance statistics relating to the Guarantee shall be posted on the XYZHost Customer Support Web Site (current customers only).

If XYZHost determines that the Network is Unavailable for one (1) or more consecutive hours during any calendar month, XYZHost, upon the customer's request, will credit the customer's monthly invoice the prorated charges of one (1) day of the XYZHost service fee for each consecutive hour, up to a maximum of seven (7) days per month.

To receive the credit if this Guarantee has not been met, Customer must contact XYZHost's customer service group within 30 days of the end of the month for which credit is requested.

Unavailability will not include Network unavailability of an hour or less, or any unavailability resulting from (a) Network maintenance, (b) circuits provided by telcos or other common carriers, (c) an external Internet Service Provider or an Internet exchange point, (d) acts or omissions of Customer or an authorized user, (e) behavior of Customer equipment, facilities, or applications, or (f) acts of God, civil disorder, natural cataclysm, or other occurrences beyond the reasonable control of XYZHost.

Here are some of the problems with this SLA. See how many of them you spotted on your own.

Vendor determination. The SLA allows the vendor to determine when the network is or is not available, so you're dependent not only on the vendor's network, but also on that vendor's systems, tools, and policies for detecting and monitoring its own problems. What happens if the network's down, but not reported as such by the vendor? What constitutes "unavailable"? Assume, for instance, the vendor monitors connectivity from 10 locations. If 90 percent of the tests are successful (i.e., you can reach the site from nine locations), is the site "available"? Suppose you can only reach the site from one location (10 percent)? The SLA apparently leaves to the vendor the right to decide what *availability* means.

TIP Don't accept SLAs in which the vendor determines whether it has achieved its performance service levels. If possible, use a third party.

Limits. Refunds in any month are limited to the equivalent of the fees paid for seven days of service. If you receive no service whatsoever for an entire month—if your web site is completely unavailable—you still have to pay 75 percent or more of the bill for that month.

TIP **Require vendors to refund or credit up to 100 percent of their fees if they miss their service levels.**

Claims. Since you've got to trust the vendor's system for tracking performance and identifying outages, you'd think that same system could notify the vendor when an outage has occurred so that you could receive the credits you're due. But no, you've got to decipher the data each month and *ask* for your credit. And if you wait more than 30 days, sorry, you're out of luck.

TIP **If you have no choice but to accept an SLA that places the burden of initiating a claim on you, make sure you know precisely what supporting data you must supply. Also watch out for time limits for making your claims.**

Granularity. In order to be considered "unavailable," your site must be unreachable for a continuous 60 minutes. If after 59 minutes there's a brief period during which your site can be reached, but it then goes offline again, the "consecutive hour" counter is reset to zero. In theory, there could be only short bursts of availability once an hour for an entire month, and you wouldn't be entitled to any credit.

TIP **Avoid SLAs whose remedies don't take effect unless failures occur continuously and over consecutive periods.**

Maintenance. What exactly is "maintenance"? It doesn't appear to be restricted to *planned outages* or *scheduled maintenance*. Suppose your site goes down for an entire day because one of your vendor's engineers makes a mistake while changing a router configuration. Is that maintenance? There's no limit as to what the vendor might consider maintenance, even retroactively.

In fact, the concepts of planned outages and scheduled maintenance shouldn't apply to a service that's supposed to be up 24/7. Given the state of the art in redundant routers and links, there's no reason why connectivity to your site shouldn't be available at all times.

TIP **Scheduled or preventive maintenance should be counted as downtime when calculating a connectivity service level.**

Circuits. Most web-hosting services don't own their own circuits. Instead, they lease long-haul fiber from the major backbone providers that manage all the routers and switches between one endpoint and the other. By excluding failures in these links, the web-hosting vendor essentially excludes its own network from its connectivity SLA.

TIP Don't accept exclusions for third-party network problems. Instead ask for an SLA that's based on objective measurements of *user experience* compared to an industry average.

Acts of God. Fire? Flood? Earthquake? Aren't these the events to which a high-end web-hosting vendor such as this one claims its facilities are immune or at least well defended? A broad exclusion such as this might make sense for a company that works out of an office building, but we expect Internet data centers to be tougher. (See the section titled *Force Majeure* in the Chapter 9, "Risk Management," for a detailed discussion of this issue.)

TIP Challenge prospective vendors to exclude from acts of God any services that they claim are particularly robust during their sales cycles or in their marketing materials. Whatever their reaction, protect yourself against acts of God by purchasing insurance.

Following is the packet-loss section of the SLA. Since the latency SLA is essentially the same, we won't go through that one.

XYZHost Packet Success Service Level Guarantee

XYZHost's packet success goal is based on the successful delivery of packets through the XYZHost IP backbone. Unsuccessful packets are deemed to be those dropped due to transmission errors or router overload before exiting the XYZHost regional IP backbone.

XYZHost's packet success Service Level Guarantee ("Guarantee") is that successful delivery of packets will meet or exceed 99% between XYZHost-designated IP backbone paths.

The measurement consists of 50 100-byte pings sent every 15 minutes. A daily average will be calculated using these 96 samples. The daily measurements will be averaged to calculate a monthly average.

Should XYZHost fail to meet the Guarantee in two consecutive calendar months, Customer is entitled to a one (1) day prorated credit for the XYZHost monthly fee for the second month and an additional one (1) day prorated credit for any consecutive month in which the Guarantee is not met.

Each month's packet success performance statistics are posted on the XYZHost Customer Support Web Site (current customers only).

Following are a few more problems:

Cause. Any cause of packet loss other than "transmission errors or router overload" is excluded. What about router failures, circuit overloading (other than just the routers), or other causes? Packet loss is packet loss. Why exclude any causes?

TIP Watch out for general exclusions of causes. Any causes that are excluded should be done so explicitly.

Consecutive periods. No matter how bad the packet loss may be in any given month, you'll receive no credits whatsoever unless the problem continues to exist in the following month as well. Even then, you'll never get a credit for the first month. Furthermore, you could experience severe packet loss in alternating months and never be entitled to a credit. This is another example of the *granularity* problem described in the previous section.

Pro rata. If you do have two months in a row of severe packet loss, you're only entitled to a maximum credit equivalent to one *day* of service, or less than 2 percent. You've still got to pay 98 percent of the bill for those two months.

TIP At the very least, require vendors to refund or credit fees for missed service levels on a pro-rata basis. An accelerated schedule will increase their motivation to deliver as promised.

Accelerated Credits

While weak SLAs often specify credits at less than a pro-rata share, some vendors are willing to go in the other direction and offer *accelerated* credits. For example, some vendors will credit their customers one day's worth of fees for *each* 15-minute outage (a 96:1 acceleration). One goes so far as to credit one day's fees for each 26 *seconds* (a 3323:1 acceleration).

When evaluating SLAs, therefore, take into account the balance between the service level and the credit acceleration. A 99 percent uptime guarantee with 96:1 acceleration may be more valuable to you than a 99.99 percent guarantee with only 1:1 acceleration.

This particular SLA was selected because it's an example of so many pitfalls in SLAs. Most connectivity SLAs are weak, but few are this bad.

The remaining examples in this chapter are not from the real world, but have been created to illustrate how one might go about better expressing the true expectations of both parties.

Creating a Better Connectivity SLA

In regard to the preceding SLA it's interesting to note that the vendor has chosen to separate service interruptions (availability) from service degradations (packet loss and latency). While the latter may be important when it comes time to diagnose a problem, packet loss and latency are at best proxies for what really matters: the user experience.

Our next example is an SLA that addresses connectivity as perceived by the end user rather than according to details such as packet loss and latency. It's based on many of the concepts presented in this book. As you read through it, note how the weaknesses of the real-world example have been addressed. (The quantitative aspects of this SLA are based on the use of a *benchmark server*, discussed in detail in Chapter 19, "Monitoring.")

SLA Title	Connectivity
Purpose Description	To ensure adequate Internet access to the Customer's web site. In lieu of separate SLAs covering details such as packet loss and latency, this integrated SLA addresses bandwidth and connectivity from the perspective of the web-site visitor. It is based on an independent, third-party measurement service and the use of a dedicated Benchmark Server that uses the same connectivity as the Customer's web site, but is independent of the Customer's production equipment.
Measurement	The Benchmark Server shall be connected to the Internet using the same infrastructure as the Customer's primary web servers. The Benchmark Server shall be configured to deliver a single-object 50-Kbyte benchmark web page (the "Benchmark Page").

Connectivity shall be measured by comparing the performance of the Benchmark Page to that of the "XYZ Benchmark Page" using the monitoring services of XYZ, Inc., ("XYZ").

Measurements shall be the mean values in seconds, using a five-minute interval (bucket size), computed each day from midnight to midnight Pacific Time.

Service levels shall be considered achieved when the performance of the Benchmark Page is better than or equal to the performance of the XYZ Benchmark Page using the "95th Percentile Rule" applied to all interval measurements over the course of the day. [*Note: The 95th Percentile Rule is discussed in* Chapter 11, "Traffic Models."]

Targets The Benchmark Page performance shall equal or exceed that of the XYZ Benchmark Page as follows ("Reachability Service Level"):

> 20% faster in 80% of measurements;
> 0% faster in 95% of measurements; and
> No more than 20% slower in 100% of measurements

Incentive Target:

> 20% faster in 95% of measurements and
> no more than 0% slower in 100% of measurements

Planned outages and scheduled downtime shall not be excluded from these targets. [*Note: The actual targets should be determined during evaluation and testing. See* Chapter 19, "Monitoring," *for details.*]

Reporting XYZ shall generate all reports. The Customer shall grant access to the Vendor for purposes of verifying XYZ's data. (XYZ will deliver via email a daily report summarizing the performance of the Benchmark Page as compared to the XYZ Benchmark Page for the previous 24-hour period.)

Fees	$900 per Mbps (megabits per second) or fraction thereof as measured using the 95% Rule, five-minute intervals, and a calendar-month period.
	The Customer shall pay an incentive bonus of an additional 5% (calculated on a daily, pro-rata basis) for each day in which the service levels achieve the Incentive Target.
Responsibilities	The Customer shall supply a Benchmark Server acceptable to the Vendor, and shall pay Vendor's normal fees associated with the ongoing maintenance of this server.
	The Vendor shall maintain the Customer's Benchmark Server.
	The Customer shall pay all fees to XYZ and shall run the XYZ reports necessary to evaluate compliance with this SLA.
	The Customer shall report deviations to the Vendor by the end of the calendar month that follows the occurrence of such deviations.
	The Vendor shall verify Customer's reports of deviations and issue any credits due within 30 days of receiving such reports.
	All other actions to be taken hereunder are the responsibility of the Vendor.
Corrective Actions	Upon being notified by the Customer of a missed service level, the Vendor shall promptly diagnose the cause and take reasonable actions to correct it.
	It is the Vendor's intention that no peering or transit link shall exceed utilization greater than one-third of its capacity. The Vendor's policy is to upgrade its links in advance as necessary to achieve this goal. However, there is no service level agreement or guarantee based on the Vendor's taking such actions.
Remedies	The customer shall receive a full pro-rata credit for each day during which the service level is not met.
Risk Transfer and Limitation of Liability	The Vendor's financial responsibility shall be limited to the Remedies presented herein. The Customer is encouraged to obtain third-party insurance to cover potential losses that are greater than those covered by the Remedies contained herein.
Contract	This Service Level Agreement is an Exhibit to the Web Hosting and Managed Services Agreement entered into by the Vendor and the Customer. The definitions, terms, and conditions of that Agreement are incorporated herein by reference.

Here are the ways in which the above SLA improves upon our previous example:

Vendor determination. This SLA uses a third-party monitoring service to determine whether the SLAs are met. In the earlier example, the vendor had both the responsibility and the sole authority to determine conformance.

Limits. The new agreement calls for credits up to the full amount paid by the customer.

Claims. You still have to ask for your credit within 30 days, but that's only because you're the one who controls the relationship with the monitoring service. Some web-hosting services have their own such relationships and can therefore take responsibility for initiating claims.

Granularity. The "59-minute downtime" loophole is gone. All measurements are over the course of a month.

Maintenance. Preventive and scheduled maintenance have been explicitly included as downtime.

Circuits. The new SLA emphasizes the end-user experience as the basis for measuring quality, rather than focusing on discrete measurements such as packet loss and latency. There's no need to exclude third-party circuits.

Acts of God. This wasn't addressed in the new SLA. It must be dealt with in the main contract to which the SLA is attached.

Incentives. This is something all new. If you expect your web-hosting vendor to make a commitment and put some skin in the game, you should be equally progressive. Don't just think of an SLA as being potentially punitive (the stick). Also consider its value as an incentive (the carrot). In this instance, the vendor can potentially earn a 5 percent bonus if it delivers service levels above and beyond those to which you've both agreed. That's a very important incentive to a web-hosting service or MSP, for it's not just an increase in revenues, but rather an increase in profits. It costs you relatively little, but it means a lot to a vendor. Most vendors would do a lot to increase their bottom lines by 5 percent. You probably give bonuses to your own employees who outperform expectations. Why not do the same for your outsourcers?

TIP Include incentive bonuses for vendors that exceed expected service levels.

Reactive SLAs

The performance SLA presented previously attempts to define a state in which everything is working properly. Because the connectivity service level is *measured*, when it's achieved, it'll be obvious to both you and your web-hosting service.

SLAs in the next category (*reactive SLAs*) are quite different. They define the actions that your web-hosting service or MSP will take when a problem occurs and your site needs attention. Reactive SLAs are based on the vendor's reaction to *events*, and the principal measurement is *time*. This is unlike performance SLAs, which describe expectations for ongoing, continuous services such as web-site uptime and connectivity. Their principal measurement is not time, but the quality of the service.

Before we study an example, let's look at two important issues that are fundamental to all reactive SLAs: the classification of incidents according to their severity, and the extent to which the vendor is directly responsible for the resolution of problems.

Incident Classification

When your web site goes down, you expect your web-hosting vendor to jump through hoops to get it up and running as quickly as possible. But not every problem needs to be addressed in such a panic mode. There are many tasks that, while still important, can be accomplished "soon," and still others that fall into the "eventually" category.

For example, if a nonredundant database server fails, causing your web site to go down, it must be dealt with immediately. But if there's a failure in the middle of the night of a single drive within a RAID array, the system will continue to operate until the failed drive can be replaced the next morning.

By definition, reactive SLAs deal with responses to *incidents,* and it's crucial that you and your web-hosting service or MSP share a common understanding of how incidents will be classified and prioritized. This is fundamental to good communications and the accurate interpretation of reactive SLAs.

Incidents should be classified according to two attributes: *severity* and *priority.* Unfortunately, they're often confused with one another and even used interchangeably, but they are very different. Severity is a property of the *problem,* while priority is a property of the *solution.* Severity describes the *impact* of a problem and isn't a judgment call. If the web site is down, it's down. If a component has failed, it has failed. Priority, on the other hand, is used to determine the order in which incidents must be addressed. For example, an incident that has gone unresolved for a long period of time may be assigned a higher priority than a more recent but higher-severity incident. Table 10.1 contains the definitions of three levels of severity.

The originator of an incident should determine its severity, and no one else should be allowed to change it. If you call your vendor's network operations center to report a problem, you're the originator, and you should decide how severe the problem is. If a problem is detected by an automated monitoring system, it's that system's responsibility to assign the severity. For this process to succeed, however, it's imperative that originators follow the guidelines in Table 10.1. When people or systems abuse their power to specify incident severity, the system collapses.

An incident should not normally be *escalated* from one level of severity to another merely because it has gone unresolved after some period of time. That's the purpose of priority. If a situation actually gets worse, then the severity may have to be increased, but an incident doesn't become more severe just because it's still outstanding. Likewise, a vendor should never *reduce* the severity of an incident without first conferring with you.

Priority, on the other hand, is very much a judgment call on the part of the web-hosting vendor's staff. Priorities may be given ratings like high/medium/low or simply be assigned numerical values. Unlike severity, the priority of an outstanding incident should be adjusted based on the length of time that incident has gone unresolved and whether the service level has been missed. In general, high-severity incidents should also be assigned a high priority; but as a customer, the manner in which a vendor defines its priorities is not particularly important to you.

TIP **Ask vendors for written definitions of the classification of incidents by severity and for an explanation of the rules for their use.**

Table 10.1   Incident Classifications by Severity

SEVERITY	CRITERIA
Critical	The entire site is down, performance has become unacceptable, or a major function affecting many visitors or buyers is inoperative. Examples: Failure of any nonredundant component such as a database server; or a critical file must be recovered.
Urgent	The site is operating normally, but a redundant component or supporting feature has failed. Examples: Failure of a redundant server where the remaining server(s) can't adequately handle the increased load; failure of one of a set of redundant power supplies, a redundant server, or a single drive in a RAID array; failure of a daemon or process where a failed-over one is temporarily adequate; failure of a reporting tool; or a noncritical file must be recovered.
Routine	The site is available and performing adequately. Examples: Preventive maintenance, upgrades, nonurgent patches, certain configuration changes.

Responses

A clear understanding of how severity and priority are defined goes a long way toward improving communications between you and your web-hosting service. The other issue you must pin down in advance is who will have responsibility for each step in the problem-resolution process. In some cases, the web-hosting service or MSP will take responsibility for a problem all the way through to its resolution. In other cases, the vendor may agree to be responsible only for detecting the problem and informing you that it has occurred.

Each reactive SLA describes the events that trigger a vendor response and the expectations for the results of that response. Web-hosting services offer responses in four classes: monitoring, dispatch, problem determination, and problem resolution.

Monitoring. The first step is for the vendor to determine that an incident has occurred, typically through automated monitoring of the service.

Dispatch. Once a problem has been identified through monitoring or other means (e.g., a phone call from you), the next step for the vendor is to contact anyone who needs to be kept in the loop until the incident is resolved. This might include calling or paging you or your staff as well as contacting third parties such as hardware maintenance vendors. In some cases, even if your staff has the responsibility for problem determination or resolution, you can still utilize your vendor's *dispatch services.* Such services also typically include tracking the follow-through of third parties and keeping you informed as to their progress.

Problem determination. Once the proper people have been dispatched (you, your web-hosting vendor's staff, or a third party), the next step is for those people to determine the likely *cause* of the problem. In some cases, for instance with hardware problems, your web-hosting vendor will diagnose the problem and then provide dispatch services to alert and track third-party maintenance staff.

Problem resolution. After determining the cause of the problem, someone must provide the final response to actually *correct* the problem.

TIP Every reactive SLA should clearly state who's responsible for monitoring, dispatching, determining, and resolving the problem.

Data Recovery SLA

Now that we've reviewed the general issues of incident classification and vendor responses, let's look at an example of a reactive SLA for *data recovery*. This SLA covers the vendor's reactions in two situations. In the first, one or more missing or damaged files are responsible for a portion of your web site being down (i.e., severity = critical). The second is used when one or more files or databases must be recovered, but the majority of your site can continue to function adequately until the recovery can be accomplished (i.e., severity = urgent).

SLA Title	Data Recovery
Purpose	To establish expectations for completion times for recovery of files and databases from backup media.
Description	In conjunction with backup services (addressed by a separate SLA) the Vendor provides file and database recovery services described in this SLA.
Measurement	The service levels are defined in terms of the time to complete (not merely initiate) a data recovery operation. The times used to determine compliance with this SLA shall be those recorded in the Vendor's incident tracking system.
	If a recovery request is initiated as a result of the Vendor's diagnostic efforts of another incident (e.g., recovery from a site outage requires that one or more files be restored), the start time for purposes of measuring conformance to this SLA shall be the time at which the determination of the previous problem is logged in to the Vendor's incident tracking system.
	If an incident is not properly recorded, it shall be assumed that the service levels were not achieved for that incident.

Targets   Resolution times below are shown as <hours>:<minutes>.

	Critical	Urgent
1. Max time to complete single (small) file recovery from on-site media	00:15	02:00
2. Max time to complete single (small) file recovery from off-site media	03:00	04:00
3. Max additional time (added to 1 and 2, above) to complete recovery of total operating system and application recovery to a clean but operational server. (If required, emergency provisioning of a clean server is covered by a separate agreement and SLA.)	02:00	04:00
4. Max additional time (added to 1 and 2, above) to complete recovery of databases with empty tables	0:30	1:00
5. Max additional time to complete file or database recovery per gigabyte	00:05	00:10

100% of all incident resolutions shall be completed within the above target times.

Incentive Target:
    20% faster in 100% of measurements and
    50% faster in 80% of measurements

Reporting   Vendor shall log (manually or automatically) all recovery activities and shall provide the Customer with web-enabled access to such logs. Logs shall include the start and end date and time of each recovery activity.

Vendor shall generate a report showing compliance with the service levels for each calendar month. The report shall be web-enabled and available to the Customer no later than 15 days after the end of the month.

Fees   The fees for Backup services (defined in the Backup SLA) include all charges for Data Recovery services. There are no fees uniquely associated with this SLA.

The Customer shall pay an incentive bonus of an additional 5% (calculated on a calendar monthly basis) if the Incentive Targets are achieved for that month. If there are no data recovery incidents in a given month, no incentive bonus shall be paid.

Responsibilities	*Monitoring:* There are no monitoring responsibilities directly associated with this SLA.
	Dispatch: The Vendor shall perform all dispatch functions, including keeping the Customer informed as to the status and eventual completion of any data recovery incidents. Generalized dispatch service levels are addressed in the Dispatch Service SLA.
	Problem Determination: The Vendor shall perform all problem determination functions.
	Problem Resolution: The Vendor shall perform all problem resolution functions.
Corrective Actions	If any recovery from on-site media cannot be accomplished within the specified times, the incident shall be escalated to Critical (if it was not already), and off-site media shall be retrieved in order to affect a recovery. [*Note: This is one of the few situations in which severity changes are permitted, as discussed earlier.*]
Remedies	The Vendor shall issue a credit to the Customer for each data recovery incident that is not completed within the target time. The amount of such credit shall be 10% of the total paid in the previous month for Backup services.
	However, in no event shall the Vendor issue credits for Backup and Data Recovery services (combined) for services in any calendar month that exceed the fees paid by the Customer for Backup services in that month.
Risk Transfer and Limitation of Liability	The Vendor's financial responsibility shall be limited to the Remedies presented herein. The Customer is encouraged to obtain third-party insurance to cover potential losses that are greater than those covered by the Remedies contained herein.
Contract	This Service Level Agreement is an Exhibit to the Web Hosting and Managed Services Agreement entered into by the Vendor and the Customer. The definitions, terms, and conditions of that Agreement are incorporated herein by reference.

Response versus Resolution

One important issue with regard to reactive SLAs is suggested in the *Measurement* section of the preceding example. It's the distinction between "time to initiate" (or respond to the problem) and "time to complete" (resolve the problem).

A typical (i.e., weak) SLA contains a vendor's commitment to respond, initiate, or *begin* working on a problem within some period of time. That's all well and good, but if your web site is down, it's not the response that counts. It's the *completion* of the task or the resolution of the problem that matters.

Some vendors just don't get it. They insist that all they can do is promise to start their diagnostic efforts within some timeframe. After all, they argue, how can they promise to solve a problem within any time limit until they know what caused it?

One would expect this attitude from a vendor that's seeing every problem for the first time. But if you and your web-hosting service are a good match for one another, your site should present few new challenges to your vendor. One reason you'll have chosen your vendor is because it has done it all before.

If a server dies, your vendor should know exactly how long it will take to replace it and reload your content and data. If your server requires only a new CPU or some replacement RAM, that's great. But the vendor should be willing to make a commitment, that 80 percent, for example, of all server failures will be *resolved* within two hours. The vendor should have more than enough statistical experience to know what it can promise.

What's an emergency for you shouldn't be one for your web-hosting service or MSP. In the same way that firefighters put out fires every day, web-hosting vendors repair and replace servers all the time. Some reactive services, such as our example of data recovery, are very easy to estimate. Every vendor should know exactly how long it takes to locate and restore a file from backup disk or on-site archive tape, as well as how long it takes to retrieve tapes from off-site storage. There's no art or rocket science here. These are everyday occurrences, and rather than promising how quickly they'll get started on a problem, there's no reason vendors can't also guarantee results.

TIP Look for SLAs that commit to resolution of problems, not merely initiation of a response.

Proactive SLAs

The first two categories of service level agreements, *performance* and *reactive*, addressed ongoing services and responses to problems. Our third and final category, *proactive* service level agreements, includes those that describe services that are intended to prevent problems from occurring in the first place.

Proactive SLAs are conceptually simpler—although not necessarily shorter—than those in the other categories. One reason is that the basis for measuring whether a proactive service has been delivered as expected is typically just a matter of determining whether the task was completed on time and error-free.

Backup Example

We'll use *backup services* as our example, since it's complementary to recovery services, described in the previous example.

SLA TITLE	BACKUP
Purpose	To ensure availability of current copies of all content, data, and code in case individual files, databases, components, or complete servers need to be restored due to errors, malfunctions, or major disasters.
Description	All standard files (operating systems, applications, utilities) on all servers shall be copied to CD-ROM (Backup CD). The format used shall be appropriate for both rapid recovery of an entire

server as well as for recovery of individual files. A new Backup CD shall be created whenever a change is made to the associated server. Backup CDs shall be retained on-site.

All other files (those that contain code or data unique to Customer's applications) shall be copied to magnetic disk (Backup Disk) on a storage unit that's on-site but physically separate from any of the Customer's servers. Backup Disk copies shall be created at least daily so that a Backup Disk copy that is no more than 30 hours old shall always exist. The two most recent copies of each file or database shall be available at all times.

A complete copy of a current error-free Backup Disk set shall be made to magnetic tape (Archive Tape) weekly so that an Archive Tape copy that is no more than nine days old shall always exist. The most recent Archive Tapes shall be available on-site at all times. The next most recent Archive Tapes shall be located at a remote location or in transit to or from that location. Long-term retention and reuse of Archive Tapes are addressed in a separate Tape Rotation SLA.

Measurement

The service levels are defined in terms of the timeliness of error-free backups as calculated each calendar month. Measurement of these criteria shall be via the review of entries in the log files.

Targets

Error-free Backup CDs shall be created within 24 hours of any change to a server (95% of the time) or within 48 hours (100%). ("Backup CD Service Level")

Error-free Backup Disks shall be created on time (all but two days per calendar month), or one day late (100%). Only one of the currently available Backup Disks may contain an error. ("Backup Disk Service Level")

Error-free Archive Tapes shall be created on time (three out of every four weeks, on a rolling basis), and no more than two days late (100%). No more than one set of Archive Tapes in a row may contain errors (i.e., files not backed up). ("Archive Tape Service Level")

To be considered acceptable, all backup media referenced in the above SLAs shall be readable for purposes of recovery or analysis, with the exception of any errors previously documented in the backup logs.

The Customer may request no more frequently than annually a "Recovery Test," whereby a full recovery to a test server is made from a Customer-designated set of Archive Tapes. The Vendor must demonstrate to the Customer's satisfaction that the restored server contains all the files necessary for full and proper operation.

Reporting

The Vendor shall log (manually or automatically) all backup activities, and shall provide the Customer with web-enabled access to such logs. Logs shall include the date and time of each backup activity, as well as reports of any backup errors (i.e., files not backed up) that occurred.

The Vendor shall generate a report showing compliance with the service levels for each calendar month. The report shall be web-enabled and available to the Customer no later than 15 days after the end of the month.

Fees

$50 per month per server covered under this SLA. ("Per-Server Fee")

$5 per gigabyte per month for Backup Disks using the high-water mark (100%) rule as measured each calendar month. Includes Backup Tapes. ("Per-Gigabyte Fee")

$200 per Backup CD created due to a change in the configuration of a server requested by the Customer (i.e., not due to changes made in the course of the Vendor's maintenance activities). ("Per-Backup CD Fee")

$5,000 per Recovery Test requested by Customer.

Responsibilities

The Customer has the responsibility of properly reporting any changes it or its applications may make to files affected by this SLA.

The Vendor shall supply all backup hardware, software, and media.

All other actions to be taken hereunder are the responsibility of the Vendor.

Corrective Actions

If a Backup CD contains an error, it shall promptly be replaced with one that is error-free.

If a Backup Disk contains an error, the following day's Backup Disk must be error-free.

If an Archive Tape contains an error, it must be replaced with one that is error-free.

Remedies

If the Backup CD Service Level for any server is not achieved in any given calendar month, the Customer shall receive a one-month credit for the Per-Server Fee associated with that server as well as for any Per-Backup CD Fees associated with that server during that month.

If either the Backup Disk Service Level or the Archive Tape Service Level are not achieved in any given calendar month, the Customer shall receive a credit for the Per-Gigabyte Fee for that month.

If any Service Level (Backup CD, Backup Disk, Archive Tape) is missed for any two calendar months out of six calendar months (on a rolling basis), the Customer shall receive a credit for all fees invoiced under this SLA that have not been previously credited for the six-month period up to and including the second missed month.

Risk Transfer and Limitation of Liability	The Vendor's financial responsibility shall be limited to the Remedies presented herein. The Customer is encouraged to obtain third-party insurance to cover potential losses that are greater than those covered by the Remedies contained herein.
Contract	This Service Level Agreement is an Exhibit to the Web Hosting and Managed Services Agreement entered into by the Vendor and the Customer. The definitions, terms, and conditions of that Agreement are incorporated herein by reference.

Note that there are no incentive targets or bonuses in this SLA. Backups must be done right, and there's no way to do them "more right."

Wimpy SLAs: Worse Than Nothing

Many SLAs contain outrageously weak time commitments. One SLA might promise to initiate a response to a critical outage within an hour. Another might guarantee a resolution within two days. What's wrong with this picture?

One reason you've decided to outsource your web hosting is because you believe a third party can do a better job of 24/7 coverage than you could do with your own staff. Suppose you accidentally delete a file from one of your servers. Let's say it didn't bring down your web site, but you can't get your job done until the file is restored. If this was under the control of your own staff, you'd have that file restored within a few minutes. So why should you accept an SLA that says the vendor will complete such a recovery within eight hours?

Vendors offer wimpy SLAs because customers let them get away with it. Talk frankly to your prospective web-hosting vendors and ask them whether they honestly think they can be as responsive as your in-house staff. If so, then why don't they put it in writing? If not, then why are they charging you so much?

Many wimpy SLAs come from vendors that have jumped onto the bandwagon just so they can tell the world they *have* SLAs. You might be tempted to brush off wimpy SLAs as merely worthless. In fact, they can actually cause you more harm than if they didn't exist at all.

If you and your web-hosting vendor end up in arbitration or litigation, someone (an arbitrator, judge, or jury) will need a basis upon which to decide the level of services to which you are entitled. Lacking anything in writing, an arbitrator will probably use some vague criteria such as "industry standard practices" or "reasonable efforts," which may or may not be to your advantage.

But if there's something in writing such as a document entitled "Service Level *Agreement*" that purports to express the original intentions of the parties, that document will most likely supercede other criteria. The whole purpose of an SLA, after all, is to clearly express the mutual expectations and commitments of the parties. If that SLA doesn't express your understanding of the service level expectations, it may be too late.

The advantage of an SLA in this situation is that it specifies the levels of service less ambiguously than if they were left unspecified. If an SLA exists, a judge, jury, or arbitrator will likely use the service levels defined in the SLA instead of more generally accepted measurements. After all, these were the levels of service that the parties agreed to at the inception of their contractual relationship.

If your contract includes wimpy SLAs, you (not only the vendor) must be willing to live with them. When push comes to shove, and the vendor holds an SLA up in front of an arbitrator, it's too late to claim that you expected something more than was written into your agreement.

> **TIP** Don't include (even by reference) an SLA in a web-hosting or managed services agreement unless it expresses the levels of service you'll accept. If you and your vendor can't agree on the wording of an SLA, it may be preferable not to have one at all. Better yet, find another vendor who will put better service levels in writing.

SLA and Web-Hosting Contractual Issues

In addition to the warning to watch out for wimpy SLAs, here are some other issues to be aware of when reviewing or negotiating SLAs and web-hosting contracts.

Exclusions

Many SLAs exclude vendor responsibility for occurrences "beyond the vendor's control." This language is common in many other types of contracts, and it's something that you may normally pay little attention to. But this phrase has significant consequences in web-hosting and managed-service SLAs.

You may be paying your vendor to manage third-party relationships as part of the services it provides. In the case of managed services, you may even be paying the vendor *specifically* to assume risks for third-party services. If your SLA contains exclusions for things that are "beyond the vendor's control" it may mean, in essence, that the vendor has no responsibility for the very services for which you're paying.

> **TIP** Don't let vendors exclude liability for the very things you're paying them to do for you.

Again, review the section on *force majeure* in the Chapter 9, "Risk Management," for more information on the scope of a vendor's liability.

Subcontracting

Another exclusion to watch out for is the vendor's responsibility for the actions of its subcontractors. If subcontracting is permitted, make sure that it doesn't let your vendor off the hook in case of problems caused by a subcontractor.

If you plan to use both a colocation service and a managed service provider, pay close attention to the three-way relationship that exists. Is one vendor the prime contractor and the other a subcontractor? If so, how do responsibility and liability pass from the sub through the prime to you, and vice versa?

TIP Insist that vendors accept responsibility and liability for the actions of their subcontractors to the same extent they would if no subcontractors were involved.

Also consider what will happen if you terminate the agreement with one of your two vendors. If your MSP lets you down, are you stuck with the colo? Suppose the colocation vendor's connectivity turns bad. Can you move to a new colo and keep the same MSP? Is your MSP allowed to bypass the colo's connectivity by bringing in connections to third-party ISPs?

TIP Ask for provisions in your contracts giving you the option to terminate in case of a problem with the vendor's colocation or managed services partners.

Price Changes

Although not strictly an SLA issue, you should consider your exposure to price increases by your vendors. Is there anything in their contracts that limits their ability to increase prices when it comes time for renewal? Make sure you don't get low-balled for the first year, only to have the price shoot up at renewal time.

As discussed in Chapter 7, "The Dark Side of Outsourcing," changing web-hosting vendors is a major event, and the vendors know it. Some of them aren't above using tactics like this to get you in the door. Others are inexperienced and just don't realize that their pricing is too low to cover their costs. But when they figure it out, you're the one who'll have to pay the difference—unless you protect yourself.

Can your vendor arbitrarily increase prices when it comes time to renew the contract? (Reread the section *Customer Dumping* in Chapter 8, "Getting It Right.")

TIP Negotiate a cap on annual price increases of 10 percent per year on a per-line item basis.

Change of Control

Web-hosting and managed-services businesses are relatively new and highly volatile. Mergers and acquisitions seem to be announced nearly every week. Do you know what it would mean to you and your web site if your web-hosting service or MSP were to be acquired?

TIP Request provisions that give you the option to cancel your web-hosting agreements in case another company acquires a controlling interest in one of your vendors.

This won't be a particularly popular idea with your vendors, since your contract is one of the assets that gives them value. But you should at least consider what might happen if such an acquisition were to occur.

Disputes

As is a good idea for any contract, review the provisions for resolving disputes. Most customers and vendors find it's beneficial to have a clear escalation path by which disputes can be resolved quickly and at the lowest cost to both parties. Here's an example of an escalation path:

Negotiate. Identify in the contract (i.e., in advance of any dispute) individuals from each party who will serve as *advocates* in case a dispute arises. The contract should require these individuals to meet promptly and at least once to attempt to resolve any dispute. The contract should furthermore require that if the named negotiators are unsuccessful after a specific period of time, the problem will be escalated to a meeting of senior executives of each party.

Mediation. If the dispute continues to go unresolved for yet another specific period of time, the contract should require formal mediation.

Arbitration. If formal mediation is unsuccessful, you may want an agreement that the dispute be submitted to binding arbitration. However, depending on your business and your risk-management strategy (e.g., does your vendor provide formal risk transfer?), you may not want binding arbitration. As with most of the issues in this section, this is one that should be reviewed by a competent attorney.

TIP Make sure contracts and SLAs include a formal process for the escalation and resolution of disputes.

Termination Rights

Ultimately, you may have such severe problems with your web-hosting vendor that you feel you must get out of the contract and take your web site elsewhere. This can be a very nasty situation. Web sites are particularly difficult to move, and doing so is almost impossible without at least some cooperation from the old vendor. If your relationship with that vendor has deteriorated (and it probably has if you're trying to leave), you may have to rely on terms and conditions that were written into the contract back in the days when all was well.

First, make sure that there's some provision for you to terminate any web-hosting or managed services agreement in case of repeated failures to meet service levels.

TIP Negotiate clear and unambiguous definitions that give you the option to terminate agreements if service levels are consistently missed.

Second, make sure that if you're forced to terminate the agreement for cause, the vendor is obligated to assist you in relocating your web site. This can include, for example, continuing to provide certain services overlapped with those provided by your new vendor, as well as cooperating with changes to DNS, and so on.

TIP Make sure vendors are required to assist you with the relocation of your site if you exercise an option to terminate your web-hosting or managed-services agreement.

As you can see, SLAs are not for the faint of heart—at least good ones aren't. After this pitch for how SLAs *should* be written, you may be ready to go out and fight for SLAs the way you think they should be. Realistically, unless you're a major customer, few web-hosting services and MSPs will even consider making changes to their standard SLAs.

If you are using a shared- or dedicated-server web-hosting service, you'll probably have neither the opportunity nor the need to negotiate your SLAs. Nevertheless, you should ask for them and read them carefully.

If you're a major customer of a colocation service and/or a managed services provider, be prepared to invest many hours in reading, analyzing, and negotiating SLAs and contracts. It'll be time well spent.

But in order to evaluate and negotiate your specific service level requirements, you'll first need to get a handle on your web site's traffic and hardware requirements, and the best way to do that is to build a dynamic model of your site. That's the subject of the next chapter, "Traffic Models."

Traffic Models

You may have a good idea of what your web site will need *qualitatively*—its features and functions—but do you know your *quantitative* requirements? How many visitors will your web site get? How many page views? How many transactions? And how much server hardware and software will it take to meet those requirements?

The best way to answer these questions is to build a *traffic model* of your web site, and that's what we'll do in this chapter. Even if your site is already live, an accurate traffic model will prove invaluable.

Nearly every aspect of planning your web-hosting solution will be affected by what you learn from your model. A complete model does more than just allow you to forecast web-site traffic. It's the fundamental tool for planning the scalability of every component of your web site. Ultimately, your web-site model will even tie into your company's business plan, ensuring that your technology decisions are, in fact, based on the actual principles driving your business.

We'll start with a basic spreadsheet to model a simple web site. From there we'll add concepts to the model in steps. Along the way we'll also increase the traffic assumptions from one example to the next in order to reflect larger and larger sites. By the time we're done, we'll have developed a fairly robust model that forecasts not only web-site traffic, but also e-commerce transactions and revenues.

As valuable as these models may be, they're still only examples, and they don't include calculations of every aspect of every conceivable web site. In particular, we won't go as far as modeling database server performance, as that's very application-specific and worthy of a book all its own. We also won't model the delivery of rich media (such as Flash) or streaming content, since most web-site owners with a substantial amount of such traffic will probably find it more cost-effective to outsource its hosting to a content delivery network (CDN), as discussed at length in Chapter 13, "Caching and Content Delivery Networks."

> **TIP** The examples described in this chapter are real, usable models, and each spreadsheet is available on the web site that accompanies this book. You can find the Excel files used in these examples at www.rds.com/books/hosting/.

A Simple, Static Web Site

We'll start with a model for a simple web site that contains only static content. Ninety-five percent of all web sites fall into this category. The most significant characteristics of such sites are (a) they don't require databases; (b) their content changes only when their owners change it explicitly; (c) they don't support any transactions (e.g., commerce); and (d) they can usually run on shared or dedicated servers.

The primary objective of this first model is to figure out how much bandwidth or data transfer such a site will require. From this, we can determine, for instance, whether the site will be able to run on a $19.95/month service supporting up to 5 GB/month of data transfer, or it will need a higher-volume service. This first simple model is shown in Figure 11.1. (A downloadable version of this spreadsheet is at www.wiley.com/compbooks/kaye.)

The model in Figure 11.1 starts with three assumptions that are constants (i.e., not formulas) in Excel. These are the values that you can change as appropriate for your own site:

B2: *Site Visits per Month.* This site will receive 3,000 visits per month.

B3: *Average Pages Viewed per Visit.* On average, each visitor will view 10 pages each time he visits this web site.

B4: *Average Page Size (Kbytes).* The average page on this web site contains 50 Kbytes of text and images.

From these three assumptions the following three values are computed:

B6: *Site Visits per Day.* This one's easy. It's just the number of visits per month divided by 30.

	A	B	C	D	E	F
1	**Assumptions**					
2	Site Visits per Month	3,000				
3	Average Pages Viewed per Visit	10				
4	Average Page Size (Kbytes)	50				
5	**Calculations**					
6	Site Visits per Day	100				
7	Page Views per Month	30,000				
8	GB Transferred per Month	1.5				

Figure 11.1 SmallStaticSite.xls.

	A	B	C	D	E	F
1	**Assumptions**					
2	Site Visits per Month	15,000				
3	Average Pages Viewed per Visit	10				
4	Average Page Size (Kbytes)	50				
5	**Calculations**					
6	Site Visits per Day	500				
7	Page Views per Month	150,000				
8	GB Transferred per Month	7.5				

Figure 11.2   SmallStaticSite.xls updated.

> **B7:** *Page Views per Month.* This is computed as the number of visits per month (B2) multiplied by the average pages viewed per visit (B3).

> **B8:** *GB Transferred per Month.* Here's the answer we're looking for. This site needs to transfer 1.5 GB per month, which is computed by multiplying the average page size (B4) by the number of page views per month (B7). Dividing by 1,000,000 converts from kilobytes (used to measure page size) to gigabytes.

A web-hosting service that offers, for instance, 5 GB per month of data transfer should be sufficient for this site. But suppose, as seen in Figure 11.2, the site's traffic increases by five times—not only possible, but perhaps desirable. To see the effect of that increase, just change the value in cell B2 to 15,000. (Download the spreadsheet and you can do this yourself.)

From this model we can see that at 15,000 visits per month, the web site will outgrow the web-hosting service's 5 GB per month limit. So what happens? Unless the site owner upgrades to the next-highest package, there are three actions the web-hosting service might take:

- The web-hosting service might not even notice and let the traffic go through without charge. (Don't gamble on this one.)

- The web-hosting service could charge an additional fee for the extra 2.5 GB of data transferred.

- The web-hosting service could shut the site down around the twentieth day of the month when the 5 GB limit is reached.

All three of these actions occur in the real world. You should know your hosting service's policies regarding overages before this happens, and make sure they're specified in your contract.

TIP If your web-hosting service is going to charge you for additional bandwidth, you should know how much in advance.

Traffic Measurement Techniques

The technique used by your web-hosting service to measure traffic can have a significant impact on how your bandwidth usage and billing are computed. The technique that yields the smallest results is to measure your traffic by processing your log files. Because the log files report the actual size of the objects transmitted, you won't be paying for any *overhead*, such as the additional bytes that are required to support TCP/IP and other protocols.

However, some vendors measure traffic according to statistics they extract from routers. In this case, the results will include the *total* number of bytes transmitted, including the overhead from protocols such as TCP/IP and HTTP. This can increase the results by as much as 5 percent. This is the measurement technique we'll assume for the models in this chapter.

Some vendors count not only the traffic your web servers transmit, but the traffic your servers receive as well. That is, they charge you for the requests and other packets that are received from your visitors' browsers. This can increase your charges by as much as an additional 15 percent.

TIP Ask prospective vendors how they measure traffic, specifically whether they include protocol overhead and inbound traffic in their measurements.

Hits, Page Views, and Bytes

Web-site traffic is measured in a variety of ways. Some people talk about *hits* while others refer to *page views, gigabytes (GB),* or *millions of bits (megabits) per second (Mbps).* Still others refer to *visitors* or *unique visitors.* In fact, all of these measurements are valuable, but not always in the same contexts.

Every time someone clicks on a hyperlink or a Submit button, and every time someone types a URL in the Address window of his or her browser, that person is requesting a page; and each time that happens, the web site receives a *page request* from the browser. The web server replies to each page request with an HTML page that counts as a *page view* for statistical purposes.

But the HTML pages are not complete. They include most of the *text* that's seen on the screen, but they include only *references* to the images and other objects that make up the rest of the page design. An *object* is anything a browser requests, such as an HTML page, an image file, a video stream, and so on. A *hit* is the event that occurs when a server receives the request for an object.

Here's a very simple page coded in HTML:

```
<HTML>
<HEAD>
<TITLE>Sample Web Page</TITLE>
</HEAD>
<BODY>
<IMG SRC="/image/header.gif">
<H1>Welcome!</H1>
<IMG SRC="/image/logo.gif">
The photo below shows how I spent my summer vacation.
<IMG SRC="/photos/vacation.jpg">
<p>
<IMG SRC="/image/footer.gif">
</BODY>
</HTML>
```

The lines that begin "<IMG. . .>" are *image tags* and tell the browser to go back to the server to request the associated images. In order to display this page, the browser will *hit* this site's web server five times: once for the underlying page and again to retrieve each of the four images: a header, a footer, a logo, and a photograph. If every page on the web site has four images, the site's ratio of page views to hits is 1:5.

Page Structure

In order to model certain characteristics that vary according to the number of hits or page views, we need to understand the *ratio* of hits to page views in more detail.

There are a number of free and easy-to-use tools on the Internet that will analyze the contents of any web page in terms of hits and bytes. The one shown in Figure 11.3 is called Dr. Watson, and is hosted by Addy & Associates at http://watson.addy.com/. On this page you can enter the URL or host name of any web page. There are many options, but for this purpose we've selected only "Compute estimated download speeds."

As examples, let's look at the home pages of two popular web sites, Yahoo! and Amazon. The home pages and corresponding Dr. Watson analyses are shown in Figures 11.4 through 11.8.

Two things are noteworthy about the Yahoo! home page. First, it's almost entirely text, which can be transmitted more efficiently than the same information sent as

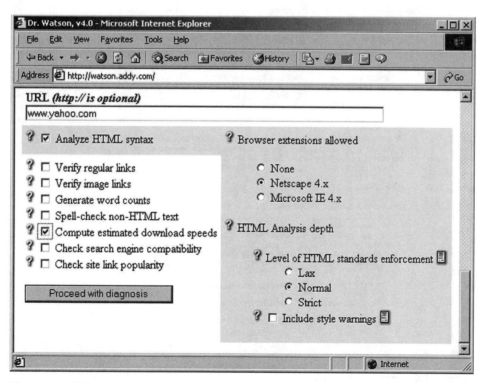

Figure 11.3   Dr. Watson.
Source: Addy & Associates

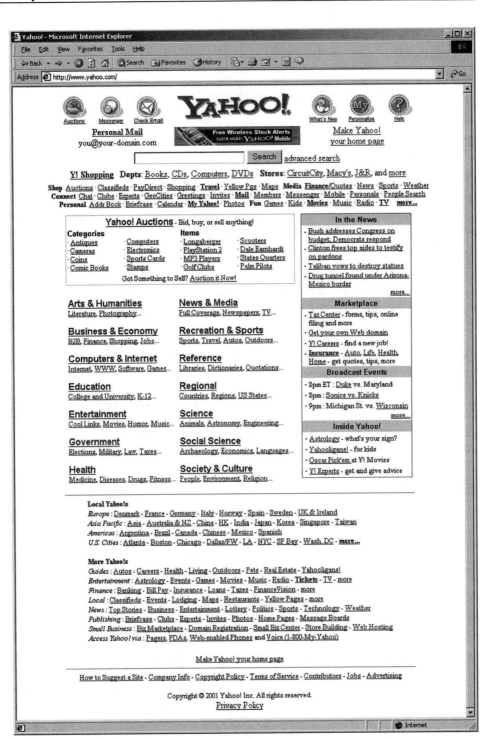

Figure 11.4 www.yahoo.com.

Figure 11.5 The Yahoo! navigation bar.

Dr. Watson, v4.0 - Microsoft Internet Explorer

File Edit View Favorites Tools Help

⟵ Back ▾ → ⊗ ▤ ⌂ | ⊘ Search ▧ Favorites ⊕ History | ▧▾ ⊜ ⊠ ▾ ▤ ○

Address ⟩ http://watson.addy.com/   ▾ ⟩Go

Checking server response …

Server response

> **http://www.yahoo.com**
> was redirected to
> **http://www.yahoo.com/**
>
> **Response code from http://www.yahoo.com/**
> OK (code 200)

Analyzing HTML …
Computing download speeds …

Estimated download speed

> These download times are estimates and should only be used as a general guideline. Many factors, such as your modem, quality of connection, ISP load, server responsiveness, and Internet routing can greatly impact the actual download times experienced by your visitors.

Object type	Number	Size in bytes	Estimated download times (seconds)					
			14.4	28.8	33.6	56k	128K	T1
HTML	1	16330	11.91	6.53	5.44	4.67	2.04	0.82
Images	2	10171	7.42	4.07	3.39	2.91	1.27	0.51
Total	3	26501	19.33	10.60	8.83	7.57	3.31	1.33

Done   ⊕ Internet

Figure 11.6 Analysis of www.yahoo.com.
Source: Addy & Associates

graphics. Second, the navigation bar (or nav bar) that appears to consist of separate graphics is, in fact, only one image, as shown in Figure 11.5.

The analysis of www.yahoo.com is shown in Figure 11.6. Note that there are only three objects: the underlying page and two images. One image is the navigation bar. The other is the ad banner that appears directly under the Yahoo! logo. Everything else on this page is simple HTML text. The entire page (i.e., all the files that make up what

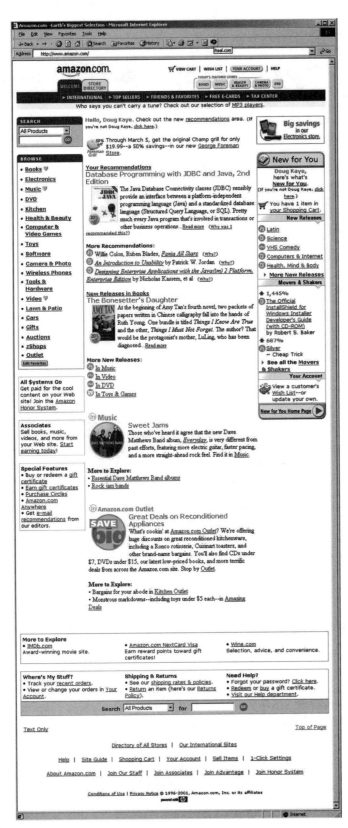

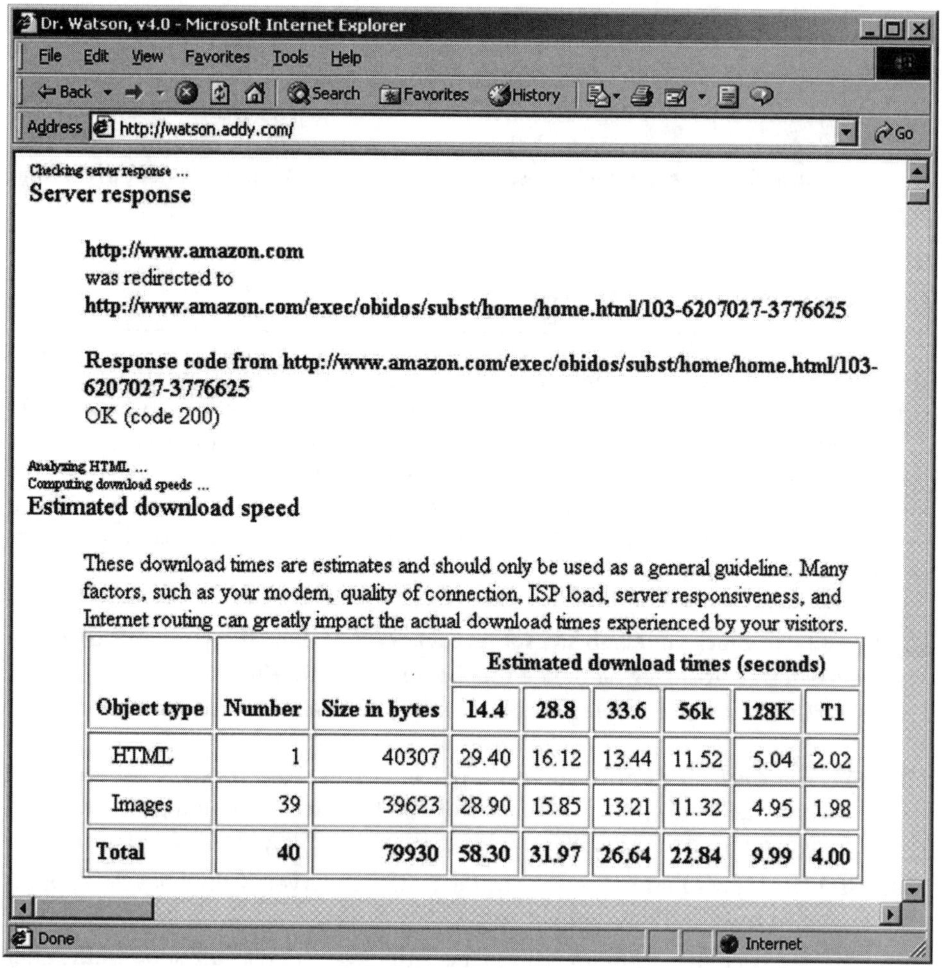
Dr. Watson, v4.0 - Microsoft Internet Explorer

Address http://watson.addy.com/

Checking server response ...

Server response

http://www.amazon.com
was redirected to
http://www.amazon.com/exec/obidos/subst/home/home.html/103-6207027-3776625

Response code from http://www.amazon.com/exec/obidos/subst/home/home.html/103-6207027-3776625
OK (code 200)

Analyzing HTML ...
Computing download speeds ...

Estimated download speed

These download times are estimates and should only be used as a general guideline. Many factors, such as your modem, quality of connection, ISP load, server responsiveness, and Internet routing can greatly impact the actual download times experienced by your visitors.

			Estimated download times (seconds)					
Object type	**Number**	**Size in bytes**	**14.4**	**28.8**	**33.6**	**56k**	**128K**	**T1**
HTML	1	40307	29.40	16.12	13.44	11.52	5.04	2.02
Images	39	39623	28.90	15.85	13.21	11.32	4.95	1.98
Total	**40**	**79930**	**58.30**	**31.97**	**26.64**	**22.84**	**9.99**	**4.00**

Done

Figure 11.8 Analysis of www.amazon.com.
Source: Addy & Associates

a user sees, combined in size) is only 26 Kbytes. Using a 56 K modem connection, this complete page can be downloaded in only 7.57 seconds.

Compare the Yahoo! home page to www.amazon.com, shown in Figure 11.7, and the accompanying analysis in Figure 11.8.

You can see that the Amazon.com home page is three times the size (in total bytes) of the Yahoo! home page. You can also see that it has nearly *20 times* as many images (37 versus 2). Most of the Amazon.com images are actually small icons or buttons, but graphically it's clearly a more complex page. Yahoo.com has a page/hit ratio of 1:3, whereas Amazon.com's ratio is 1:38. By comparison to Yahoo!'s home page, Amazon's is graphic-intensive.

Page views are a common metric applied to web sites, particularly for advertising-based sites that charge advertisers according to ad *impressions*. If there's one ad per page, then the number of page views and the number of impressions are equal.

But if advertisers are interested in page views, and users care about the overall page size and download speed, why do we care about hits and objects? When it comes to planning for the resources required to *deliver* those pages, there's a certain amount of overhead (processor power, etc.) associated with each object, regardless of its size. Likewise, there's overhead associated with the page, regardless of how many objects it contains. To accurately model our web sites, we therefore need to know about both hits and page views.

The Effects of Caching

As we'll explore in detail in Chapter 13, "Caching and Content Delivery Networks," caching in browsers, corporate proxy servers, and ISP access caches can have a substantial impact on the traffic your web servers receive. You can easily see this effect by examining your logs. You'll probably find, for example, that the images on your web pages receive fewer hits than the underlying pages themselves. This is because the images are more likely to be cached. In Figure 11.9, we've added the capability to compensate for the effects of caching.

> **TIP** You can check your web site for its *cacheability*—how the Internet's cache servers will treat it—using an online tool hosted by CacheFlow, Inc., at www.cacheflow.com/technology/tools/friendly/cacheability/tool/index.cfm.

B5: *Effective Cache Hit Ratio.* This is the percentage of objects that browsers request but never make it to your web servers due to the effects of caching. You can find your actual effective cache hit ratio by studying your log files.

B9: *GB Viewed per Month.*This is the traffic your web servers would have to support if there were no caching.

B10: *GB Transferred per Month.* This is the actual web server outbound traffic after taking the effects of caching into consideration.

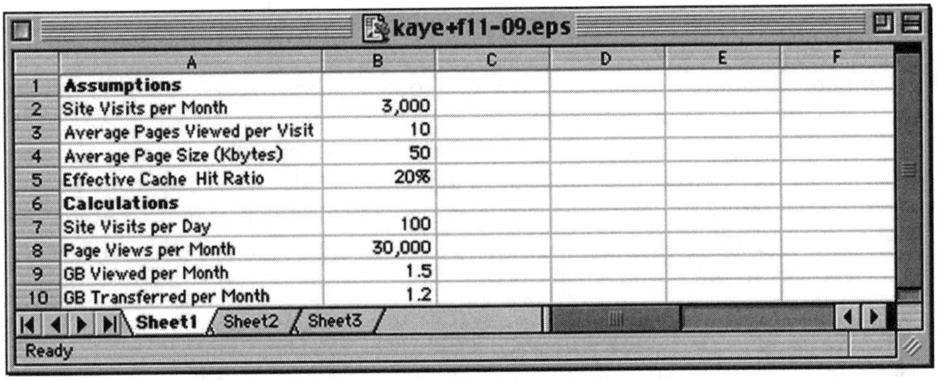

	A	B	C	D	E	F
1	**Assumptions**					
2	Site Visits per Month	3,000				
3	Average Pages Viewed per Visit	10				
4	Average Page Size (Kbytes)	50				
5	Effective Cache Hit Ratio	20%				
6	**Calculations**					
7	Site Visits per Day	100				
8	Page Views per Month	30,000				
9	GB Viewed per Month	1.5				
10	GB Transferred per Month	1.2				

kaye+f11-09.eps

Sheet1 / Sheet2 / Sheet3

Ready

Figure 11.9 CacheHits.xls.

Estimating Log-File Space

Another reason you should know the number of hits your web site will receive is to predict the disk space you'll need for storing log files. It's remarkable how many web sites crash only because the web server's disk drive fills up with log-file entries. This has probably happened to almost every webmaster at least once.

Most web servers are configured to write various access and error log files to disk. These files grow and grow until a log-file reporting program eventually analyzes them, then they're deleted. Typically, the web server writes one line of text for every hit (not just page request) the web server receives. Figure 11.10 shows a few lines from a sample log file.

As you can see, each log-file entry is on the order of 100 characters. If your web site is like Amazon's, that means every page view generates 38 $\times$100 or 3,800 bytes of log-file data. If your site gets 15,000 site visits per month, your log files will be 3,800 $\times$15,000 or 570 MB (that's *megabytes!*) per month. If your web-hosting service allows you only 100 MB of disk storage, you're going to burn through that in less than a week. Similar to what it may do when you exceed your data transfer limits, your hosting service may take any of the following actions with regard to your exceeding your disk storage quota:

- Not notice and let the log files grow without charge.
- Charge you an additional fee for the additional disk storage used.
- Shut down your web site when you exceed the 100 MB limit.

Again, all three scenarios are practiced. Make sure you know which your service provider will do. If your web site is on a server of its own, a full disk will likely crash the whole server. (See Chapter 19, "Monitoring," for information on systems that can monitor disk capacity and notify you of an impending problem before it becomes critical.)

Log-file rotation is a common practice that reduces the requirements for log-file storage, and therefore reduces the risk that you'll fill a disk drive or exceed your allotment of disk space because of huge log files. There are many complex log-file rotation techniques available, but a simple one is to generate reports once a day, and to retain the most recent seven days of log files.

TIP Most sites generate log files that take up much more disk space than their content. Plan ahead for log-file space requirements, and develop and follow a log-file rotation and deletion plan.

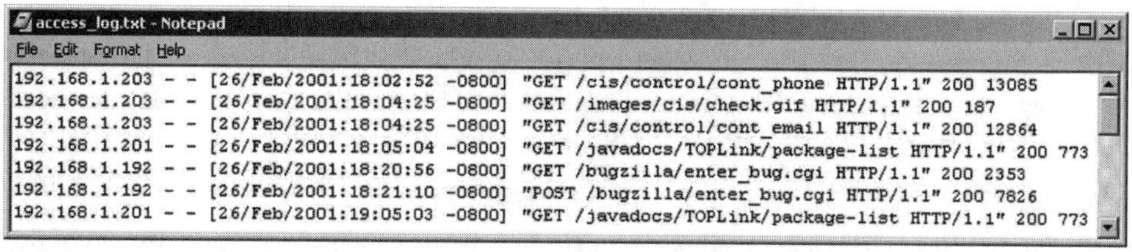

```
access_log.txt - Notepad                                               _| □| x|
File  Edit  Format  Help
192.168.1.203 - - [26/Feb/2001:18:02:52 -0800] "GET /cis/control/cont_phone HTTP/1.1" 200 13085
192.168.1.203 - - [26/Feb/2001:18:04:25 -0800] "GET /images/cis/check.gif HTTP/1.1" 200 187
192.168.1.203 - - [26/Feb/2001:18:04:25 -0800] "GET /cis/control/cont_email HTTP/1.1" 200 12864
192.168.1.201 - - [26/Feb/2001:18:05:04 -0800] "GET /javadocs/TOPLink/package-list HTTP/1.1" 200 773
192.168.1.192 - - [26/Feb/2001:18:20:56 -0800] "GET /bugzilla/enter_bug.cgi HTTP/1.1" 200 2353
192.168.1.192 - - [26/Feb/2001:18:21:10 -0800] "POST /bugzilla/enter_bug.cgi HTTP/1.1" 200 7826
192.168.1.201 - - [26/Feb/2001:19:05:03 -0800] "GET /javadocs/TOPLink/package-list HTTP/1.1" 200 773
```

Figure 11.10 Web server access log file.

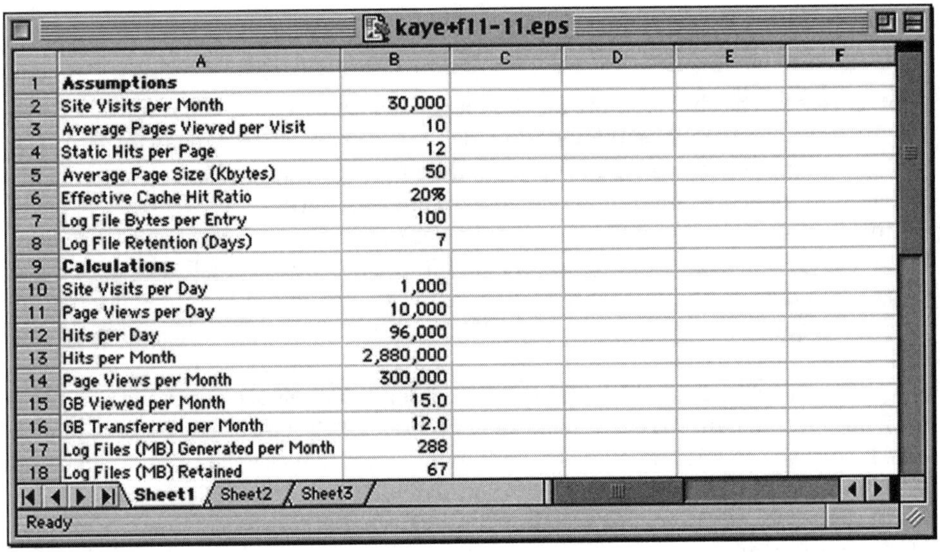

	A	B
1	**Assumptions**	
2	Site Visits per Month	30,000
3	Average Pages Viewed per Visit	10
4	Static Hits per Page	12
5	Average Page Size (Kbytes)	50
6	Effective Cache Hit Ratio	20%
7	Log File Bytes per Entry	100
8	Log File Retention (Days)	7
9	**Calculations**	
10	Site Visits per Day	1,000
11	Page Views per Day	10,000
12	Hits per Day	96,000
13	Hits per Month	2,880,000
14	Page Views per Month	300,000
15	GB Viewed per Month	15.0
16	GB Transferred per Month	12.0
17	Log Files (MB) Generated per Month	288
18	Log Files (MB) Retained	67

Figure 11.11 LogFileSize.xls.

Now let's enhance our model to deal with hits and log files, and at the same time double the traffic to 30,000 visits per month. This next version of our model is shown in Figure 11.11.

In this new version we've added eight rows:

B4: ***Static Hits per Page.*** This is the ratio of the number of images per page. If your site is designed like Yahoo!'s home page, you'll have a very low ratio. If it's more like Amazon's, you'll have a value of 30 to 40 here. Use an online tool to sample your own web site, or a site you think is similar to yours, to come up with this number. We've used 12 as a typical value.

B7: ***Log File Bytes per Entry.*** This constant is used to compute the size of the web-server's log files. Adjust it according to how your web server is configured. If the server is managed by your web-hosting service, ask it for this value.

B8: ***Log File Retention (Days).*** This is the number of days log files are retained on the site before being deleted.

B11: ***Page Views per Day.*** This intermediate result is used to calculate hits/day, but it's often valuable in its own right. The formula is Site Visits per Day (B10) times the Average Pages Viewed per Visit (B3).

B12: ***Hits per Day.*** This is the most important new calculation, which we get from Page Views per Day (B11) times the number of Static Hits per Page (B4), reduced by the Effective Cache Hit Ratio (B6).

B13: ***Hits per Month.*** This is another intermediate result.

B17: ***Log Files (MB) Generated per Month.*** This is the total size (in megabytes) of the log files the site will create each month.

B18: *Log Files (MB) Retained.* This is the calculation of how much disk space (in megabytes) you'll need on an ongoing basis to retain the log files that are not deleted.

In this example, the sample site receives 30,000 visits per month and 96,000 hits per day, net the effects of caching. It will generate 288 MB worth of log files each month, but since the logs are only retained for seven days, only 67 megabytes need be set aside for their storage. Transferring 12 GB per month, the sample web site may now be too busy for a shared server. It's time to consider a dedicated or colocated server. It's also time to start measuring bandwidth in a new way.

Average, Peak, and Burst

Some web-hosting services measure bandwidth not by counting the total number of bytes transmitted over the course of a month, but by the data *transmission rate* measured in bits per second. The standard method for measuring traffic in this way is called the *95th Percentile Rule.* Here's how it works:

1. The bandwidth being downloaded is retrieved from a router or switch every five minutes over an entire month (about 8,640 samples).

2. Each sample is converted to *bits per second* by counting the total number of bytes during the five-minute sample and dividing by 30 (5/60 of an hour times 10, to convert bytes to bits and account for protocol overhead). So, for example, if a site transmitted 1.5 megabytes during a five-minute period, the system would record a sample of 50,000 bits per second.

3. The highest 5 percent (about 432) samples each month are discarded. These are referred to as *bursts.*

4. The customer is billed according to the next highest sample recorded for the month—the 95th percentile sample.

Whereas shared and dedicated services are usually billed according to the actual number of bytes transmitted (which makes it somewhat easier to forecast), colocation vendors typically use this 95th Percentile Rule.

If web sites pumped out data at a steady rate, it would be easy to calculate the 95th percentile value directly from the total number of bytes transferred each month. In reality, web-site traffic goes up and down all the time, so the relationship between bytes per month and bits per second is always in flux.

Take a look at the graph in Figure 11.12, which shows the traffic through a typical Internet router. (Note that the graph shows time increasing right to left.) The upper graph shows traffic for a single 24-hour period, while the lower one shows an entire week. You can see in both graphs that there's a repeatable pattern with a roughly 4:1 range in traffic, from a low of about 15 Mbps to a high of 60 Mbps, depending on the time of day.

The quietest period is between 2:00 to 4:00 A.M. with the peak period running 10:00 A.M. to 9:00 P.M. (This particular router primarily carries traffic where both the sender and receiver are located in the same time zone.) The peak value is 65 Mbps. The 95th percentile rate for this router is approximately 60 Mbps. The average data rate, however, is about 40 Mbps, or about two-thirds of the peak value. This is a fairly typical curve for web sites.

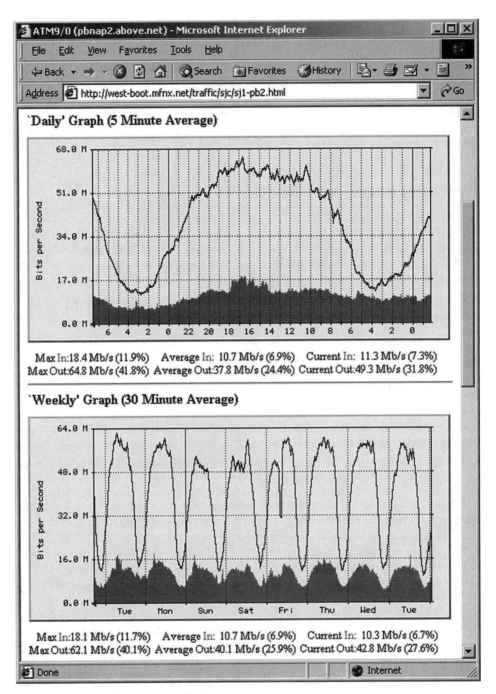

Figure 11.12   Typical router traffic.

In modeling a web site we need to track both peak and average activities. For example, when we talk about page views per day or page views per month, we realize that within a single day there will be substantial variations. For performance purposes, we need to design our systems to handle the peaks; but for business purposes, such as managing advertising revenues, we must deal with averages over longer periods, such as days or months. We handle this in two ways.

First we maintain a *peak/average ratio*. The router just described shows a ratio of about 3:2 (1.5). But when measured within short periods (such as a minute), the load on a web site isn't steady. When a user clicks, he or she wants the page immediately, so the server must handle short bursts of activity. Therefore, when designing a site, we also calculate and use a *burst ratio* that further increases the server's capacity. A burst ratio of 5 is a good place to start. Very busy sites, such as Yahoo!, receive less bursty traffic and can plan using burst ratios as low as 2.

Let's now enhance our model to account for both the peak/average and burst ratios. At the same time, let's assume that our site is now receiving 100,000 site visits per month, as seen in Figure 11.13. In this version of our model we've added the following rows:

B7: *Peak/Average Ratio*. This is the ratio of peak traffic to average traffic. All daily, weekly, and monthly values are assumed to already be averages. Hourly, per minute, and per second values are in some cases shown as both average and peak values. Average values are most important for applications such as estimating advertising or other commerce activities. Peak values are more helpful for planning hardware and bandwidth requirements. A peak/average ratio of 3 is fairly common.

B8: *Burst Ratio*. This is the ratio of burst traffic to peak traffic. It's used to provide some headroom above the forecasted peak levels that are measured over five minutes. One purpose of the burst ratio is to accommodate variations within those peak five-minute periods. It also ensures some capability for the site to handle more than the immediately forecasted volume.

B12–14: *Site Visits*. We've added per hour (avg) and per minute (avg), which are computed directly from the per day value by dividing by 24 (hours) and then again by 60 (minutes).

B16–21: *Page Views*. We've added per hour (avg), per minute (avg), and per second (avg, peak, burst). The per hour and per minute values are again computed directly from the per day value by dividing by 24 and again by 60. The per second (avg) is computed by dividing the per minute value again by 60. The per second (peak) value is the average value multiplied by the Peak/Average Ratio. The per second (burst) value is the peak value multiplied further by the Burst Ratio.

B22–28: *Hits*. We've added per hour (avg), per minute (avg), and per second (avg, peak, burst) the same as we did for Page Views.

B29–31: *Megabits*. Here we've added the calculation of actual bandwidth required. The Megabits per Second (avg) value is computed by multiplying the Page Views per Second (avg) by the Average Page Size (Kbytes) and then dividing by 100 to convert from Kbytes to megabits, and to account for protocol overhead.

	A	B	C	D	E	F
1	**Assumptions**					
2	Site Visits per Month	100,000				
3	Average Pages Viewed per Visit	10				
4	Static Hits per Page	12				
5	Average Page Size (Kbytes)	50				
6	Effective Cache Hit Ratio	20%				
7	Peak/Average Ratio	3				
8	Burst Ratio	5				
9	Log File Bytes per Entry	100				
10	Log File Retention (Days)	7				
11	**Calculations**					
12	Site Visits per Day	3,333				
13	Site Visits per Hour (avg)	139				
14	Site Visits per Minute (avg)	2.3				
15	Page Views per Month	1,000,000				
16	Page Views per Day	33,333				
17	Page Views per Hour (avg)	1,389				
18	Page Views per Minute (avg)	23				
19	Page Views per Second (avg)	0.39				
20	Page Views per Second (peak)	1.16				
21	Page Views per Second (burst)	5.79				
22	Hits per Month	9,600,000				
23	Hits per Day	320,000				
24	Hits per Hour (avg)	13,333				
25	Hits per Minute (avg)	222				
26	Hits per Second (avg)	3.70				
27	Hits per Second (peak)	11.1				
28	Hits per Second (burst)	55.6				
29	Megabits per Second (avg)	0.15				
30	Megabits per Second (peak)	0.46				
31	Megabits per Second (burst)	2.31				
32	GB Viewed per Month	50.0				
33	GB Transferred per Month	40.0				
34	Log Files (MB) Generated per Month	960				
35	Log Files (MB) Retained	224				
36						

Figure 11.13 AveragePeakAndBurst.xls.

Web-Server Scaling

If your web site runs on a shared server, your web-hosting service has at least some responsibility for providing a server with adequate power to meet your needs. This includes making sure that there aren't too many web sites on each server.

Once you decide to switch to a dedicated or colocated server, you bear the full burden of determining how many web servers you need and how powerful each must be.
Rather than finding out the hard way (i.e., waiting until it's too late), let's continue to
enhance our model to include the scaling of web servers. At the same time as we en-

	A	B	C	D	E	F
1	**Assumptions**					
2	Site Visits per Month	1,000,000				
3	Average Pages Viewed per Visit	10				
4	Static Hits per Page	12				
5	Average Page Size (Kbytes)	50				
6	Effective Cache Hit Ratio	10%				
7	Peak/Average Ratio	3				
8	Burst Ratio	5				
9	Log File Bytes per Entry	100				
10	Log File Retention (Days)	7				
11	Static Hits per Second per CPU	300				
12	Max CPUs per Web Server	2				
13	**Calculations**					
14	Site Visits per Day	33,333				
15	Site Visits per Hour (avg)	1,389				
16	Site Visits per Minute (avg)	23.1				
17	Page Views per Month	10,000,000				
18	Page Views per Day	333,333				
19	Page Views per Hour (avg)	13,889				
20	Page Views per Minute (avg)	231				
21	Page Views per Second (avg)	3.86				
22	Page Views per Second (peak)	11.57				
23	Page Views per Second (burst)	57.87				
24	Hits per Month	108,000,000				
25	Hits per Day	3,600,000				
26	Hits per Hour (avg)	150,000				
27	Hits per Minute (avg)	2,500				
28	Hits per Second (avg)	41.67				
29	Hits per Second (peak)	125.0				
30	Hits per Second (burst)	625.0				
31	Megabits per Second (avg)	1.74				
32	Megabits per Second (peak)	5.21				
33	Megabits per Second (burst)	26.04				
34	GB Viewed per Month	500.0				
35	GB Transferred per Month	450.0				
36	Log Files (MB) Generated per Month	10,800				
37	Log Files (MB) Retained	2,520				
38	Static Content CPUs Required	3				
39	Static Content Web Servers Required	2				
40						

Figure 11.14   WebServerScaling.xls.

hance the model, let's also look at increasing the traffic to reflect a busier site—one that receives 1 million page views per month

One reminder: We're still only dealing with a static web site, and one that's deployed in a one-tier architecture. In other words, we're assuming there are no database or application servers.

As you can see in cell B29 of Figure 11.14, receiving up to 1 million visits per month means we should expect a peak of 125 hits per second, with a potential burst up to 625 hits per second (B30). [Note that for this example, we've reduced the Effective Cache Hit Ratio (B6) to 10 percent.]

Since we want to be able to handle the burst level, not just the peak level, we need to calculate our web server processor power based on the burst values. In this version of our model, we've added the following:

B11: *Static Hits per Second per CPU.* The standard way to measure the capacity of a web server is according to how many hits per second it can accept and respond to. Since a hit is an individual request for something smaller than a complete page (such as an image), this number will vary greatly depending on the size of the object being transmitted, but most servers are still rated in this manner. (You should ask your web-hosting service or MSP how many hits per second your web-server software can handle for the size of objects your site will deliver.) Also, since good web-server software can scale reasonably well when run on servers with multiple CPUs, we track the capacity on a per-CPU basis.

B12: *Max CPUs per Web Server.* This is the number of CPUs that can be installed in each web server.

B38: *Static Content CPUs Required.* This tells us how many CPUs we'll need to handle the burst loads. The value is computed by dividing the Hits per Second (burst) by the Static Hits per Second per CPU and rounding up to the next whole number.

B39: *Static Content Web Servers Required.* This tells us how many physical web servers we'll need. It's the number of Static Content CPUs Required divided by the Max CPUs per Web Server rounded up to the next whole number.

From this example, we can see that in order to support 1 million site visits a month (B2), this web site will require three CPUs (B38) spread across two physical web servers (B39).

Dynamic Pages and Application Servers

Well before your site receives 1 million hits per month, you'll probably also be generating your pages dynamically, using database and application servers—the standard three-tier architecture as described in Chapter 12, "Web Site Architectures." On such a site, the static objects (images, navigation bars, etc.) are still handled by a web server, just as with an all-static site, but each page request received by a web server is passed along to an application server so that the HTML can be created dynamically—on the fly.

A dynamic page request requires substantially more processing power than a request for a simple static page. On the other hand, application servers don't have to handle the more frequent requests for images and other small files. It's possible to estimate the number of dynamic pages that can be built per second by an application server CPU. We've used the number 55 here, which was found by testing a large site running a Java application server on 600 mHz CPUs. If you can't actually determine this number on your own system (e.g., if you haven't built it yet), contact your application server software vendor and get a value from them. Then get in touch with other web-site owners using that software and find out what results they're seeing in the real world.

In the version of the model in Figure 11.15, we've added constants and calculations for the application servers that are required to run the dynamic part of the site. Let's

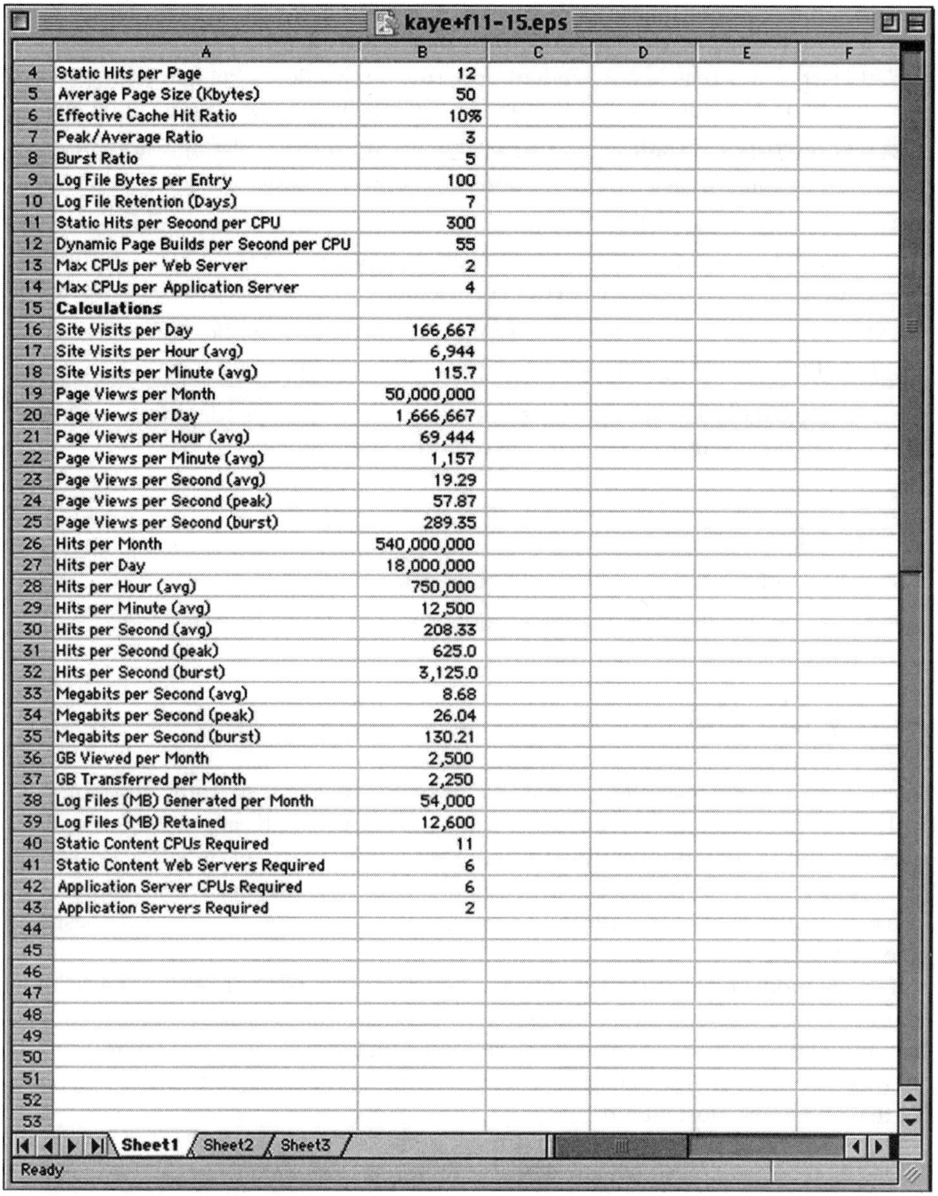

Figure 11.15   AppServerScaling.xls.

look at this using an example of a site that receives 5 million visits per month. This version includes the following new rows:

B12: *Dynamic Page Builds per Second per CPU.* This is that all-important number of how many pages your application server CPUs can each build per second. We've used 55 for a particular platform/application combination, but you need to find your own value for this constant. The number is dependent upon the application at least as much as it's dependent upon the application server software, so you should try to model your application in the same way as you model your servers.

B14: *Max CPUs per Application Server.* As with the web servers, this is the number of CPUs you can install in your application server chassis.

B42: *Application Server CPUs Required.* This value is determined by dividing the Page Views per Second (burst) by the number of Dynamic Page Builds per Second per CPU. In this example, we'll need six CPUs running the application server software.

B43: *Application Servers Required.* This is the number of Application Server CPUs Required divided by the number of Max CPUs per Application Server.

In order to handle 5 million visits per month (about 167,000 per day) with a 5:1 burst ratio, the model tells us that this site will require the following:

- Six 2-CPU web servers
- Two 4-CPU application servers
- 26 Mbps of bandwidth (at the 95th percentile peak)
- Access to 130 Mbps burst bandwidth

Sanity Checks

The value of a model goes well beyond just being able to estimate traffic. It should also be the basis of budgeting for your web-hosting expenses (both capital equipment and services), and it should be coupled to your company's revenue model. You should share your web-site traffic model with others in your organization, particularly those who forecast the expense and revenue aspects of your business. A model is *the* best way to communicate with nontechnical executives.

If you're modeling an existing web site, you'll have some degree of confidence in the accuracy of your model. You can, after all, go back and correct and refine the assumptions until you get the same results in the model that you're seeing in the real world. But what about modeling a site that isn't already up and running, or one that's running, but that will grow substantially?

You're responsible for your model's calculations, but you should collaborate with the rest of your management team on its assumptions. It's easy to build a terrific model with great formulas, only to discover that the assumptions (hence, the results) are all wrong. In addition, you should collaborate with the programmers who are responsible for the development of the application to get their input as to how it will perform and about its resource requirements.

Correlating your assumptions with your company's business plan is the best way to provide a *sanity check* for the model you've constructed. Business plans include financial models that are very similar to the web-site traffic models we've built, and you should link your model to those in the business plan to see if everything makes sense together.

When you compare your technology assumptions to those in your company's business plan, you may find (as we'll see in a real-life example later in this chapter) that

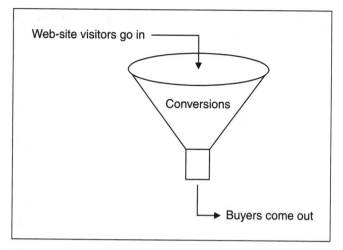

Figure 11.16 E-commerce conversions.

there's a major discrepancy. When that happens, alarms should go off in your head. Either the business plan is wrong or the web-site plan is wrong or both.

Think of the web site (or any business, for that matter) as a funnel. People visit the web site (or walk in the door, in the case of a retail shop), and some of those visitors are *converted* into buyers. The percentage of visitors that become buyers is called the *conversion rate*. Any business that has achieved some scale, such that randomness is minimized, can track its conversion rate. There's no magic conversion rate that's right for all web sites. Some sites with a lot of tire-kicking visitors have conversion rates well below 0.1 percent, while others may be as high as 10 percent. This effect is illustrated in Figure 11.16. You may hear salespeople talk about "keeping their funnel full," because they know that only a small percentage of leads will be converted to buyers.

In Figure 11.17, the next version of our model, we've added e-commerce transaction data. The new objective of this model is to determine whether the web site's capacity projections are in line with the business model. In particular, this model starts with assumptions of a *purchase conversion rate* and an *average sale price*. When combined with the projections of traffic to the site, we can calculate the expected e-commerce revenues. The new cells in this model are:

B4: *Purchase Conversion Rate.* This value should come from the business plan. If it's not there, or if there's no business plan, solve that problem before going any further with your web-site plans!

B5: *Average Sale.* This value should also come from the business plan. As with the conversion rate, it makes no sense to proceed with building an e-commerce web site without at least some forecast for this number.

B46–52: *Sales Transactions.* These values (monthly, daily, hourly, per minute, and per second) are derived by multiplying the number of site visits by the conversion rate and the average sale price. The per-second peak and burst values are useful for estimating credit card processing and other back-end transaction requirements.

	A	B	C	D	E	F
1	**Assumptions**					
2	Site Visits per Month	5,000,000				
3	Average Pages Viewed per Visit	10				
4	Purchase Conversion Rate	15%				
5	Average Sale	$25.00				
6	Static Hits per Page	12				
7	Average Page Size (Kbytes)	50				
8	Effective Cache Hit Ratio	20%				
9	Peak/Average Ratio	3				
10	Burst Ratio	5				
11	Log File Bytes per Entry	100				
12	Log File Retention (Days)	7				
13	Static Hits per Second per CPU	300				
14	Dynamic Page Builds per Second per CPU	15				
15	Max CPUs per Web Server	2				
16	Max CPUs per Application Server	4				
17	**Calculations**					
18	Site Visits per Day (avg)	166,667				
19	Site Visits per Hour (avg)	6,944				
20	Site Visits per Minute (avg)	115.7				
21	Page Views per Month	50,000,000				
22	Page Views per Day	1,666,667				
23	Page Views per Hour (avg)	69,444				
24	Page Views per Minute (avg)	1,157				
25	Page Views per Second (avg)	19.29				
26	Page Views per Second (peak)	57.87				
27	Page Views per Second (burst)	289.35				
28	Hits per Month	480,000,000				
29	Hits per Day	16,000,000				
30	Hits per Hour (avg)	666,667				
31	Hits per Minute (avg)	11,111				
32	Hits per Second (avg)	185.19				
33	Hits per Second (peak)	555.6				
34	Hits per Second (burst)	2,777.8				
35	Megabits per Second (avg)	7.72				
36	Megabits per Second (peak)	23.15				
37	Megabits per Second (burst)	115.74				
38	GB Viewed per Month	2,500				
39	GB Transferred per Month	2,000				
40	Log Files (MB) Generated per Month	48,000				
41	Log Files (MB) Retained	11,200				
42	Static Content CPUs Required	10				
43	Static Content Web Servers Required	5				
44	Application Server CPUs Required	20				
45	Application Servers Required	5				
46	Sales Transactions per Month (avg)	750,000				
47	Sales Transactions per Day (avg)	25,000				
48	Sales Transactions per Hour (avg)	1,042				
49	Sales Transactions per Minute (avg)	17.4				
50	Sales Transactions per Second (avg)	0.29				
51	Sales Transactions per Second (peak)	0.87				
52	Sales Transactions per Second (burst)	4.34				
53	Equivalent Annual Revenues (avg)	$225,000,000				
54						

Figure 11.17 Ecommerce.xls.

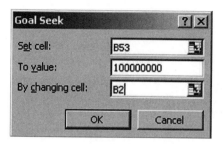

Figure 11.18   Excel's Goal Seek input.

> **B53:** *Equivalent Annual Revenues (avg).*This value is calculated by multiplying the number of transactions per month by 12 and then by the value of the average sale. The model of our sample web-site projects annual revenues of $225 million.

That final number, annual revenues, is the key to our sanity check. If it isn't close to the projected revenues in the business plan, something's amiss. It's critical that this discrepancy be resolved before going further.

Goal Seeking

When things don't add up, you need to decide which numbers to believe. For instance, suppose you believe that the projection of annual revenues and the conversion rates are both correct, but you aren't sure about the web-site traffic you should expect in order to achieve those numbers.

Excel has an important feature called Goal Seek that allows you to specify the result of a calculation and adjust an input value until the desired result is achieved. It's like the television game show *Jeopardy:* You start with the answer rather than the question.

For example, suppose we believe that our site won't generate $225 million in revenues, as suggested by our model, but rather only $100 million. Using Excel's Goal Seek feature (found on the Excel menu at Tools, Goal Seek) we can enter the desired result (100,000,000) along with B2, the cell to be adjusted in order to achieve these results. This is illustrated in Figure 11.18.

Excel then adjusts cell B2 (Site Visits per Month) until cell B53 (Equivalent Annual Revenues) equals $100,000,000. It announces that it has found a solution, as shown in Figure 11.19. In this instance, the model tells us that in order to generate annualized revenues of $100 million per year, the site must plan for 2,222,222 site visits per month.

A Case Study

The model in Figure 11.17 (Ecommerce.xls) is a good starting point on which to build a model for any web site, and I've personally used this model (or one like it) many times when planning major e-commerce sites. But it's just a start, and you should expand the model to reflect the realities and priorities of your own business.

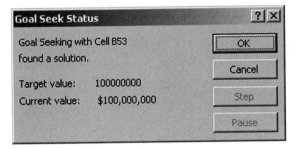

Figure 11.19 Excel's Goal Seek status.

Models such as this are invaluable for making sure an organization's business and technology plans are, at the very least, in the same ballpark. It amazes me how many e-commerce initiatives are launched when the goals of technology are not in sync with those of finance or marketing.

The following is an actual case study that illustrates this point perhaps better than any other I've seen. The models used in this real-world example are also available on-line at www.wiley.com/compbooks/kaye.

I was asked to assist with the architecture of an e-commerce web site for a major re-tailer that already had more than 4,000 storefront outlets in the United States. My first question (as always) was "How much traffic will the site get?" The client had not de-veloped such a projection, so I used a variety of criteria to try to get a handle on reality. The approach that made the most sense was to look at the volume of sales the company expected to generate from its web site. From that, I looked at the design of the site and made some educated guesses about user behavior. I developed a bottom-up spread-sheet that modeled web-page size, page views per minute, and hits per second, and then factored in various ratios such as visitor-to-buyer conversion rates, and so on. I thought I had a pretty good model for the web-site traffic, and since it was in the form of a what-if Excel spreadsheet, I could change any of the assumptions to instanta-neously see different results.

As often happens, however, this major e-commerce project was the brainchild of the client's marketing department, whose members had developed it to this point without involving their IT (information technology) folks. Well, the politics turned ugly. The IT people were not at all happy that they hadn't been consulted from the beginning, and they decided to set a "gold standard" for this new e-commerce project. Why not? They could make the requirements as rigorous (even ridiculous) as they liked. Since they were, in a sense, independent auditors of the project, why not set the bar as high as possible?

I took the call from the company's CIO. "Doug, we just want to make sure the site can handle 120 credit card transactions per second with no customer waiting more than five seconds for a transaction to clear. You need to prove to us that your team's design can support that."

Numbers like that can be abstract and meaningless, so I didn't initially have a reac-tion to that number one way or another. Is it high? Is it low? At first I wasn't sure. I dug through my notes, and came across an interesting fact: At its peak on Mothers' Day, the year before, the 1-800-FLOWERS web site was processing *three* credit card transactions per second. Our client was asking us to build an e-commerce site that could handle 60 times that transaction volume.

To double-check my initial reaction, I called one of the credit card transaction-processing companies and learned that even if the client were to lease a dedicated line to its service (i.e., bypass the Internet altogether), the processing company wouldn't be able to handle this volume of transactions. Clearly, the CIO had presented me with some unreasonable expectations, but how could I show him the errors of his thinking?

I decided to use the top-down model and the sanity check concept. The result the company wanted was a burst of 120 credit card transactions per second. The question I decided to answer was, "How many page views per minute should one assume in order to generate that many credit card transactions?"

Here's why it's so important to correlate the technology and business plans. There's no point in building the systems to handle that number of credit card transactions unless you also build the rest of the web site to handle the other parts of the user experience. It's like a drive-through restaurant. There's not much point in building a kitchen that can crank out 2,000 burgers an hour if you can only move 150 cars per hour past the drive-through window. There should be no single bottleneck. Ideally, all components should operate at the same percentage of their peak capacities.

My goals were to (a) determine how much traffic this web site would have to support in order to generate a burst of 120 sales per second, and then (b) determine how many servers and other components it would take to build such a site.

One thing was in my favor, which made the modeling somewhat simpler than usual: The client's IT department had specified a burst load, not an average load. When you develop a model for an average load, in order to also take a stab at the peak and burst loads, you have to make all sorts of guesses about the time of day or day of the week people will visit the site. When you're given a burst load, you can (for the most part) ignore those fluctuations and pretend that the burst load must be sustained 24 hours a day, 7 days a week. After all, most of the components such as servers and bandwidth must be capable of handling the burst load, not just the average or peak.

I asked the client to provide the remainder of the assumption values: page views per visit, the conversion rate, and so on. As the preliminary site designs were already complete, I was able to get actual data for page size and hits per page. I then plugged those values into the assumptions using my e-commerce model. Finally, I used Excel's Goal Seek feature, and had it adjust the number of site visits per month that would be required to generate a burst load of 120 sales per second. The results are shown in Figure 11.20.

Instantly, I had the data I needed. I called the CIO back. "Yes, we can build a site that can handle 120 credit card transactions a second, but let me tell you what I think the implications of that design will be. The good news is you can do it with only 6 web servers and 10 application servers. The bad news is that each one will have to be a Sun E10000 Starfire with 64 CPUs. They cost about $1 million apiece. The software licenses for the application servers alone (600 CPUs) will cost about $30 million.

"So on just the hardware and software alone, and not even counting the database servers and their software licenses, we're at $46 million. I know the *total* budget for the entire project is about $5 million, so there's no way we can build the system to your requirements."

I asked him how many credit card transactions their bricks-and-mortar stores processed per second. It turned out that all 4,000 stores worked fine on a network that

	A	B	C	D	E	F
		kaye+f11-20.eps				
1	**Assumptions**					
2	Site Visits per Month	207,360,000				
3	Average Pages Viewed per Visit	10				
4	Purchase Conversion Rate	10%				
5	Average Sale	$25.00				
6	Static Hits per Page	12				
7	Average Page Size (Kbytes)	35				
8	Effective Cache Hit Ratio	10%				
9	Peak/Average Ratio	3				
10	Burst Ratio	5				
11	Log File Bytes per Entry	100				
12	Log File Retention (Days)	7				
13	Static Hits per Second per CPU	400				
14	Dynamic Page Builds per Second per CPU	20				
15	Max CPUs per Web Server	64				
16	Max CPUs per Application Server	64				
17	**Calculations**					
18	Site Visits per Day (avg)	6,912,000				
19	Site Visits per Hour (avg)	288,000				
20	Site Visits per Minute (avg)	4,800				
21	Page Views per Month	2,073,600,000				
22	Page Views per Day	69,120,000				
23	Page Views per Hour (avg)	2,880,000				
24	Page Views per Minute (avg)	48,000				
25	Page Views per Second (avg)	800				
26	Page Views per Second (peak)	2,400				
27	Page Views per Second (burst)	12,000				
28	Hits per Month	22,394,880,000				
29	Hits per Day	746,496,000				
30	Hits per Hour (avg)	31,104,000				
31	Hits per Minute (avg)	518,400				
32	Hits per Second (avg)	8,640				
33	Hits per Second (peak)	25,920				
34	Hits per Second (burst)	129,600				
35	Megabits per Second (avg)	252				
36	Megabits per Second (peak)	756				
37	Megabits per Second (burst)	3,780				
38	GB Viewed per Month	72,576				
39	GB Transferred per Month	65,318				
40	Log Files (MB) Generated per Month	2,239,488				
41	Log Files (MB) Retained	522,547				
42	Static Content CPUs Required	324				
43	Static Content Web Servers Required	6				
44	Application Server CPUs Required	600				
45	Application Servers Required	10				
46	Sales Transactions per Month (avg)	20,736,000				
47	Sales Transactions per Day (avg)	691,200				
48	Sales Transactions per Hour (avg)	28,800				
49	Sales Transactions per Minute (avg)	480				
50	Sales Transactions per Second (avg)	8.0				
51	Sales Transactions per Second (peak)	24.0				
52	Sales Transactions per Second (burst)	120.0				
53	Equivalent Annual Revenues (avg)	$ 6,220,800,000				
54						

Sheet1 / Sheet2 / Sheet3

Ready

Figure 11.20 BigRetailer-1.xls.

could handle a combined maximum of 80 transactions per second. They had in mind that their web site should be able to handle 50 percent more than all of their existing stores combined.

I then pointed out that a site that could handle a burst of that volume of transactions would also be able to handle over $6 billion per year in revenues. He said that they were projecting annual revenues from the web site to be only $4 *million* per year—the equivalent of one of their most successful bricks-and-mortar stores. We agreed that it made better business sense to therefore plan on the same volume of transactions as they would expect from a successful store, and to spend about the same amount of money building their e-commerce site as they would when building a major store. In fact, this was what they had in mind when they created a $5 million project for the web site.

Subsequently, I sent the client a few more observations about the site they had *thought* they wanted to build:

- The traffic would be one-quarter that of AOL's total traffic at the time.

- The required 3.78 *gigabits* per second of bandwidth was more than was used by all of Exodus' data centers combined.

In the end, I convinced the client to launch with a site that had the burst capacity for three (not 120!) credit card transactions per second, and be upgradeable to twice the capacity (six transactions per second) by adding only CPUs and RAM. The site went live running on a pair of half-loaded Starfire servers.

The final model for the web site as delivered is shown in Figure 11.21. In this instance, the model was probably the only way to resolve the mismatched expectations of the marketing and IT departments. One should never plan a web site using numbers that are based solely on a single perspective: business or technology. It's only when the assumptions and calculations from both groups align that you can have confidence that you're even in the right ballpark.

This concludes our look at the nontechnical issues surrounding web hosting. In this third part of the book, we've seen the dark side of outsourcing, and how to get it right. We've explored a strategy for risk management that will allow you to deal with risks and losses as comfortably as you deal with the more upbeat aspects of developing your web site. We've even had a look at SLAs—not as they are today, but as they ought to be.

The traffic models we've developed in this chapter built the bridge between these nontechnical issues and those we'll address in the next section, Part Four, "Technologies." You'll find the next section to be very different, beginning with a survey of website architectures, followed by in-depth looks at caching, CDNs, connectivity practices, storage, backup and recovery, and security. These are the specific technologies that you should consider when selecting your web-hosting vendor and when planning your web site for outsourced hosting.

	A	B	C	D	E	F
		kaye+f11-21.eps				
1	**Assumptions**					
2	Site Visits per Month	10,368,000				
3	Average Pages Viewed per Visit	10				
4	Purchase Conversion Rate	10%				
5	Average Sale	$25.00				
6	Static Hits per Page	12				
7	Average Page Size (Kbytes)	35				
8	Effective Cache Hit Ratio	10%				
9	Peak/Average Ratio	3				
10	Burst Ratio	5				
11	Log File Bytes per Entry	100				
12	Log File Retention (Days)	7				
13	Static Hits per Second per CPU	400				
14	Dynamic Page Builds per Second per CPU	20				
15	Max CPUs per Web Server	64				
16	Max CPUs per Application Server	64				
17	**Calculations**					
18	Site Visits per Day (avg)	345,600				
19	Site Visits per Hour (avg)	14,400				
20	Site Visits per Minute (avg)	240				
21	Page Views per Month	103,680,000				
22	Page Views per Day	3,456,000				
23	Page Views per Hour (avg)	144,000				
24	Page Views per Minute (avg)	2,400				
25	Page Views per Second (avg)	40				
26	Page Views per Second (peak)	120				
27	Page Views per Second (burst)	600				
28	Hits per Month	1,119,744,000				
29	Hits per Day	37,324,800				
30	Hits per Hour (avg)	1,555,200				
31	Hits per Minute (avg)	25,920				
32	Hits per Second (avg)	432				
33	Hits per Second (peak)	1,296				
34	Hits per Second (burst)	6,480				
35	Megabits per Second (avg)	13				
36	Megabits per Second (peak)	38				
37	Megabits per Second (burst)	189				
38	GB Viewed per Month	3,629				
39	GB Transferred per Month	3,266				
40	Log Files (MB) Generated per Month	111,974				
41	Log Files (MB) Retained	26,127				
42	Static Content CPUs Required	17				
43	Static Content Web Servers Required	1				
44	Application Server CPUs Required	30				
45	Application Servers Required	1				
46	Sales Transactions per Month (avg)	1,036,800				
47	Sales Transactions per Day (avg)	34,560				
48	Sales Transactions per Hour (avg)	1,440				
49	Sales Transactions per Minute (avg)	24				
50	Sales Transactions per Second (avg)	0.4				
51	Sales Transactions per Second (peak)	1.2				
52	Sales Transactions per Second (burst)	6.0				
53	Equivalent Annual Revenues (avg)	$ 311,040,000				
54						

Sheet1 / Sheet2 / Sheet3

Ready

Figure 11.21 BigRetailer-2.xls

PART Four

Technologies

In Part Three, "Strategies," we examined the challenges of outsourcing web hosting and how to overcome them. In this part, we turn our attention to specific web-site technologies, specifically how you should take them into consideration during (and after) your vendor-selection process. We'll begin our explorations of technology in Chapter 12, "Web-Site Architectures," with an explanation of the differences between *server architectures* and *application architectures.* We'll then survey multiserver configurations including the two- and three-tier models and the use of application servers. We'll quantify the concept of scalability and see how it's affected by architecture. Next we'll consider redundancy and reliability, single points of failure, common mistakes such as *redundant redundancy,* and the economics of redundant systems. We'll then look at database architectures and performance, and end with an introduction to geographically distributed architectures.

In Chapter 13, "Caching and Content Delivery Networks," we'll continue our discussion of geographically distributed architectures with a tutorial on caching theory, followed by an overview of the various forms of Internet caching and how they can affect the delivery of your content. Next, we'll take an in-depth look at content delivery networks (CDNs) and how you can use them to improve the performance and scalability of your web site. We'll consider how much effort it takes to adapt your content for delivery by various CDNs, and how you can keep your options open during development of your web site in case you later decide to use a CDN. Finally, we'll look at the economics of CDNs and suggest a vendor-selection process.

Whether or not you use a CDN, you should evaluate how effectively potential vendors manage their Internet bandwidth. In Chapter 14, "Connectivity Practices," we'll explore the practices and procedures to look for when selecting a web-hosting service, including multihomed routing, peering versus transit, internal networks, satellite data centers, and capacity planning. Then we'll look at some poor practices you may encounter—hopefully during your vendor selection rather than after—including *bandwidth choking* and *bandwidth lowballing*.

In Chapter 15, "Storage," we'll explore the options for managing your web site's data. Although most sites need only simple disk drives, or direct attached storage (DAS), many larger sites require other technologies such as network attached storage (NAS) or storage area networks (SANs). We'll compare and contrast these storage technologies and introduce global storage systems (GSS).

Of course, if you have data to store, you need to protect yourself from its loss. In Chapter 16, "Backup and Recovery," we'll look at why the solutions offered by most web-hosting services address the vendors' own needs for *archiving*, but are insufficient as solutions for your *backup* requirements. (We'll also see why it's so important to separate these concepts.) We'll explain the risk of *propagation of corrupted data,* and why the backup strategy you're using may not be as fail-safe as you think. But we won't leave you without a solution. We'll look at an integrated strategy using archiving, backup, version control, and media rotation.

Finally, we'll look at the topic on which perhaps more Internet books have been written than any other. In Chapter 17, "Security," we'll focus our attention on the practices that lure web-site owners into a false sense of security. We'll start by considering why it's so important to plan for certain security risks rather than to attempt to eliminate them all. Next, we'll examine the weaknesses of Internet security practices including the use of firewalls and intrusion detection systems (IDSs), passwords, administrative networks, encryption, and patches. We'll end with a discussion of third-party managed security services and whether such services are right for you.

Web-Site Architectures

We concluded the previous part by developing models to forecast your web-site traffic; within those models you learned how to estimate the number of servers you'll need in order to handle your web site's traffic. But spreadsheets don't tell you where those servers should be located, how to interconnect them, or which software components should run on which servers. These are the issues addressed by *web-site architecture.*

Web-site architecture is a complex and often-debated topic, one that we can't do justice to in only one chapter. Yet we can't ignore it, for it's a topic that has a substantial effect on the successful operation of any web site. So, though we can't look at every architectural possibility and analyze every technical detail, we're going to explore the broader concepts and consider some subtleties that you may not find discussed anywhere else.

If you're a nontechnical manager, this chapter will give you an understanding of the complex issues surrounding the architectural design of web-site configurations. If you're a hands-on techie, you'll recognize the architectural issues but be able to see them from a new, more strategic perspective.

We'll start by looking at the difference between *server architectures* and *application architectures.* Next we'll consider the challenges of application complexity, capacity, scalability, reliability, and performance (security will be covered separately in Chapter 17, "Security.") We'll end this chapter with discussions of database architecture and geographic redundancy.

Servers and Applications

Every web site actually has two overlapping architectures. One is the *server architecture* that specifies the hardware and its physical organization (how many servers? where should they be located? how should they be interconnected?). The other is the *application architecture* that defines how the logical components (the software and data) interact in much the same way as the servers on which they run.

Take, for instance, a web site running on two servers. The server architecture defines how these boxes are to be interconnected, perhaps using 100baseTX links and a high-speed switch. This architecture guarantees that the servers can communicate efficiently and reliably with one another.

In much the same way, the application architecture determines how the software components will communicate. The application architecture might specify a two-tier model in which one computer runs the web-server software and the other handles the database. The interconnection in this case might be via a pool of ODBC connections (it doesn't matter whether you fully understand what that is; you get the idea).

As we explore various configurations, we'll be looking simultaneously at both the system and the application architectures.

Application Complexity

The earliest web sites contained little more than simple documents. They used only one type of server: a web server that delivered HTML pages and image files in response to visitor requests. There were no *applications* to speak of, no programs, just web pages. In fact, the vast majority of web sites still fall into this category.

These early web sites may have included Common Gateway Interface (CGI) scripts for processing simple forms, but typically they weren't sufficiently complex to require, for example, databases. These simple sites stored their data in the host operating system's file system and were therefore based on the *one-tier application model,* as illustrated in Figure 12.1. Note that this figure is also an example of a *one-tier server model*—there's only one physical server.

Database Support

Some web sites, on the other hand, are as complex as any preweb data-processing application. In some cases, web applications are even more complex, since they have to deal with a rather hostile application environment: a clunky user interface, weak security, and the requirement that the software run 24/7/365. For instance, delivering a stock-trading application over the Internet is a lot more difficult than delivering the same application to in-house, behind-the-firewall desktop computers.

As sophisticated applications began to appear on the web, developers realized they could benefit from using the same database packages (such as Oracle and Microsoft's SQLserver) they were already using for traditional applications. For instance, web pages could be created on the fly from the contents of a database via CGI and other application program interfaces (APIs). The resulting *dynamic* web sites are based on the *two-tier application model,* as illustrated in Figure 12.2.

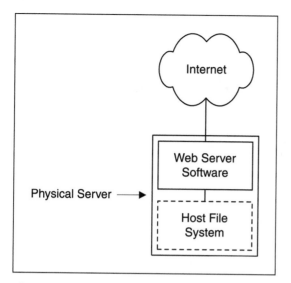

Figure 12.1   One-tier application and server model.

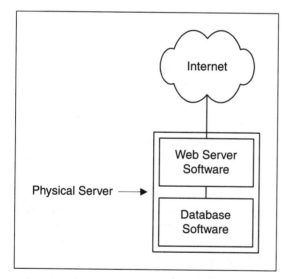

Figure 12.2   Two-tier application model.

The Two-Tier Server Model

As the traffic and complexity of a two-tier application running on a single server increases, the web server and database components begin to compete with one another for computer resources. They have such different requirements that they can no longer efficiently share a single system.

Therefore, as soon as there's enough traffic to justify the cost, it makes sense to split the web and database software and run each of them on its own physical server. The resulting two-tier server architecture is shown in Figure 12.3.

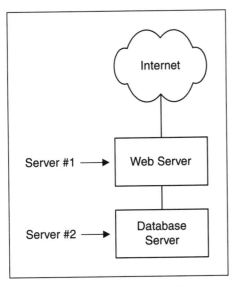

Figure 12.3 Two-tier server architecture.

Application Servers: The Three-Tier Model

Although the two-tier model works well for simple database-driven web applications, this architecture has some well-known problems that remain difficult. These problems include:

Limitations of CGI. Applications based on the Common Gateway Interface run as separate *processes* from the web server software with which they typically share physical servers. This is very inefficient, and such applications are inadequate for complex or high-volume web sites.

Common components. Using CGI, each dynamically generated page is controlled by a separate *script,* and there's no good mechanism by which CGI scripts can share code and data. It's bad enough on a single server, but when an application is deployed on more than one web server—either for increased reliability or capacity—it's difficult for the two instances to communicate.

State and sessions. It's difficult to maintain *state* between one web page request and the next using CGI. State and sessions are discussed in detail in the next subsection.

Database connections. If a database is used, each script (i.e., for each page) has to open and close its own connection to the database. This typically takes longer than the actual function of the script.

To address these problems, high-end sites use separate *application servers* (or simply *app servers*) that sit between their web and database servers, creating a *three-tier application architecture,* as illustrated in Figure 12.4.

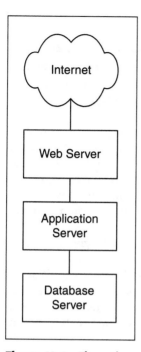

Figure 12.4   Three-tier application model.

Note that the three application tiers shown in Figure 12.4 may be deployed on one, two, three, or even more physical servers, depending on the performance, capacity, and security requirements. In fact, another advantage of the three-tier application model is that each tier can be scaled independently. For instance, a web site that contains primarily static content may grow through the addition of web servers, but without increasing application or database capacity. On the other hand, a site with extensive application logic may require more physical application servers, but relatively few web servers.

Application servers provide run-time environments (i.e., application-support services and libraries) specifically designed for the web-based application programs. These environments substantially lower the cost of application development by including built-in features that the application programmer would otherwise have to develop and maintain. As an analogy, consider how an operating system provides features such as device drivers, memory management, and a file system. If the OS didn't provide these facilities, each programmer would have to develop his or her own features. The built-in solutions provided by application servers (which we'll discuss further in the following sections) reduce the amount of customized code that must be developed, thereby increasing a web site's reliability.

In the sections that follow, we'll explore the specific problems that are solved by the use of application servers and the three-tier application model. In subsequent sections, we'll also see how application servers can be used to address requirements for scalability and reliability.

State and Sessions

The web is an inherently *stateless* application environment, meaning that each time a visitor requests a web page (or even an individual object within a page for that matter) that visitor's web browser, in effect, must knock on the web server's door and reintroduce itself. Every request/response exchange is a standalone transaction, not related to the exchanges that immediately precede or follow it.

Likewise, since the web server is "done" after delivering each object, there's no concept of web-site visitors saying goodbye. They just don't come back for more. There's no way to know that visitors have left the web site other than to simply wait until so much time has passed that it doesn't appear they'll be asking for more web pages. Unless the web developer goes to some trouble or gets help from additional software (such as an application server), the web server won't be able to remember a visitor from one web-page request to the next.

This lack of statefulness is a problem for many applications that depend on the concept of a *session*—some persistence of knowledge of things about visitors between one click and the next. The most common example is an electronic shopping cart. Without statefulness and session management, an online shopping site would not be able to remember the contents of a visitor's shopping cart as that visitor navigated from one web page to the next. The concept of a session and the management of state are two built-in benefits of application servers.

Functional Segmentation

As applications become increasingly complex, they likewise become more difficult to manage. Good software design requires *modularity*—organization of the parts of the application into smaller units based on function or data structures—to avoid large, monolithic programs and tangled messes of so-called spaghetti code that become difficult to maintain and debug as they evolve.

We looked at how the two-tier application model isolates the very different functions of serving web pages and files from database management. This is a good first step, but complex application programs need a separate place to call their own as well. Neither a database server nor a web server is a good environment in which to develop or run complex applications. Application servers provide such an environment.

Database Connection Management

A notorious challenge for any web-based application that uses a database is how to connect to the database server. Each application that needs to use the database must first establish a *connection* to the database software. This can be a fairly expensive operation in terms of time and computer resources. The time it takes to connect to a database is typically much greater than the time it takes to perform most read or write operations. Plus, there's always the chance that a database connection won't be available because all of the connections are in use by other applications that, while not necessarily using them at the moment, have not yet released them. In such cases, applications requiring database connections have no choice but to signal errors or wait until connections become available.

This problem is exacerbated by the fact that an application may need to use the database for only the few milliseconds it takes to generate a single web page. The result is that, unless something is done to avoid it, the typical database-driven web site will spend more time opening and closing database connections than actually using them. Creating and managing a *pool* of database connections that can be shared efficiently by applications (a solution to this problem) is yet another service provided by application servers.

Capacity and Scalability

One of the fundamental requirements for any web-site architecture is that it must be able to handle increases in *capacity*. If you expect that next year your web site will receive twice as many visits per second as it can handle currently, you need to find a way to add hardware and/or software to double its capacity. But some architectures on which sites are based can be grown more economically than others. They're, simply, more *scalable*.

The term scalable is most frequently used to describe web sites and architectures whose capacity can easily be increased by adding more hardware and software. More specifically, the *scalability ratio* of a web site or architecture is the ratio of the increase in capacity to the cost of achieving that increase. For example, suppose that in order to double your site's capacity you must spend twice as much again as you've already spent on hardware and software (3 times total). That would be a scalability ratio of 2:3 or 0.67.

Figure 12.5 illustrates some of the *scalability curves* one can find in real-world web sites. We'll look at the characteristics of each curve.

Typical Scalability

The *typical* curve represents the scalability of most web-site architectures. If you were to smooth out the steps in this curve, you'd find that the average scalability ratio approaches 1.0 (the chart in Figure 12.5 isn't drawn to scale).

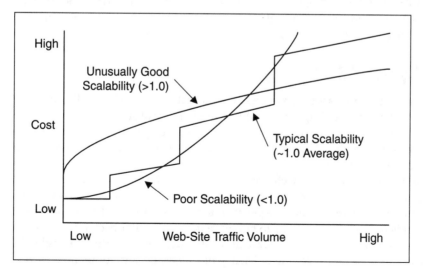

Figure 12.5 Web-site scalability.

But the curve is jagged. There are steps or breaks at certain traffic thresholds where the cost suddenly increases. These are due to upgrades made to the web site over time in order to accommodate increases in traffic. You can't, for instance, buy a fraction of a new server. You've got to make most upgrades in realistic increments.

There's nothing inherently wrong with this curve but, depending upon an organization's financial situation, it may be beneficial to plan an upgrade path that contains a larger number of smaller steps. At the moment an upgrade is completed, there's usually some temporary excess capacity. If the upgrade increments are smaller and more frequent, there may be less unused (wasted) capacity. For example, large steps will occur when replacing servers, whereas smaller steps will occur when adding additional CPUs or RAM to existing servers. We'll discuss this concept further when we look at the economics of redundancy later in this chapter.

Poor Scalability

The *poor scalability* curve in Figure 12.5 illustrates what can go wrong. Here we have a so-called nonscalable web site with an exponential curve. For every doubling of traffic, the cost of handling it increases by a factor of 4. The only way to keep a site like this alive is to hope and pray that it doesn't become too popular. Success could be fatal.

Most poor scalability is caused by bad application architecture, usually from poor database design or applications that access databases inefficiently. On the other hand, some applications are fundamentally nonscalable. For example, consider an online dating service that matches its visitors to one another. To test each member for compatibility with each other member requires $n2/2-1$ tests, where n is the number of members. Every time the number of members doubles, the computing requirements to match them increases by a factor of 4.

Another example of an application that poses scalability challenges is *collaborative filtering,* a technology for matching visitors to products. Sites like Amazon.com use it as the basis for recommending a book you might like to read. It takes some very creative solutions to simplify these problems so that they can be scaled linearly, rather than as a square function. Vendors of off-the-shelf software products that perform functions such as matching and collaborative filtering have attempted to do just that.

Unusually Good Scalability

The target for most web sites is to achieve a scalability ratio of 1.0, meaning that it's possible to double the capacity simply by doubling the number of servers. Only very unusual applications can achieve scalability ratios substantially greater than 1.0. No matter what visitors do at a web site, handling twice as many visits usually requires twice as much hardware and software.

But wouldn't it be great if your web site could scale like the *unusually good scalability* curve in Figure 12.5? Is there some way to gain some *leverage,* so that as the volume of traffic to your site increases, your cost-per-visit actually decreases? From a business perspective, this means finding a way to get more than one dollar back in savings for every dollar you invest in server hardware and software. Certainly this is possible in bricks-and-mortar businesses. It's the efficiency of *volume.* Because of their sales volumes, large warehouse retailers can afford to offer steeper discounts and still make more money than the small neighborhood stores. The warehouses are highly scalable businesses.

It turns out there *are* opportunities to achieve a scalability ratio of better than 1.0 for nearly any web site, but not through changes in application architecture. Greater scalability can often be achieved by using *caching* and *content delivery networks* (CDNs), which we'll explore further in Chapter 13, "Caching and Content Delivery Networks."

Redundancy and Reliability

Among pilots of light airplanes there's a never-ending debate: Which is safer, a single-engine airplane or a twin? The enthusiasts of the twin-engine claim their airplanes are safer because they can maintain altitude in case an engine fails. They point out that an airplane with just one engine has a *single point of failure,* whereas the twin-engine airplane has *redundant* power sources.

Single-engine proponents, on the other hand, point out that their airplanes are only half as likely to have a failure in the first place, and that if a twin loses an engine while flying at a low airspeed, the airplane becomes uncontrollable due to asymmetric thrust with often-fatal results. A single-engine airplane that loses an engine (even at low speed) simply becomes a controllable glider that can be landed more safely than a comparable twin.

Because no one tracks the accident statistics that would allow this controversy to be settled once and for all, pilots will sit around airports and argue this point forever, and not one of them will ever admit he or she is wrong. But there's a lot to be learned from this debate that relates to web architecture.

Single Points of Failure

There's no question that single points of failure are weak links in web-site architectures, and that eliminating them through redundancy is a key component of any high-availability strategy. There are two ways to deal with single points of failure:

Component-level redundancy. Within a server, you can use redundant components to eliminate many single points of failure. For example, because power supplies tend to fail more frequently than many other components, some servers can be purchased with redundant (dual or triple) power supplies. Likewise, servers can be configured using RAID systems (redundant disks, as described in detail in Chapter 15, "Storage") to keep the failure of an individual disk drive from bringing down an entire system or site.

System-level redundancy. Redundancy can also be deployed at the system level by including multiple instances of each type of server. For example, you can have multiple web servers, multiple application servers, and multiple database servers. If configured properly, a failure of a single server won't cause the web site to fail. You can even deploy servers to multiple locations. Again, if you configure things properly, one location can fail completely, and your web site will still be available.

Common Mistakes

Although redundancy is one of those universally good things like Mom, apple pie, and the flag, it's quite common for well-meaning architects to adopt it incorrectly. Redundant components or systems aren't always the right answer. Following are descriptions of three common errors made in designing redundant web-site architectures.

Consistency

Murphy's Law guarantees that if one server has a redundant twin, while another does not, the nonredundant server will always fail first. In other words, whatever your strategy for redundancy, it must be applied in all cases and consistently. You've got to look at your entire configuration and find *all* of the single points of failure. If you can't afford to eliminate every one of them, spend your money in the places where failures are the most likely to occur or where their impact will be the greatest.

TIP Apply redundancy consistently. Don't just address some single points of failure. Begin with the most vulnerable systems and components.

Redundant Redundancy

Some architects go too far. They waste money by creating overly redundant or *redundantly redundant* systems. Let's say, for instance, that you've decided to use three web servers. That way, if one fails, you'll still have two-thirds of your full capacity to deliver static content. You've created redundancy *across* your web servers. This is a good configuration: reliable and easy to manage. So far, so good.

Your next decision is the configuration of the individual web servers. Should you create additional redundancy *within* each server? Should the servers have dual power supplies? RAID arrays? Obviously, you want to do things right, and you want your site to be reliable, but you don't want to waste your money. You've already planned for the failure of an individual server. There's no need to invest in redundancy both across *and* within your web servers.

Instead of buying expensive internally redundant servers, go for web servers that are fast yet inexpensive. Don't bother with dual power supplies. What if one fails? Let it. That server will fail and the others will handle its load. *Just as you planned.* A RAID configuration? Why bother, unless you need increased performance? Don't waste your money. Go ahead and let one bad drive bring down an entire server. It's okay. The site will still survive. In many cases, the money you save by not building redundancy at the component level may be enough to allow you to buy a third server. Not only will this further increase the reliability of your site, it will also give you greater capacity before and after the failure of a single server.

On the other hand, because it's so difficult to distribute a database across multiple servers, it usually makes more sense to apply redundancy within a database server, rather than by trying to link multiple, less robust servers. You should make the within/across decision separately for each tier in your server architecture. We'll look at database architectures later in this chapter.

TIP Don't waste money by applying redundancy at both the component level *and* across multiple servers within the same architectural tier.

The Cheap Speakers Phenomenon

Just as it doesn't make sense to deploy redundancy both within servers and across them, there's also no point in building a web site that's substantially more reliable than the data center in which it resides. For instance, if your web-hosting service has only one fiber link to the Internet, it takes only one scoop of the back-hoe to take you offline for many hours.

It's like the guy who spends thousands of dollars on a new stereo amplifier, DVD/CD, cassette deck, tuner, and surround sound decoder, but runs out of money when it comes time to buy the speakers. The fancy components won't matter if you can't hear the difference.

Audiophiles suggest spending as much on speakers as you spend on all other components combined. Likewise, when it comes to your web-site configuration, be careful not to build the ideal configuration only to house it in an unreliable data center.

TIP Include an analysis of the reliability of your web-hosting service's infrastructure when developing your plans for redundancy.

If your web-hosting service's facilities aren't sufficiently redundant (and you can't switch facilities), it may make sense to start thinking about a *geographically distributed* architecture for your site. This means you would replicate some or all of the components at different locations, perhaps even in different countries. All of the component- and system-level redundancy you can include won't do you much good if there's no electricity in California and your web-hosting service runs out of diesel fuel for its generators (we'll look at architectures for *geographic redundancy* later in this chapter).

The Economics of Redundancy

Like the debate of the merits of one airplane engine versus two, there's an ongoing debate among web architects: Is it better to run a web site (or any application for that matter) on a small number of very powerful but expensive computers or on a larger number of slower but cheaper computers? Of course, there's no one right answer, but consider the following:

- After years of trying to run multiple web sites on large multi-CPU Sun and SGI computer systems, many shared-server web-hosting vendors have switched to using a larger number of much smaller devices.

- Some portions of Yahoo! run on hundreds of small, inexpensive Intel-based servers running the Apache web server and the FreeBSD operating system. In many cases, the Yahoo! staff performs no preventive maintenance of any kind. For example, they rarely upgrade the software to new releases (if it ain't broke, don't fix it). There are so many redundant servers for each function, that when one fails, there is no noticeable effect on performance or availability. The defective computer is removed and replaced by another equally inexpensive server.

- Most so-called high-availability components and servers (i.e., those designed for particularly low failure rates) are sold at a premium. For example, a pair of hot-swappable, mirrored disk drives costs more than twice as much as a single non-swappable drive, if you take into consideration the cost of the hot-swappable carriers and the processor overhead or special hardware to manage the mirroring.

TIP All other things being equal (and except in the case of database servers—an exception that's discussed in more detail later in this chapter), it's better to use a larger number of redundant inexpensive servers than a smaller number of high-reliability ones.

Unfortunately, it's not a perfect world. "All other things" are not equal. As we'll discuss in the next subsection, quirks in software licensing and web-hosting fees may complicate an otherwise straightforward decision.

Redundant Software Licenses

The first quirk is the cost of software licenses. If your web servers are based on free or inexpensive software, such as the Apache web server package, the aforementioned strategy of using a greater number of smaller servers works very well. But suppose your application servers are running an expensive commercial package that cost $20,000 to $50,000. What then?

If the software license fee is *per server* (i.e., per box or per chassis), you've got a difficult decision, because then you're motivated to use an architecture containing as few boxes as possible and to load them up with as many CPUs as you can. On the other hand, most application servers are licensed on a *per CPU* basis (i.e., per microprocessor, many of which can be installed in a single server), in which case it doesn't matter to the software vendor whether you have two CPUs in one server or one CPU in each of two servers. If the cost of the software is the same in both cases, the two-server configuration should give you more redundancy per dollar.

TIP Consider software license fee peculiarities when trying to optimize your web-site architecture. Expensive licenses may favor the use of a smaller number of larger servers.

Rackspace and Management Fees

Unfortunately, the economic challenges of redundancy don't end with the software. There are two other per-server costs that may sway you from an otherwise optimal design: the cost of rackspace and per-server management fees.

Part of your web-hosting fee will be based on the number of racks or cabinets you use. Although it may vary with the actual hardware you've selected, in most cases two small servers still take up more space than a single server that has twice as much capacity. That means you may pay more in rackspace charges for a configuration using smaller redundant servers.

Similarly, your web-hosting vendor may charge you a per-server management fee. Again, this would shift the economic decision toward a smaller number of larger servers. It may not be technically preferable, but at the end of the day, as long as you have the required degree of redundancy, the decision should be based on which is the cheapest way to get it.

TIP Web-hosting service and MSP fees for rackspace and server management may also favor the use of a smaller number of larger servers.

Clustering and Load Balancing

You might think that only the big sites need to deal with capacity, scalability, and reliability, and that owners of web sites on shared servers have few choices in these areas. But as we'll see, web-site architecture is important to everyone, even the owner of a web site running on a shared server.

In Chapter 4, "Shared and Dedicated Servers," we looked at the basic shared-server architecture in which a single physical server houses multiple web sites—perhaps hundreds of them. Although shared-server technology has improved to the point that sites can coexist reasonably well, the fact remains that the failure of a single box can bring down all of the sites running on it.

Some web-hosting services offer a configuration that can substantially improve the reliability of shared-server hosting. This configuration, referred to as *server clustering*, is common in higher-end configurations, such as those supported by MSPs, but is being used increasingly by some shared-server vendors as well. A clustered configuration is shown in Figure 12.6. Note that each of the five web sites exists on each of the two servers. This is, therefore, a redundant configuration.

Requests from users' browsers are received by the *load balancer,* which then directs the requests to one server or the other (we'll look at redundant load balancers shortly). Load balancers are hardware devices that make request/dispatch decisions based on three criteria:

- If one web server is down or offline, all requests will be sent to the other server.

- If one web server responds more slowly (the load balancer watches the server response times), more requests will be sent to the faster server, hence tending to balance the load between the two servers.

- If both servers are responding equally, requests will be sent alternately to each server. This is referred to as *round-robin dispatching.*

Where available, shared-cluster hosting is somewhat more expensive than single-server shared hosting, but it's a good choice if you want a slight increase in the availability (uptime) of your web site.

TIP If your site will be hosted on a shared server, but you need increased reliability, look for a web-hosting service that offers clustered servers. It's usually only slightly more expensive than using nonclustered servers.

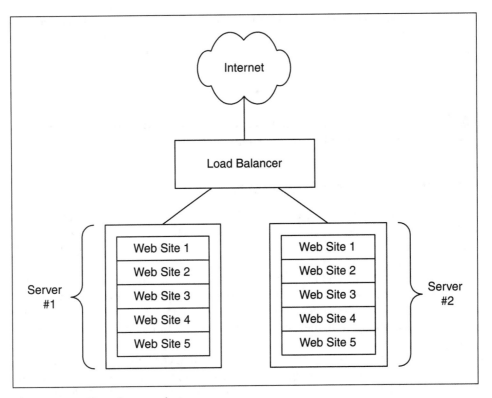

Figure 12.6   Shared-server cluster.

Load balancers can also be used to improve the reliability and scalability of web sites using dedicated or colocated servers, as shown in Figure 12.7.

Figure 12.7 presents a configuration with two web servers and a single load balancer. It's similar to the clustered shared-server configuration discussed earlier and shown in Figure 12.6, with the exception that in Figure 12.7, each web server is dedicated to a single web site.

When any component in one of the web servers fails, the other server will take on the full responsibility for responding to visitors' requests for web pages. Overall, this configuration is therefore more reliable (providing greater availability) than the single-server configuration that would be offline in the case of a single failure.

When both servers are running, the combination of the two can handle twice the volume of requests that can be handled by a single server alone. When one server is down, the remaining server can handle only half the load that the pair can handle, but it's better than nothing. Three, four, or even more servers may be added to the load balancer to further increase capacity. If there's a failure of one server, only $1/n$ of the total capacity is lost (where n is the number of servers).

TIP Add a load balancer (or use load-balancing services from your web-hosting service) as a cost-effective way to increase reliability.

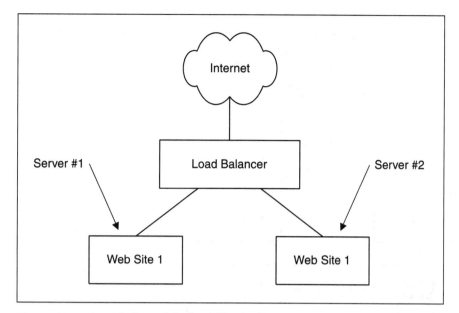

Figure 12.7 Load-balanced dedicated servers.

Redundant Application Servers

Application servers can also be configured redundantly as shown in Figure 12.8. State-of-the-art application servers communicate among themselves and synchronize their data so that users being serviced by one application server can share data in real time with users on another. This link (shown as a line connecting the app servers in Figure 12.8) is also used to keep the application servers in sync and to allow each one to monitor the other. When one application server fails, the other automatically picks up its tasks. This is known as *failover.*

Note that there's no similar link connecting the web servers. While each of the web servers must be able to communicate with either application server (in case one of either type fails), there's no need for the web servers to communicate with one another.

Redundant Infrastructure

The configuration shown in Figure 12.8 still has two single points of failure: the load balancer and the database server. Figure 12.9 shows a *fully redundant* configuration. Looking first at the top of the diagram, note that the web site now has multiple connections to the Internet via the web-hosting service's routers—ideally via two *different* routers. Each Internet link is connected to a pair of redundant load balancers via high-speed switches. The load balancers are linked to one another, enabling them to coordinate their load-balancing activities and to "fail over" in much the same way as application servers do. Each load balancer is linked to both web servers.

So what happens when things fail? If a switch fails, the associated link to the web-hosting service's Internet connections will be unusable. But that's okay, because there's

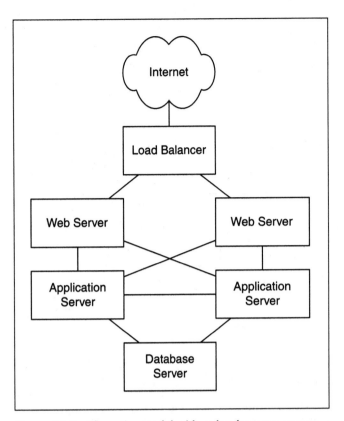

Figure 12.8 Three-tier model with redundant app servers.

another switch and link that will continue to operate. If one of the load balancers fails, the link between them allows the good load balancer to learn that the bad one has stopped working and that it must assume sole responsibility. Since the good one can still communicate with both switches and with all web servers, the site stays up.

TIP An architecture is not fully redundant unless it includes redundant switches, load balancers, and links to your web-hosting service's routers.

Databases

As with the load balancers at the top of Figure 12.9, the database servers at the bottom are also shown in a redundant configuration. Of all the components of a web site, database servers are by far the most difficult to scale. Because databases are highly volatile (their content changes continuously), you can't merely put copies on two or more separate database servers as you can with web servers. In the case of databases, you've got to keep any such multiple copies in sync—and not just synchronized within a few seconds, but right down to the level of the individual transaction. For example, if an inventory database indicates there's only one item left, that item had better not be sold to

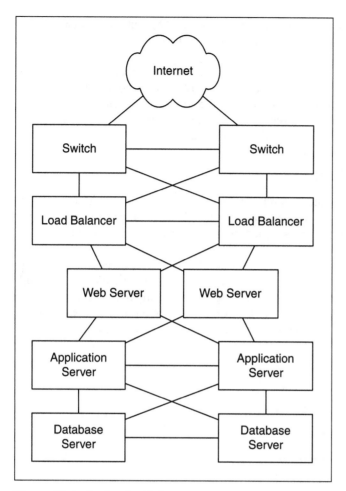

Figure 12.9 Redundant infrastructure.

two different visitors who just happen to be shopping at the same moment but who are connected to separate copies of the database.

Because of the need for real-time synchronization, and unlike web and application servers that can be scaled cost-effectively by adding additional servers, it's almost always better (or at least cheaper) to use a larger database server than to try and distribute the database over multiple servers. Unless you really do need to get close to 100 percent uptime (in which case you have no choice but to implement fully redundant database servers, possibly even at multiple locations as we'll consider shortly), do everything you can to avoid the need for multiple database servers.

Instead, start by improving the reliability of your single database server using redundant components. A solitary database server is the best place to spend your money on redundant power supplies, RAID, and the most reliable server hardware you can afford. When it comes time to upgrade, rather than add a second server, replace the one you have with one that's more powerful. Ideally, buy one to which you can continue to add CPUs and RAM as your requirements increase. All databases are hungry for RAM—primarily for caching data—so make sure your server has a high capacity for add-in memory.

> **TIP** Database servers are the one case where it's best to build redundancy into a single server before going to a multiserver architecture.

Unlike multiple application servers that need share only a subset of the entire database, multiple database servers must share and maintain synchronization for everything they store. It can be done, but it's a tall order, and a very complex and expensive one to fill. For these reasons, many web sites use one of two somewhat less robust, but far less expensive solutions: *hot-* and *cold-standby* databases.

Cold-Standby Databases

Figure 12.10 illustrates a cold-standby database configuration. The second server is *cold* because it may literally be shut down most of the time. When a failure occurs in the primary database server, current data is copied to the cold standby, which is then brought online in place of the primary.

There are three fairly obvious disadvantages of this architecture. First, the web site will be down between the time the primary database server fails and the time the cold-standby server is brought online. The second problem is that any transactions that were in progress at the time of the failure will be lost. Finally, depending on exactly what failed, data may have to be restored from backup disks or slower magnetic tape. The

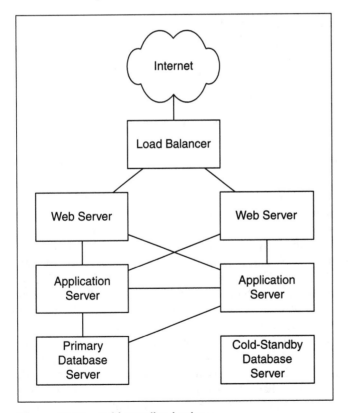

Figure 12.10 Cold-standby database.

magnetic tape might even be stored off-site, hours away. Depending on the size of the database, the restoration process also could take many hours, during which time the site will remain offline.

Still, the advantages of a cold standby remain. It's better than no redundancy at all, and the only additional costs as compared to the single database-server architecture are the cost of the second database server and the database software. Some vendors even discount the latter so long as the server is used for cold standby only.

It's interesting to note that disk drive failures are not the most common causes of database failures or of the need to recover data from backups or archives. The RAID storage systems typically used with databases are remarkably reliable. A far more common cause is database corruption due to application errors, and that can't be eliminated by *any* architecture.

Hot-Standby (Failover) Databases

With a cold-standby database, it's frustrating to have the hardware and software going to waste when, for only a little more money and only a bit more complexity, you can further reduce your exposure to downtime by using that second server as a *hot-standby* database, shown in Figure 12.11.

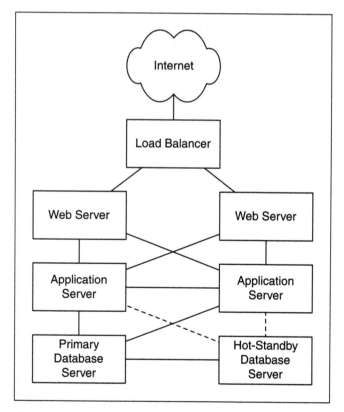

Figure 12.11   Hot-standby database.

In this hot-standby configuration (so-called because the standby database server is always powered up and ready to go), there's a special link between the primary and hot-standby database servers, similar to the failover link between the application servers. The hot-standby server maintains a near-real-time copy of the database, and receives *updates* over this link.

Unlike cold-standby configurations that require manual intervention in the case of an outage, the hot-standby configuration handles failures unattended. When the primary database fails, the hot standby is ready to take its place almost immediately. It's connected to the application servers, but those links remain unused until the failover event occurs, at which time the application servers communicate with the standby database server as though it were the primary. With some failover systems, the application servers may not even be aware that the change has occurred. Some hot backup database systems can fail over within 5 or 10 seconds, which is usually fast enough that user sessions don't time out.

> **TIP** A hot-standby database configuration is a good intermediate step between a single-server design and a fully redundant architecture.

Database Clustering

The final step in single-location database architectures is the use of *database clusters,* as illustrated in Figure 12.12. As with the hot-standby configuration, database clusters use special software to keep two or more databases in sync. In clusters, however, all of the database servers are servicing requests from application servers. None of the database servers are relegated to standby mode. As shown in Figure 12.12, each application server has a path to each database server through a pair of redundant high-speed switches.

Database clustering can offer near-perfect reliability, but at a very high cost. Most site owners who require database clustering find they pay more for the database hardware, software, and clustering package than they pay for all other web-site hardware and software combined.

> **TIP** Use a database cluster to achieve the highest levels of single-location database redundancy.

The servers in a database cluster share a single storage system, not shown explicitly in Figure 12.12. We'll discuss storage in more detail in Chapter 15, "Storage."

Performance

We've looked at examples of web-site architectures that address application complexity as well as improve reliability, capacity, and scalability. But what about performance? The architectures we've already discussed address performance in the following ways:

Tiers. The two-tier architecture allows web and database servers to function without competing for resources.

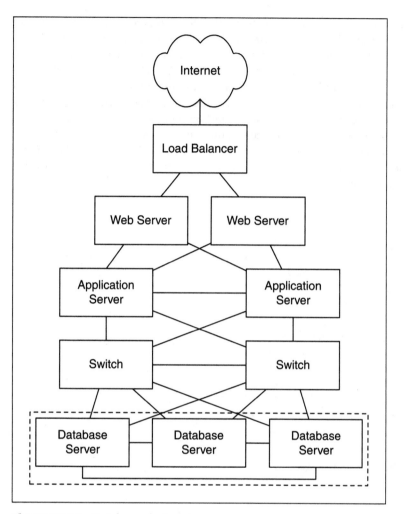

Figure 12.12 Database clustering.

Application servers (using the three-tier model). Improve performance by caching frequently used data, thereby minimizing the number of requests to the database. Application servers also pool database connections, again, improving performance.

Application and database design. Good database schema design and efficient (scalable) use of the database by the custom application can eliminate the majority of web-site performance problems.

Getting Closer to the Users

Once you've deployed a multitier architecture based on scalable application servers, and addressed any flaws that may exist in your application and database designs, what else can you do to improve the performance of your web site? The next step is to move your content closer to your web site's visitors.

Most web sites are based on the *hub-and-spoke* model in which the web site is located at the *hub,* and all of the visitors are located at the perimeter, as shown in Figure 12.13. Fundamentally, the hub-and-spoke model of a centralized web site is weak. Every request to your server, every response it sends, and all of the packets to support these exchanges must traverse the full distance between the visitor and the web site. The problem is most evident to web-site visitors from other countries. Moving data across continents and oceans can be slow, expensive, and unreliable.

Figure 12.14 illustrates an alternative to the hub-and-spoke model in which the capacity of the centralized web site is reduced. The load is shifted to additional instances of the site (indicated by circles containing Ws), which are located at the edges of the Internet, closer to the visitors.

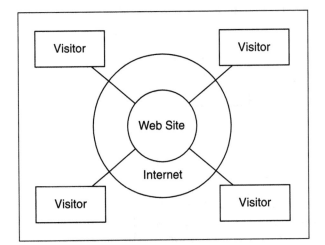

Figure 12.13   The hub-and-spoke model.

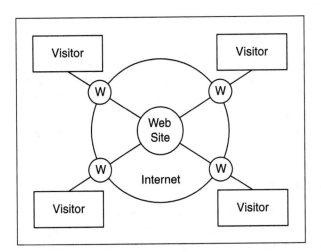

Figure 12.14   Moving content toward the edge.

There are two ways to move your content closer to your visitors. The first is through *geographic redundancy,* described in the next section. The second is through *caching* or a *content delivery network.* These topics are important enough that we've dedicated all of Chapter 13 to discussing them.

Geographic Distribution

In addition to improved performance, many web-site owners want or need the extra reliability they can get only from running their servers at multiple locations. Geographic redundancy (as opposed to redundancy within a single location) can buy you at least some immunity from all those natural disasters and Internet routing problems. Although most modern data centers can withstand tornados, hurricanes, floods, and moderately strong earthquakes, the towns in which the data centers are located and the web-hosting service's employees may not be so lucky.

Mirroring and Load Balancing

The most basic geographically redundant architecture is called *mirroring.* In this model, shown in Figure 12.15, all of the web site's files are simply copied to one or more *mirror sites* whenever the contents of files change.

The objective of mirroring is to improve availability and performance. It improves availability by ensuring that if one location goes down or can't be reached, the other location will continue to operate and be reachable via alternate routes.

Similar to the local load balancers used in redundant one-site architectures, the *distributed load balancers* shown in Figure 12.15 direct traffic to the location that can deliver

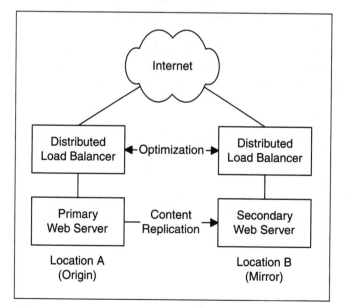

Figure 12.15 Mirrored web servers.

content most quickly, using the least expensive bandwidth. These devices communicate with one another in order to optimize site selection in much the same way as redundant local load balancers do. Furthermore, by participating in the management of a web site's Domain Name Service (DNS), the distributed load balancers can ensure that if one site goes down completely, all traffic will be directed to the other.

Mirroring just a portion of any site (e.g., the images, audio files, etc.) is a common practice. In fact, the only sites that can be mirrored entirely are those that either don't have a database at all or that have a database that's read-only, such as those used strictly to generate dynamic content. If your site needs to *write* to a database (as is the case with most e-commerce sites), basic mirroring probably won't work. You're going to need a *fully distributed* architecture.

Fully Distributed Architectures

Some applications built on three-tier architectures—using application and database servers—need very high uptime service levels. For example, financial services (banks and brokerages) simply can't afford to go down in the middle of a trading session, and these companies will spend extraordinary amounts to make sure they don't. As you might imagine, geographically distributing your *entire* site (as illustrated in Figure 12.16) can be quite expensive and complex.

Earlier in this chapter we mentioned that database clustering wasn't for the weak of heart, and that anyone planning such a configuration should obtain the assistance of someone who has done it many times. This is even more true for fully distributed architectures that require real-time *data replication* as shown in Figure 12.16.

Keeping multiple side-by-side database servers that are synchronized is hard enough. Keeping them in sync when they're thousands of miles apart is substantially more difficult—entire books are devoted to the subject. But in the real world, distributed databases border on science fiction; they're few and far between.

> **TIP** Unless you need the very high availability that can be achieved only through fully distributed architectures, you can probably get the other benefits of such a configuration at a much lower cost by using a content delivery network.

In this chapter we've looked at a wide range of server and application architectures that address application complexity, capacity, redundancy, and reliability. We've looked at the economics of redundancy and some of the common mistakes people make when designing redundant systems.

The one architectural issue we've touched on only briefly is performance scalability. Every configuration we've considered so far is designed to achieve a scalability ratio approaching 1.0. In the next chapter, we'll look at technologies you can use to achieve even greater scalability ratios.

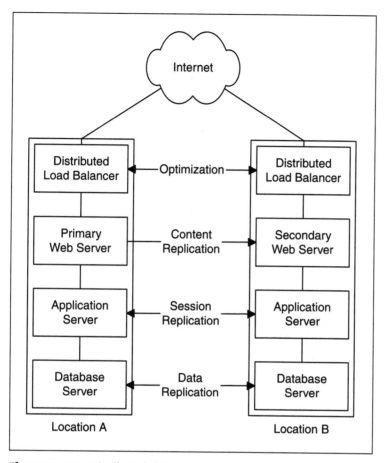

Figure 12.16   Distributed database.

Caching and Content Delivery Networks

We've been looking at architectures that can scale linearly, but how would you like a way to achieve even better scalability and, at the same time, improve the performance of your web site? *Caching* and its younger cousins, *content delivery networks* (CDNs), are technologies that can do just that. They can, simultaneously, make your web site appear faster and increase its capacity without a commensurate increase in cost.

We'll begin this chapter with a look at how caching works on the Internet and how you can install a *cache server* to offload traffic from your web servers. Then we'll explain how you can speed up your web site by using a CDN to deliver your content from locations much closer to your visitors.

Caching

Caching has been an important (but behind-the-scenes) part of the Internet for a long time. Your web browser, for instance, includes a cache that makes web sites appear faster than they really are. It does so by maintaining local copies of web pages and images that you've recently seen, so that the next time you ask for the pages or images, it can display them without having to retrieve them from the web.

ISPs and their corporate customers similarly use cache servers to minimize repetitious traffic and thereby make their Internet links more efficient. But their caches exist for the benefit of those ISPs and businesses that own them. They may happen to make

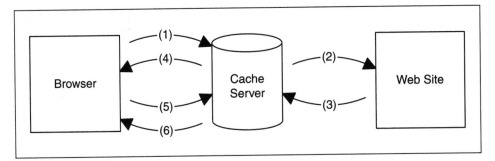

Figure 13.1 Caching.

your web site appear faster, but only if you're an AOL, Yahoo!, or Amazon.com—one of the top 50 web sites in terms of traffic. If your web site isn't among those top 50, it's unlikely that caches owned by third parties are improving your content delivery.

As you'll learn from this chapter, even if your web site isn't among that top tier, you can still get the scalability and performance benefits of caching by deploying your own *reverse-proxy cache* or by using a CDN. But before you can decide whether caching, a content delivery network, or both are right for your web site, it's important to understand how these technologies work.

All caches and CDNs use the same basic algorithm as illustrated in Figure 13.1. The algorithm works as follows:

1. When a *cache server* receives a request for an object, it checks its own storage first.

2. If it doesn't find the object, or if the object has expired, the cache server sends a request to the web site.

3. When the web site returns the object, the cache server saves a copy in its local storage and notes that this is now the most recently requested object in its cache.

4. It then returns the object to the browser.

5. The next time the browser requests the same object, the cache server again checks its own storage.

6. If it still has the requested object, and the object hasn't yet expired, it returns that object to the browser without forwarding the request to the web site.

A *cache hit* occurs when a cache returns an object directly from its local storage. A *cache miss* is what happens when the cache doesn't have a current copy and must therefore request the object from the web site. The number of requests that result in cache hits is referred to as the *hit ratio*, and is usually expressed as a percentage. For example, if 146 out of 200 requests result in a cache hit (i.e., 54 of the other requests generated cache misses), the hit ratio would be 73 percent.

Caches are like traffic checkpoints along the information superhighway. They're not part of the official infrastructure, and they don't appear on the Internet's road map—or *routing tables* as they are called. Caches depend entirely on being in the right place to intercept traffic between browsers and web sites. Like highway checkpoints, therefore, they're *passive*, waiting for traffic to come to them. We'll see why this distinction is so important when we look specifically at CDNs.

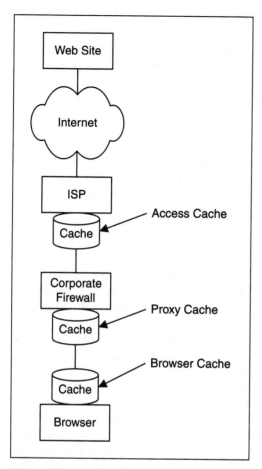

Figure 13.2 Cache hierarchy.

Caching has three beneficial effects:

- From the perspective of a visitor to your web site, caching reduces the time it takes to retrieve objects, thereby increasing the perceived speed of the visitor's Internet connection.

- From the perspective of your web site, caching reduces the number of requests it must process, thereby increasing the number of visitors it can accommodate with a given hardware configuration.

- Finally, caching reduces the total amount of traffic on the Internet, thus improving both the performance and the economics for all of us.

The Cache Hierarchy

So far we've only looked at caching generically. But caching is deployed in many different ways and at many different points between the browser and the web site to solve a number of different, but interrelated problems. Figure 13.2 illustrates three types of caching that we'll explain in the following sections.

Browser Cache

Most web browsers include a cache within the browser software itself. When a browser requests and receives an object from your web site, the browser saves a copy of the object in its own cache, which is located on the user's disk drive.

If that same object is requested again, either explicitly by the user (e.g., he or she enters a URL for a page he or she has recently viewed), or is referenced in one of your underlying web pages (e.g., it's an image that's used on more than one page), the browser checks its cache. If the cache finds a valid copy of the requested object, it returns that copy to the browser rather than requesting another copy from your web site. If the cache doesn't find a valid copy, the cache forwards the browser's request for the object to your web site.

Neither the user nor the browser is aware that the request may not have gone all the way to the server. Caching is, therefore, a *transparent* operation.

Proxy Cache

As we move up from the browser and toward your web site (in Figure 13.2), the next cache we encounter is near the corporate firewall where many organizations use *proxy caches* to improve the performance of their Internet connections and to enforce their security policies. A proxy cache works in exactly the same way as a browser's cache (or any other cache for that matter), but instead of caching the requests of just one browser, it does so for *all* of the browsers attached to a corporate network. If any browser being serviced by the proxy cache recently requested a cacheable object, then subsequent requests by that browser or any other browser may be served from the proxy cache.

The primary beneficiary of a proxy cache is the company that owns it, but the web sites whose content is repeatedly stored and served by a proxy cache benefit as well. Unfortunately, as we mentioned earlier, the secondary beneficiaries tend to be only those 50 busiest web sites, although if individuals served by a single proxy cache tend to view any site, whether it's among the top 50 or not, that site will appear to perform better for those users.

Access Cache

Just as businesses use proxy caches to maximize the throughput on the Internet links they purchase from ISPs, those ISPs use *access caches* to optimize the performance of the links they use to reach other ISPs. Not only does an access cache reduce an ISP's cost by reducing the number of requests that are forwarded to its peering partners, but it also improves performance (as perceived by its customers) by delivering objects more quickly.

Like a proxy cache, an access cache *aggregates* the requests of multiple customers on the network it serves. Look again at Figure 13.2. The first time an object is requested by the browser, that request will pass through all of the caches on its way to your web site. Each cache will take a cache miss and forward the request. On the return trip, the requested object will also pass through all of the caches, and each cache in the hierarchy will have an opportunity to grab the object and save it in order to fulfill later requests. Therefore, one user requesting, for example, the Amazon.com logo, causes it to be cached for all other users within his or her company *and* all other users of his or her company's ISP.

The primary beneficiary of an access cache is the ISP that installs it. And once again, the secondary beneficiaries are the busiest web sites whose contents tend to be stored in the access caches.

Reverse-Proxy Cache

Browsers have caches to make themselves faster; businesses install proxy caches to improve the effectiveness of their Internet connections; and ISPs use access caches to reduce their costs. While it's important to know that these caches are out there and to understand how they work, none of the caches we've looked at so far (browser, proxy, and access caches) is a type that you, as a web-site owner, can deploy in order to improve the performance of *your* web site. That's the job of a *reverse-proxy cache*.

Reverse-proxy caches use the same technology as proxy and access caches. In fact most caches, including reverse proxies, are based on Squid, a free software package that was derived from the ARPA-funded Harvest project (see www.squid-cache.org).

Unlike proxy and access caches that are used to reduce traffic in the links immediately above them in the hierarchy shown in Figure 13.2, a *reverse-proxy cache* is used to offload the delivery of static content from your web servers, as illustrated in Figure 13.3. It's called a reverse-proxy cache because it appears to your web server as though it were a

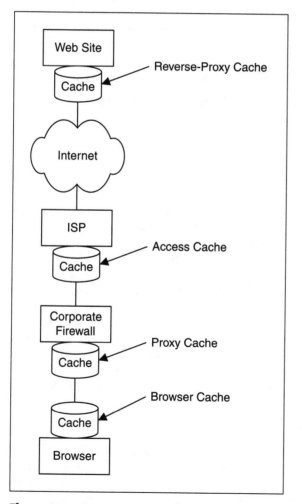

Figure 13.3 Reverse-proxy cache.

browser, whereas a normal proxy cache appears to a browser as though it's your server. And unlike proxy and access caches that are deployed for the benefit of those who install them, your reverse-proxy cache will specifically benefit you and your web site.

When a request comes into your web site (either from a browser or from an intervening cache), the reverse-proxy cache intercepts it to see whether it can be fulfilled from the cache's store of web-site objects. If the reverse proxy has the object in its cache, it masquerades as your web site and returns the object to the visitor. If the requested object isn't in the reverse proxy's cache, the reverse proxy requests the object from the web site, delivers it to the requestor, and retains a copy in its cache so the object is available the next time it's requested.

Reverse proxies are simpler and faster than the web servers they offload. Reverse proxies can even be preloaded with content, to further improve their performance, or (because they include standard caching logic) they can automatically retrieve updated content from web servers, and thus eliminate the need to manually replicate that content across multiple servers. Furthermore, multiple reverse proxies can communicate with one another via the Internet Cache Protocol (ICP), so that if one cache misses (i.e., doesn't have a current copy of a requested object), it can retrieve the object from a sibling rather than from the web server. Reverse proxies can reduce your cost of delivering static content and therefore increase the scalability of your web site.

TIP If you need to deliver more static content than your current web server(s) can handle, consider adding a reverse-proxy cache instead of another web server.

The Distributed Cache Problem

A reverse-proxy cache can do wonders to offload traffic from your web servers, but because it's located near your servers (rather than close to your web-site visitors), it doesn't do much to improve the *performance* of your web site as perceived by those visitors.

If the top 50 web sites get a performance boost from all of those proxy and access caches installed by ISPs and businesses, there must be some way for you to get a similar benefit. If you could move *your* caches away from your web site and place them closer to your visitors, your web site would appear to be much faster. Wouldn't it be great if you could place a whole collection of *distributed caches* at strategic points around the Internet, so that requests from each browser would be serviced by the closest distributed cache server, as shown in Figure 13.4?

It's a great idea, and it's the fundamental concept behind content delivery networks. But unfortunately you can't do this with simple caches. Remember, they're transparent. Browsers wouldn't know your distributed caches existed, and there would be no way to tell a browser to direct its requests to one of your caches. The distributed caches would be ignored, and all requests would continue to be sent to your web site rather than to the distributed caches.

The only way a browser's request manages to reach any cache is by happenstance. If there happens to be a cache along the route between the browser and your web site, that cache can intercept requests. Unfortunately, the access cache shown in Figure 13.4 doesn't know that the nearby-distributed cache exists, so the access cache isn't going to send the distributed cache any requests. The access cache will continue to send its requests directly to your web site. If you have a reverse-proxy cache, it may service the

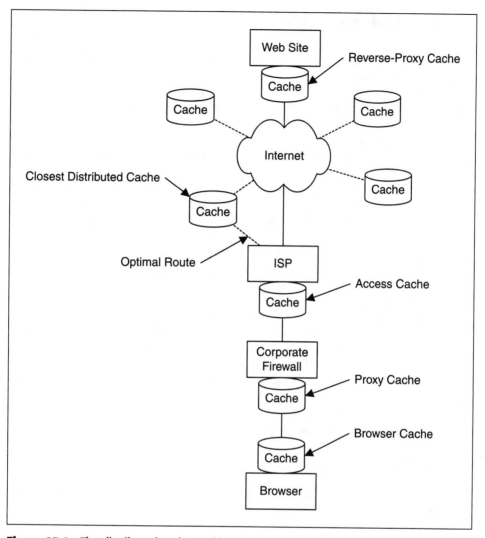

Figure 13.4 The distributed cache problem.

access cache's requests, but that's only because it can intercept the requests on their way to your web site. The distributed caches aren't in a position to intercept anything.

The distributed caches aren't part of the hierarchy. Just because you've put one somewhere on the Internet that's closer to the user's web browser doesn't mean any of the routers or other caches along the way will use it. A cache doesn't normally have the ability to advertise its availability in the same way a web site does (via routing tables), so it can't get any traffic other than what it can intercept.

Caches are like fishing nets; they're *passive*. Unless they're in the river where all the fish happen to swim by, they won't catch a thing. Ultimately, what's needed is an *active* approach in which requests (like fish) are explicitly directed toward those strategically located distributed caches. That's the concept behind content delivery networks.

Content Delivery Networks

A content delivery network solves the distributed cache problem by using a *CDN controller* to actively manage distributed cachelike devices called *edge servers* and by taking control of part of your web site's infrastructure—typically its Domain Name Service (DNS). In this way, visitors' requests for content can be explicitly directed to the edge server that can best fulfill them.

You can build your own content delivery network or you can outsource content delivery services to an existing CDN vendor in much the same way as you outsource web-hosting services. In fact, some web-hosting vendors also own and operate their own content delivery networks. Since building a CDN is beyond the budgets of all but the largest web-site owners, our discussions will focus on the use of existing commercial CDNs, although the architecture and components of a CDN are the same in either case, as illustrated in Figure 13.5.

CDNs use another new term, *origin server,* to refer to the site that acts as the *authoritative source* for the CDN's content. The origin server is the place from which an edge server will request objects that it doesn't find in its cache. In most cases, your existing web site will be the origin server.

Traditional caches and the edge servers of CDNs differ in fundamental ways. Caches are passive devices that work independently and are only effective when they can intercept content requests. Caches don't make any optimization decisions. They either have a requested object or they don't. If they have it, they use it. If they don't have it, they get it.

Edge servers, on the other hand, are always deployed in a group and are actively managed by a CDN controller. The edge servers and the CDN controller cooperate with one another and use the infrastructure of the Internet (typically DNS) to force requests to the edge server that is optimal for each visitor.

CDN Differentiation

Now that we've seen how a content delivery network in general solves the distributed cache problem, let's look at some of the questions you should ask in order to determine the type of CDN that's best for your web site:

- What's the optimal number of edge servers in a CDN for *your* site?
- What must you do to prepare your site for distribution by various CDNs?

The Optimum Number of Locations

If you build a private CDN, the number of edge servers will likely be relatively small. But among commercial CDN vendors, there is great debate over what's the optimal number of edge servers. Let's look at the two most common models for deployment of edge servers: distributed and centralized.

The Distributed Model

Vendors using the *distributed* approach place relatively small edge servers in the points of presence (POPs) of as many ISPs around the world as they can. As of this writing, for

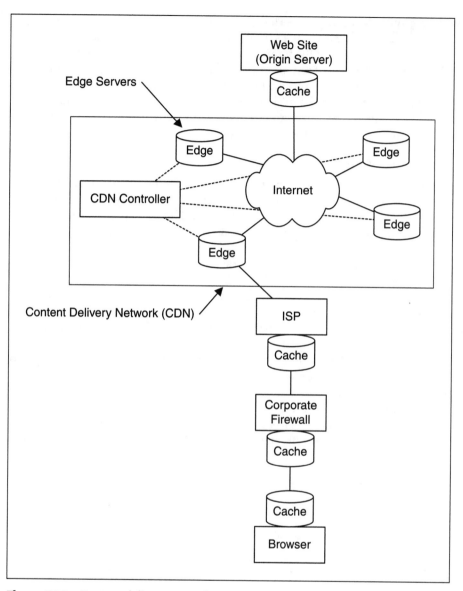

Figure 13.5   Content delivery network.

example, one such vendor had deployed more than 8,000 edge servers on 460 networks in 54 different countries, and was adding more servers literally every day.

The theory behind the distributed model is that edge servers should be as close as possible to the user in order to deliver content quickly and reliably; and the more edge servers you have, the closer you can get them to users. When it works, this is the fastest model, and it's particularly effective for high-volume web sites.

On the other hand, critics of the distributed model (i.e., competitors) point out that while it's a good architecture for the top 50 web sites, it doesn't fare nearly as well for sites that receive less traffic. Because there are so many edge servers, each one receives relatively few hits. With 8,000 edge servers, for example, each edge server would receive, on average, 1/8000th of the traffic of a centralized web site serving the same visitors. The larger the number of servers, the closer they can be to the users, but the lower will be each server's hit ratio. And the lower the hit ratio, the poorer the performance of the CDN, since for each cache miss, an edge server must retrieve the requested object from the origin server. Furthermore, there's the general consideration that the larger and more complex a network is, the more difficult it is to maintain.

The Centralized Model

The competing *centralized* architecture is based on deploying a much smaller number of edge servers (from 4 to 40), but with each one having the capacity to hold many more objects than the distributed model's edge servers. Although there are variations from one vendor to the next, the most common strategy is to deploy edge servers at one or two locations in each major country—perhaps a few additional in the United States. By comparison, some large distributed CDNs have more than 200 servers in the United Kingdom alone.

Given the same budget, a CDN that uses the centralized model and fewer edge servers can afford to configure those edge servers with much larger caches. The larger the cache, the higher the hit ratio will be for those edge servers; the higher the hit ratio, the better the performance of the CDN.

Figure 13.6 illustrates the differences in performance between the centralized and distributed CDN models for sites with different traffic volumes. As you can see, the distributed model works poorly for sites with low to medium traffic volumes. There are two reasons for this. First, because there are so many edge servers, their average hit ratios are low. Second, because caches favor the objects that are requested most frequently, the low- to medium-traffic sites are at a substantial disadvantage when competing for storage space in the edge servers.

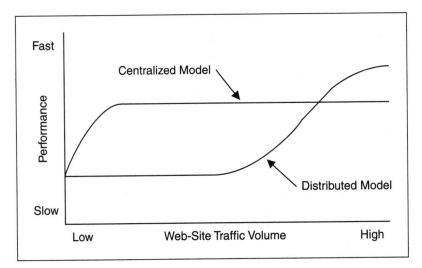

Figure 13.6 Comparison of CDN models.

Once the volume of traffic increases, however, and the distributed model begins to leverage its caches (which are closer to the browser than those of the centralized model), things change. When the web-site traffic increases to the point at which the distributed model begins to experience a high hit ratio, it starts to deliver better performance than the centralized model.

TIP CDNs using the centralized model (4 to 30 edge servers) tend to work best for web sites with low to medium traffic volumes. High-volume sites may do better with a CDN based on the distributed model.

Preloading

Note in Figure 13.6 that the curve for the centralized model rises quickly and then flattens out. This is because, with a relatively small number of edge servers, it doesn't take much traffic for an object to be cached in all of them. In the distributed model, it's not until there's substantially more traffic before an object is cached in every edge server.

Some centralized-model vendors offer to *preload* content into their edge servers, so that even the first request for an object will get a cache hit. Preloading increases an edge server's hit ratio to 100 percent. Distributed-model vendors offer a preload option less frequently because their edge servers are typically too small to support it.

TIP For guaranteed performance levels, look for a vendor that offers preloading of your content.

Which model is better for *your* web site? There's really only one way to know for sure, and that's to run tests using your site's actual content and visitor distribution patterns. There are simply too many variables to accurately predict the outcome.

Site Preparation

Another way in which CDNs vary greatly is in the extent to which you must modify your existing web site in order to use them. Some CDNs require literally no changes whatsoever to your site, whereas others require rather extensive modifications. In the following sections, we'll examine some of the modifications that may be required.

On-the-Fly URL Rewriting

Some CDNs use a technology called *URL rewriting* that doesn't require any modification of your existing web site. It's particularly popular for use by shared- and dedicated-server web-hosting vendors, because it can be very easily deployed for any of their customers. In fact, some shared- and dedicated-server vendors include a basic CDN capability at no additional charge for all of their customers, and offer an enhanced or upgraded version to those customers who want even better performance.

URL rewriting is performed by an *agent*—software that's added to a web server—that intercepts and modifies URLs embedded within HTML web pages *on the fly,* as they're being transmitted to browsers. Following is a simple HTML web page fragment before being modified by a rewriting agent:

```
<HTML>
<HEAD>
<TITLE>Sample Web Page</TITLE>
</HEAD>
<BODY>
<IMG SRC="/image/header.gif">
<H1>Welcome!</H1>
<A HREF="intro.html">
    <IMG SRC="/image/logo.gif"></a>
<p>
<IMG SRC="/image/footer.gif">
</BODY>
</HTML>
```

Now here's how that same fragment might look after being rewritten by the agent (the changes have been underlined):

```
<HTML>
<HEAD>
<TITLE>Sample Web Page</TITLE>
</HEAD>
<BODY>
<IMG SRC="http://sfo2.some-cdn.com/www.rds.com/image/header.gif">
<H1>Welcome!</H1>
<A HREF="http://sfo2.some-cdn.com/www.rds.com/intro.html">
    <IMG SRC="http://sfo2.some-cdn.com/www.rds.com/image/logo.gif"></a>
<p>
<IMG SRC="http://sfo2.some-cdn.com/www.rds.com/image/footer.gif">
</BODY>
</HTML>
```

The agent has modified all of the embedded URLs. Instead of referring to the /image directory on the same host as the underlying web page (*relative addressing*), the IMG tags now refer to a directory on one of the CDN's edge servers named sfo2.some-cdn.com. Likewise, the HREF has been changed so that if the visitor clicks on the logo, the web page intro.html will be retrieved from the edge server rather than from the origin server.

The most important advantage of the URL rewriting technology is that it can be deployed without your having to manually modify your web-site content. As mentioned earlier, this makes it suitable for shared- and dedicated-server web-hosting vendors to offer as a way to speed up all of their customers' web sites without the customers' involvement.

One disadvantage of URL rewriting is that the rewriting process itself takes time to scan the HTML and therefore slows delivery. Furthermore, web pages with rewritten URLs (i.e., those that have passed through the rewriting agent) are not themselves cacheable. This is because these web pages are potentially customized for each individual user, and the decision of which edge server to use (as manifested in the rewritten URLs) may change over short periods of time.

Despite these disadvantages, CDNs that use URL rewriting can dramatically improve the performance of a web site. You need to run your own tests to determine whether this technology is better or worse than any other. And remember, URL rewriting is perhaps the only CDN technology that allows you to take advantage of a CDN without altering your content or applications.

TIP Vendors that use URL rewriting allow you to get up and running on their CDNs with very little investment and little risk of lock-in.

Content Segregation

Except for those CDNs that use on-the-fly URL rewriting, most CDNs require changes to the organization of your web site's content. In particular, they typically require that the objects they cache be stored on a server with a separate host name so that the CDN can control the DNS for that host.

For example, suppose you decide to use a CDN to cache only your images—GIF and JPEG files. Let's further assume that you've been storing your image files in a web-server directory—www.rds.com/images. While this isn't a problem for simple web sites that don't use a CDN (or even for CDNs that use URL rewriting), it won't work for most other CDNs, since the CDN can't take control of the /images directory without taking control of everything else on your web server as well.

So, if it's not too late, start preparing now by segregating your content, just in case you decide to use a CDN at some time in the future. It won't cost you any more to do it right if you start now.

The best approach is to store your images and other highly cacheable objects (such as audio and video files) with URLs that refer to dedicated hosts. For example, rather than storing your logo as a file in a directory on your primary web server:

```
http://www.rds.com/images/logo.gif
```

store it as a file on a web server dedicated to images:

```
http://images.rds.com/logo.gif
```

This doesn't require a separate physical server for "images." If your web site is small and doesn't receive much traffic, you can use the same hardware as you use for "www"; create another virtual server or "server instance" for the "images" host; and configure DNS to resolve both server names to the same IP address.

There's another reason you should store images and other static objects in this way. If you need to add another web server to keep up with increases in your traffic, you'll then have the option of dedicating one or more servers to handling these objects, and all you'll have to do is move the files and change one DNS entry. Once you store your images using a dedicated host, you can use a virtual server, a dedicated server, or a CDN without having to change the URLs.

TIP Create separate virtual servers for images and other types of static objects (e.g., audio and video files). This will give you the option of moving these objects to dedicated servers or having them managed by a CDN without making any changes to your HTML or applications.

Aliases and Subdomain Delegation

Unlike the few CDNs that use the URL rewriting technique, most CDNs must take control of all or part of your DNS infrastructure. Think of the implications of this. Because all of your external *and internal* servers (not just those used for the web), and perhaps your company's email *MX records,* are managed through DNS, once you give control of your DNS to a CDN, you'll be dependent on them for making any DNS changes, even if those changes have nothing to do with your web site.

In general, it's a good idea to limit the extent to which a CDN takes over the management of your DNS. There are two better ways to accomplish this. The first is to create an *alias* using DNS. For example, consider two DNS records:

```
images.rds.com   IN   A      64.165.81.112
```

is an A (address) record that defines "images" as a host with the IP address 64.165.81.112, whereas

```
images.rds.com   IN   CNAME   images.some-cdn.com
```

is a CNAME (canonical name) record or *alias.* In the latter instance, any browser requesting the IP address of images.rds.com will be told to instead look for the CDN's host named images.some-cdn.com, which is under the control of the CDN's own DNS. Whatever kinky DNS practices your CDN vendor chooses to follow should be on its own DNS servers, not yours, thereby minimizing the risk to your other DNS records.

Subdomain delegation is the second way to give a CDN segregated control of DNS. For more information on both CNAME aliases and subdomain delegation, refer to Chapter 21, "Domain Names and DNS."

TIP Create aliases with CNAME records, or delegate subdomains to your CDN rather than give it control over all of your DNS.

Custom URLs

In addition to their need to make DNS changes, CDNs tend to be still more intrusive because they require that you modify your URLs to explicitly refer to their servers in their domain. For example, the image originally referenced by:

```
http://images.rds.com/logo.gif
```

may need to be referenced as:

```
http://some-cdn.com/images.rds.com/logo.gif
```

Most CDNs that require changes such as this usually supply software that will crawl your content and make the changes semiautomatically. Some vendors even provide utilities that look at the objects themselves to determine their type, size, and how best to manage them. In some cases this *metadata* is encoded within the URL itself. Here's an example of a URL that has been constructed in this manner:

```
http://a1572.g.some-
cdn.com/7/1572/608/20614144426/images.rds.com/logo.gif
```

Vendors that use such elaborate methods claim they can achieve superior results. Their competitors, of course, say otherwise. The only way to know for sure is to run your own tests. In any case, there are some additional disadvantages to CDNs that require batch modification of your URLs.

Dynamic content. If your web pages are generated dynamically, it can be difficult to locate and modify the embedded URLs. In fact, the URLs may be derived algorithmically, and therefore require modification of your application software.

Lock-in. Once you change your site to meet the requirements of a particular CDN, you're locked in to that CDN unless and until you change your URLs once again.

TIP Be wary of CDNs that require you to modify your URLs in ways that are unique to one vendor. If you decide to use a CDN that requires modification of your URLs, try to make the changes in a manner that's automatically reversible, for instance by changing an *environment variable* or configuration parameter.

CDN Technologies

Since running your own tests is the only good way to determine which commercial CDN is best for your web site, we could just stop here. But in the process of evaluating content delivery networks, you'll likely encounter vendor arguments over more issues than simply the optimal number of edge servers or what you need to do to prepare your content for delivery by a CDN.

In the next few sections, therefore, we'll explore some of the inner workings of CDNs, not so much because this information is all that critical when selecting a vendor, but because, with this knowledge, you'll be a more informed buyer. You'll also see how the gurus of CDNs have come up with a number of pretty clever ways to use the Internet's own technologies to overcome some of its many flaws. We'll answer the following questions:

- How does a CDN decide which edge server is best?
- Having made that decision, how does a CDN tell the web browser which edge server to use?
- How do CDNs deliver streaming content?
- What are the effects of caching and CDNs on your web-server log files?
- How do CDNs work together to exchange content (similar to how ISPs exchange packets)?

Finding the Best Edge Server

CDNs try to deliver content from the best edge server. *Best* doesn't always mean the closest, the fastest, or the most reliable, but often a combination of all of these attributes and more. The best edge server is the one that has the closest *topological proximity* to the visitor's browser. Topological proximity is an abstract measurement that takes into account a wide variety of criteria such as physical distance, speed, reliability, and data transmission costs.

Following are some of the considerations that a CDN may take into account in determining topological proximity:

Server availability. Is the edge server running and able to deliver content?

Server load. How busy is the edge server? As compared to other edge servers on the CDN, how quickly can it transmit requested objects?

Hop count. How many routers or switches are there between the edge server and the browser? (A *hop* is the segment of a route from one router or switch to the next.)

Latency. How long does it take packets to reach the browser from the edge server?

Packet loss. What's the reliability of the route between the edge server and the browser?

Cost of bandwidth. What's the cost of delivering the object from one edge server as opposed to using another? What's the least-cost routing (LCR)?

Some systems allow edge-server selection to be made by balancing multiple criteria. For example, a CDN may choose to give 60 percent weight to round-trip time (latency) and 40 percent to the hop count.

Directing the Browser

Now that we've identified the criteria by which content delivery networks measure the topological proximity of edge servers to browsers, let's look at how CDNs receive requests from those browsers in the first place and how they direct the browsers to the optimum edge servers.

You may recall that one can't just drop caches at the edges of the Internet and expect them to work. They wouldn't be able to receive requests. Most CDNs solve this problem either by acting as the web site's DNS nameserver or by masquerading as one of the site's web servers. These techniques allow a content delivery network to intercept DNS or HTTP requests and to formulate responses that will thereafter direct browsers to the correct edge servers.

There are many ways in which CDNs accomplish these tasks, and we'll look at three of them in the following sections: DNS redirection, DNS racing, and HTTP redirection.

DNS Redirection

The majority of content delivery networks use DNS-based schemes that receive requests to locate a *host* or *subdomain* such as image.rds.com. Let's look at one such scheme known as *DNS redirection*, while referring to Figure 13.7.

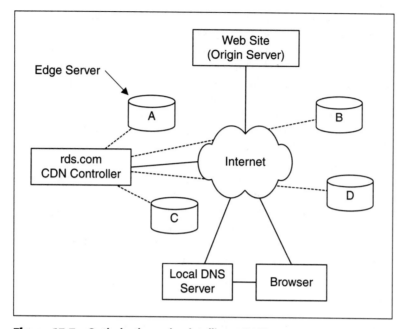

Figure 13.7 Optimization using intelligent DNS.

In order to locate the image server for the www.rds.com web site, the user's local DNS server sends a DNS request to the CDN controller, which is acting as the name-server for the subdomain images.rds.com. The CDN controller then sends queries to each of the edge servers, asking them to test the route between themselves and the local DNS server. Each edge server sends a test packet to the local DNS server and measures the round-trip delay. (The theory is that the local DNS server is fairly close to the browser and that testing the link to the local DNS server is an adequate way to determine how well an edge server can reach the browser.)

The edge servers reply to the CDN controller with the results of their measurements along with the other criteria that may be used to compare their topological proximities to the local DNS server. The CDN controller receives and sorts the replies from the edge servers—we'll assume edge server C came up the winner—and the CDN controller finally sends a reply to the local DNS server telling it that edge server C is, in fact, images.rds.com.

DNS Racing

In the example described in the preceding subsection, the decision of which edge server the CDN should select was somewhat elaborate. It involved the CDN controller's asking the edge servers for information that they, in turn, needed to collect by communicating with the local DNS server. This takes time, of course, which can degrade the performance of the delivery of content—the very problem CDNs are trying to solve.

Another DNS-based scheme, called *DNS racing*, is somewhat faster than DNS redirection. DNS racing makes use of a side effect of DNS by having the *local DNS server* determine which edge server can reach it most quickly.

Here's how it works. Referring again to Figure 13.7, you'll see the user's local DNS server tries to find images.rds.com and is directed to the CDN controller. The CDN controller then sends a message to each of the edge servers, instructing them to reply directly to the local DNS server's request. The command from the CDN controller includes a synchronized start time a few milliseconds into the future so that all of the edge servers will transmit their DNS replies at the same time.

At the appointed moment, all of the edge servers simultaneously send their DNS responses to the local DNS server. In their responses, the edge servers each claim to be the true images.rds.com. The local DNS server is satisfied as soon as it receives the first DNS response from any edge server. The other responses are ignored no matter how quickly they arrive. In this way, the edge server that was able to reach the local DNS host the fastest is the one that will be used to deliver the content. This is a Darwinian approach to edge-server optimization: natural selection by survival of the fastest.

Although DNS racing makes the edge-server decision more quickly than the earlier approach, it makes its decision on the basis of a single test, and it's not able to take into consideration additional variables such as cost-of-bandwidth and edge-server load.

HTTP Redirection

Our third and final example, *HTTP redirection*, is not used as frequently as those based on DNS. Referring again to the diagram in Figure 13.7, here's how this one works: The CDN controller in this case is masquerading not as a DNS nameserver, but as the web server images.rds.com. The browser, therefore, sends its first request for an image file directly to the CDN controller. The CDN controller then sends a query to each of the edge servers, asking them for information regarding their topological proximity to the browser. Each edge server then measures its topological proximity to the browser and replies to the CDN controller.

The CDN controller receives and sorts the replies from the edge servers—we'll assume edge server C again came up the winner—and the CDN controller replies to the browser's request for the web page with an HTTP Redirect (status code 302) telling the browser that it should reissue the request to edge server C.

One reason HTTP redirection is used less frequently than DNS-based schemes is that it's specific to the HTTP protocol. You can't use it, for example, to optimize the delivery of file downloads using the File Transfer Protocol (FTP) or to deliver most streaming content.

We've presented only three examples of how CDNs determine topological proximity and thereby select an optimum edge server. There are many more techniques—far too many to cover in this chapter. From the examples presented here, however, you should have a sense of the range of technologies on which real-world CDNs are based.

Dynamic Content and ESIs

Most web-site owners use CDNs only for the delivery of their static content such as images and multimedia files. They tend to consider their *dynamic* content that's *personalized* or modified for delivery to each web-site visitor to be noncacheable, and hence unable to be served by a CDN.

But there's a trend toward moving more and more of a web site's application logic and database content to the edge of the network, and hence closer to the visitor. Part of this trend is the advent of edge-side includes (ESIs) that allow edge servers to dynamically assemble complex, personalized web pages in much the same way as has traditionally been done only at the origin site. The technology is called edge-side includes because it works very similarly to the server-side includes (SSIs) that have been available ever since some of the first web servers were developed.

ESIs are an excellent way to deploy certain dynamic applications such as product catalogs, stock quotes, and auctions that perform simple on-the-fly substitutions and lookups from tables or small databases. The resulting web pages are assembled more closely to the web-site visitors, thereby improving the pages' perceived performance. Furthermore, ESIs make such applications far more scalable by reducing the centralized infrastructure necessary to support a dynamic web site (see www.edge-delivery.org for more information on ESI and edge-site includes).

TIP Look for a CDN that supports ESIs to deliver dynamically generated content directly from its edge servers.

Streaming Content

Most of what we've considered so far relates to all types of content. But streaming content such as audio and video present some unique problems, and content delivery networks are particularly good platforms for solving them. Not only do CDNs get the content closer to the visitor, they're also much better equipped than centralized servers to handle the peaks in traffic that often occur with event-based content for which streaming is used, such as the next presidential election debacle or Victoria's Secret fashion show.

If you use a CDN to deliver your streaming content, the CDN can even handle the origin-server functions so that you don't have to deal with the specialized server software that's required. Managing streaming servers isn't typically a core competency that's worth your acquiring in-house.

There are two very different types of streaming data: live versus on-demand content. We'll explore them in the following subsections.

Live Streaming

Live streaming content is essentially the same as live radio or television programming. There are one or more real-time content *feeds* from the source to the CDNs point of origin, and from there to the edge servers. The edge servers then stream the content to the web-site visitors. Because it's live, this type of streaming content is not stored or cached by the CDN; it's just distributed and delivered. The edge servers merely act as *stream multiplexers* to split the single feed they receive into as many streams as are necessary to deliver the content to the visitors they serve. Edge servers may also change the stream to lower-bandwidth versions (an operation called *transcoding*) so that visitors with lower-speed links can still view the stream.

Some CDNs that specialize in live streaming content own, or partner with, satellite-based networks that are excellent for distributing live content to multiple edge servers

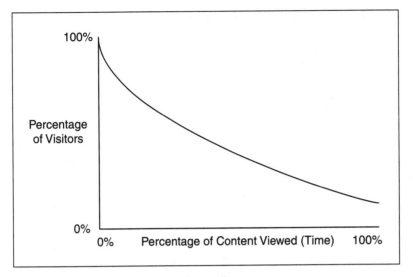

Figure 13.8 Streaming content drop-offs.

simultaneously. It's inexpensive (far cheaper than terrestrial delivery), more reliable, and produces lower *jitter*—something particularly problematic for streaming protocols (see Chapter 18, "Connectivity Performance," for more on the topic of jitter).

On-Demand Streaming

On-demand streaming content (as opposed to live-event streaming) is likewise appropriate for a CDN, but it works in a very different way. Unlike live content, on-demand content is stored and cached in files, just like any other object. However, unlike other cached objects, which are always received and delivered in their entirety, sometimes only fragments of streamed objects might be used.

Think of the times that you've viewed on-demand streaming content. How often have you watched or listened all the way through to the end of the content? Are you like most people who *drop off* at some point before seeing or hearing the end? Figure 13.8 shows a typical distribution of the habits of streaming content viewers. All visitors see or hear the beginning of the content, but relatively few stick with it all the way to the end.

So what effect does this have on caching? When a user drops off in the middle of receiving on-demand streamed content, the file transfer is incomplete. Edge servers that aren't prepared to handle streaming content properly may simply delete the incomplete file from their caches on the assumption that they didn't receive the file correctly. Better edge servers will store whatever they've received for later use, but since they didn't receive the entire file before the drop-off occurred, they have only the earliest portion.

When another user requests the same object, the edge server can do a good job of delivering the portion that it has stored, but if the user is still requesting more when the cached portion runs out, the edge server must go back and request the remaining portion from the origin server. Suddenly the quality of the stream deteriorates because the data can't be delivered directly from the edge server, and this may in turn require that the client software "renegotiate" the streaming session parameters.

To get around this problem, CDNs that specialize in the delivery of on-demand streaming content use a strategy by which they preload their edge servers with complete copies of the files. This allows such CDNs to deliver results that are truly superior to delivering the same content from the origin site. As with the distribution of live streaming data, satellite networks are an excellent way to accomplish preloading because of their low cost.

TIP If you're considering using a CDN for the delivery of on-demand streaming content, look for one that offers preloading as an option.

Log Files

The effect of caching on log files is an important issue whether you employ your own caching solution or use a CDN. Because traditional cache servers effectively bypass or short-circuit requests to your web servers, your log files don't reflect the actual number of times your content is requested. When an object is delivered from a browser cache, proxy cache, or access cache, the event doesn't appear in your logs. If you have a reverse-proxy cache sitting in front of your web server, you at least have the ability to merge its logs with your web-server logs; you can't do that with the downstream cache servers over which you have no control.

Because a content delivery network is under your control, or at least that of a vendor with whom you have a relationship, you can get log files from the CDN's edge servers and merge them with those from your origin servers and reverse-proxy caches. You still won't be able to track requests that are handled farther downstream by third-party caches, such as those that are requested and that never even reach the CDN's edge server.

Note that this is only an issue for content that is actually cached. If your HTML pages are noncacheable—for example, they're dynamically generated or time-sensitive—all requests for them will reach your web site and will appear in your logs. If only your images are cacheable, then only the logging of your images will be inaccurate. (Under normal circumstances, it's not important to log requests for images except as a security measure or to verify the performance of a CDN. Furthermore, must customers use CDNs only to host their images, not the underlying web pages, so their existing web-page logs are usually sufficient.)

TIP Be aware of the effects of third-party caching on your log files, particularly if your web site generates revenues from advertising.

CDN Peering

A relatively new development is *CDN peering* by which multiple commercial CDNs can deliver content on behalf of one another. For example, suppose you select a CDN vendor that's particularly strong in most of Europe but not in the Middle East. Your CDN could decide to *peer* with another CDN that does cover the Middle East so that your content can be delivered efficiently there as well. For business purposes, you would only need to deal with your original vendor.

The concept of CDN peering creates an entire *content-delivery value chain* similar to that which exists for the handling of telephone calls. Peering includes capabilities for one CDN to automatically report traffic to another so that you can receive a single, integrated set of log files no matter how many CDNs participate in the content value chain.

Also similar to the telephone network, CDN peering includes the capability to process *settlements* that allow CDNs to be paid by one another for their share of the cost of delivering your content. Even ISPs operating their own caches can eventually participate. As we've seen previously, without peering and settlements, the ISPs operate caches, but only as a cost-saving measure. Caches reduce their need for upstream connectivity. With CDN peering, ISPs can also deliver content on behalf of the web-site owner and therefore get a share of the CDN's revenues.

As a result, when ISPs and others have the opportunity to derive revenues from content delivery settlements, they'll be motivated to improve the capacity of their caches. As the use of CDN peering continues to increase, we can all look forward to faster download speeds.

TIP Ask prospective CDN vendors if they participate in any content peering initiatives or if they plan to do so in the future.

CDN Economics

A CDN isn't something you use *instead* of a web-hosting service. Think of it more as an extension to your existing site. But when edge servers deliver content from their caches, the load on your origin server is reduced. When this happens, you'll be paying your CDN to deliver your content, but you won't be using (or paying for) bandwidth from your web-hosting service. To achieve the promises of scalability and reduced costs with which we began this chapter, the total cost of distributing content via CDN must be less than the total cost for equivalent delivery directly from your origin site.

Most commercial CDNs base their charges on bandwidth, using either the 95th Percentile Rule or a per-gigabyte fee. On average, the fees charged by CDNs are roughly twice what you'd pay for the same bandwidth from a colocation service. Is it worth it? It's hard to assign a value to the performance improvement you'll receive from a CDN, but you can at least compare the cost savings you'll receive.

As you can see in Figure 13.9, using a CDN will initially be more expensive. But at some point it becomes less expensive to deliver content in this way than to deliver it from your own servers. CDN costs decrease due to volume pricing—yielding a scalability ratio greater than 1.0—while the cost of delivering the same content from the origin site will scale at something equal to or less than 1.0. Furthermore, CDN costs scale more smoothly since they don't incur the step-function jumps that are caused by the incremental upgrades required if you host your content on your own servers.

Using a CDN should actually reduce costs at the same time it provides improved delivery. Although the CDN bandwidth charges are higher than those of a colocation service, with a commercial CDN you don't have any of the other charges such as those for server hardware, software, maintenance, monitoring, and management.

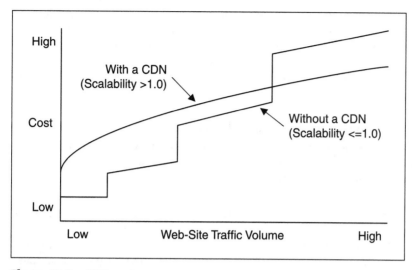

Figure 13.9 CDN costs.

Using a CDN you can build a very high-volume site that's based on a very small origin configuration. If your site contains only static content, for example, and you preload all of your content to all of your CDN's edge servers, you can even shut off your origin site and no one will notice, no matter how much traffic your site receives.

If your content is more dynamic in nature (e.g., yours is an e-commerce site) by using a CDN and thereby eliminating concerns about scalability, you can instead focus your time and attention on the transactional aspects of your web site that most likely must remain at the origin site.

CDN Vendor Selection

We've explored some of the technical and economic issues surrounding CDNs, and to wrap up our discussion, let's look at the right way to go about selecting a vendor.

Don't focus on the technology; run tests! CDNs are all about performance, and the only way to know how well a particular vendor's network will help your web site is to test it. Your tests should be based on your actual content and include both small and large objects (GIFs, large files, and streams) in the same proportion as you expect them to be used on your live site.

TIP Running your own tests, using your own content, is the only good way to evaluate the performance of CDNs.

Use third-party testing cautiously. It's a good idea to use an independent performance-measurement company to perform your tests, but give a great deal of thought to how the tests are being run. Remember that, as compared to your web servers, edge servers are much closer to your visitors. Since measurement services are trying to get a handle on the visitor's experience, their monitoring *probes* are also located close to your visitors. This means that a measurement service's probes may be located very close to a CDN's edge servers—possibly within the same third-party colocation facility. A monitoring probe and the edge server it's measuring may, in fact, be closer to one another than either is to your visitors, which could generate inaccurate results.

TIP When evaluating CDNs, use third-party measurement services that measure from locations as close as possible to the visitor's browser. Ask the measurement-service provider how it addresses the problem of the proximity of its monitoring probes to the CDN's edge servers.

Ignore industry and vendor reports. A CDN that's the best for one web site may be one of the worst for another site, and vice versa. Therefore, don't rely on published third-party reports to determine which CDNs will perform best for you. For that, once again: Run your own tests. Tests conducted by the CDNs themselves are even less reliable than independent reports and may be misleading. Vendors are competing for milliseconds, and it's easy for them to create tests that show their solutions in the best light.

TIP Don't use published comparisons of CDNs or vendor-supplied test data as the basis for comparing content delivery networks in lieu of running your own tests.

Get references. Go to other web sites like yours, and see who's using which CDNs. Chapter 20, "The Net Detective Toolkit," will help you identify what CDN a web site is using. Contact the owners of those web sites and find out how they like their vendors. Did they consider others? Why did they select the vendors they did?

TIP Do some snooping on web sites that appear to have content and traffic volumes similar to yours. Find out which CDNs they use, then contact the site owners to find out their levels of satisfaction with those CDNs.

Get a list of supported formats and file types. Some CDNs support only images, and some support only certain streaming formats. Some vendors support only certain formats in certain countries.

TIP Make sure prospective CDNs support the file types and streaming formats you intend to use, and that they operate edge servers capable of handling those content types in the regions from which your visitors will access your web site.

Determine how CDNs deliver content to AOL. If your site caters to consumers and you've ever analyzed your log files, you may have noticed that as much as 40 percent of your traffic seems to come from Manassas, Virginia. That's the home of America Online (AOL). All of AOL's users reach your web site through AOL's elaborate caching system, so if AOL's users are important to you, pay special attention to how well a CDN delivers content to AOL users.

TIP If consumers are important to your business, ask prospective CDNs how they optimize content delivery to AOL users.

Review financial stability. Like the dot-com fallout in 2000–2001, not all CDN vendors will survive. Even if a vendor can keep itself alive, the performance of a network whose owner can't afford to increase the capacity of its edge servers can deteriorate very quickly. If you're not comfortable reading 10-K and 10-Q filings on FreeEDGAR (www.freeedgar.com), get help from someone who is. In particular, look at its available cash (how much money it has in the bank that can be used to operate its business) and its burn rate (how quickly it's spending that money). If it doesn't have enough money in the bank to support its operations for at least six months, ask the vendor how it plans to stay in business.

TIP Evaluate the financial stability of prospective CDNs in the same way as you would a web-hosting service or MSP.

Ask your web-hosting company. In many cases your web-hosting company or MSP will already have a business and technology relationship with one or more CDNs. Not only might that mean better multivendor support, but you may also be able to get better pricing by purchasing CDN services through your hosting vendor.

TIP Include in your evaluation of vendors any CDNs that have relationships with your web-hosting service or MSP. But don't limit your tests to only those CDNs; you may find another that's better for your site.

Whether your web-site configuration is a small one (e.g., hosted on a shared server) or one that fills a large cage, you'll likely be able to benefit from caching or a content delivery network. At the very least, these technologies can improve your visitors' experiences; and if your site is one that will grow substantially, caching and CDNs may be the least expensive way to achieve your scalability objectives.

CDNs are the future of Internet content delivery. CDNs today are adjuncts—add-on optimizations—to centralized web-site architectures. But soon, CDNs and their descendents will no longer be adjuncts to web hosting; they'll replace it. Instead of building a centralized web site or even a distributed one, a web-site owner will create his or her content, data, and code, and simply deliver it to a *content distributor* in much the same way that a television producer delivers a completed TV show to CBS, FOX, or HBO.

Connectivity Practices

The quality of a web-hosting service can be measured in many ways, but no criterion is more critical or as esoteric as how well a web-hosting service is connected to the rest of the Internet. In this chapter we'll look at the *qualitative* issues of connectivity and their impact on web-hosting service policies and practices. We'll explore issues such as *peering* versus *transit* services, internal web-hosting service networks, capacity planning, the nasty practice of *bandwidth choking*, and finally the waterbed theory of network outages. (No reading ahead!)

Later, in Chapter 18, "Connectivity Performance," we'll explore the *quantitative* aspects of web-site connectivity, including performance monitoring and the lower-level measurements of *reachability*, *packet loss*, and *latency* that are helpful in understanding why the connectivity of one vendor is better or worse than that of another.

Multihomed Routing

Unlike a typical Internet data center, your home and office are connected to only a single ISP that provides access to the Internet. When it works, everything's fine. But when that one link goes down, you're completely offline.

For more reliability, you can buy separate connections from two different ISPs and combine them in one of two ways. The first way is *warm standby/failover* mode. In this case, the second link isn't used until the first one fails. The router's decision is a fairly simple all-or-nothing one.

The second method, called *multihomed routing*—in which both links are always active—is more complex. The advantage of this method is that—when both links are active—they can both be used to carry traffic. How does a router decide which link to use for any given transmission? If there's only one active link, there's really no decision: the packet is sent out on the active link. But if there are two active links, the router must be far more sophisticated (i.e., expensive).

Another seemingly small, but very nasty problem with multihomed routing has to do with the ownership of your IP addresses that are now theoretically reachable via two ISPs. If you have only one ISP, you're probably using a block of IP addresses that belong to that ISP. With two ISPs, you have a problem, because the second ISP isn't allowed to tell other Internet routers that you can be reached over its network using the IP addresses that belong to the first ISP. This can be solved, but it's not for the faint of heart. Don't try it at home.

A web-hosting service has the same set of problems, but on a much larger scale than you have in your home or office. For the large web-hosting services, connecting to many ISPs (not just two) is something they deal with on a daily basis. They have little choice. But poor economies of scale make this difficult for the smaller web-hosting services, which is important to consider when evaluating them.

If you want to work with a smaller web-hosting service, try to find one that's colocated within a data center operated by a larger vendor, and that, therefore, depends on the larger vendor for connectivity to the Internet. There is nothing wrong with this arrangement so long as the larger vendor continues to provide high-quality connectivity.

If you decide to use a smaller web-hosting service that operates its own data center, you should dig deeper into its connectivity. Confirm that it has *transit* service (explained in the next section) to at least two ISPs.

Peering versus Transit

Web-hosting services exchange packets with ISPs via two types of arrangements: *peering* and *transit*. There's a lot of debate about which is better. You can talk to one hosting service and come away convinced that peering is best, then speak to another, equally good vendor and change your mind entirely. In fact, there's no right answer to this debate. Peering and transit are primarily business relationships, not technological distinctions. The routers that move packets around the Internet don't know the difference. Certainly, exchange points may be more or less efficient, but it's not due to the distinction between peering and transit.

Transit is the simplest and most fundamental service for which you pay an ISP for a connection to the Internet. In exchange for a fee, the ISP guarantees to accept packets bound for any host on the Internet, and to provide a return path for any packets trying to reach you. The amount you pay is somehow related to the volume of traffic you send and receive. For example, you may pay based on the raw speed of the connection or according to the amount of data actually transmitted to and from your location.

When a business or consumer customer buys transit service, it's called *access*. This is the service that most of us use from our homes and offices to reach the Internet. Anyone can buy transit/access services from a wide variety of ISPs. Transit may be used for any application, including general access to the Internet and web-server hosting. Most web-hosting

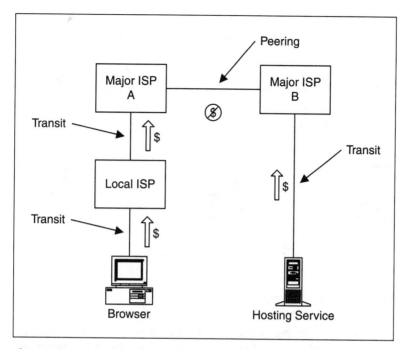

Figure 14.1 Transit and peering.

services (particularly those not operated by the ISPs themselves) buy transit services from one or more ISPs to carry Internet traffic to and from their customers' web servers.

If you purchase transit from a local or regional ISP, that vendor will, in turn, buy transit service from a larger ISP, and so on up the Internet food chain. But there's no "master" ISP at the top from which the major ISPs all buy transit services. Instead, the major ISPs have had to figure out a way to exchange packets in order to guarantee that all of their transit customers can reach one another. Because the major ISPs consider themselves peers of one another, the arrangements to exchange packets are known as *peering*.

Figure 14.1 illustrates a typical situation involving both peering and transit. The arrows with the dollar signs indicate who pays whom. The site visitor (Browser) pays his or her local ISP for transit services. That local ISP in turn purchases transit services from a major ISP (A). The hosting service purchases transit services from a different major ISP (B).

The two major ISPs, A and B, both have responsibility to effect delivery on behalf of their transit customers, so they've agreed to a peering relationship that permits them to exchange packets with one another without the exchange of money.

Peering is a relationship that's usually limited to ISPs, since pure web-hosting services aren't considered peers by the ISPs. However, some web-hosting services do have opportunities "to peer" with ISPs. This occurs in the following three situations:

- Some major ISPs themselves offer web hosting, so their web-hosting traffic gets to piggyback on their existing peering relationships.

- Some large web-hosting services have national or international backbone networks that effectively make them ISPs. They're therefore able to negotiate peering agreements with other major ISPs.

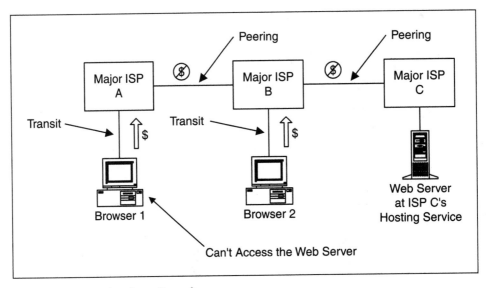

Figure 14.2 Peering doesn't reach everyone.

- Some intermediate-sized web-hosting services peer with local or regional ISPs and hence bypass the major ISPs for moving that portion of their traffic that doesn't require long-distance transmission.

An important point to remember about peering is that it provides access only to customers who buy transit from the peering partner. For example, if a web-hosting service has a peering relationship with Sprint, that link can only be used to reach Sprint's transit customers. It can't be used to reach customers of other ISPs.

This restriction of peering is illustrated in Figure 14.2 where ISP B peers with both of its neighbors, A and C. Browser 2 (a transit customer of ISP B) can reach the web server hosted by ISP C through the peering between ISPs B and C. Browser 1 (a transit customer of ISP A), however, can't reach the web site. ISP B uses its peering relationships only for the benefit of its transit customers who pay for the privilege. ISP B won't carry traffic between ISPs A and C because it isn't compensated for doing so. As long as a web-hosting service is buying transit service instead of (or in addition to) depending on peering, however, it can count on being able to use that service to reach the downstream customers of *all* ISPs.

The starting point for any new web-hosting service is to purchase transit service from a single ISP. The next step—and what you should consider to be the minimum requirement for your web-hosting service—is for that web-hosting service to also purchase transit service from a second ISP. Without at least two transit services, the loss of a single transit connection will always cause some subset of Internet users to be unable to reach your web site.

It's not possible to reach all customers on the Internet through peering alone. No matter how many peering relationships a web-hosting service may have, some ISPs will not be included. Therefore, at least one transit relationship is always required in order to guarantee that all users can reach your site. A second transit service is the only way to guarantee that a single failure cannot make your site inaccessible to some visitors.

TIP Don't use a web-hosting service that doesn't purchase transit service from at least two major ISPs unless the web-hosting service is, itself, one of the major ISPs.

Internal Networks

Some web-hosting vendors operate multiple data centers, possibly one on each coast of the United States. Others have a half-dozen or more strategically placed around the world. And then there are folks like IBM, which, at the time of this writing, had 130 data centers worldwide, 60 of which handled web hosting.

Most of these web-hosting services operate some sort of private network between their data centers. These *internal networks* may be for administrative purposes only or they may be full-fledged international backbones, capable of carrying all sorts of Internet traffic.

If the architecture of your web site is distributed (i.e., you have servers at multiple data centers or you use a CDN), your vendor's internal network is indeed important, and you should evaluate it as thoroughly as you do other aspects of your vendor's connectivity.

But if all of your content is served from a single location (as is the case for the vast majority of web sites), such interfacility networks are, in fact, of little value; therefore, it's best not to attribute much importance to vendors' claims regarding their internal networks.

What's more important is how well the data center in which *your* web servers are located is connected to your customers and other web-site visitors. In most cases, a link to another facility owned by the same vendor doesn't help accomplish this.

If your web-hosting service has a direct link to the major ISP that also provides transit services to your customers, you want to be connected to *that* link as directly as possible. If the link to that ISP occurs at a data center other than the one in which your servers are located, your traffic may depend on your vendor's internal network to reach that ISP. While the vendor may claim the benefit of the direct connection to that ISP, it's not truly direct as far as your web site is concerned.

When evaluating a web-hosting vendor's claims for its internal network, the question to ask is when, if ever, will data to or from your web site actually travel on your web-hosting service's own backbone. The following are four possible answers:

Never. If the web-hosting service's network is for administrative purposes only, it will never carry your web site's traffic. This is okay. It just means that you need to evaluate the connectivity between the data center where your site will live and the major ISPs.

For distributed architectures. If your site is based on a distributed architecture or a CDN, and a single vendor hosts all your remote locations or edge servers, you'll be dependent on that vendor's internal network for the replication of content between databases or edge servers (which were described in more detail in Chapter 13, "Caching and Content Delivery Networks") or for database or commerce transactions. Evaluate the internal network thoroughly.

Always. If the web-hosting vendor is either a major ISP itself, or has built an ISP-grade backbone in order to justify its peering relationships by carrying its share of long-haul traffic, your data *will* traverse the vendor's internal network. Again, this isn't a bad idea, but you need to check out the web-hosting service's network as thoroughly as you would that of a major ISP.

Sometimes. This is the worst possible answer. In this scenario, the web-hosting vendor proudly tells you that your traffic will be carried by its backbone in case of failures of the direct links between any of the major ISPs and the data center in which your web site is housed. This implies that the web-hosting vendor has configured its routers so that if, for example, its link to Sprint goes down, traffic destined for Sprint customers will instead be sent over the web-hosting vendor's network to another one of its data centers and be put onto the Sprint network from there.

It all *sounds* good, and it *is* an extra level of redundancy. But the first problem is that since a "standby" connection such as the one described in the "sometimes" scenario isn't used all day, every day, it's difficult to know how well it will work when it's really needed. Second, suppose the extent of the outage at the data center in which your web site is housed is so substantial that the standby links to the vendor's other data centers are inadequate for the load. Not all failures are as simple as the loss of a connection to a single ISP. For example, one fiber cut can take down many transit links, and possibly overwhelm the standby links.

If a web-hosting service offers the "sometimes" scenario, does it have enough capacity in its internal network to handle outages such as these? It would be surprising if the answer were yes, for what vendor can afford to keep a network like that available in standby mode all the time? The "never" and "always" strategies are much more economical for the vendor, and hence are probably better for you as well.

> **TIP** If a vendor has multiple, linked data centers, ask how those connections are used. The best answers are "never," "always," and "for distributed architectures." Stay away from "sometimes."

See Chapter 17, "Security," for a discussion of the security aspects of internal networks.

Satellite Data Centers

Another problem related to internal networks is the one of *satellite data centers*—data centers that receive some or all of their connectivity from other data centers rather than directly from ISPs. The clue that a data center may be a satellite data center, as opposed to a primary one, is when the web-hosting service brags that it doesn't have just one, but *two* data centers in the same metropolitan area.

Why would they do that? Simple. They had more business than they could handle in the first one, so they built another. Or perhaps they acquired another vendor with facilities in the same area.

Like the internal network, it *sounds* great. Your web site gets the privilege of being located in the new data center. The vendor has learned a lot from running its first data center, and the new one is much better. It also has more expansion space, should you need it. If you dig deeper, the conversation may go something like this:

"But how is that data center connected to the Internet?" you ask.

"Ah! We have three OC-12s coming into this town from three major ISPs," the vendor replies.

"Show me where they enter the building."

"Well, they actually come into our *old* data center; then we have redundant connections between the buildings, each at different physical points of entry."

It's not a bad answer. The extra hop between your servers and the Internet will probably go through a fast switch, so the latency will not be significant.

The real issue is one of reliability. Although the satellite data center may be reliable enough to meet your needs, the fact that there's yet another link and another set of routers or switches to maintain means that it probably isn't quite so reliable as the older, primary data center. This isn't the worst situation, but all other things being equal, it would be better not to be in a satellite data center.

Figure 14.3 shows two fully independent data centers. A failure in one will not affect the other. They are as independent as if separate vendors operated them.

Figure 14.4 illustrates the satellite (or *secondary*) data center problem. Data center B is dependent on data center A, but not vice versa.

Figure 14.5 illustrates a similar problem in which the data centers are codependent. An outage in either facility will affect the other. Neither of these is actually a satellite of the other, nor is either of them fully independent.

TIP Ask a prospective vendor if it has more than one data center in the area. If so, investigate how the data centers are connected to one another, and where the links to the major ISPs enter each of the buildings. Try to locate your servers in a facility that is as independent as possible from problems in another facility.

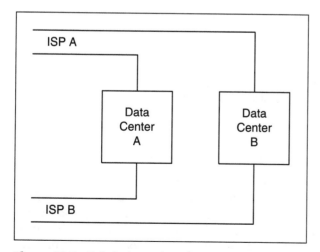

Figure 14.3 Fully independent data centers.

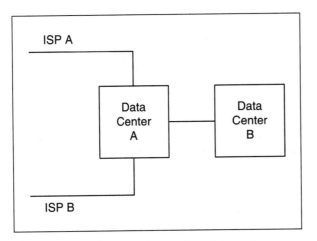

Figure 14.4   Primary and secondary data centers.

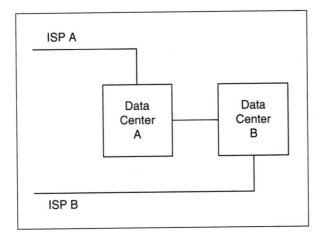

Figure 14.5   Codependent data centers.

There's nothing fundamentally wrong with keeping your servers in a satellite data center. Just make sure to check it out as described in this section.

Capacity Planning

As the Internet continues to grow, and as more and more users upgrade to DSL and cable access, every web-hosting service must continually increase and improve the capacity of its connectivity. To get it right requires sophisticated forecasting and experience. Many web-hosting services have been caught flat-footed, victims of their own success, and unable to add bandwidth to their data centers in order to keep up with their customers' requirements. Many customers have been trapped by web-hosting services that can't handle increases in traffic, a situation that forces customers to either move or add their own, independent Internet connections.

Generally, this problem is most common among the smaller web-hosting services, but that's not always the case. Many of the major web-hosting services—some even run by the top-tier ISPs—have, at one time or another, not kept up with their customers' demand for bandwidth.

In evaluating a vendor's capacity planning practices, there's no magic number, but a good guideline is for a web-hosting service to never let any link peak at more than one-third of its total capacity. This is referred to as a *capacity/load ratio* of at least 3:1. For example, a DS-3 circuit has a data rate of 45 Mbps (megabits per second). If the traffic on a DS-3 exceeds 15 Mbps, the web-hosting service should upgrade that link to at least the next level, an OC-3 link that runs at 155 Mbps.

One major web-hosting service (Exodus) reported that at the end of 2000 all of its data centers combined had a capacity of 73 Gbps (gigabits per second), and that according to the 95th Percentile Rule it was using 14.5 Gbps (a capacity/load ratio of 5:1) *averaged* across all of its links. While that's an excellent number (well above the 3:1 guideline), it doesn't guarantee that some of the *individual* links aren't overloaded.

> **TIP** Ask your vendor what its policies are for upgrading the speed of its links. They should have such a policy in writing. Better yet, get an SLA that states that any link that exceeds one-third of its capacity when measured using a monthly 95th Percentile Rule will promptly be upgraded.

No matter how small a web-hosting service's data center may be, your site should never be connected to the Internet via anything slower than a DS3. If your site is small, you might think a T1 (1.544 Mbps) would be adequate. But suppose you have just one visitor at a time and that visitor has a 6 Mbps DSL or cable Internet connection? In that case, your web site's connection to the Internet will be the weakest (slowest) link in the chain. Your site will look slow to this visitor, even if you have a T1 line all to yourself. T1 links that cost on the order of $1,200 per month were considered *commercial grade* connections for many years. But once DSL allowed consumers and businesses to access the web at T1 speeds or higher for just a few hundred dollars per month or less, T1s became useless for web hosting.

> **TIP** Don't use a web-hosting service that has any link slower than a DS-3.

On the other hand, don't be too easily impressed by vendors' claims that, for example, it has "multiple OC-12s." Once the lines are at least DS-3s (45 Mbps) it's the peak load, not the raw speed that matters. A small web-hosting service with a near-idle DS-3 can provide better connectivity than a large service with multiple, heavily-loaded OC-12s.

Data Rates and 3:1 Capacity/Load Levels

Table 14.1 shows the data rates and 3:1 capacity/load levels for the most common data services used by web-hosting services.

Table 14.1   Common Data Rates

DESIGNATION	DATA RATE	3:1 CAPACITY/LOAD
T1/DS-1	1.54 Mbps	514 Kbps
T3/DS-3	45 Mbps	15 Mbps
OC-3	155 Mbps	51.7 Mbps
OC-12	622 Mbps	207 Mbps
OC-24	1.24 Gbps	415 Mbps
OC-48	2.45 Gbps	817 Mbps
OC-96	4.98 Gbps	1.66 Gbps

TIP Evaluate vendors' connectivity by capacity/load ratio, not by capacity alone.

Bandwidth Choking

Just as you shouldn't select a web-hosting service that uses circuits slower than DS-3s, you should also avoid any web-hosting service that uses any type of *bandwidth-choking* technology. In an effort to enforce peak bandwidth limits, some web-hosting services use these technologies to *throttle* or *choke* the burst bandwidth your web site can access.

One bandwidth-choking scheme creates *virtual T1s* that insert a link that can't exceed 1.544 Mbps between your servers and the web-hosting service's router. Other schemes use router features and configurations to limit the throughput on individual ports.

Your servers should have at least a 100 Mbps connection to your web-hosting service's router or switch, and an unrestricted, high-speed path from there to the Internet. If you're paying for bandwidth according to the total number of bytes transferred each month, there's no reason the web-hosting service should limit how many of those bytes you pump out over a short period of time. Likewise, if you're paying for bandwidth using the 95th Percentile Rule, let the rule work. If your site needs the next increment of bandwidth more than 5 percent of the time, make sure it's available. The 5 percent window should be enough to protect you from being charged for outrageously high and rare peaks.

TIP Don't use a web-hosting service that makes use of any bandwidth-choking technologies.

Price

As with everything else, price is also an important criterion when evaluating web-hosting services. Figure 14.6 illustrates the range of pricing for bandwidth using the 95th Percentile Rule. The costs shown are per month per megabit per second.

ISP transit service, such as you'd purchase for your office, can cost as much as $1,500 per month per Mbps if purchased at low volume such as 1 Mbps or 2 Mbps. If you start

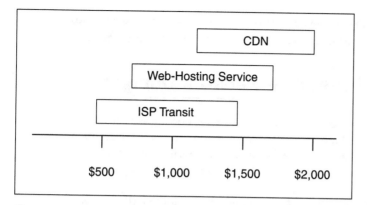

Figure 14.6 Bandwidth pricing (per Mbps per month, 95th Percentile Rule).

purchasing bandwidth at the level of DS-3s, you can find it for as little as $400 per Mbps, and if you step up to an OC-3, the price can drop to $250 per Mbps.

Bandwidth purchased from web-hosting services costs more than when purchased directly from an ISP. The reasons for this are (a) the web-hosting service provides a higher level of management, (b) the service includes the web-hosting company's router, so you get a direct 100 Mbps link, and (c) the service includes redundant (multi-home) routing, whereas transit service from a single ISP is less redundant. At low volumes (1 or 2 Mbps) you can pay as much as $1,700 per Mbps to web-hosting services. At much higher volumes the price decreases to as low as $700 per Mbps.

At the high end of the spectrum, content delivery networks will deliver your data for prices in the range of $1,500 to $2,000 per Mbps. CDNs were discussed in detail in Chapter 13.

TIP Be aware of the market pricing for bandwidth. It's a commodity, and prices continue to drop.

Bandwidth Lowballing

Be particularly careful about the bandwidth component of your pricing. If you exceed your monthly limit, you may be charged very high *bandwidth overage fees*. Whether you're paying for bandwidth using the 95th Percentile Rule (used by colocation and managed service providers) or according to actual data transferred (used by shared- and dedicated-server vendors), your hosting package will include a certain base level of monthly bandwidth. This might, for instance, be 5 GB per month for shared-server hosting, or 2 Mbps per cabinet for colocation.

There will also be a separate charge (the overage fee) for any bandwidth you use above and beyond the base level called for in your agreement. Sometimes the rate for bandwidth overages is exorbitant. Customers often don't notice this, because they're focused on the base rate and perhaps assume their needs will never grow to require additional bandwidth.

Study the details. Some vendors include a very low level of bundled bandwidth in their packages, and make their money on the overages.

TIP Plan for (or at least consider) success. Calculate what you'll pay for bandwidth if your web site is successful beyond your wildest dreams.

The Waterbed Theory of Network Outages

One phenomenon I've noticed is that whenever ISPs, hosting services, or web sites experience outages of one kind or another, competitors rarely criticize them, although you might hear about it behind closed doors. When Sprint, for example, has a failure, WorldCom doesn't point at them and gloat. Why? Because it's only a matter of time before it happens to them.

Network problems remind me of the bubbles in a waterbed. (If the analogy doesn't work, you obviously didn't have a waterbed in the '60s or '70s.) When bubbles appeared in one part of the bed, you could try to make them go away by pressing down on the bed at that point. This was a futile process, however, as the bubbles simply popped up in another part of the bed. They never really went away.

Until we can come up with a worldwide replacement for the asphalt-digging backhoe (the Internet's single greatest enemy), outages will continue to be a fact of life. No ISP, and therefore no hosting service or web site, will be immune to them.

I mention this as a caveat. The most informative time to evaluate the Internet infrastructure is when there's a problem—when it's possible to see how well the Internet body is responding to an injury. It's all too easy to find the current culprit (or victim) ISPs and chastise them, but because of the waterbed phenomenon, this approach solves nothing. More valuable is to analyze any vendor or situation over an extended period of time, at least many days, and preferably months.

I remember helping a client select a hosting facility one autumn. I did my research in September and made my recommendation in October. This location looked terrific: a world-class data center and all the connectivity and redundant fiber one could want. The servers were installed in November and went live in December.

In three months, the bubble in the waterbed had moved. The hosting service had failed to keep up with its bandwidth expansion plan, and by the time this web site moved in, the hosting service was experiencing terrible packet loss on many of its most critical links. My due diligence was for naught. Even with the best of intentions and methods, I was unable to predict that it was now this hosting service's time to suffer.

Unfortunately, because it takes so long to provision large bandwidth pipes such as OC-12s and OC-48s, and because this particular hosting service was so far behind the eight ball, it took more than six months for it to resolve its problems. In the meantime, my client had no alternative but to bring in additional transit service from an outside ISP to work around the problem.

From this lesson I hope you'll learn to (a) make your evaluations over as long a period as possible, (b) dig into your prospective hosting service's *policies* for proactively upgrading their bandwidth, and (c) recognize that no amount of due diligence can prevent all problems.

In this chapter we've considered connectivity that is external to an Internet data center. Increasingly, however, networks are being used not only within a data center, but between servers and storage subsystems. In the next chapter we'll look at the rapidly evolving world of storage technologies, and consider how to best utilize them for your web site.

Most web-site owners don't think of storage as a discrete service provided by their web-hosting vendor. Indeed, storage for the vast majority of web sites means no more than a disk drive or two. But at the high end of the market—for sites with 100 GB or more of content and data—the world of storage is changing rapidly.

In this chapter we'll look at the four storage technologies that are used for Internet applications:

Direct attached storage (DAS). The common individual disk drives or arrays directly connected to an individual server.

Network attached storage (NAS). High-performance general-purpose file servers connected to web-site servers via LANs.

Storage area networks (SAN). Ultra-high-performance special-purpose storage systems.

Global storage systems (GSS). A technology for geographically replicated file systems.

Table 15.1 presents a summary of the suitability of each of the storage technologies to the requirement of capacity and the capability to handle static content, shared read/write files, and databases.

Table 15.1 Storage Technologies

	CAPACITY	FOR STATIC CONTENT	FOR SHARED READS/WRITES	FOR DATABASES
DAS	<= 200 GB	Yes (for one or two web servers in a single location)	No	Yes (good reliability if RAID is used)
NAS	<= 10 TB	Yes (for more than one server in a single location or for more than 200 GB)	Yes	Yes (high reliability if clustered)
SAN	100 GB–100 TB	No (too expensive)	No	Yes (high reliability)
GSS	300 GB–100 TB	Yes (for more than one location or in conjunction with a CDN)	Yes	No

*NOTE The capacity assumptions in Table 15.1 and throughout this chapter assume that the largest standard disk drive is in the 70 GB range. As the size of drives continues to increase, so will the maximum capacity of DAS and other storage technologies.

We'll begin our exploration of storage with an overview of Redundant Array of Inexpensive Disks (RAID) then consider each of the technologies listed in Table 15.1 in detail.

RAID

Virtually all storage systems that include more than one disk drive are based on the brilliant invention of RAID. In 1987, David Patterson, Garth Gibson, and Randy Katz—three University of California graduate students—proved how these configurations of multiple, small, cheap disk drives could outperform larger, more expensive Single Large Expensive Disks (SLEDs).

Furthermore, RAID systems provide greater reliability. Although a single disk drive may have a mean time to failure (MTTF) of 100,000 hours (11-plus years), the equivalent mean time to data loss (MTTDL) for a RAID system can be as high as 2.5 *billion* hours (or more than 250,000 years), as long as one replaces a redundant drive within an hour of its failure. Table 15.2 highlights the features of each of the RAID configurations. Note that only RAID-0 (no redundancy), RAID-1 (mirroring), RAID-0+1, and RAID-5 are typically used in web-site applications.

Interfaces

The storage systems we'll examine use a variety of SCSI and LAN interfaces to connect servers to disks and disk subsystems. Table 15.3 shows the speeds of the various interfaces.

Table 15.2 RAID Configurations

	STRENGTHS	**WEAKNESSES**	**WEB-SITE APPLICATION**
RAID-0 (Striping)	Fast	Low reliability	Only if additional redundancy is provided through multiple servers
RAID-1 (Mirroring)	Fast	Expensive (always doubles the number of disk drives)	For high reliability if datasets are small enough to fit on a single disk drive
RAID-0+1	Fastest of all	Expensive (same cost as RAID-1)	For high speed, high reliability, and high capacity
RAID-2	None	Complex	None
RAID-3	Fast	Slow random access	None
RAID-4	Fast sequential reads and writes and random reads	Slow random writes	None
RAID-5	Fast reads; inexpensive	Slow writes	Mostly read file systems and databases
RAID-6	More reliable than RAID-5	Very slow writes	None

Table 15.3 Interface Transfer Speeds

INTERFACE	**TRANSFER SPEED**
10baseT (Ethernet)	1.25 MB/sec
SCSI-1	4 MB/sec
Fast SCSI	10 MB/sec
100baseT LAN	12.5 MB/sec
Ultra SCSI	20 MB/sec
Fast/Wide SCSI	20 MB/sec
Ultra2 SCSI	40 MB/sec
Ultra-Wide SCSI (SCSI-3)	40 MB/sec
Wide Ultra2 SCSI	80 MB/sec
Fibre Channel	100 MB/sec
Gigabit Ethernet	128 MB/sec

Note that even the fastest SCSI interface (wide ultra2 SCSI) is 38 percent slower than gigabit Ethernet. But also consider that if multiple drives in a RAID system are each connected to their own bus, the resulting performance may be equal to the total speed of all the busses combined, depending on the type of RAID used. For instance, three wide ultra2 SCSI disk drives in a RAID-0 configuration or six such drives in RAID-0+1, connected to separate interfaces, can achieve transfer rates as high as 3×80 MB/sec, or 240 MB/sec.

Direct Attached Storage

DAS is just a fancy name for the familiar disk drives we use in most of our desktop computer systems and servers alike. As illustrated in Figure 15.1, DAS drives are installed within servers (*internal*) on a SCSI bus, or connected to those servers via SCSI or Fibre Channel cables (*external*). The disks may be configured as standalone drives or in one of the various RAID configurations described in Chapter 12, "Web-Site Architectures."

The largest storage system you can build using DAS depends on how you achieve redundancy. As we discussed in Chapter 12, there are two ways to do this. If you have only one server of each type—for example, one web server or one database server—you must create redundancy *within* that server by using RAID. However, if you have multiple servers—say, two or more web servers or two or more application servers—you can build your systems without RAID and rely on the redundancy afforded by the multiple servers. In other words, if you have only one server in a given role, you need to make sure it has its own redundancy. But when you have more than one server in a role, then you have the option of *not* using redundant disks with each server, thereby saving the cost of extra disk drives. With this configuration you accept that a disk failure will bring down an entire server, and you rely on the other server(s) to carry the load until the failed drive is replaced and its content restored.

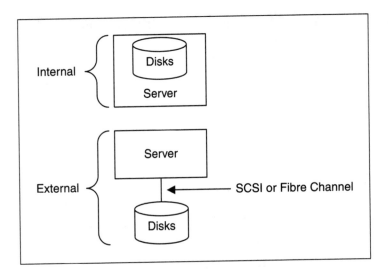

Figure 15.1   Direct attached storage (DAS).

As the capacity of disk drives continues to increase, so does the maximum size of storage systems for which DAS is appropriate. A typical RAID-0+1 (mirrored-striping) configuration with six 36.7 GB drives provides 110 GB of usable storage. Six 73.4 GB drives deliver a usable 220 GB. Without per-server redundancy, seven 73.4 GB drives can be used to provide more than 500 GB of usable space.

DAS, particularly with a RAID-0+1 configuration, can be used for high-performance single-server databases up to 200 GB or so. But because only one server can access a DAS system, DAS isn't appropriate for use with database clusters—that is, multiple database servers.

Likewise, since multiple web servers can't share a single DAS system, each server must have its own storage. If two or more servers must access a single storage system, DAS won't work, and you should consider one of the other storage technologies.

TIP Use DAS unless you (a) have more than 200 GB of data, (b) need access to a single file system from multiple servers, or (c) need very high performance.

Network Attached Storage

All but one of DAS's limitations are addressed by NAS. NAS systems can be larger and faster than most DAS, and they can be shared by multiple servers. The only thing NAS doesn't offer is built-in geographic redundancy. A typical NAS configuration is illustrated in Figure 15.2.

NAS is implemented in dedicated file servers that are attached to web, application, or database servers using a dedicated high-speed local area network connection. (For security and performance reasons, the LAN used for NAS shouldn't also be used for other purposes such as server-to-server interconnection.) If you use a gigabit Ethernet LAN (128 MB per second), you can read and write data faster using a NAS server than you can with single-controller DAS configurations.

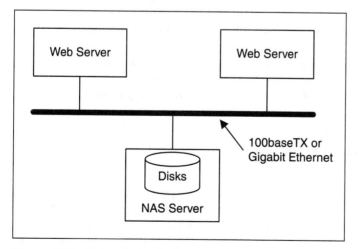

Figure 15.2   Network attached storage (NAS).

You can configure NAS servers from standard components or you can buy NAS servers as preconfigured, turnkey *appliances*. These appliances include a wide range of features and management tools that would take much longer to assemble and configure individually.

In addition to improved performance and appliancelike convenience, NAS offers the following advantages over DAS:

Higher capacity. Using clustering, NAS systems can be configured with as much as 10 terabytes (TB) of storage. Although DAS storage can support many hundreds of gigabytes, NAS is typically used instead for applications requiring more than 200 GB.

Data sharing. NAS supports the same sharable file-locking capabilities that exist for multiple applications sharing DAS on a single server. But because a NAS server is on the LAN, it can be reached by applications on different servers. For instance, if you have two or more web servers attached to a single NAS file server, you only need to update a single copy of an image or other file for the new content to then be available to all web servers. Note, however, that NAS servers are not appropriate for storing database files for multiple database servers unless you're also using specialized database-clustering software and hardware.

Multiple OS access. NAS servers can be used by Unix servers as NFS (Network File Service) devices or by Windows servers as Common Internet File System (CIFS) devices. NAS servers even appear as NFS and CIFS servers *simultaneously*, allowing for real-time file sharing between Unix and Windows systems.

Snapshots. Many NAS servers include *snapshot* capabilities that allow versions of the contents of the file system to be frozen in time. There are three important uses for snapshots. First, they allow applications to read old versions of files. Second, it's an excellent way to manage backups. By creating a snapshot, one can then back up the snapshot so as not to interfere with the ongoing reads and writes to the live data. Third, snapshots can be used as the basis for mirroring multiple NAS servers by synchronizing the snapshot between them.

> **TIP** Use NAS if you have between 200 GB and 10 TB of data or you need access to a single file system from both Unix and Windows operating systems.

NAS is an excellent storage technology when the majority of the operations are *reads* as opposed to *writes*. This makes NAS servers ideal for the storage of static content such as images and streaming-data files, or databases that are entirely or mostly read-only, such as catalogs.

Storage Attached Networks

The one application for which NAS is weak is as a storage system attached to a transactional database, one that performs at least a moderate amount of write/update operations. A newer technology, called—somewhat confusingly—SAN addresses this requirement. Like many NAS servers, SAN systems are sold as complete ready-to-go appliances. The architecture of a SAN is shown in Figure 15.3.

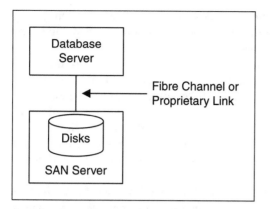

Figure 15.3 Storage attached network (SAN).

Unlike NAS servers that are based on standard file-service protocols (NFC and CIFS), SAN servers are proprietary systems that are specially tailored to mate with specific server hardware and software for maximum performance.

The primary application for SAN-based systems is not web sites, but rather large, complex, corporate back-end applications. As you might expect, this enterprise class solution carries a hefty price tag, and usually comes complete with its own staff of on-call technicians.

There are three situations in which SANs may be appropriate for use with your web site:

Corporate databases. If your web site is driven by a database that supports nonweb applications, that database may already be using a SAN, in which case it will, de facto, be part of your web site.

Transactional databases. SAN storage will support web sites built on transactional databases that require (a) higher reliability and read/write performance than you can achieve with NAS, or (b) more than the 200 GB of usable storage you can expect from DAS.

Storage farms. Some web-hosting vendors offer storage services based on SAN technology (see the next section on storage service providers for further discussion).

TIP Use SAN-based storage for database servers and clusters if you need (a) maximum performance and reliability, (b) more than 200 GB of database storage, or (c) a significant volume of write/update operations. Stick with DAS and NAS for the storage of static content, and DAS for smaller databases.

Storage Service Providers

In the same way that managed service providers (MSPs) offer to manage your web site, an even newer group of *storage service providers*—SSPs, of course—will manage your storage. As with the SANs that SSPs typically manage, the target market for SSPs is not web sites, but rather the traditional, large-scale, back-end, database-driven applications that are common in Fortune 500 companies. Very few Internet-only applications justify the use of an SSP, and certainly the vast majority of web sites don't need storage to be managed independently from other services.

Some SSPs create large *storage farms* at the data centers of one or more of the major colocation vendors. From there, these SSPs connect their storage systems to your web servers using high-speed fiber. In some cases, an SSP's storage farm will be located in the same building as your web site. In other cases, your web site will be in a different location, and hence require a longer (but still very high-speed) fiber connection to reach the storage farm. Some SSPs also offer to manage your private storage systems that you buy or lease from the SSP and that are located alongside your other servers, perhaps in your corporate data center.

Some MSPs and colocation vendors offer *shared* managed storage themselves or through a third-party arrangement with an SSP. However, very few web-site owners find this to be an attractive solution. Typically, any web-site owner who needs storage on the scale of a NAS or SAN server, finds that he or she doesn't want to share storage with other web sites. So while managed storage makes sense for web-hosting vendors (it lowers their costs and adds another source of revenues), it doesn't make sense for their customers.

If you need an SSP for other corporate storage needs, there's no reason not to include your web site within the scope of what the SSP manages. However, there's rarely a reason to use an SSP for only your online applications.

> **TIP** Don't use an SSP for your web site unless you have truly extraordinary storage or uptime requirements. Even then, consider that management of your storage may be a core competency that you must maintain in house.

Global Storage Systems

GSSs are a recent development in high-end storage, and they're a particularly good option for web-hosting applications with large volumes of static or streaming content. The architecture of a GSS system is illustrated in Figure 15.4.

A GSS is essentially a *distributed NAS*. It offers transparent access to a single geographically redundant virtual file system via multiple NAS-like storage cache servers located anywhere in the world. That's a bit of a mouthful, but it will make sense after looking at a GSS piece by piece. A GSS consists of the following:

GSS storage site. GSS vendors build large storage farms (GSS Storage Sites in Figure 15.4) at multiple locations. The number of locations ranges from as few as two to as many as a dozen or so. Each GSS storage site contains a complete copy of your files.

GSS cache server. At each location where you want access to your data, you install a *GSS cache server*. This device appears to your other servers as though it were a standard NAS server, except that it has a *virtual capacity* (on the GSS storage sites) of 100 terabytes and a large local cache. A web server or other client attached to the GSS cache server can read and write files using the same NFS and CIFS pro-

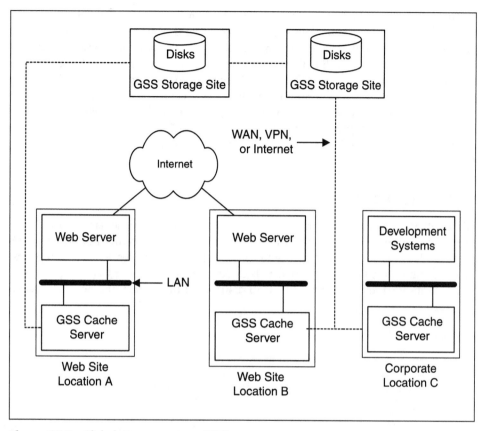

Figure 15.4   Global storage system (GSS).

tocols it would use if it were communicating with a standard NAS server. Invisible to these clients, the GSS cache server communicates via a high-speed VPN connection to the remote GSS storage sites.

When a GSS cache server receives a read request for a file not already in its cache, it transmits the request via the virtual private network (VPN) to the topologically closest GSS storage site. The storage site returns the requested data over the VPN to the GSS cache server that, in turn, delivers the data to the requesting web server or other client. Likewise, when a GSS cache server receives a write request, it's communicated to all GSS storage locations so that each one can maintain a current copy of the data.

You can install GSS cache servers at as many locations as you like, anywhere in the world, and each one will present its local clients with the same high-speed view of your file system. Your data is stored redundantly and at multiple locations, so there's no need for a backup and recovery system other than to protect you from unintentional deletes that would, of course, be propagated to all GSS storage sites. Depending on a GSS cache server's location and its connection to the Internet (and hence the VPN), data stored in this manner can be accessed nearly as quickly as data stored on a local NAS server. This requires that the GSS storage site and the GSS cache server be connected via a route with no links slower than OC-3 (155 Mbps).

The GSS model allows transparent access to files from multiple locations, and like NAS, GSS supports both Unix and Windows operating systems. You can have a Unix server in one country accessing the same files as a Windows server in another, all transparently.

The one limitation of GSS is that it can't be used as storage for a database, for two reasons. First, databases require block-level access to the storage system, and a GSS is based on file-level access. Second, the GSS latencies over a WAN, VPN, or the Internet are too great for the high-volume transaction processing that's required to support databases. GSS is a *distributed file system,* not a distributed database, and updates are not truly real-time. That is, it takes a while for changes to propagate from one GSS site to another.

GSS HTTP Access

Although many applications can use GSS storage, web sites in particular can use GSS in an even more valuable way, as illustrated in Figure 15.5. In this configuration, each GSS site includes a farm of web servers, and can therefore deliver files such as web pages, images, or multimedia objects *directly* to browsers, cache servers, or CDN edge servers.

For example, the file stored in the GSS distributed file system and accessible via a GSS cache server as:

```
/images/logo.gif
```

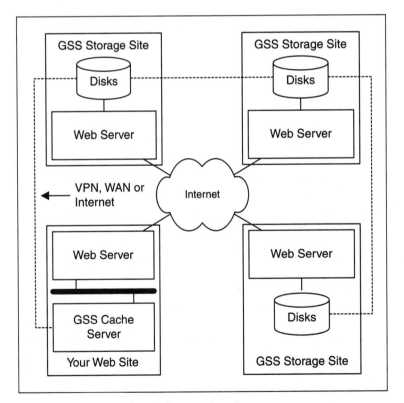

Figure 15.5   GSS with a web-server interface.

can, if permitted, also be accessed from any web browser via a URL similar to the following. The string of digits is an *authentication code:*

```
http://storage.gss-vendor.com/300646025/images/logo.gif
```

This has the simplicity of a content delivery network (discussed in Chapter 13, "Caching and Content Delivery Networks"), but it's not quite the same thing. The GSS storage sites aren't located particularly close to visitors; they're not edge servers. The selection of GSS storage-site locations is instead based on their access to high-speed and high-quality Internet connectivity. This makes a GSS system a great companion for a CDN. You can store your content with a GSS vendor, then use one or more—possibly competing—CDNs to deliver that content. The CDN will treat the GSS storage sites as a single, but distributed, high-speed origin server. The GSS system will cause the CDN to retrieve objects from the topologically closest GSS storage site, just as the CDN does with its own edge servers.

A GSS system is particularly good for large files such as music, video, and medical images. The file system gives you instant mirroring. You also get extraordinary scalability. If the size or quantity of your files increases quickly, it's no problem. You can go from a few hundred gigabytes to a 100-terrabyte file system with no additional capital expense and no advance preparation. You get instant provisioning without the need for forecasting or planning. If you need storage or content delivery for a short time—say, for an event—you won't need to make the one-time extraordinary investment in infrastructure.

GSS vendors base their pricing on two components: the storage of data and the transmission of that data. Prices start at about $30 per gigabyte per month for storage, assuming a 300 GB minimum (i.e., $9,000 per month). Data transfer costs are comparable to those charged by colocation vendors.

> **TIP** If your web site includes more than 300 GB of combined static and streaming content, consider using a GSS, perhaps in combination with a CDN.

In this chapter we've explored a wide range of storage systems that can be used to support web sites, whether those web sites are hosted in house or outsourced. In the next chapter, "Backup and Recovery," we'll look at systems for archiving and backup that can support recovery from failures of the storage systems we just examined, in addition to file and disaster recovery.

Backup and Recovery

Backup and recovery services are among the most frequently ignored topics of web-site outsourcing. By the time most web-site owners get around to thinking about backup and recovery, they typically just check the yes box and move on to the next issue. Unfortunately, many web-hosting services and MSPs haven't given the topic much more thought than these customers. So if you don't invest the time to plan a backup and recovery strategy, you can easily end up paying for services you don't need; or worse, you may learn the hard way that you're not getting the backup and recovery services you do need.

In this chapter we'll first examine the most common vendor-supplied backup and recovery systems and identify their weaknesses. Then we'll look at some of the things that you can do—both with and without involving your web-hosting service or MSP—to improve upon them.

Backup and recovery are easy to do incorrectly and hard to do correctly. Depending on your outsourcer's default backup system to independently handle your requirements is risky at best, and disastrous at worst. While its default system will generally do a reasonable job of backing up a simple static site for disaster recovery purposes, it will *not* properly handle complex sites (such as those containing databases) unless you work closely with the team handling this function to define your requirements for backup. Be prepared to spend significant time and money here, because, as just mentioned, backup/restore is very hard to do correctly!

Archives

Although they're usually referred to as "backups," most of the services you'll find from web-hosting vendors and MSPs are actually *archives,* optimized for disaster recovery and long-term storage of data and intellectual property. Archives are like homeowner's insurance policies: Everyone should have them, but most people will never have to use them.

Archival copies are stored off-site in order to make sure that even if the data center housing your web site is totally destroyed, you'll still have copies of your code, data, and content. All archival systems are, therefore, based on removable media, usually magnetic tape, but in some cases recordable CD-ROMs (CD-R) or Data-DVDs. When tapes are used, they may be erased and recycled, so a good *media-rotation plan* is a critical aspect of most archive systems.

The Typical Approach

Figure 16.1 illustrates the architecture of the archive systems you're most likely to find at a web-hosting service or MSP. The design is fairly straightforward. On a regular basis (typically each night) all of your content, data, and code are copied to removable tape, CD-R, or Data-DVD media. From there, copies are transported to an off-site storage facility for safekeeping. Recovery follows the opposite path. If an appropriate copy isn't on-site, one is retrieved from the off-site facility. In either case, the missing files, database, or complete disk structures are then recovered from the tape/CD/DVD media.

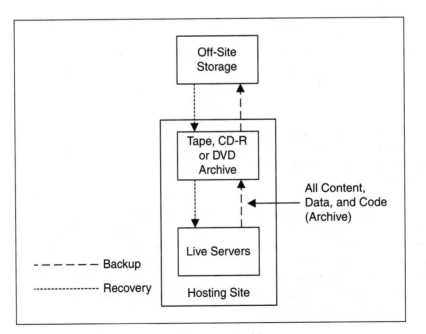

Figure 16.1 Typical backup and recovery architecture.

Most web-hosting vendors and their customers consider this archival form of backup and recovery to be sufficient, so few of them bother to investigate alternatives. But they should. There are some significant problems with this approach that often don't show up until it's too late to correct them. The most severe, the *propagation of corrupted data,* is described next.

Propagation of Corrupted Data

Using an ideal backup strategy, you should be able to recover any version of any file forever. With a *revision control system,* you can do just that, as we'll see later in this chapter. But archiving software packages don't work like revision control systems. Instead, they make *full archives* and *incremental archives.* The incremental archives include all files that have changed since the most recent full archive.

The full/incremental approach makes sense until you consider the problem of *data corruption.* Let's use the manuscript for this book to illustrate this problem. The manuscript is stored in 24 separate Microsoft Word files, one per chapter. The chapters that are currently in development are modified daily, whereas completed chapters may not be touched for weeks or even months at a time. Using the full/incremental method of archiving, one might make a complete tape archive every two weeks and incremental tape archives once a day. Copies of the older chapters would then be on the full archives, and copies of the most recent versions of the more rapidly changing chapters would be on the incremental archives. So far, so good.

Now, consider what happens if the original (disk) version of an older chapter file becomes corrupted—perhaps due to faulty hardware or software—but the corruption goes undetected. The corrupted version of the file will be copied to the next full archive tape. That's okay, though, as long as there's still at least one other, older full archive tape that contains an uncorrupted copy of the file.

But let's see what happens when we add a media-rotation scenario. For instance, let's assume there are only two full-archive tapes and that they're being alternated. (Each week, the tape with the oldest full archive is erased and reused.) Two weeks after the corrupted file is copied to the first full archive tape, the corrupted file will be copied to the second one. At that point, *both* of the full archive tapes will contain the corrupted version of the file, and the uncorrupted version will be lost forever. Since a chapter of the book may go untouched for months, there's no way to know this has occurred until it's too late. You can use more than two full archive tape sets to postpone this problem, but so long as you reuse media, you'll always have some risk of loss due to this *propagation of corrupted data.*

There are two ways to solve this problem. The simplest is to always make full archives and keep all of them forever. In the case of this manuscript (a total of 20 megabytes), that's quite practical since adding a new copy of the entire manuscript to a rewritable CD-ROM (CD-RW) every night requires less than one new $1 disk every 30 days.

Even if you have hundreds of megabytes of content, code, and data, this may be a good strategy for your web site due to the low cost of CD-R media. For example, you can do a full archive of a 1 GB file system every day for a year for less than $500 in media costs, and the required 730 CD-Rs would fit in a one-cubic-foot container. Using this approach, you'll never have to worry about corrupted files. You can recover any day's version of any file, for as long as the CD-Rs last—40 to 250 years.

TIP For maximum protection against the propagation of corrupted data, make full archives daily and keep them forever.

Media Rotation

The second solution is to develop a media-rotation plan that reuses media but that attempts to retain multiple versions of files. Such a solution is less than ideal since there's usually no way to know which versions might be corrupted until you try to read them. So the only reason you should use a media-rotation solution is if the media costs of an always-full/keep-forever archive strategy are prohibitive.

If you can't justify the media costs to make full daily archives and keep them forever, or if your web-hosting service won't do this for you, then you'll have no choice but to adopt a media-rotation plan for the erasure and recycling of your disks or tapes. While no such plan is as simple and as safe as always making and retaining full archives, you can partially reduce the risk of loss due to data corruption by using a *hierarchical* method. Since an always-full/keep-forever strategy is the first choice (Plan A), let's call this rotation strategy Plan B:

- Make a full archive once a month (instead of daily), and retain each monthly archive forever. This reduces your media costs by nearly 30:1.

- Make incremental archives once a day and keep them until you make the next full (end-of-month) archive.

The worst-case risk of Plan B is that if a file becomes corrupted on the last day of a month—that is, just before the next full archive—the most recent uncorrupted version (if any) will be nearly one month old.

If you still can't justify the media costs of Plan B (keeping a full archive for every month) you'll have to rotate your full-archive media as well as your incremental media. You might consider something similar to Plan C:

- Make a full archive once a week.

- Make incremental archives once a day and keep them until you make the next full archive.

- Retain the four most recent full archives (four weeks).

- Retain the last full archive made each calendar month for one year (12 sets).

- Retain the last full archive made each calendar year forever.

Plan C uses approximately 10 times less media than Plan B and roughly 300 times less than Plan A. But it's also a riskier strategy. If a file is corrupted on the last day of a year, for instance, the next-most-recent uncorrupted version will be a year old, if it exists at all.

There are many other media rotation strategies. What's important to realize is that they *all* carry some risk of the propagation of corrupted data.

TIP Make sure your archive strategy addresses undetected data corruption. If you can't afford to retain all your full archives in perpetuity, adopt a plan for media rotation. But be aware that any time you reuse or rotate media you have some risk of loss due to the propagation of corrupted data.

Recovery Performance

Aside from the serious risk of the propagation of corrupted data, the other problem with an archive system is its slow performance. Think of how often you need to recover from a substantial disaster (such as a fire or the complete loss of a server) as opposed to how frequently you need to simply restore an accidentally deleted file or two. Most web-site owners find that the latter requirement occurs far more frequently.

But the typical system just described, including its associated processes and procedures, is optimized for *disaster recovery*, not *file recovery*. With this archival approach to backup and recovery, the relatively common task of recovering a single file or two can be painfully slow.

Consider why you need to back up your data in the first place. The backups have no inherent value in and of themselves. The only reason you make backups at all is for the sake of the *recoveries*. But the two types of recovery, disaster recovery and file recovery, are very different, and a backup system that's optimized for one is usually not very good for the other.

Disaster recovery. This is what first comes to most people's minds when they hear "backup and recovery." Disasters include anything that has the potential to wipe out your entire web site, and perhaps even destroy the server hardware. Such threats include fires, floods, earthquakes, explosions, and malicious attacks. They're characterized by the potential of major losses but they occur relatively infrequently. In other words, disaster recovery is rarely needed but critically important. A system optimized for disaster recovery must be reliable above all else. Speed and convenience are secondary.

File recovery. This is the restoration of individual files or directories that may have been deleted or corrupted by bugs, human error, or other causes. File recoveries occur much more frequently than disaster recoveries. Convenience and speed are the most important characteristics of a system optimized for file recovery. Reliability is somewhat less important so long as a good archival plan is also in place.

Note, by the way, that whether a system is optimized for one type of recovery or the other, it doesn't matter *why* a recovery is necessary. That is, it makes no difference

DATABASE BACKUP AND RECOVERY

Complex databases have their own unique backup and recovery requirements. *Row recovery,* for instance, is the process of restoring one or more rows or records to individual database tables. *Storage checkpointing, block-level incremental backups, transaction logging,* and *storage rollback* are examples of other database-specific technologies.

Database packages and third-party products include specialized backup and recovery utilities that write to and read from the file system, so although an extra step in reading from the file system may be required during a recovery, for the sake of this discussion we'll assume that database recovery lies within the scope of file recovery. This is an oversimplification, however, as a thorough exploration of database backup and recovery is beyond the scope of this book.

whether data is lost due to human error, buggy software, a hardware failure, or a breach of security. When the time comes that you need to recover your data, all that matters is that you can complete the recovery completely, reliably, and as quickly as possible.

TIP Ask prospective vendors how long it will take them to recover a single file from tape. Check their data-recovery SLAs, if they have them.

Most vendors will tell you it will take them a number of hours to recover even a single file. Add a few hours if an archival copy must be retrieved from an off-site storage facility, and you'll see why an archive system that's optimized for disaster recovery is inadequate for file recoveries.

Backup

In this section we'll look at two things you can do to overcome the weaknesses of a web-hosting vendor's archive system. The first is specifically for small, static web sites. It uses your existing development system as an integral part of your backup and recovery strategy. The second is for larger and more complex web sites. It's based upon an intermediate magnetic disk backup system that sits between your live servers and your vendor's archive system.

Backup and Recovery for Static Sites

The archiving systems we've discussed so far are intended to protect your code, data, and content *as they exist on your live web site.* But copies of many of these assets also exist on your web-site development computers. If your web site consists only of static content (e.g., you have no visitor-specific files or databases), your development system can play a significant role in your web site's backup and recovery strategy. If you create and maintain your web site using one of the popular development packages such as Microsoft's Front Page, Macromedia's Dreamweaver, or Adobe's Go Live!, you're probably using the built-in site-management features of those packages. Or you may just be using FTP to move your files from the development environment to your live site. In any case, your content-publishing process represents a way that you can restore code, content, and data to your web site, as suggested by Figure 16.2.

The dotted line linking your development system and your live servers in Figure 16.2 represents the method by which you already publish your code and content to your live site. Assuming all of your content is uploaded from your development system to your live servers, you can use this same process to recover that content, should it become necessary.

As long as you have this ability to recover your web site's content from your development system, you're not dependent on a vendor's archiving system, and you're not, therefore, subject to the risks of propagation of corrupted data due to media rotation in the vendor's archiving system. If your development system includes copies of every proprietary object, then even in a worst-case scenario, you can rebuild your site from your development system. In this situation, the archive system exists only to meet your

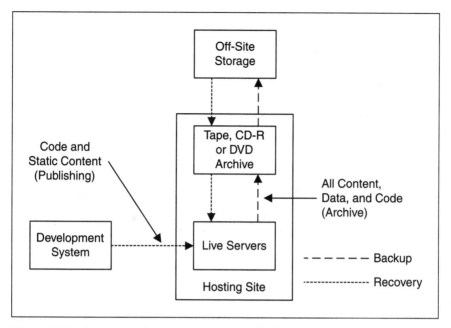

Figure 16.2 Backup and recovery for static web sites.

vendor's needs. If the vendor must recover a file or a complete server, it can turn to its archives. But you've got your own backups. You might consider not using your vendor's archiving system at all.

TIP If your site is small and simple, consider using your development system to back up your content in lieu of some of your vendor's extra-cost services, such as archiving, tape rotation, and off-site storage.

Revision Control

If you have a significant amount of static content, and certainly if you have custom application software, the best way to back up your development environment is with a *revision control system*, such as the open source *concurrent versions system* (*CVS*) shown in Figure 16.3.

A revision control system tracks all of the changes you make on your development system during the processes of building and enhancing your web site. The revision control system stores the changes you make in a treelike file structure; the associated branches of the tree represent the various versions of files. As indicated in Figure 16.3, you can make archival copies of the entire revision control file structure itself and store them off-site. A revision control system is much more valuable than a simple full/incremental backup or archiving solution because it allows you to *tag* a *release* (take a *snapshot* of every file in the tree as of a point in time) and to later re-create that release or any other on demand.

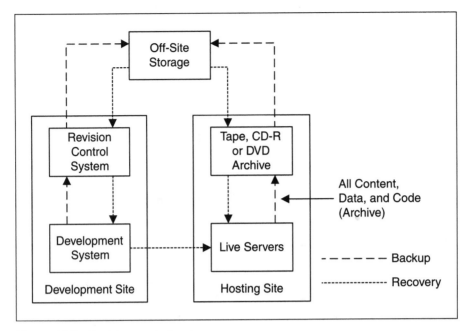

Figure 16.3 Revision control system.

TIP Use a revision control system in your development environment as part of your complete backup and recovery strategy.

Backups on Disk

Our next improvement to an archive-only system is for sites that are too large or complex to depend on their development systems for the rapid recovery of individual files. Such sites should consider an intermediate magnetic disk backup system, as shown in Figure 16.4. We refer to this as a *backup* system rather than an *archive* because its primary purpose is for file recovery, not disaster recovery. With such a system, you can recover deleted or corrupted files without waiting for your vendor to retrieve a tape, install it in a tape drive, and then search the tape for the lost file. Tape is excellent for your off-site archives, but magnetic disk is ideal for on-site backup. This concept, combined with the other systems we've discussed, is illustrated in Figure 16.4.

In this configuration, your live servers are backed up to magnetic disk either daily or even more often, depending on your application. From there, files are archived to your web-hosting vendor's system. Again, recovery works by reversing the process. You can recover individual files, entire directories, or the complete contents of a disk drive or system directly from the magnetic disk backup. In case of a disaster that damages the live servers *and* the magnetic disk backups, you can recover from the archives, either directly to the live servers or to the intermediate disk backup.

Why do most web-hosting vendors and MSPs use only archiving? One reason is that they don't take into consideration how frequently you may need to recover just a portion of a web site. As mentioned at the beginning of this chapter, neither customers nor vendors tend to look at these issues early in the outsourcing relationship.

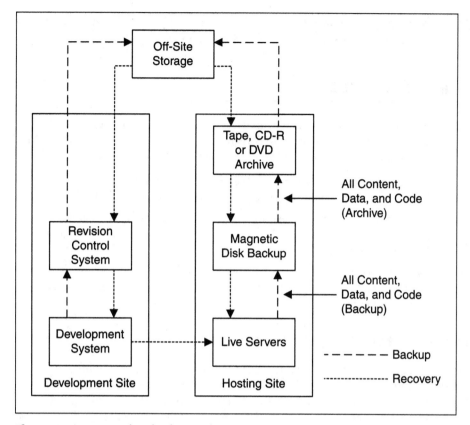

Figure 16.4 A complete backup and recovery system.

Another reason web-hosting services and MSPs use tape is to keep their costs down. Vendors typically archive multiple customers to a single *tape library* that can store as much as 100 TB of data. Your web-hosting vendor or MSP can save itself a lot of money this way.

The final reason that archiving to tape is still the standard is that's how vendors have always done it. In the old days, disks were too expensive to be used for backups, and the media costs for tape were far lower than for nonremovable disks. But we've come a long way from the early 1970s when a 10 megabyte disk drive weighed 150 pounds and cost $5,000 (that's right—$500,000 per gigabyte). Magnetic disk storage now costs less than $10 per gigabyte, and at 50 cents for a blank disk, CD-R media costs only $0.71 per gigabyte. In 30 years, the cost of random-access storage has come down by a factor of 1 million, so it's definitely time to consider it as part of a modern backup and recovery strategy.

As far as specific disk media are concerned, if your backup requires less than 2 GB, it can be stored on a single, removable Iomega Jaz disk. Got 20 GB or less? A Peerless disk will suffice. You can store more than 73 GB on a single standard disk drive; and using RAID, you can store more than 500 GB on seven 73 GB drives, a configuration that will cost less than $10,000. Speed is not critical for this application, so you can even use slow, inexpensive IDE disk drives.

TIP Use magnetic disk backup as intermediate storage between your live site and your web-hosting vendor's tape archiving system.

Backup Practices

Backups and archives are of no value if they're incomplete or otherwise unusable for recovery, so here are three final issues to consider when evaluating the backup and recovery services of a web-hosting service or MSP (we'll discuss each one in detail):

Where to store the archives. Unless you've included magnetic disk backup in your configuration, you may want to keep your most recent archive media on site.

Logs and reports. You'll need these to audit your vendor's backup and recovery services. Does the vendor actually perform the backups and archives as promised? Are they error-free?

Recovery tests. Tests are the only way you can be confident that you or your vendor can recover complete systems as well as individual files and do so within the times specified in the service level agreement.

Where to Store the Archives

An archiving strategy must include a plan for where to keep the archive media. If you have an intermediate magnetic disk backup system, as described earlier, it's generally okay to keep all of your tapes off-site. But if you don't have intermediate storage, it may be smarter to keep the most recent archive copy in the data center. In many cases, system administrators are in such a hurry to get the most recent data to an off-site storage facility, they lose sight of the fact that the archive system must support file recovery as well as disaster recovery.

The disadvantage of off-site storage, of course, is that the time it takes to retrieve archival media from far away substantially increases the total time it takes to effect a recovery. Consider the recovery requirements once again. Assuming you're using redundant storage (e.g., RAID) or redundant servers, you'll rarely lose an entire file system. It's much more common for you or your web-hosting service to accidentally delete a file during maintenance, so most data recoveries will involve restoring only a few files or a directory.

If archives are your only backups, it's usually better for you to keep your most recent copies close to your servers rather than in some underground vault two hours away. With your media close at hand, a simple file recovery can be accomplished in minutes rather than hours.

If a true disaster such as a fire does occur, you'll be glad you have off-site full and incremental backups, even if they're a day or two old. It's important to ensure that there's *always* a reasonably recent copy off-site. And remember that off-site doesn't mean media sitting in the data center awaiting pickup by a courier. A fire can destroy the loading dock as well as your servers. To qualify as off-site, media must at least be en route to or from the vault. This means you'll probably need at least three sets of media at all times: one in the vault, one possibly in transit, and one in the data center.

TIP Unless you have intermediate magnetic disk backups, make sure you have copies of your most recent data and content nearby, and another almost-as-recent copy off-site at all times.

Logs and Reports

The most common problem you'll find with backup and recovery is that many backups or archives will not be executed correctly. In most instances, the copies will merely be incomplete, possibly due to errors that occur during the backup process. But in some cases, the backups or archives may never be run at all, due to some mistake on the part of your vendor's staff. Nothing will ruin your whole day like discovering that the copies you thought you had all along never existed. And at times like that, not even the best-written SLA can get your files back.

Second to having no backups or archives at all, the most common problems are omissions due to two causes:

Open files. Some backup utilities can't copy files that are open (i.e., in use), and there's no guarantee that if such a file is skipped on one day's backup or archive, it will necessarily be saved the next day. This problem is compounded if media are rotated.

Changes in the file system. Over time, you'll add and delete files and directories on your web site's servers. But you may never know that such a file or directory isn't being saved. If it doesn't get added to the backup or archive list, the logs won't indicate that an error occurred. Even a full recovery test (described next) may not identify that a new, but rarely used, file hasn't been added to the list and therefore isn't being copied to your backup disks or archive media.

The only solution to these problems is for someone to read the backup and archive logs every day. Your web-hosting service should give you web-enabled access to your site's backup and archive logs, and you must study them vigilantly to make sure your vendor is making error-free backups and archives as promised.

TIP Review your backup and archive logs daily. Check that any recently added files and directories are included.

Recovery Tests

It's not enough to know that your vendor has apparently copied everything to backups and archives. The ultimate test is: Can your vendor recover a system from those copies? A *recovery test*, in which a freshly provisioned server is restored from backups or archives, is the only way to be certain.

Remember, just because no errors appear in the logs doesn't mean that everything was backed up or archived. Entire directories or file systems may be skipped. Important Unix configuration files or Windows registry database entries may have been omitted. A rigorous strategy would include repeating recovery tests periodically and after any major changes are made to the site.

Some backup techniques (such as low-level track and sector copies) are good for copying entire disk drives but nearly useless for recovering individual files. Likewise, some file-oriented backup techniques (e.g., simple file copy) don't include certain critical system and configuration files, so it's a good idea to make sure that you can recover both individual files and entire disk systems.

> **TIP** Run data recovery tests before servers are brought online, and on a regular basis thereafter. Test for both complete recovery to a virgin server as well as recovery of individual files and databases.

As you've learned from this chapter, the backup and recovery solutions offered by many web-hosting services and MSPs are often inadequate or more than you need. In either case, these vendor-provided solutions tend to be based on older strategies that meet vendors' needs rather than yours, so it often makes sense to deploy separate backup and recovery solutions in addition to, or instead of, those provided by your vendor.

In the next chapter, "Security," we'll see how important a good backup and recovery strategy is to your security plan, and how—in some instances—it may be all you need.

CHAPTER
17
Security

"I can improve the security in a bank by strip-searching every customer."
Bruce Schneier, CTO and cofounder, Counterpane Internet Security, Inc.

Web-site security is another topic that's worthy of its own books, so in these few pages we won't attempt to cover everything you'll ever need to know about security. Instead, we'll look at a few of the classic myths of web-site security: things that people think and do—with honorable intentions—that give them a false sense of security. In the process of exposing these myths, we'll support four recommendations:

Don't try to avoid all threats. You won't succeed anyway. Find the right balance between threat avoidance and risk management.

Watch out for a false sense of security. Firewalls, intrusion detection systems, and audits can lull you into complacency.

Beware of risky web-hosting practices. Vendors' use of administrative (back-door) networks and their poor management of software updates and patches increase your risk of security breaches.

Make sure you have good backups. They won't keep the bad guys from getting in, but good backups and archives (as discussed in Chapter 16, "Backup and Recovery") will reduce the impact of attacks by ensuring that you can get a preattack version of your web site up and running as quickly as possible.

Taking Risks

As Bruce Schneier's intentional sarcasm suggests, it doesn't make sense to eliminate all threats at all costs. You've got to make some very conscious decisions as to which threats are worth living with and which ones aren't. Managing risks (discussed in detail in Chapter 9, "Risk Management") means first determining your potential losses and then having a plan that's based on sound risk/reward analysis to deal with them.

Risk isn't necessarily a bad thing. We knowingly take risks all the time. There's a risk that by driving your car tomorrow you might have an accident. A strategy based solely on threat avoidance would suggest that you stay home. Good risk management, however, tells you that the benefits of driving outweigh the risks, so you decide to take your chances and drive your car anyway. And to cover the eventuality of an accident, you buy insurance and thereby share the risks with other drivers.

In business, one often needs to take risks in order to generate profits. When you were hired for your current job, your employer took a risk. The company knew it would be paying your salary for some time before you did anything useful. (It was a worthwhile risk, wasn't it?)

Credit card companies are examples of good risk managers. Just think about all the risky things they do. They generously issue cards to people of questionable creditworthiness. When customers don't pay on time, the credit card companies extend them even more credit, of course. Their credit loss rates are in the 5 percent range, but does that really concern them? No. They *manage* their risk. They know exactly what it would cost them to reduce that 5 percent loss rate to 4 percent, and they know that doing so would reduce their profits more than it would save them.

How about retail merchants? Have you ever thought about the grocery store that leaves beautiful fresh produce out in front of the market where anyone can just pick up an apple and walk away with it? How about the bookstore that has bins of not-too-popular books sitting out in front? What are these businesspeople thinking? Are they fools? No, they're managing their risk. They know that the losses they incur from these promotions will be outweighed by the profits from the incremental business they attract.

The same risk-management approach should be applied to web-site security. In the rest of this chapter we'll use this strategy as we evaluate the risk/reward trade-offs of security technologies such as firewalls, intrusion detection systems, passwords, administrative networks, and encryption.

Data Recovery: An Important Defense

A good backup and recovery plan is an important cornerstone of any web-site security strategy, since as long as you have a complete and uncorrupted copy of your web site's data and content, you can recover from *any* attack. Good backups won't prevent the initial losses you may suffer, nor will they prevent collateral damage such as loss of goodwill, or liability for the disclosure of your customer's confidential data, but they'll minimize the effect of *cascading losses* due to extended web-site downtime, as described in Chapter 9.

You should know (with your web-hosting vendor's help) how long it would take you to restore your site from backups after a complete loss of all code and data. Once you have that information, you can compute the potential loss due to the downtime during which you would accomplish a recovery.

In many cases, you'll find that no additional security-related actions prove to be worthwhile, and that you get the most bang for the buck by doing nothing more than maintaining good backups. For example, if your site contains only static content and perhaps a few forms, good backups could be the entire extent of your security plan. Certainly, if your web site is a small one (e.g., running on a shared server), you're not going to spend thousands of dollars for a firewall or fancy intrusion detection system. But even if your site is large and complex, you may find that you don't need many of the security products and services that are being pitched to you.

TIP Consider a good backup and recovery plan as the starting point for any security defense. Anything more should be justified on a cost-benefit basis.

Firewalls

One of the first options you'll have to consider is if and where to use firewalls—perhaps the most hotly debated web-site security topic of all. We'll look at the technological issues of firewalls in a moment, but first let's consider the psychological aspects.

Too many web-site owners and system administrators install firewalls (correctly or otherwise) and stop there. They believe they've adequately secured their web sites. Firewalls are perceived (and sold) as a panacea. There's something about them—particularly those that come as dedicated *appliances*—that make people believe in them. It's very easy to look at the firewall logs every morning and pride yourself on the fact that your firewall prevented so many attacks the day before. It's very reassuring, but it's a false sense of security. Remember, most of the bad guys know how firewalls work. The logs only show you what the firewall caught; they don't even hint at the more sophisticated attacks that went right through the firewall.

TIP There's only one good way to deploy firewalls: Configure your web site as though you didn't have a firewall, and then add one anyway.

Once you've *hardened* your servers (the process of removing or at least disabling all unnecessary or known hackable software), you can consider where to place firewalls. The conventional wisdom is to place them at the so-called point of maximum leverage, where your web site connects to the Internet. The theory is that if you can keep someone from getting past your first line of defense, it's much easier to defend the next level. This makes sense if your web site is for authenticated "members only." But here's a reality check: most major web sites don't use firewalls in front of their web servers.

To see why, let's return to the bank analogy. As with a multitier web-site architecture, a bank has multiple levels of security. To enter the branch you need virtually no authentication. Strangers are encouraged to walk in the door; they may want to open an account. It doesn't take much more authentication to make a deposit. If you know the account number and you have the money, the bank is happy to take it. Withdrawals, however, require that you show some identification. And if you want to get into the vault, you're going to need even more robust authentication: a safe-deposit box key and your signature.

A traditional strategy suggests that the bank could increase security by moving the robust authentication requirement from the vault to the front door of the branch. After all, some proponents would suggest, if you keep unauthenticated people from even entering the branch, you not only protect the vault, you also keep them from harassing the tellers (just think how secure we could make a bank if it weren't for those darned customers!). But not only would moving robust authentication to the front door discourage visitors, it would also be very expensive. The bank would have to issue keys to every customer, and hire staff to check everyone's signature. By authenticating only when necessary (e.g., for access to the vault), the cost scales with the risk, and the solution is applied only where needed.

The same applies to a firewall in front of your web site. Is it the web servers you're trying to protect (like the front door of the bank) or is it your data (the vault)? Certainly you're not trying to protect your HTML pages or images. These are the very files you're encouraging visitors to access. Your risk of losing these files is relatively low.

And what about the cost? Firewalls in front of web, cache, and streaming content servers are very expensive because the processing power required by a firewall to thoroughly examine packets is often greater than what it takes to create and transmit those packets in the first place. Even firewalls built using expensive servers are slow, sometimes much slower than the less-expensive servers they're trying to protect. So protecting your front-line servers with firewalls will likely reduce the performance of your site, cost you more than they're worth, or both.

> **TIP** Don't use a firewall in front of your web servers unless access to your static content is restricted to authenticated visitors, and unauthorized access would cause a substantial loss.

Back-End Firewalls

Although it doesn't make sense to require that visitors authenticate themselves to enter a bank branch, it's still important to do so for access to the vault. If your web site is large and complex enough for you to even be thinking about a firewall (i.e., you have something worth protecting), the chances are good that you're also using at least a two-tier (and perhaps a three-tier) architecture. If so, there's probably no valuable data stored on your web servers; it's most likely in a separate database. So while it usually doesn't make sense to use firewalls in front of your web, cache, and streaming servers, it may be a good idea to use them at points *within* your configuration that contain more valuable data and that receive a lower volume of traffic—for instance, in front of your application servers. Such a configuration is illustrated in Figure 17.1.

Like the number of bank visitors who require access to the vault, the amount of traffic in and out of the application servers is much less than the volume of traffic in and out of the front door to your web site. Therefore, a firewall in front of the application servers requires far less computer power than one that sits in front of the external servers.

> **TIP** In three-tier architectures, install a firewall between your web servers and your application servers.

Note that in place of a full-fledged firewall in front of the web and cache servers, the configuration shown in Figure 17.1 includes a *packet filter* running in a router, intelli-

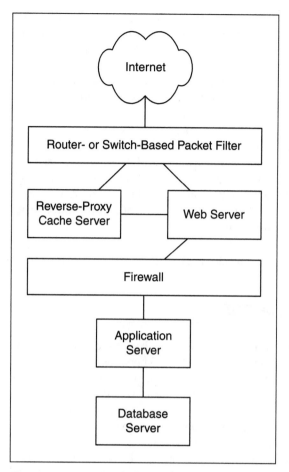

Figure 17.1 Back-end firewall.

gent switch, or load balancer. A packet filter is simpler, faster, and less expensive than a full-fledged firewall. It restricts access by IP address and port number. This technology is virtually mandatory as basic defenses against certain attacks. (For more information on packet filtering, refer to any good book on Internet security, some of which are listed in the appendix, "Resources.")

> **TIP** Always use packet filtering in the switches, routers, and load balancers that connect your web site to the Internet.

Shared Firewalls

Some dedicated-server vendors and MSPs offer *firewall services* that enable you to connect your web servers to their firewalls rather than purchase or lease firewalls of your own. These services may sound like a good deal, but they make even less sense than installing your own firewall in front of your web servers.

As discussed earlier, placing a firewall in front of a web server adds little value, and it creates a false sense of security. A *shared firewall* in this manner has the additional disadvantage that the performance of your web site will be affected by the load placed on the firewall by other web sites.

And don't even *think* of using a shared firewall between your web server and your application servers, or in any other back-end position. A shared firewall used in this way creates a potential path between your application servers and the servers of the other sites using the firewall. This path leaves you susceptible to weaknesses in your neighbors' security practices. If there happens to be even a one-line error in the firewall configuration file (an easy mistake to make and overlook), and if someone breaks into a neighboring web site's server, he or she can get to your application servers through the firewall. Your risk increases with each site that's added to the shared firewall, since each additional site increases the chance that an error will be made or exploited. And, yes, firewalls can be broken into, just like servers.

TIP Don't use shared firewalls under any circumstances.

Intrusion Detection Systems

Like firewalls, another highly touted security technology is that of intrusion detection systems (IDSs). The purpose of an IDS is to sound an alarm whenever it detects either a successful attack or an attack in progress. Proponents of intrusion detection systems point out that it's better to know about an attack while it's underway than after your site has been breached. But, like firewalls, an IDS may give you a false sense of security, for it can't report what it can't detect, and it certainly won't be able to detect *all* intrusions.

In theory, an IDS offers two benefits. First, it may allow you to stop an intruder before he or she can cause additional damage. Second, you may be better able to determine how the break-in was perpetrated and, hence, prevent the use of similar attacks in the future.

Intrusion detection systems come in two flavors: host-based and network-based. A *host-based IDS* (also called a *data integrity monitor*) looks for files and configuration data that change unexpectedly. It alerts you to the fact that your systems have already been compromised. A *network-based IDS* watches the network traffic coming into the web site and tries to identify *behavior* that might be associated with an attack.

Network-Based Intrusion Detection

The biggest problem with network-based IDSs is that they just don't work very well. They have a weakness that's similar to those described when putting a firewall in front of your entire site. Like a firewall, the IDS must examine every packet in detail in order to look for the peculiarities it associates with an attack. Also like a firewall, a network-based IDS must keep track of the relationship of one packet to the next, so it's a far more complex—that is, slower—application than a web server. Therefore (again, as with a firewall), you may need more powerful computers to run a network-based IDS than you need to actually operate your web site.

All too often, a network-based IDS can't keep up with the traffic, and once it falls behind, it becomes useless. This fact is not unknown to hackers, so if they suspect that a web site is using a network-based IDS, the first thing they do is *flood* the IDS with packets so that the IDS loses track of what the hackers are up to. It's way too easy to do.

On the other hand (and, again, as with firewalls), a network-based intrusion detection system may be valuable if it's installed in front of your application servers rather than in front of your web site. It's the application servers and database that contain the assets that are most valuable to you and to hackers. Furthermore, because the volume of traffic to your application servers is far less than the traffic between the outside world and your web site, an IDS in front of the application servers is less susceptible to flooding.

With a well-designed, three-tier architecture, the configuration alone helps to defend your database. Hackers must get into your web servers before they can launch an attack on your application servers. The patterns of traffic between your web servers and your application servers are more predictable than the traffic from the Internet to your web servers. This greater predictability makes it easier for a network-based IDS located in this position to detect anomalies and therefore sound fewer false alarms.

> **TIP** If you want to deploy a network-based intrusion detection system, consider placing it in front of your application servers rather than in front of your entire web site.

Network-based IDSs are prone to substantial false alarms. This triggers the boy-who-cried-wolf syndrome, in which valid alarms are ignored because they can't be distinguished from the high volume of false ones. It's like car alarms going off in New York City. They're practically useless because everyone ignores them.

Should you pay someone on your staff or elsewhere to respond to every alarm, real or false? Is it worthwhile? Like a car alarm, there's little point to installing an IDS unless someone is going to react to every IDS alert. Therefore, if you do decide to deploy a network-based IDS, consider using a managed security service (MSS), discussed later in this chapter, to install and monitor it. Most MSSs have experience with one or more network-based IDS packages. In some cases, the developer of the IDS software also provides the managed security services.

> **TIP** If you decide to use a network-based IDS, consider outsourcing the reaction services to an MSS.

Host-Based Intrusion Detection

While host-based IDSs and simpler data-integrity monitoring packages don't attempt to do what network-based IDSs claim to accomplish, they are a lot more successful at achieving their humbler objectives. These programs track all changes to files and notify your security experts of any unanticipated changes. They can also track changes to file size, access permissions, and other file attributes.

Data-integrity monitoring has the added benefit that it helps to minimize the *private knowledge syndrome* described in Chapter 6, "Managed Services." These packages generate log files of all changes made to the directories and databases they protect. The logs show who changed what, when, and (by requiring all changes to be annotated) why. This is particularly important if you co-manage your servers with an MSP. Some data-integrity packages also support the capability to *roll back* the objects they manage to a state that was known to be safe prior to a security breach.

A host-based IDS or data-integrity monitoring package can provide most of the value of a network-based IDS, but at a fraction of the cost.

> **TIP** Use a host-based IDS or data-integrity monitoring package as a low-cost substitute for a network-based IDS.

Passwords

Most people think of passwords as a form of protection, but hackers see them as opportunities. Passwords are, in fact, one of the weakest aspects of any security system. Think of all the web sites for which you've registered with a username and a password. Have you ever used the same username/password combination at more than one site? If so, imagine what would happen if someone (perhaps an employee of one of those companies) learned your username/password combination. He or she could then log in as you to any other site at which you've used this combination, perhaps even to your online brokerage or bank account.

> **TIP** Never reuse the same password on more than one server or account.

Of course, coming up with new passwords for every application (and remembering them) is truly a burden, and the temptation to reuse passwords is just as great for an MSP or web-hosting service as it is for you. But imagine if the root password on your servers was the same as the root password on every other server managed by that vendor. This certainly would be convenient for the MSP's system administrators, but an incredible opportunity for any hacker who could somehow learn that one magic password.

Vendors shouldn't reuse passwords any more than you should. In fact, good MSPs and web-hosting services don't use normal passwords at all. Instead, they use either *one-time passwords* (i.e., the passwords literally work only once) or they use a *token-based authentication* scheme. The latter requires their staff to log in using constantly changing access codes that they get from small electronic *tokens*. These devices display a unique code that changes every minute or so, and they're synchronized with a centralized *authentication server*. Token-based authentication requires "something you have and something you know"—the token and a PIN. It's the same type of authentication used for ATM machines. You need the ATM card (something you have) and your PIN (something you know). Neither alone is sufficient to gain access.

> **TIP** Ask prospective vendors how they manage passwords. Give the highest marks to those that use token-based authentication systems.

Social Engineering Attacks

Unless a vendor uses one-time passwords or token-based authentication, it's suscepti-ble to the greatest risk of passwords: a *social engineering* attack, which exploits the weak-nesses of people. Even the best-intentioned employees do remarkably stupid things, and the bad guys know how to manipulate them. For instance, employees may give out passwords to one another or to supposed customers over the phone or through unen-crypted email. All of these bad practices are easy to exploit. If your site is otherwise well designed, the risks from such social engineering attacks are statistically greater than those from hackers using technology to break into your site.

One way to evaluate a vendor's social engineering defenses is to telephone its NOC, pretending to be an employee of one of the customers you were given as a reference ac-count. Tell the NOC personnel that you've lost a password. If the vendor has a *customer portal* web site, just ask for the password to that site. If not, say that you can't find the root passwords to one of your servers. Does the first person immediately tell you, "No!" or do you have to go through a few helpful people before you're finally turned down? A particularly alert NOC will politely transfer your call to its security depart-ment, where good sleuths may ask you for your phone number and then call you back to "discuss" your request. Hopefully, you'll never get a password.

TIP As a way to evaluate a vendor's security policies, telephone the vendor's NOC, pretending to be an existing customer. If you're able to get a password to a customer's server or to the vendor's administrative web site, there's a serious problem.

Administrative Networks

To support remote management of your web site, you may want to implement an *ad-ministrative network* (also called a *back-door network*). It will allow you to reach the servers that are normally inaccessible from the outside world, such as your application and database servers. An administrative network can be based on either a physical net-work connection (such as a T1) or by creating a *virtual private network* (*VPN*) superim-posed on the public Internet. In general, a well-designed private administrative net-work (i.e., one that's available only to your organization, not to your web-hosting vendor) is a good way to reach your servers.

But while it's okay for you to have a private administrative network, it's a potentially dangerous practice when a web-hosting vendor or MSPs uses a single back-door network to reach more than one customer's web site by linking each customer's site to the ven-dor's NOC. As with a shared firewall, such a shared network link creates a potential path by which hackers can gain access to your servers by first breaking into those of other web sites. This risky configuration is illustrated in Figure 17.2.

A better design is a configuration in which the network itself is not shared by multi-ple web sites. Instead, each site has a separate dedicated connection to the vendor's NOC, as illustrated in Figure 17.3.

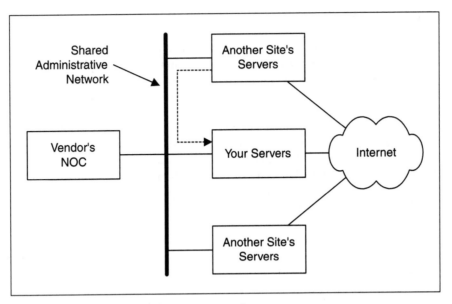

Figure 17.2 Multisite administrative network.

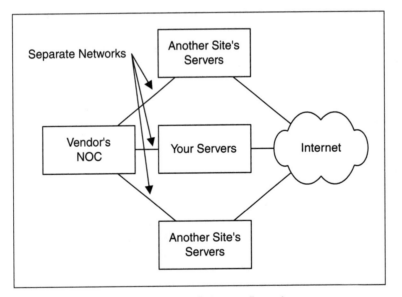

Figure 17.3 Administrative network star configuration.

TIP Be wary of vendors' shared administrative networks. Configurations in which the network itself is not shared are safer.

Some web-hosting services and MSPs use their administrative networks for backup and recovery by connecting each of their customers' systems to a centralized backup server. This creates yet another path by which hackers can reach your site through the back door. It's important to watch out for this configuration as well.

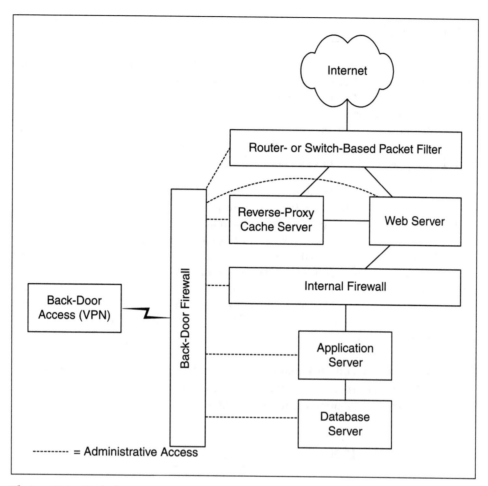

Figure 17.4   Back-door access.

Back-Door Firewalls

No matter what topology you use for a back-door network (even if it's used only by you and not by a web-hosting vendor), it's a good idea to use a firewall between the back-door network and your servers, as shown in Figure 17.4. Since the volume of traffic is quite low as compared to that which comes in through the front door of your web site, a firewall in this application doesn't need to be of particularly high performance. You can typically use a low-cost firewall appliance in this application.

Also, as shown in Figure 17.4, a back-door link through a firewall is a good way to gain administrative access to your routers, switches, and internal firewalls, in addition to your servers.

TIP If you have an administrative network, secure it with a firewall.

Encryption

Encryption (the process of scrambling data so that it can't be read easily by unauthorized people or applications) is an important and valuable technology. It's necessary for many tasks, but by itself, encryption is not usually sufficient. Encryption, like firewalls and intrusion detection systems, can create a false sense of security. For instance, you can use the most powerful encryption algorithms to protect credit card numbers and other personal data, but your application will still need the *key* to access those records. If the key is available to your application, the bad guys can probably find it and use it to unlock your data.

In 1999, the online music vendor CD Universe lost more than 300,000 of its customers' credit card numbers to a Russian hacker. A year later, another hacker stole the credit card numbers of up to 3.7 *million* customers from Egghead.com. The moral of these stories is simple: *never* store credit card numbers (even with encryption) on any server that's part of your web-site configuration. Instead, store your customers' credit card numbers and other confidential data with the same service that processes your credit card transactions. You can retrieve this data later, one record at a time, using customer ID numbers that you can store *unencrypted* in your web site's database. Since the credit card services are not directly accessible via the web, they're inherently more secure than your web site.

TIP *Never* store credit card numbers in your web-site database, even if they're encrypted. Use a third-party credit card processing service that will store your customer's credit card numbers for use in future transactions.

Security Patches

Credit card number theft is an ongoing problem. In March 2001, the FBI reported that 40 companies had lost a total of more than 1 million credit card numbers and other customer data to hackers from Eastern Europe. How did the hackers get in? They exploited a known vulnerability in Microsoft's Windows NT operating system for which Microsoft had published a patch *three years earlier.* If the system administrators responsible for these 40 web sites had followed standard industry practices, they would have installed that patch and those attacks would have been prevented. By the way, many of those web sites had firewalls. They didn't help.

Any time a new type of attack is discovered, it's reported by various security organizations such as the CERT Coordination Center (CERT/CC), a federally funded research and development center operated by Carnegie Mellon University (www.cert.org). This is a great web site to visit if you want to get an idea of how really vulnerable the Internet is to attacks.

Another important security resource is the BugTraq mailing list (see www.securityfocus.com/). BugTraq is a *full-disclosure* moderated mailing list for the detailed discussion and announcement of computer security vulnerabilities: what they are, how to exploit them, and how to fix them.

Along with reporting attacks, BugTraq, CERT, and other sites and services also publish fixes to vulnerabilities, including patches to specific applications. Someone (you or your vendor) must track these reports *daily* and install the appropriate patches. It's not just the good guys that read CERT and BugTraq; so do all the bad guys. And remember, these services are only reactive. The entire hacker community knows about these vulnerabilities before you do.

You need to ask your vendor two questions about how it handles patches:

Are patches installed promptly? Ask your vendor how quickly it installs patches once they're released. If you're using an MSP, you may even want to address the timeliness of patch installation in a service level agreement.

Are patches tested first? Patches that fix one problem can often break something else. Vendors should run *regression tests* to determine that new patches don't interfere with existing applications.

TIP Ask vendors what security services they monitor or subscribe to, how promptly they install security-related patches, and if they test patches for compatibility with applications before installing them.

Managed Security Services

Many of the security issues we've addressed in this chapter raise one additional question: Who should be responsible for the security of your web site? There are three possible answers: You can manage security yourself; you can let your web-hosting service or MSP take care of it; or you can outsource security to a third-party MSS.

What's right for you is based on what you can afford and the extent of your risk. You can use your budget as a guideline, since it's also a reasonable indicator of the financial losses you might incur if your web site were to be brought down by an attack. The more a company spends on its web site, the more it usually stands to lose when the site is compromised.

If you're running on a shared server or a low-end dedicated server, your risks are likely very low, and third-party services will cost more than the threats they could help you avoid. Your best bet in this situation is to use whatever services your web-hosting vendor provides as part of its standard package. Just make sure you have good backups (as we discussed earlier in this chapter) to cover you in case an attack wipes out your code and content. And keep in mind that shared-server hosting will always be inherently vulnerable.

If you're using an MSP, but the *total* budget for your web site is below $1 million per year (about $75,000 per month), the optional security services provided by your MSP may be worthwhile. You may also want to pay an independent security guru for periodic audits, but be careful to avoid the false sense of security that audits may give you. (Some security experts believe things change so quickly that an audit is invalid in as little as one week.) Neither your budget nor your total risk exposure (up to the amount that's covered by your worst-case scenario recovery plan) justifies the minimum $5,000 or so per month that it would cost to use an independent managed security service.

If your total web-site budget is $1 million per year or more, *and* you have risks substantially greater than the loss of your static content, you should consider using an independent MSS in addition to your colo and/or MSP.

TIP **Ask your hosting company if it has passed an SAS 70 Level I or Level II audit. Even if you don't use your MSP's security services, you'll get the benefit, since the requirements to obtain SAS 70 certification apply to all of the systems under the MSP's control, even yours.**

An MSS doesn't replace your MSP's security services, but rather works with them. For example, an MSS doesn't take on the responsibility of most threat-avoidance activities. Most MSSs expect that you or your MSP will track and install security patches as if the MSS weren't involved. What an MSS will do, however, is monitor your site on an ongoing basis, and provide the following services:

On-call intrusion detection response. If something is caught by your intrusion detection system, your MSS will be notified by email and pager and respond immediately, 24/7.

Security logs review. An MSS will scour the daily logs of your IDS and firewalls (if any), looking for anomalies and recommending courses of action as appropriate.

SECURITY AUDITS

There's a lot of controversy surrounding security audits. As discussed, even the best audits are only valuable for a very short period of time. Once you or your web-hosting vendor make a change to your web site or to the routers and other devices connecting your site to the Internet, you've invalidated the audit. All bets are off.

Another arguable practice is using simulated attacks to audit a web site. You're likely to find vulnerabilities using this approach, but once again, you may develop a false sense of security. It's easy to find *some* vulnerabilities. It's impossible to find them all.

One type of audit that may have value is one performed not on your web site, but on your web-hosting vendor's processes, An *SAS 70* audit allows service organizations to disclose their control activities and processes to their customers and their customers' auditors in a uniform reporting format. *Statement on Auditing Standards (SAS) No. 70, Service Organizations,* is an auditing standard developed by the American Institute of Certified Public Accountants (AICPA).

SAS 70 is a widely recognized standard. It signifies that a service organization has had its control objectives and control activities examined by an independent accounting and auditing firm. A formal report including the auditor's opinion ("Service Auditor's Report") is issued to the service organization at the conclusion of an SAS 70 examination. A *Type I* report describes the service organization's description of controls at a specific point in time. A *Type II* report includes not only the service organization's description of controls, but also detailed testing of the service organization's controls over a minimum six-month period.

Review your MSP's activities. An MSS will constantly be looking over your MSP's shoulder to make sure your MSP does everything right, including the timely and correct installation of security-related patches.

Your MSP may try to convince you that it can provide all of the security services you need. But when done right, security is a specialty that goes beyond what most MSPs are willing to invest in. If yours is a high-budget/high-risk web site (i.e., at least a $1 million per-year budget *and* a potential for significant losses), you should consider working with independent experts.

Another reason to use a third party to manage security is to leverage the healthy tension that's created between the independent security specialists and the system administrators and technicians that work for your MSP. It's a lot like the tension that exists between programmers and quality assurance (QA) engineers. Like programmers, an MSP's sysadmins and techs are under pressure to get things done quickly, to respond to deadlines, and to move on to other tasks. But security experts, like QA staff, are there to occasionally put on the brakes in order to guarantee that things are done right. It's important to have advocates of both positions on your team, if you can afford it.

The same tensions that exist at the staff level ripple all the way up to senior management. MSS executives understand that it's their companies' role to act as independent auditor of your system's security. As auditors, their responsibility actually exceeds that of your MSP.

TIP If your total annual web-site budget is greater than $1 million, and your risks are substantially greater than just the loss of your static content, use an MSS to add knowledge, experience, and objectivity beyond what an MSP can provide.

Attacks are like hardware failures—they *will* happen. You've got to assume that the bad guys will get in no matter what you do, so you must practice risk management—not just threat avoidance—to deal with the attacks that do get through.

But as you develop and update your security plan, don't lose sight of your customers and your business. Avoid spending money to tighten security only to make your web site so unusable that visitors are needlessly discouraged. Sure, banks could dramatically reduce robberies by strip-searching everyone that comes through their doors, but not too many customers would come back for more.

Although we've looked at some of the most common web-site security myths, we've only scratched the surface of this topic. Refer to the bibliography in the appendix for recommendations of books that address this important topic in greater detail.

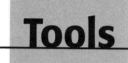

PART

Five

Tools

In Part Four, "Technologies," we looked in depth at some of the service components provided by web-hosting services and MSPs. In this final part of *Strategies for Web Hosting and Managed Services,* we'll look at some of the things you can and should do yourself.

We'll start in Chapter 18, "Connectivity Performance," with a look at the tools and techniques for measuring the quality of the connectivity to your web site. In particular, we'll make the case for the use of *benchmark servers* during your vendor evaluation and for as long as you operate your web site. We'll also explain the low-level connectivity metrics of reachability, packet loss, and latency, and how and why to measure them.

Chapter 19, "Monitoring," continues with an exploration of the various products, services, and strategies for monitoring your web site. Using the benchmark servers we introduced in the previous chapter, you'll see how to establish *baselines* and *service levels* and how to use monitoring technologies for notification, competitive analysis, diagnostics, internal monitoring, and trend reporting.

In Chapter 20, "The Net Detective Toolkit," you'll learn how to use a variety of desktop and online tools to analyze a competitor's web site or one given as a reference by a web-hosting service or MSP. You'll also find out how to discover which web sites—other than those given to you as references—are hosted at a web-hosting service. And you'll learn techniques for finding out whether some of the claims a vendor makes about its infrastructure are, in fact, true.

Chapter 21, "Domain Names and DNS," looks at two important issues associated with your Internet domain. First we'll look at a way to *delegate a subdomain* to your web-hosting service or MSP rather than give it complete control over your DNS infra-structure. Then we'll examine the right way to register and manage your domain names.

We'll wrap things up with "Resources," an appendix that contains some biblio-graphic references and lists online tools and services.

Connectivity Performance

The Internet is like a living, breathing, organic being. "How's the Net doing today?" is a question you'll hear one network engineer ask another. The Internet has its good days and its bad days. The Internet can be unhealthy (e.g., slow) in one part of the world, yet healthy in others. There are even web sites that monitor and record the "pulse" of the Internet using metaphors such as "Internet health reports," "Internet traffic reports," and "Internet weather reports."

But there's only one Internet health criterion that really counts: the user experience. Can visitors reach your web site? Is your web site fast enough to meet their needs? Will they come back again and again, rather than switch to a competitor's site? These are the issues that truly matter.

The best way to evaluate a web-hosting service according to this criterion (both during vendor selection and on an ongoing basis) is through the creative use of independent performance measurement services. Normally, these services monitor existing web sites, but in this chapter we'll also look at ways to use them to compare hosting services' Internet connectivity during your vendor-selection process.

We'll start with the most important performance measurements, those that approximate the user experience and that can be used as the basis for service level agreements after you've selected a vendor. Then we'll explore the lower-level measurements of *reachability, packet loss,* and *latency,* which are helpful in understanding why the connectivity of one vendor is better or worse than that of another.

In Chapter 19, "Monitoring," we'll look at how the measurement tools we introduce in this chapter can also be used to monitor your site once it's up and running.

Benchmark Sites and Servers

Measuring web-site connectivity is complex and even controversial, yet without such measurements, the tasks of objectively evaluating and selecting vendors and of monitoring service levels would be impossible. There are two requirements for measuring the performance of web sites. The first is to identify metrics that approximate the actual experience of users. The second requirement is to isolate the measurement of connectivity performance from that of the performance of your servers. This requirement will become critical once your site is up and running. When a user reports that your web site is slow, you need to know whether the problem is caused by your web site or by something along the path between your site and the user. Unless you have a way to separate these measurements of server and connectivity performance, you won't have a clue how to solve the problem.

In this chapter, we'll explore the use of *benchmark sites*—surrogate web sites or stand-alone servers whose only purpose is to be measured remotely—as a way to meet these requirements of measuring the user experience and separating the measurements of connectivity and server performance. If your web site will run at a shared-server facility, you'll use benchmark sites. If your site will be hosted at a dedicated-server or colocation facility, you'll use dedicated *benchmark servers.*

You might think that the best way to evaluate the connectivity performance of multiple vendors would be to run an instance of your actual web site from each vendor's location and measure the performance, but doing so has three disadvantages. First, it probably isn't financially practical, particularly if you have a multiserver architecture. Second, you probably want to complete your vendor evaluation before your web site is finished, since your web-hosting vendor may play a substantial role in your deployment process. Finally, ironically, and perhaps most critically, measuring a live site is *not* the best way to evaluate connectivity performance, because when measuring a live site, it's difficult to separate connectivity performance from other performance-related issues. For example, if your measurements show that it suddenly takes twice as long to download a web page as it did the day before, how do you know whether the problem is with the vendor's Internet connectivity or caused by your own servers?

When you've reduced your list of prospective web-hosting vendors to two or three, tell each of them that you want to run a test for two weeks or a month. Then create a very simple, one-page web site. It can be representative of your web site's design (i.e., it may have multiple images or other objects on the page) or it can just be a simple 50 Kbyte HTML text file. If your site will include significant large-object or streaming content, you should configure your benchmarks to deliver samples of those object types as well.

If you're using benchmark sites (i.e., you're evaluating shared hosting), simply upload the identical web page file(s) to each of your vendors' servers. For dedicated-server hosting or colocation, you'll want to use small, inexpensive servers. They don't need to run the same software or applications as your actual web site. The goal of this evaluation isn't to analyze the performance of the servers, but rather the performance

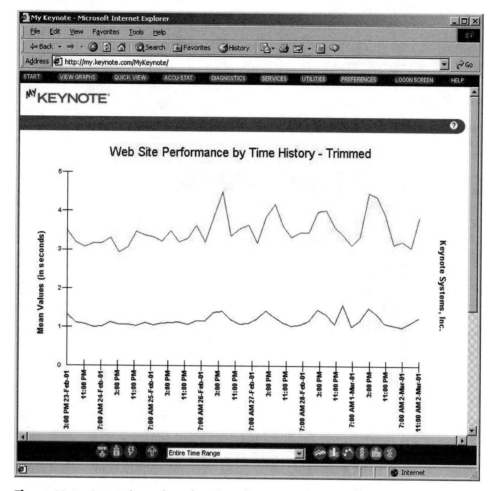

Figure 18.1   Comparison of two benchmark servers (one week, by time).
Source: Keynote Systems, Inc.

of the links *to* the servers. The least expensive Intel-based Linux servers you can find are ideal for this task. All that matters is that they be identical.

Your prospective vendors should be willing to let you park these servers in their facilities for a one-month test at no charge. (This is a great way to take advantage of those one-month free trial offers.) The servers require no management or maintenance. If one fails, it need not be repaired quickly.

Next, sign up with an independent measurement service to monitor your benchmark sites during the test period. The examples given in Figures 18.1 and 18.2 are based on two identical benchmark servers at two different web-hosting services. Each benchmark consisted of the same single 50 Kbyte web page, and each ran on identical servers with identical software.

Figure 18.1 shows a comparison of two benchmarks by download time. Note that one (represented by the lower line) was consistently faster than the other. The data was

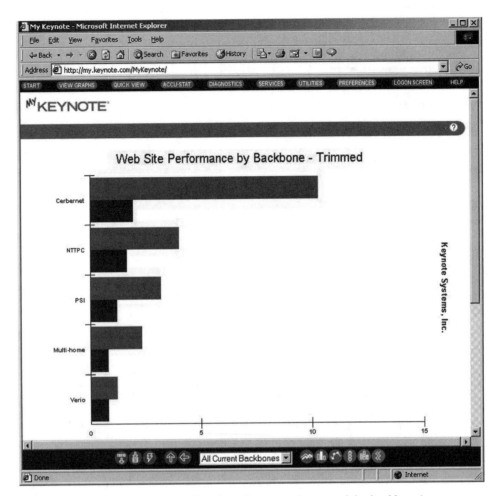

Figure 18.2 Comparison of two benchmark servers (one week by backbone).
Source: Keynote Systems, Inc.

collected using an assortment of a measurement service's agents located worldwide on various Internet backbones.

The graph in Figure 18.2 is driven by the same data, but presents it by ISP backbone. Note in this version that the slower benchmark was particularly slow when accessed from the Cebernet backbone in the United Kingdom. The actual numbers in such tests aren't important. What we care about is the consistent difference between the ability of two web-hosting services to deliver the identical content.

The beauty of measuring benchmark sites is that you can isolate connectivity performance from other variables. So long as benchmarks are based on identical hardware and software, any differences must be attributable to variations in connectivity. Clearly, all other considerations being equal, the faster web-hosting service would be the one to select.

> **TIP** Use benchmark sites or benchmark servers and sign up for third-party reports to monitor them as a way of evaluating the connectivity of the vendors on your short list.

Performance Component Criteria

By using benchmark sites to approximate the user experience, you'll also have a platform for more in-depth analysis of performance problems. In this section, we'll look at the criteria most often used to measure such problems: *reachability, packet loss,* and *latency.* While these are valuable criteria, it's important to keep them in perspective. Specifically, don't fixate on the numbers. These are primarily diagnostic concepts, and the values can change from day to day, or even minute to minute.

It's also important to understand which measurements really make a difference. For example, when evaluating web-page delivery, packet loss is more important than latency, whereas in Internet telephony applications, quite the opposite is true (this will be discussed in more detail later in this chapter).

With these caveats in mind, let's look at the three criteria for the measurement of the quality of a web-hosting service's connectivity.

Reachability

The most basic requirement of connectivity is to answer, "Can I get there from here?" Your web site should be accessible by all of your customers, all of the time; but the reality is that outages on the Internet are still a fact of life, and you can't always "get there from here."

Reachability is a measurement of the ability to communicate from one point on the Internet to another. Reachability doesn't judge the quality, reliability, or speed of a path, only that the path exists and that it can carry at least some data from one end to the other.

Reachability is a difficult concept to quantify. Should a site be considered unreachable if one customer has a problem getting to your site, but all others can reach it just fine? Suppose everyone except AOL users can reach you? That might be a nonissue for a B2B company but traumatic for some B2Cs.

When evaluating vendors, it's important to understand exactly how they define their reachability service levels. What does a guarantee of 99.9 percent uptime mean in regard to reachability? If your site can be reached from any location, is it considered up? Suppose it can be reached from some locations on the Internet but not from others? Is that considered up or down? Suppose everyone can reach your site except your most important customer? Suppose you can't reach it from your own home or office?

> **TIP** An SLA should include a clear definition of uptime in terms of which locations can or cannot reach your web site.

Proximity to Access Providers

In some cases, access to your site from one region or through a particular ISP may be more important than from the rest of the Internet as a whole. If you know how users will access your web site, take that into consideration when evaluating vendors' connectivity.

The most obvious example is visitors using America Online (AOL). Some consumer-oriented sites receive 40 percent or more of their traffic from AOL users. If you expect a substantial percentage of your traffic to come through one access network, ask prospective vendors to show you how well they're connected to that network. Some web-hosting services, for example, have a *private peering* relationship (i.e., a dedicated connection that doesn't pass through public access points or other ISPs) with AOL.

TIP If you know that access to your web site via certain ISPs or from certain locations is particularly critical, evaluate vendors on this basis and negotiate your connectivity SLA to reflect this requirement.

Packet Loss

Reachability is the first and most basic measurement of Internet performance, but just being able to get packets from one location to another isn't enough. The *quality* of the path between visitors and your web site can be degraded in two ways: through packet loss and latency.

Packet loss is a measurement of the percentage of data packets that are dropped by routers and switches on a path between one location and another on the Internet. There are many potential causes of packet loss, but the most common is congestion. To get from your web site to a user's browser, packets may traverse 20 or more *hops* between routers that are owned by a number of different ISPs. Congestion occurs because Internet traffic runs over fiber optic, copper, satellite, and microwave links, each of which has a finite capacity. When the number of packets exceeds the number that a link can handle, something has to give, and packets are simply discarded by the routers at one end of the link or the other.

Not all ISPs are as aggressive as they should be in upgrading their links and routers to keep up with the demand. It's important, therefore, to evaluate both a vendor's current connection as well as its policies for future upgrades, as discussed in Chapter 14, "Connectivity Practices."

Packet loss is the most common symptom of a congested link. When packets are lost, it's not that the link is entirely down. If that were the case, the vendor's routing infrastructure might well be able to find an alternative route. But most routers and switches aren't capable of switching to alternative routes when packet loss occurs. They only change routes when they detect complete link failures.

Some degree of packet loss is unavoidable. The Transmission Control Protocol (TCP) assumes, in fact, that packets will be dropped from time to time. One of the jobs of TCP is to keep track of which packets have been received, and to request retransmissions of any that were lost. TCP makes sure that as long as you're receiving data, you're guaranteed that you haven't lost any intermediate packets. In other words, if a user receives the end of a file, he or she can be assured that a piece of it wasn't lost halfway through the file transfer. Although TCP handles retransmissions reliably, they're remarkably inefficient.

As an example, let's take a look at the transmission of a single 5 Kbyte image. The sending end (a web server) breaks the image into five packets, each containing ap-

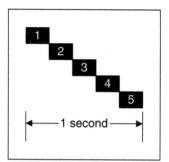

Figure 18.3 5 Kbytes at 56 Kbps.

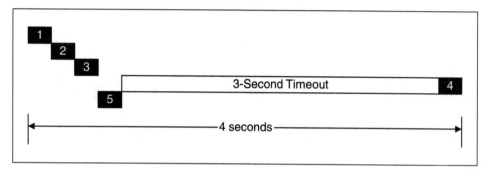

Figure 18.4 Packet loss at 56 Kbps (viewed at receiving end).

proximately 1 Kbyte. These packets are sent out in sequence, one immediately after another. Figure 18.3 illustrates a timeline for the transmission at 56 Kbps. The total time is approximately one second.

Now let's take a look at what happens when one packet (number 4 in the example shown in Figure 18.4) is lost along the way. As shown, the receiving end (let's assume it's a web-site visitor's computer) waits up to three seconds for the dropped packet to arrive. When that packet doesn't arrive at the destination after three seconds, a *timeout* occurs, and the receiving end asks the transmitting end to retransmit the lost packet.

At 56 Kbps, this timeout period extends the total time to transmit the image from one second to four seconds. One can see that the delay caused by even a single dropped packet is far greater than merely the time it takes to retransmit the packet. This is because the entire data transfer process is halted while the protocol waits for the timeout to occur. During this time, the TCP connection remains idle.

The effect of lost packets is even greater at higher speed. This is because the timeout period (typically three seconds) is the same regardless of the data transfer rate. A pause of three seconds has a far greater *relative* impact at a high speed than it does at a lower one.

Figures 18.5 and 18.6 illustrate what happens at T1 speeds. When there's no packet loss, the five 1 Kbyte packets are transmitted in approximately 33 milliseconds total. When just one packet is lost, however, the time jumps to 3.04 seconds, or an increase in elapsed time of more than 92 times.

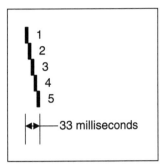

Figure 18.5 5 Kbytes at 1.5 Mbps.

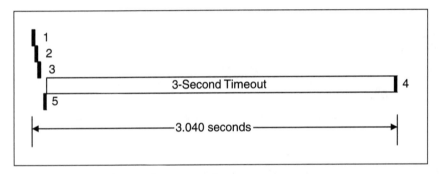

Figure 18.6 One lost packet at 1.5 Mbps.

The extent of the effect of lost packets is determined by the speed of the slowest hop between the sender and receiver. In most cases, the slowest hop is the user's connection to his ISP. Business users are often connected at T1 (1.544 Mbps) or DSL (up to 6 Mbps) speeds, and consumers are switching to DSL or cable modem connections as quickly as the carriers can install them. This trend toward higher *last-mile* speeds means the importance of packet loss will increase over time.

Packet Loss Statistics

All good web-hosting services track their packet loss, and if you ask, you should be able to get copies of their packet loss statistics. We'll look at some examples of vendor reports shortly.

Ideally, packet loss should be addressed by a service level agreement. Some vendors do have SLAs that cover packet loss, but these SLAs are typically limited to packet loss within the vendor's own network. Ultimately, this is all a vendor can do, however. No vendor can guarantee the performance of other vendors' networks. Note, however, that it *is* reasonable for a vendor to guarantee the *average* performance of its third-party peering arrangements, particularly as compared to industry averages. This concept will be explained in detail in Chapter 19, "Monitoring."

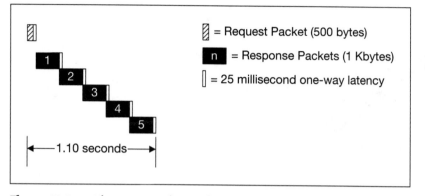

Figure 18.7 5 Kbytes at 56 Kbps with 50 msec round-trip latency.

When it comes to the delivery of web pages, as opposed to other types of data, such as streaming audio or video, no amount of packet loss is acceptable. Any percentage of packet loss should be considered a problem.

> **TIP** Use packet loss as the next most important measurement (after user-perspective performance measurements) for evaluating a web-hosting service's current capability to deliver web pages.

Latency

Following reachability and packet loss, latency is the third criterion of performance that affects web sites. Latency is a measure of how long it takes individual packets to traverse an Internet route. Individual latencies are the delays that are introduced at each hop along the route. The most important latency measurement is that of the overall time delay from one end of the connection to the other. (Note that packets that never make it from one end to the other due to packet loss are not even considered in measurements of latency.)

Latency is the measurement that most ISPs and web-hosting services point to when bragging about their networks. But when it comes to the delivery of web pages (as opposed to other content on the Internet such as streaming audio or video), latency is not nearly as critical as packet loss.

Consider this example: Suppose a visitor's web browser requests the same 5 Kbyte object that we used in our examples of packet loss. Figure 18.7 shows the request-response timeline. Unlike the simplified examples we used for packet loss, this illustration includes the request packet sent by the browser in addition to the server's response packets that contain the actual data.

Figure 18.7 illustrates the HTTP request packet (about 500 bytes in this example) and the five 1 Kbyte response packets that carry the requested 5 Kbyte object. The 25-millisecond latency attached to the request packet represents the delay that occurs when the request is held up in the various routers between the visitor's computer and the web server. Likewise, the latencies tacked onto each of the response packets show how each of them is delayed during the return trip.

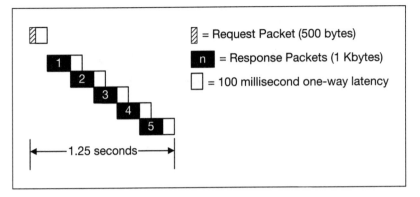

Figure 18.8 5 Kbytes at 56 Kbps with 200 msec round-trip latency.

The server can't begin to transmit its response until it has received the request in its entirety, so the latency associated with the request will always be realized. Note, however, that the latencies for all but the final response packet actually overlap the packets that follow. This is due to the workings of the TCP protocol. It allows the sender (the web server in this instance) to transmit a limited stream of packets—one right after the other—without an acknowledgment from the receiving end. Therefore, although each packet is delayed along its route, the delays are not cumulative. The net effect is that the latency is added only twice: once for the request and again (but only once) for the response.

With zero latency, the exchange illustrated in Figure 18.7 would take 1.05 seconds. A one-way latency of 25 milliseconds (50 milliseconds round-trip) increases the total time to 1.10 seconds. Now let's look at what happens when the latency increases to 100 milliseconds each way, or 200 milliseconds round-trip, as illustrated in Figure 18.8. Although the latency increases by 4 times, or 300 percent, the total elapsed time to complete the exchange increases only 0.15 seconds, or only 14 percent.

As with packet loss, however, the effect of latency does increase with the data rate. In Figure 18.9 we see the effect of a 200-millisecond round-trip latency on the same 5 Kbyte exchange at T1 speeds. With zero latency, this exchange (including the request packet) takes 37 milliseconds, but with a 200-millisecond round-trip latency, it takes 6.4 times longer—a 540 percent increase.

The three lessons to be learned from the examples in Figures 18.8 and 18.9 are:

■ The actual effect of the total round-trip latency is determined by the slowest-speed link between the browser and the server, which is typically the user's local access speed.

■ As with packet loss, the effects of latency are much more significant at higher data rates.

■ The effects of latency generally increase relative to the number of objects on a web page. A web page with twice as many separate objects will incur twice the delay due to latency. Good web-page design, therefore, suggests a smaller number of larger objects over a larger number of small objects.

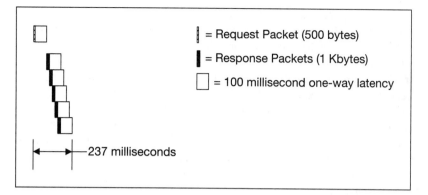

Figure 18.9   5 Kbytes at 1.5 Mbps with 200 msec round-trip latency.

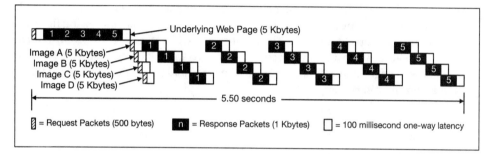

Figure 18.10   Web page with four images at 56 Kbps and 200 msec round-trip latency.

Latency Mitigation

Certainly latency is a potential problem, but for the delivery of web pages, it's not as critical as it might be. The effects of latency are to some extent mitigated by the design of most web browsers that open four simultaneous TCP/IP connections to the servers from which they request web-page objects. These *logical* connections share the *physical* connections that the browser and server have to the Internet. The logical connections essentially time-share the physical connection.

If a web page contains four images, for instance, the browser will first read the underlying page, and will then request all four images at the same time, using four separate TCP/IP connections. In this case, the effect of latency will occur first while retrieving the underlying page, then again (but just once) when reading the four images.

This example is illustrated in Figure 18.10, which shows a 5 Kbyte underlying web page that includes references to four 5 Kbyte images. Each row in this figure represents the request, responses, and latencies associated with a single object. The first row is the request/response for the underlying web page itself. Once the page has been received, the browser fires off requests for each of the four images (A through D). The requests, responses, and latencies for each image are shown as the next four rows of packets respectively.

Because the browser opens four TCP connections as soon as the first packet for image A starts along its way, the server can keep the *pipe* (the physical connection) filled with data. If the browser were to open only one TCP connection, it would have to receive all of image A before it could even request image B.

The data transmission rate for the example in Figure 18.10 is 56 Kbps, and the round-trip latency is 200 milliseconds. Note that the total effect of the latency is only 400 milliseconds, or only 7 percent of the total transmission time. Although there are substantial latencies associated with each response packet for each image, once the underlying web page has been entirely received (200 milliseconds total latency), the pipe is always full. Only the 100 millisecond delays associated with the underlying web page, first image request, and the last image response actually affect the performance of the overall exchange.

Again, the effects of latency are accentuated at higher transmission speeds, but they continue to be minimized by the fact that browsers typically open multiple connections to servers.

What's considered acceptable latency? To some extent, it depends on distance. It takes a theoretical minimum of 17 milliseconds to move data 3,000 miles using fiber optic cables and high-speed switches. In reality, an excellent transcontinental (North America) hop adds at least 25 milliseconds. Here are some latency guidelines for the delivery of web pages that are the average of the thresholds used by a number of third-party measurement services:

Good	75 ms
Acceptable	150 ms
Unacceptable	>150 msecs

TIP Use latency as the third most important criterion for evaluating a web-hosting service's capability to deliver web pages.

A Real-World Example

Figure 18.11 illustrates many of the issues we've discussed so far in this chapter. This figure was captured from a third-party analysis of a single download of Amazon.com's home page. It illustrates the following issues:

- The underlying page (www.amazon.com) is downloaded in its entirety before the objects it contains are requested.

- The browser opens four TCP connections and attempts to download four objects at a time.

- While attempting to download the twelfth object, a single packet is lost. (The timeline for this object is actually the last one shown, since this particular report displays them in the order completed, not the order started.)

- The total download for this object (a GIF image) takes an additional three seconds due to the TCP timeout and retransmission period. (We don't actually see an indication of a lost packet, but this is what it looks like.)

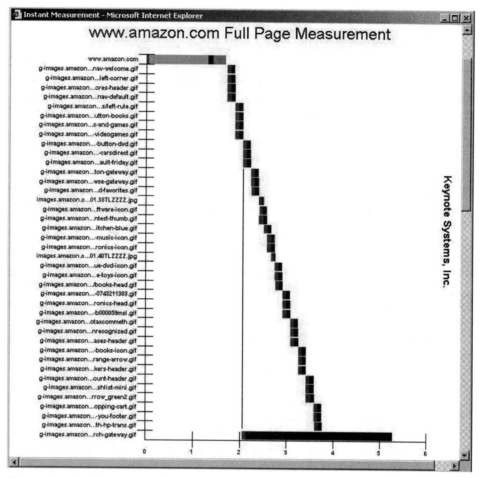

Figure 18.11 Diagnostic showing packet loss.

Source: Keynote Systems, Inc.

- During this time, one of the TCP connections is unavailable for other purposes, so from the time the packet is lost (just after two seconds into the entire process), only three images—not four—can be downloaded at a time.

- Although it appears graphically that without the loss of a packet this page would download in approximately four seconds, in fact it takes only slightly more than three seconds. The difference is that the fourth TCP connection is then available, and the physical pipe is therefore used more efficiently.

- A total of 164 packets were transmitted or received during the request and download of this web page, so the loss of a single packet represents a packet loss rate of less than 1 percent.

In the example shown in Figure 18.11, the loss of just a single packet is responsible for approximately a 60 percent increase in the download time of the page.

TCP Slow Start and Congestion Avoidance

Packet loss is a good indication of possible *congestion* along a route. When a link becomes congested, the only quick fix available to a web server or browser is to reduce the amount of traffic on the link. It's like what happens when the electrical supply is low. If everyone reduces their demand by a small amount, more serious problems for all can be avoided. To support a similar kind of good network citizenship, the TCP specification includes *congestion avoidance* to help reduce the traffic on congested routes.

When a TCP/IP connection is first established, both ends are initialized to transmit only two packets in the first *window*. This is referred to as the *slow start* process, intended to get some congestion-avoidance help from the TCP/IP protocol implementations at either end of the connection. (Before the adoption of slow start to the TCP specification, all hosts began transmitting a larger burst of packets as soon as possible.)

As packets are successfully received and acknowledged, the sender increases the size of the window in stages, which improves the efficiency of the connections. But TCP uses packet loss as an implicit indication of congestion, and as soon as just a single packet is lost, the sender drastically reduces the rate at which it sends packets. Furthermore, the sender then increases that rate much more slowly than it did when the connection was first established.

The theory (and it works) is that by reducing the load on a congested link, more data can get through without packet loss. Therefore, all of the connections using that link will experience better overall throughput than if they all tried to stuff packets onto the link as quickly as possible.

Because of slow start, it takes a while before a connection runs at full speed, so efficient use of TCP requires that connections exist for a reasonable period of time. The scheme works particularly well for file transfer operations such as program or music file downloads that move thousands or even millions of packets. When used to move web pages, however, TCP connections may be very short-lived. For instance (particularly when using the older version, 1.0, of HTTP), a brand-new connection may be created for each object on a web page. Once a single packet is lost on such a short-lived connection, the damage is done, since (as we've seen) the three-second timeout period can be a substantial percentage of the lifetime of the connection. Furthermore, due to congestion avoidance, it's possible that the speed of the connection will never return to its maximum before that connection is terminated.

> **TIP** Recognize that the effect of lost packets is not limited to just the retransmission time, but that they're also used implicitly to reduce the effective speed of connections.

Jitter

We've seen how packet loss is the biggest problem for web pages. On the other hand, streaming protocols, such as those used by RealNetworks' RealPlayer or Microsoft's Windows Media Player, are most vulnerable to another phenomenon called *jitter*—variations in latency.

When a streaming client starts receiving data from a server, it fills a buffer with a number of packets. While doing so, the client communicates with the server to adjust the rate at which the server will transmit data, based on the measured speed and latency of the connection. The buffer acts as a reservoir that allows the software to deliver audio or video to the user at a steady rate, even if the data arrives at a not-so-steady rate.

It all works well, as long as the throughput and latency of the connection remain relatively constant. If the data rate drops or the latency increases, not enough packets may get to the client in time, and a *buffer underflow* condition may occur. If that happens, the playback of audio or video must stop in midstream while the buffer is refilled and the connection is reoptimized for the now-different throughput.

If the data rate increases substantially or the latency decreases, there's a potential for *buffer overflow,* and hence packet loss, in which case the received data is either lost (if UDP is used) or the connection goes into retransmit mode (if TCP is used).

TIP Beware of jitter (variations in latency) for streaming media applications.

Performance Analysis Tools

Now that we understand the performance criteria (reachability, packet loss, and latency) and bandwidth measurements (from the models we developed in Chapter 11, "Traffic Models"), let's look at some of the tools available both for evaluating connectivity during the vendor-selection process and for monitoring these criteria once a site is up and running.

In general, there are two sources for connectivity data:

Vendors' reports. Vendors should be able to give you access to reports that show the uptime, latency, and packet loss on their links to the major ISPs. You shouldn't use a vendor that doesn't track these things, so the only question is whether the vendor is willing to share this data with you.

Third-party reports. There are a number of independent web sites that measure, record, and report various data regarding the major ISPs. Although these sites tend to focus on ISPs, and don't track many of the web-hosting services, with a little analytical thinking you can use their data to get some idea of how well a hosting service can be reached by the customers of the ISPs that are monitored.

Vendor Reports

Every good web-hosting service monitors its Internet connections on an ongoing basis, and shouldn't hesitate to provide you with access to the reports from its monitoring system. Outages are a fact of life in the web-hosting business, and how a vendor's systems handle outages and peak traffic demands are fundamental criteria for your evaluation.

Two styles of vendor reports are available: *summary* and *detailed.* Figure 18.12 contains an example of an online summary report showing vendor's reachability, packet

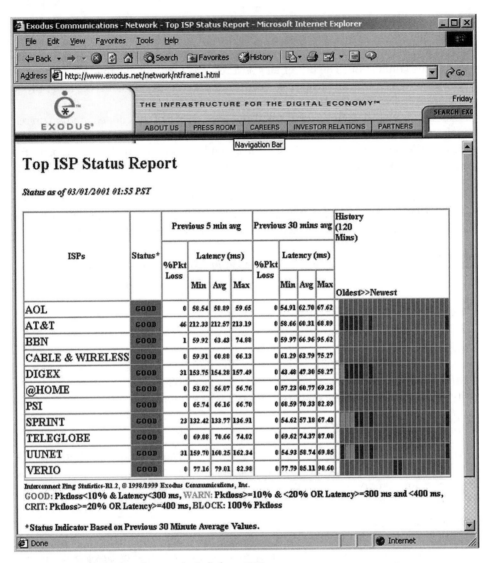

Figure 18.12 Web-hosting service's links to ISPs.

Source: Exodus Communications, Inc.

loss, and latency from selected ISPs. This example contains numerical data for the 30 minutes immediately preceding, and an iconic representation of the past two hours. Other web-hosting services have similar reports.

In many cases, you can get access to graphs that show the actual performance of each of a vendor's Internet links over extended periods of time. Figures 18.13 and 18.14 are graphs from one vendor's real-time network status page.

Figure 18.13 displays the traffic for a one-week period on a DS-3 (45 Mbps) peering connection between a web-hosting service and a major ISP. There appears to have been an outage on this link early Tuesday morning. (Note that these graphs indicate time in right-to-left order.)

`Weekly' Graph (30 Minute Average)

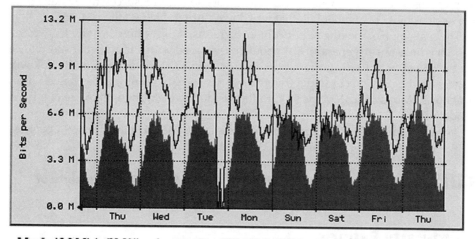

Max In:10.0 Mb/s (22.3%) Average In: 4401.8 kb/s (9.8%) Current In:4820.7 kb/s (10.7%)
Max Out:13.2 Mb/s (29.3%) Average Out:7175.1 kb/s (15.9%) Current Out:9078.0 kb/s (20.2%)

Figure 18.13 DS-3 peering (week).
Source: Metromedia Fiber Network, Inc.

`Yearly' Graph (1 Day Average)

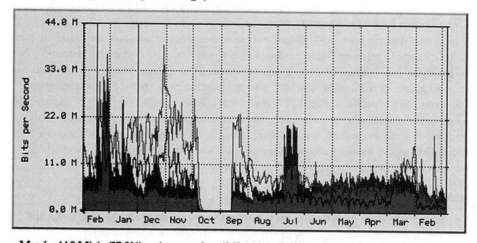

Max In:44.0 Mb/s (97.8%) Average In: 4068.1 kb/s (9.0%) Current In: 4057.8 kb/s (9.0%)
Max Out:38.9 Mb/s (86.5%) Average Out:5244.7 kb/s (11.7%) Current Out:8198.7 kb/s (18.2%)

Figure 18.14 DS-3 peering (year).
Source: Metromedia Fiber Network, Inc.

Figure 18.14 shows the traffic on this same link for an entire year, and it looks like the link was down for more than a month from mid-September through the end of October.

While outages are interesting to observe, they don't necessarily imply that a hosted web site has become unreachable or even slow. Good web-hosting services have multiple routes and excess capacity that allow them to bypass most of these problems. Note in Figure 18.14 that traffic doubled for about two weeks in mid-July, then returned to its previous level. This may have been due, in fact, to this link successfully taking over the responsibility of another link that was down during that period.

The real value of looking at performance graphs is to see how heavily loaded the vendor's links are. In general, a link should be replaced with one of higher speed once the sustained peak traffic is more than about one-third of the maximum the link will handle. In the previous example (referring to the weekly graph), the sustained peak is about 12 Mbps on a 45 Mbps link, so the vendor is operating within the one-third guideline.

Another benefit of having access to graphs such as these is that it fosters openness between a web-hosting service and its customers.

TIP Ask prospective vendors to show you their traffic and outage reports, or (even better) give you access to their real-time traffic graphs.

Third-Party Reports

In addition to reports and graphs made available by vendors, there are also third-party reports available online, notably the Internet Health Report and those from Matrix.net.

Matrix.net

Matrix.net (www.matrix.net) monitors a growing list of ISPs and web-hosting services using a system based on *beacons* (off-the-shelf computers running special software) that are deployed around the world. These beacons attempt to reach tens of thousands of destinations every 15 minutes. Matrix sells its data to vendors and corporate customers, but also makes an interesting summary available online at no charge. The Matrix.net web site is a good source of information on interpreting Internet performance measurements.

Figure 18.15 is a partial screenshot of one of the online reports generated by Matrix.net, including the results of tests for latency, packet loss, and reachability. This is a helpful and objective tool for evaluating web-hosting services or the ISPs to which they are connected. This report shows, for example, that Telia Net (Northern Europe) is experiencing long latencies (324 msec average) on this particular day.

TIP Use Matrix.net's free reports to gain a high-level perspective on the performance of major ISPs and web-hosting services. Reports are also valuable for evaluating the ISPs used by small and midsized web-hosting services.

Internet Health Report

Another useful tool is the Internet Health Report, provided at no charge by Keynote Systems at www.internethealthreport.com. Both hourly and daily reports are available.

The top-level matrix shown in Figure 18.16 indicates the latencies between some of the major Internet backbones. The numbers in the grid are the aggregate measured latencies in milliseconds for round-trips. The table is symmetrical, so the latency from

ISP	Latency Day			Packet Loss Day			Reach-ability Day		
	Week	Month		Week	Month		Week	Month	
Jump (46)	58.4			0			100		
	62.3	65.7		0.0776	0.309		100	100	
Infonet (Europe) (37)	132			0			100		
	128	132		0	0.487		100	99.6	
Exodus (51)	69.5			0.192			100		
	70.9	70.3		0.248	0.258		100	100	
Broadwing (49)	66.2			0.204			100		
	68.6	69.5		0.175	0.676		100	99.6	
Cable & Wireless plc.. (83)	62.7			0.241			100		
	64	64.7		0.327	0.503		100	100	
IBM.net (31)	162			0.323			100		
	163	159		0.507	2.28		100	98.3	
Telia Net (64)	324			0.452			100		
	170	152		0.385	1.37		100	99.3	
Qwest Communications (156)	54.7			0.513			100		
	55.7	55.3		0.527	0.801		100	100	
AppliedTheory (65)	51.3			0.769			100		
	52	61.7		0.715	1.34		100	99.4	

Figure 18.15   Internet ratings.

Source: Matrix.net, Inc.

C&W to Sprint, for example, is the same as from Sprint to C&W. Clicking on any value in the grid displays the Internet Health Report's second level, as shown in Figure 18.17.

At the second level, the Internet Health Report site shows the latencies between individual agents. For instance, Figure 18.17 illustrates that the worst case between the C&W and Sprint exchanges (384 milliseconds) is occurring between the Keynote *agent* connected to C&W in San Francisco and the agent connected to the Sprint network in New York City.

TIP Use the Internet Health Report as a cross-check when diagnosing short-term (day or month) performance problems.

This chapter introduced the first of our tools, notably vendor-specific and third-party online reports for Internet connectivity as measured by packet loss, latency, and reachability. We also studied the issues of packet loss and latency in depth, and saw

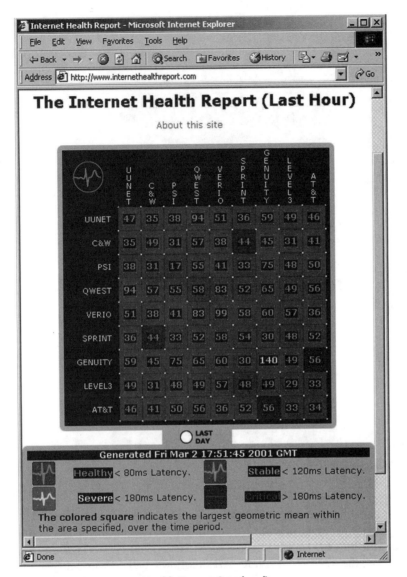

Figure 18.16 Internet Health Report (top level).

Source: Keynote Systems, Inc.

why (at least for web pages) packet loss is much more critical than latency. This chapter also introduced the concept of benchmark sites and servers as a way of isolating connectivity from other issues, and of comparing the quality of the connectivity of multiple vendors.

In Chapter 19, we'll continue our exploration of tools by looking at how the same benchmark site concept can play an important role in monitoring your web site once it's up and running.

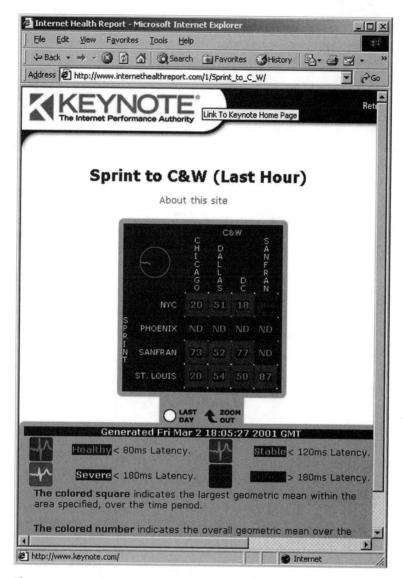

Figure 18.17   Internet Health Report (second level).

Source: Keynote Systems, Inc.

Monitoring

In Chapter 18, "Connectivity Performance," we introduced the concepts of using benchmark servers and benchmark sites, and how they can be monitored by a third-party service to measure the performance of your web site. In this chapter we'll look more closely at the various types of monitoring systems, both software packages and third-party services, that are available to help you and your web-hosting service or MSP manage your web site.

We'll look at how to monitor your web site in these two ways:

External monitoring. As presented in Chapter 18, external monitoring is usually provided by a third-party commercial service. This type of monitoring is used to track your web site's performance and availability from the perspective of your visitors. External monitoring answers questions such as: Is your site working? Is it fast enough? Is the content correct? Are the communications links between your site and your visitors working properly?

Internal monitoring. This type of monitoring tracks the individual hardware and software components that make up your web site. Internal monitoring answers questions such as: Are the proper programs running? Is there sufficient disk space and RAM and CPU capacity? Internal monitoring watches individual servers, while external monitoring watches the entire site. Internal monitoring looks for causes, while external monitoring tests results.

As we'll see, it's important to use both types of monitoring for your web site, and we'll keep this distinction in mind as we examine various monitoring solutions, categorized according to the purposes they serve:

Comparisons. Monitoring can be used to compare your live site to a benchmark site, such as described in Chapter 18.

Competitive analysis. You can use monitoring to make sure your web site is as available and performing at least as well as your competitors' web sites.

Notification. A monitoring system can alert your web-hosting service staff via email and pager whenever a problem occurs.

Diagnostics. Once a problem has been detected, monitoring tools can help identify its cause. They can also help determine who (you, your web-hosting service, or a third party) should take responsibility for solving the problem.

Trend reporting. Monitoring can help you anticipate the need for server upgrades or corrective actions before serious problems develop.

Comparisons: Baselines and Service Levels

In Chapter 18, we looked at the use of benchmark servers and benchmark sites as a way to compare the connectivity of different web-hosting services during the vendor-selection process. But the usefulness of benchmark servers and sites doesn't end once you've selected a vendor. If you continue to operate and monitor the benchmark server or site at your selected vendor's facility, you'll have a tremendous advantage when it comes time to diagnose problems and determine who's responsible for solving them.

During the vendor-evaluation period, you'll have developed a certain expectation of how well your actual web site will perform based on the performance of your benchmark site. Even before your site goes live, you'll have established a *baseline*—a measurement that can serve as a future reference point. Once your site is live, you can continue to measure connectivity performance using the same benchmark site and monitoring system you used during your evaluation.

However, don't expect your live web site to perform as well as your benchmark site did during the evaluation. There are two reasons for this. First, your live web site won't be as efficient as your benchmark site. The actual web site and web pages will typically be more complex. Second, once visitors begin to access your site, the performance of your live servers will likely diminish due to the loads placed on them. In any case, the performance of your live site will certainly vary as it experiences fluctuations in site traffic. Your benchmark site is immune to such variations, since the only hits it receives come from your external monitoring service. This stability is what makes it so valuable.

You can't ask your web-hosting service to guarantee that your live web site will be as fast as your benchmark site was during your vendor selection process. But because your benchmark site is simple, it never changes, and it's not affected by fluctuations in traffic (it only processes requests received from your monitoring service), you *can* ask the web-hosting service to guarantee the performance of your *benchmark site* rather than your live site. You're saying, in effect, "My benchmark site receives very little traffic and I promise not to change it. I want you (the web-hosting service) to guarantee the consistency and performance of your services as measured by the external performance of this site." This is why it's so valuable to run a benchmark site perpetually.

> **TIP** Keep your benchmark site running at your selected web-hosting service beyond the vendor-evaluation period and throughout the lifetime of your web site.

The SLAs covering connectivity should, therefore, be written with respect to your benchmark site, not your live site. If the connectivity is good to your benchmark site, it will be good to your live site. And if there's a problem that's associated only with your live site—not your benchmark site—you'll know it's not due to a connectivity problem. Not only is such an SLA strategy for connectivity fair to both parties, it also clearly separates responsibilities where they should remain separate. On one hand, there's the responsibility for your web site that consists of one or more servers that *generate* web pages. On the other hand, separate from the servers, there's the responsibility for the communications infrastructure that *delivers* those web pages. When it comes time to assign responsibility, it's important to keep these separate.

> **TIP** Use the measured performance of the benchmark site as the basis for your connectivity SLA.

Let's look at exactly how maintaining a benchmark site, entirely independent from your live site, allows you to quickly determine whether a problem is within your site or beyond it. The series of three images shown in Figures 19.1, 19.2, and 19.3 illustrate how effective this can be.

In Figure 19.1, everything is running smoothly. The bottom line represents the benchmark site. The middle line is the live site. The top line represents the performance of the Business 40 Average, an average of 40 major web sites, that provides a reference for what may be happening elsewhere on the Internet.

In Figure 19.2, however, something has clearly gone wrong between approximately 3:00 A.M. and noon on February 28. If the cause of the problem were within the live web-site servers (middle line), the benchmark site (bottom line) would not have been affected. Yet we can clearly see that *both* the live site and the benchmark site were affected. Therefore, we can be reasonably certain that the problem was somewhere within the web-hosting service's connectivity infrastructure. The fact that the Business 40 Average was not affected during this period further suggests that the problem was not on an even wider scale, as would happen if the problem were caused by one of the Internet backbone ISPs.

We have a very different situation in Figure 19.3. In this instance we see that around midnight on February 25, the live web site became very slow and stayed that way until the morning of February 26. But this time the benchmark site appears unaffected. We can conclude, therefore, that in this instance the problem was indeed within the web site's own servers.

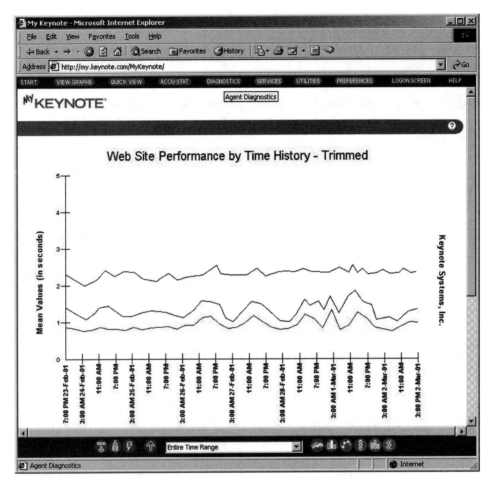

Figure 19.1   Business 40 Average, live site, and benchmark site.

Source: Keynote Systems, Inc.

From these examples we can see two benefits of maintaining your benchmark site or server beyond your vendor evaluation period, and, in fact, forever. First, when a performance problem occurs, you can immediately determine whether its cause is within your site's servers or in the connectivity. The distinction is critical, as it determines responsibility for resolving the problem. Without this data, even the problem determination—let alone the resolution—can take hours or even days.

Second, by retaining the data captured during your vendor-evaluation process, it's possible to hold your selected vendor accountable for maintaining the performance observed at that time. Without the early benchmark data, there would be no baseline; and unless the benchmark site continues to run, there are no data, independent of the live web site, that can be compared to the baseline.

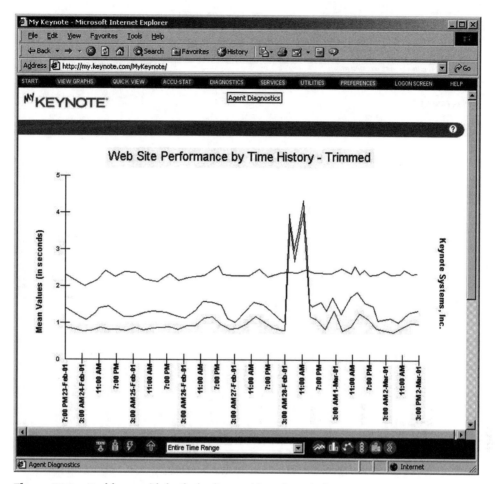

Figure 19.2   Problems with both the live and benchmark sites.

Source: Keynote Systems, Inc.

Competitive Analysis

An external measurement service can also be used to compare the performance and availability of your web site with those of your competitors. Figure 19.4 is an example of this, showing the performance of the web sites of three competitors in the same industry.

This graph shows the response time (performance) of three different weather-related web sites, plotted over a three-day period. As you can see, there are performance variations that affect all three sites, such as a slowdown at approximately 4:00 A.M. on the second day. But accuweather.com—represented by the lowest of the three curves—was the fastest site in every measurement.

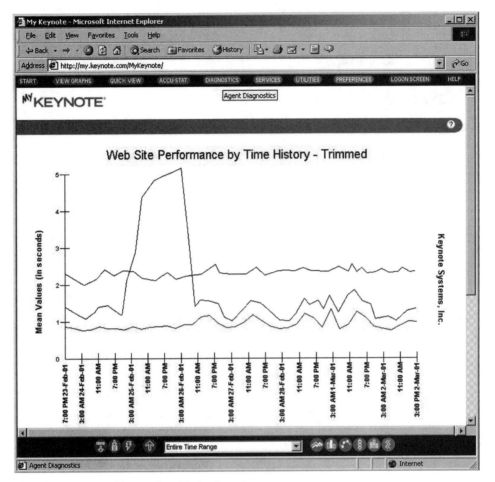

Figure 19.3   A problem only with the live site.

Source: Keynote Systems, Inc.

Not only can you use competitive analysis measurements like these after your web site is up and running, you can also use them before your web site is built and before you've selected your web-hosting service or MSP. This will help you communicate your objectives and expectations both within your organization and with prospective vendors.

TIP Measure the performance of your competitors' web sites. Use this data before your site goes live to communicate your expectations both within your own company and to your vendors. Use it after your site goes live in order to see how responsive your web site is to your customers relative to the responsiveness of your competitors' sites.

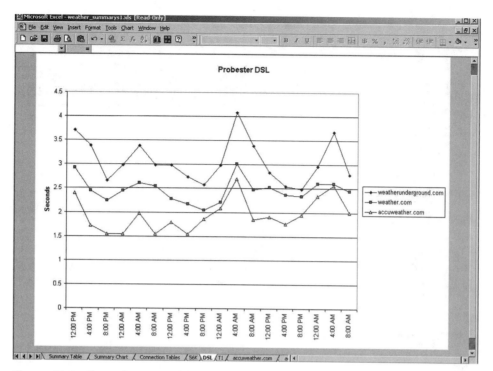

Figure 19.4   Three-site competitive analysis.

Source: SolidSpeed Networks, Inc.

Notification

The most important of all monitoring systems are those that detect problems and notify the appropriate personnel. There are two types of notification monitors: those that monitor internally (we'll discuss them later in this chapter), and those that monitor the web site externally. The same external monitoring systems that measure the performance of your benchmark site can be used to alert your web-hosting service or MSP to availability and performance problems of your live site.

Figure 19.5 shows the average response time of a single web server over a 24-hour period. The horizontal axis is the time of day, and the vertical axis is the average time to download the benchmark page, in seconds. There are two threshold levels, as indicated by the horizontal dotted lines. The lower level represents the *warning* threshold, which is set at three seconds. In this instance, the web site being monitored exceeded that level at 3:00 A.M., and the alarm was sounded. An hour later, at 4:00 A.M., the four-second *critical* threshold was exceeded and another alarm was sounded.

Third-party notification systems can be configured to send alerts via email and pager. Email can be automatically routed into your web-hosting service or MSP's incident tracking system.

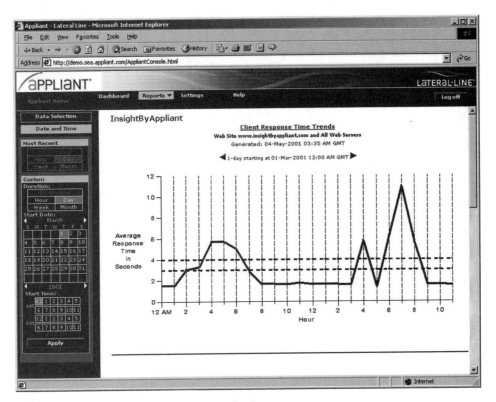

Figure 19.5 External response-time monitoring.
Source: Appliant.com, Inc.

TIP Ask your prospective web-hosting service or MSP if it uses the notification capabilities of external services. If so, you should be able to get access to the reports and be added to the notification address list. If they don't use such services (i.e., they depend entirely on their own monitoring systems), consider contracting for external monitoring yourself in order to track your web site and the responsiveness of your web-hosting vendor.

Content and Functionality

One thing to watch out for with any product or service that monitors your web site's reachability is that it doesn't just look for the absence of an error code, but actually checks the *content* returned by your servers. Monitoring packages issue HTTP *requests* to web servers, and then await the *responses.* If the responses contain no explicit error codes, some simplistic monitoring systems don't check further, and report that all is well.

Although no HTTP error is signaled, there may be a problem internal to the web site that causes the *wrong content* to be generated. For example, many applications servers will generate web pages containing cryptic messages when they can't access the web site's database. Although the web site is severely broken in this situation, no HTTP errors are reported. Because the error messages are contained in legitimate HTML web pages, a monitoring system that merely checks for the presence or absence of an error code will assume the web site is operating properly.

TIP **Make sure that any monitoring system that tests your site's response to HTTP requests checks the accuracy of the returned content.**

One way to check the accuracy of content is to create a special *monitoring page* whose sole purpose is to be checked by the monitoring system. By doing this, you can monitor the functional components deep within your web-site architecture. For instance:

Application servers. You can check that your app servers are alive and well by including in your monitoring page some content that's dynamically generated by your app servers. Just make sure the content is regenerated for each request, rather than served from your app servers' cache.

Database servers. Likewise, your monitoring page can include content that requires retrieval from your database. Again, watch out for caching in the database and the app servers to make sure that the links to the database and the database itself are being exercised and tested. If your application uses database pooling, make sure your monitoring page does so as well.

The actual content displayed on your monitoring page isn't critical, and should, in fact, be as simple as possible. Its only purpose is to be read and verified by the monitoring system and compared to the expected results. You also don't need to get fancy and create separate web pages to monitor separate components. A single notification alerting you to any problem with a single page is entirely adequate. Once the alarm is sounded, you can look at the monitoring page or use other techniques to pinpoint the actual problem. The key to success with this concept is to exercise as many internal components of the system as possible in the generation of a single page.

TIP **Develop a special monitoring page on your web site, the content of which depends on as many of the internal components of your web site as possible. Use the monitoring system to test the generated content of the monitoring page as a means of verifying that the internal components are operating properly.**

Diagnostics

Once your web-hosting service or MSP determines there's a problem, the next step is to begin diagnosis. Again, third-party monitoring services can play a role in this part of the process. For example, Figure 19.6 shows a diagnostic tool that displays the delivery of a web page in detail.

The deliveries of the web objects (the underlying web page and 12 images, identified on the vertical axis) are shown according to time (on the horizontal axis). The deliveries are broken down into the time spent in DNS lookups, establishing TCP/IP connections, possible HTTP redirections (there are none in this example), the time spent waiting for

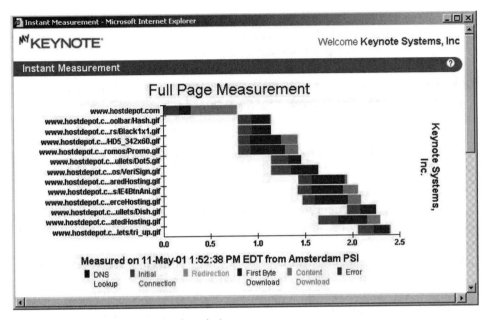

Figure 19.6 Detailed download analysis.

Source: Keynote Systems, Inc.

the server to process the request ("First Byte Download"), the actual download time, and any errors (none in this example). Figure 19.6 illustrates that this particular page is downloading properly; it takes about 2.4 seconds.

Figure 19.7 shows the downloading of the same web page when something is wrong and after a performance alarm has occurred. In this example, the alarm went off because the apparent performance of the site (in this case, as measured from a location in Amsterdam) was such that the page was consistently slow to download due to packet loss problems. The alarm—although not shown graphically in this instance—was set to go off whenever the download time consistently exceeded five seconds.

In Figure 19.7 note that the Content Download times for four objects seem particularly long. First, the underlying web page took three seconds longer than usual (as compared to Figure 19.6), and until this underlying page is downloaded completely, no other object can be requested. Two other images (.gif files) required an extra three seconds each. Finally, one image took six extra seconds to download.

As explained in Chapter 18, these three-second delays (including two that combined to create the six-second delay) are almost always a symptom of packet loss. The next step a web-hosting service or MSP might take would be to determine whether the packet loss was also present when this site was accessed from other locations and via other ISPs, and whether the web-hosting service's other customers were experiencing the packet loss. In some cases, the entire problem can be diagnosed, or at least identified, through the use of this type of third-party external diagnostic tools.

TIP Use the diagnostic capabilities of third-party monitoring tools to begin the problem determination process for performance problems.

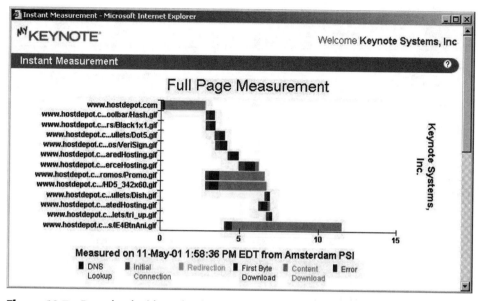

Figure 19.7   Download with packet loss.

Source: Keynote Systems, Inc.

Internal Monitoring

The external web-site monitors we've looked at so far are like having a nurse come into your hospital room every five minutes to take your pulse and make sure you're still breathing. They're important, but they track only the most general aspects of the systems under test. They won't indicate, in the hospital example, if you're suffering from a subtle condition that's about to result in a major heart attack.

An internal monitor, on the other hand, is more like being hooked up to a continuous heart monitor and EKG. It checks a number of specific measurements, alerting you or your web-hosting service to problems at a more detailed level than is possible with external monitoring alone.

Figure 19.8 shows an online status page from a system that monitors web sites internally. In this example, there are two problems, indicated by the *trouble* icon. First, there's something wrong with the disk on web server 2. Clicking on that *trouble* icon displays the details and trends of this particular problem, and would likely show that the server is about to run out of disk space. The display also indicates that there's a problem communicating with the email/DNS server using the SMTP protocol. Clicking on the icon for this problem might tell you, for example, that the server is unable to receive email from the outside world because SMTPD (the email process) has stopped running.

Internal monitors serve two very important purposes. First, like heart monitors, they can detect subtle problems before they become more significant. In the preceding example, for instance, web server 2 is not out of disk space quite yet, so the web site isn't

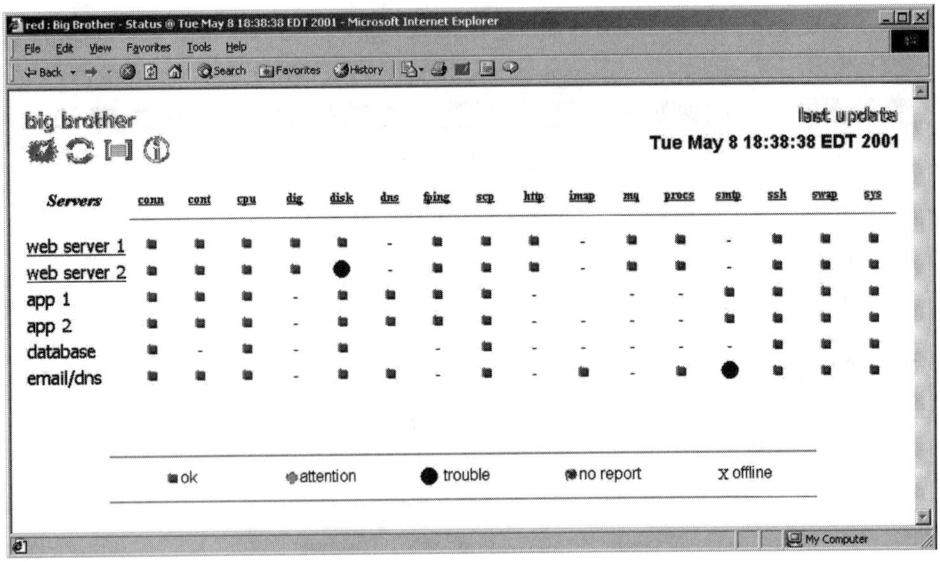

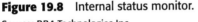

Figure 19.8   Internal status monitor.

Source: BB4 Technologies Inc.

affected and no external monitoring would, therefore, indicate a problem. But if this situation continues to worsen, web server 2 might stop due to lack of disk space, and hence affect the performance or availability of the entire web site.

The second purpose of an internal monitor is to support the diagnosis of problems. Again referring to the previous example, someone may have reported that he or she was not receiving email. A quick look at the monitor's display shows that the email/DNS server isn't responding to SMTP requests, so this server would be the first place to look in order to further diagnose the problem.

TIP Ask prospective vendors to show you the internal monitoring systems they use. You should be able to get web-enabled access to view the status of your servers. If you're using pure colocation, install such a monitoring system for yourself.

Trend Reporting

A good internal status-monitoring package will also create reports that allow you to see trends in the various measurements over time. Figure 19.9 is an example of such an online report. This report shows when a threshold was exceeded (represented by the darker bands) during the most recent 24 hours, the most recent week, the most recent four-week period, and for the past year.

Another report from a typical internal monitoring system is illustrated in Figure 19.10. In the upper section, this report shows the percentage of time that the measure-

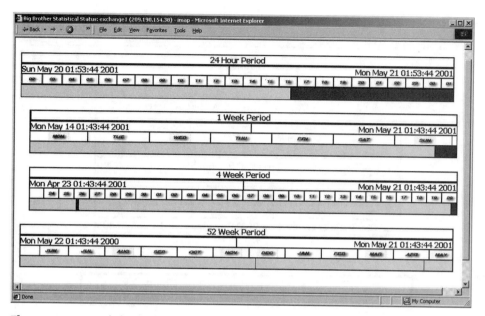

Figure 19.9 Trends by timeline.

Source: BB4 Technologies Inc.

ment taken rose above various thresholds (indicated by the six columns with unique icons) for the most recent week, four weeks, and year. The lower section of this report shows the date and time for every time the measurement crossed any threshold in either direction. For instance, looking at the second row of the "Last 50 log entries" table, the service being measured didn't change for 2,102,805 seconds from Thursday April 26, 08:42:11, 2001 until Sunday May 20 at 16:48:56.

> **TIP** Use the trend-reporting capabilities of internal monitoring systems to identify impending capacity problems. Compare this empirical data with the projections from the spreadsheets you developed in Chapter 11, "Traffic Models."

Reports for the Management Team

How often does someone inside your own company (particularly someone not familiar with the technological issues of the web) say to you, "Gee, our web site seems slow today." If you're the one responsible for keeping the web site running, even if you're outsourcing your hosting, this can be one of the most frustrating comments you hear.

The first few times this happens, you'll ask the important follow-up questions: "Can you be more specific? Are you accessing from your office or from home? Who's your ISP? Are you on DSL or dial-up? Do other web sites appear slow from your location,

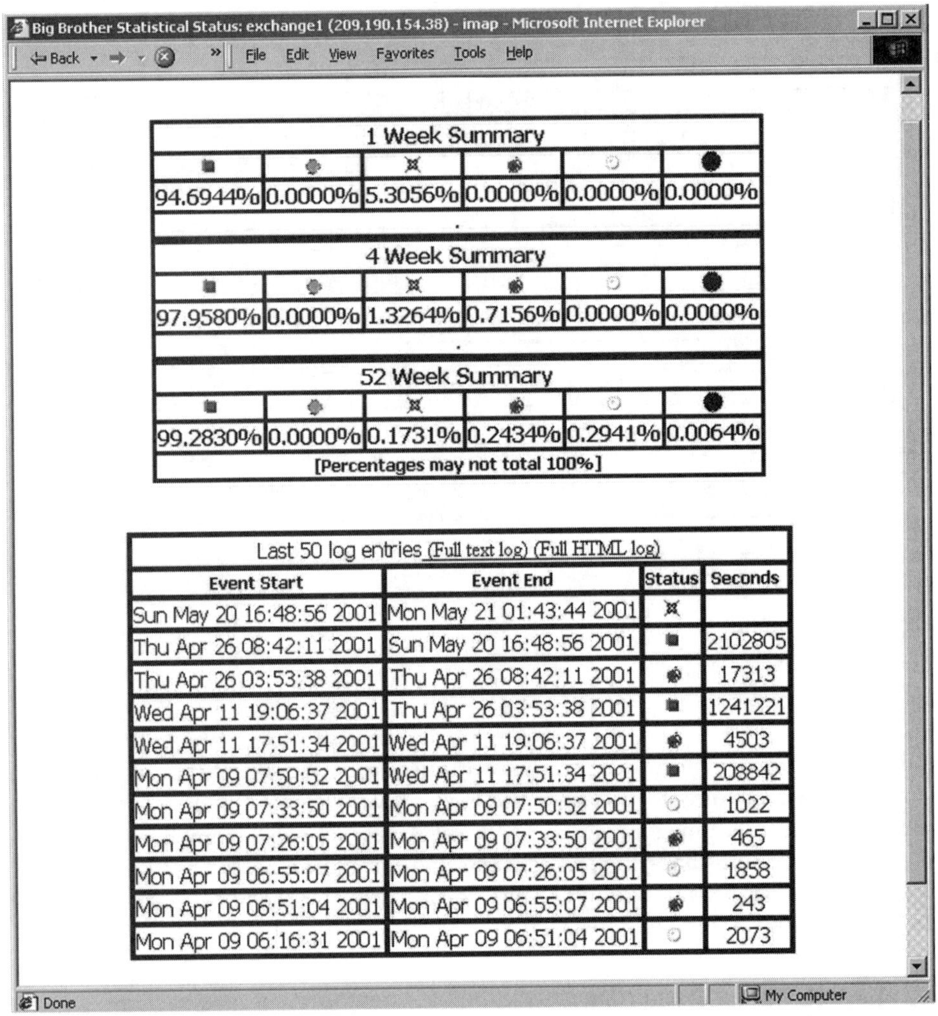

1 Week Summary					
94.6944%	0.0000%	5.3056%	0.0000%	0.0000%	0.0000%

4 Week Summary					
97.9580%	0.0000%	1.3264%	0.7156%	0.0000%	0.0000%

52 Week Summary					
99.2830%	0.0000%	0.1731%	0.2434%	0.2941%	0.0064%

[Percentages may not total 100%]

Last 50 log entries (Full text log) (Full HTML log)

Event Start	Event End	Status	Seconds
Sun May 20 16:48:56 2001	Mon May 21 01:43:44 2001		
Thu Apr 26 08:42:11 2001	Sun May 20 16:48:56 2001		2102805
Thu Apr 26 03:53:38 2001	Thu Apr 26 08:42:11 2001		17313
Wed Apr 11 19:06:37 2001	Thu Apr 26 03:53:38 2001		1241221
Wed Apr 11 17:51:34 2001	Wed Apr 11 19:06:37 2001		4503
Mon Apr 09 07:50:52 2001	Wed Apr 11 17:51:34 2001		208842
Mon Apr 09 07:33:50 2001	Mon Apr 09 07:50:52 2001		1022
Mon Apr 09 07:26:05 2001	Mon Apr 09 07:33:50 2001		465
Mon Apr 09 06:55:07 2001	Mon Apr 09 07:26:05 2001		1858
Mon Apr 09 06:51:04 2001	Mon Apr 09 06:55:07 2001		243
Mon Apr 09 06:16:31 2001	Mon Apr 09 06:51:04 2001		2073

Figure 19.10 Statistics.
Source: BB4 Technologies Inc.

too?" But soon you'll learn that these vaguely expressed concerns happen all the time, and while some of them are indicative of actual problems with your web site, others (perhaps most) are caused by external problems or don't turn out to be problems at all. Is it the site that's slow? Is it the user's ISP or the web-hosting service's connectivity? Or is it, perhaps, just another of those occasional Internet meltdowns?

There's nothing quite as good as objective (i.e., third-party) information to both allay the fears of others and to give you confidence in your own web site. The reports from your external monitoring service can play an important role in how you manage the expectations and comments from others on your management team and throughout your organization. In particular, third-party data convert people's qualitative concerns to quantitative (and quantifiable) issues, which otherwise tend to be emotional and inconsistent.

TIP Make the real-time and trend reports from external monitoring available to your management team and perhaps to your entire organization.

You can explain to people that when they have a concern about the performance or availability of the web site, they should first look at these reports. You can even provide a link to your monitoring systems on your intranet home page. You'll find this substantially reduces the number of offhand comments you receive about the performance of your web site.

When you publish these reports, it's important not to position them defensively. That is, be careful not to say, "Don't bother me unless you've checked the reports first." Instead, highlight the proactive advantages these reports offer: They're available day and night, and from any web browser, given proper authentication. By showing others that you also use these tools, and that you're on top of issues surrounding the web site, their confidence in you and your web-site operations will increase.

There are two issues you must consider, however. First, be aware that people will use these reports far more frequently than you might expect, and nontechnical managers will bestow upon the reports far more value than they deserve. Senior executives in particular have voracious appetites for data and charts such as these. Financial types will look at the reports every morning like clockwork, and some managers might even use the real-time status page as though it were a screensaver.

The last thing you want is someone looking at your reports and calling you every 20 minutes while you're in the middle of trying to solve the very problem they're observing. If you've already published access to the reports, and a problem appears for an extended period of time, publish a "we're working on it" status report next to the hyperlink for the reports. Some third-party monitoring services allow you to post such a notice on the web page containing an index of the reports for your site.

TIP Don't enable access to your reports until your web site has achieved some degree of stability.

The other issue to consider is that the results of your monitoring are effectively a report card for your personal performance. While that might seem scary at first, in fact it's a liberating concept. One of the challenges of managing a web site is defining your own success. There's nothing worse than going home at the end of the day, confident that you've done your job well, only to come back to work the next morning to learn that others (particularly your boss) felt otherwise. Publishing reports of your web site's availability and performance, including a comparison of your site relative to those of your competitors, is a good way to make sure that you and everyone else within your organization share a similar understanding of how well your site (and you) are doing. It's another case of ensuring matched expectations.

Monitoring systems—both internal and external—are valuable tools for understanding the performance of your web site and for alerting you and your web-hosting vendor to problems and potential problems. As we've seen, monitoring can also be used to compare the performance of your web site to a benchmark web site and to those of your competitors.

Monitoring is a passive tool; that is, once it's installed, it does its job in the background. In Chapter 20, "The Net Detective Toolkit," we'll look at tools you can use to actively research web sites and web-hosting vendors, and to diagnose the problems discovered by your monitoring systems.

The Net Detective Toolkit

"On the Internet no one knows you're a dog."
Dogbert

Earlier in this book we learned that a vendor that owns a beautiful data center isn't necessarily qualified to manage the servers housed inside. We also learned that many web-hosting services and MSPs don't even own their own facilities; and while some of them are very up front about this, others are not. Dogbert's corollary might be, "Things in web hosting aren't always what they appear to be."

In this chapter you'll become a Net detective. You'll learn how to discover secrets that vendors won't tell you, and how you can dispute or confirm some of the claims they make. In particular, you'll see how to find out what software a competitor is using for its web site, where its web site is hosted, and which (if any) content delivery network it uses. You'll also learn how to research a web-hosting service or MSP to find out who really owns its data center and what sites are hosted there.

Our Net Detective Toolkit includes the following:

- The capability to read and write HTTP as though you were a web browser.
- An online tool from Netcraft.com for analyzing web sites.
- The *traceroute* utility.
- The *whois* utility.
- Page-component diagnostics from Keynote Systems that we used in previous chapters.

Researching a Web Site

For our first example, we're going to investigate a live web site. Some of the questions we'll answer are: What operating system and web-server software is the site using, and where's the web site hosted?

Speaking HTTP

The HyperText Transport Protocol (HTTP) is the language that browsers use to request web pages or other objects, and the language that web servers use to send their responses. When a server replies to a request for a web object, it includes a description of itself in the *HTTP headers* of the response. HTTP is intended for computer-to-computer communications; it's normally invisible to humans. While you can use the View, Source feature of your web browser to see the HTML code that's returned by any web site, you still can't see the underlying HTTP headers. If you could "speak" HTTP, you could see those headers and, therefore, discover some interesting information about web servers.

The first web detective skill you'll acquire in this chapter (and the one that truly entitles you to proudly wear the Geek merit badge) is the ability to read and write HTTP as though you were a web browser. HTTP is based on the TCP/IP protocols, and most connections between browsers and servers use Internet Protocol (IP) *port 80* on both ends. *Telnet*, a remote-terminal utility, also uses TCP/IP, but it normally communicates over port 23. However, by instructing telnet to use port 80 instead of port 23, you can use it to communicate with a remote web server as though you were a web browser. In this way, and by typing HTTP commands by hand, you can see the actual HTTP responses and headers that are normally invisible, and thereby see the information a web site transmits about itself. Let's see how to perform this trick on a computer running Windows 2000 or NT, as shown in Figures 20.1 through 20.4.

We're going to use telnet.exe—a program that's shipped with all recent versions of Windows. But because the telnet program will halt as soon as we complete a single exchange with the remote web server, we need a way to see telnet's output even after the program terminates. Therefore, we'll start the program within a Windows *shell.*

As illustrated in Figure 20.1, begin by clicking on the Windows Start button, then on Run. Next, type "cmd" in the text box, as illustrated in Figure 20.2, and click OK. (Note: On older versions of Windows you'll have to type "command" instead of "cmd".)

We're going to use the Starbucks web site (www.starbucks.com) as our example, so at the Windows command prompt, as shown in Figure 20.3, type the following command, then press the Enter key:

```
telnet www.starbucks.com 80
```

It may appear as though nothing has happened, but you've initiated a TCP/IP connection to www.starbucks.com on port 80. The Starbucks web server now believes it has been contacted by a web browser and it's waiting to receive requests via the HTTP protocol. As this isn't normally a protocol for humans, the web server doesn't respond

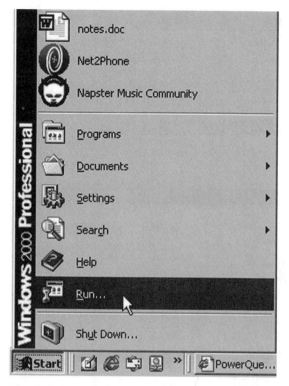

Figure 20.1 Windows Start button.

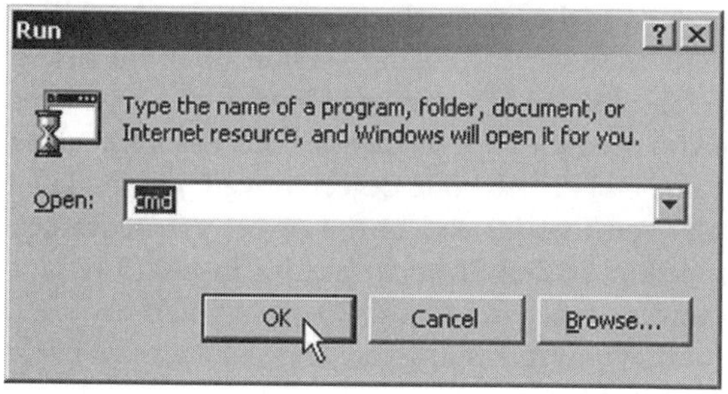

Figure 20.2 Windows 2000 Run.

with anything readable, or echo what you type. It just sits there, waiting for the web browser—in this instance, you.

The next step is to type the following command. You must type it exactly as shown here, using capital letters, spaces before and after the solitary slash (/), and no other spaces. Remember, you won't see it on your screen as you type.

```
HEAD / HTTP/1.0
```

Finally, press the Enter key *twice*, thereby following your request with a blank line.

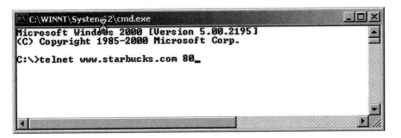

Figure 20.3   Running cmd.exe.

Figure 20.4   Response to HTTP HEAD request.

You've just sent an HTTP *HEAD* request to the Starbucks web server. You've asked it to respond with the headers for the *root document* (/) using version 1.0 of the HTTP protocol. In response, you'll get something like what's shown in Figure 20.4.

There's more information here than you need for your purposes, but let's look at a few of the more interesting lines. The first line ("HTTP/1.1 302 Object moved") is an HTTP *Temporary Redirect* (code 302). This tells you that instead of the object you requested (/), you should request the object specified in the *Location:* header in line 5 (www. starbucks.com/Default.asp); and if you were a real browser, that's what you'd do.

The second line contains the information you're looking for: The Starbucks web site is running the Microsoft-IIS/5.0 web server software.

Other items of interest include (a) the *Pragma* and *Cache-control* headers that instruct cache servers not to cache this particular URL, and (b) the *Set-Cookie* header that instructs the browser to store a cookie.

That's an awful lot of work just to learn that www.starbucks.com is running on Microsoft's IIS software, but it's good to know how browsers and servers communicate with one another via HTTP, and to know that you can emulate this interaction by hand-implementing telnet. Try doing the same thing to your own web site and see how it responds.

TIP Use telnet to send an HTTP HEAD command to competitors' web sites to learn what software the sites are using.

![Netcraft Web Site Finder - Microsoft Internet Explorer window showing the Netcraft home page at http://www.netcraft.com/ with "Explore 27,585,726 web sites", "23rd May 2001", a Simple Search field containing "www.starbucks.com" and a "Lookup!" button]

Figure 20.5   Netcraft home page.
Source: Netcraft

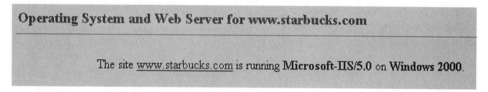

Operating System and Web Server for www.starbucks.com

The site www.starbucks.com is running Microsoft-IIS/5.0 on Windows 2000.

Figure 20.6   Netcraft OS and server report.
Source: Netcraft

Netcraft

Now that you've apprenticed using the hand tools, it's time to step up to the easier-to-use power tools. My favorite online tool for checking out a web site is run by Netcraft, in the United Kingdom, at www.netcraft.com.

On Netcraft's home page, shown in Figure 20.5, we'll begin by entering the host name of the site we want to check out, www.starbucks.com in this case.

After a few seconds, Netcraft tells us that it has discovered what you see in Figure 20.6. As shown, this is essentially the same information you retrieved using telnet, except that Netcraft also knows how to determine that the web server is running the Windows 2000 operating system in addition to the IIS/5.0 web server.

Netcraft also knows how to ask most operating systems how long they've been running since last being rebooted. A site that has been running for a long time may be better designed or managed than one that needs to be restarted frequently. While not the only indicator, this information can at least give you a clue as to a web site's stability.

TIP Use Netcraft to find out which operating system software a web site is running and how long the site's web server has been up since last being rebooted.

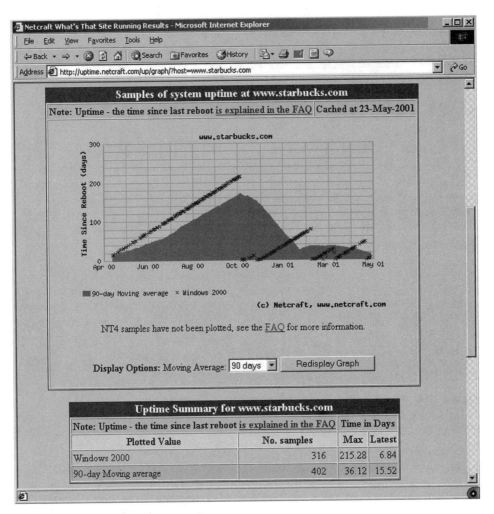

Figure 20.7 Netcraft uptime report.

Source: Netcraft

Figure 20.7 shows more of the Netcraft report on www.starbucks.com. Underneath the graph on the Netcraft report page is a tabular summary of www.starbucks.com's uptime. In the graph itself, the data points (small x's) indicate measurements by Netcraft. The Y-axis indicates the uptime for each measurement, and the dark area represents the uptime 90-day moving average.

The table below the graph summarizes the data. Note that for as long as Netcraft has monitored www.starbucks.com, the longest uptime period is 215 days, and the most recent uptime period is just under seven days. For some reason, Starbucks rebooted its web servers a week before this query. Running 215 days without a reboot is okay, but the 90-day moving average is only slightly more than two weeks (15.52 days). In other words, the trend is toward more frequent restarts of the web servers. We can't tell *why* the www.starbucks.com web server has been rebooted five times in the past six months,

Figure 20.8   Hosting history for www.starbucks.com.
Source: Netcraft

but it might be a question worth asking of its web-hosting service or MSP if we're considering it to host our web site.

Speaking of which, where is Starbucks' web site hosted? Scrolling down further on the Netcraft page we learn the answer, as shown in Figure 20.8.

Here we see that the IP address of the web server is 64.14.140.210. But more important, we learn that the IP address is within a *netblock* of addresses that belongs to Exodus Communications, one of the largest web-hosting services. Since the Starbucks web server has an IP address that's owned by Exodus, it's reasonable to conclude that Exodus hosts the Starbucks web site. This is, in fact, the case.

TIP Use Netcraft to find out where a web site is hosted.

While we've got our Netcraft tool handy, let's use it to learn a bit more about Exodus. If you click on one of the hyperlinks for Exodus Communications in Figure 20.8, you'll see up to 50 other web sites hosted at Exodus, as shown in Figure 20.9.

In fact, Exodus hosts thousands of sites, but Netcraft only lists the 50 sites that have been running for the longest continuous time. Note that many web servers at Exodus have long average uptimes.

What does this actually tell us about Exodus? For one thing, they host some web servers that haven't gone down in more than 20 months. The first five servers—all belonging to eBay—have been running for at least 625 days. That's an impressive run. You won't find too many web servers that have run nonstop for more than a year.

(Nobody's perfect, though. As I was writing these few paragraphs, I learned that on May 9, 2001, web sites belonging to 50 customers—including Yahoo!—went down when

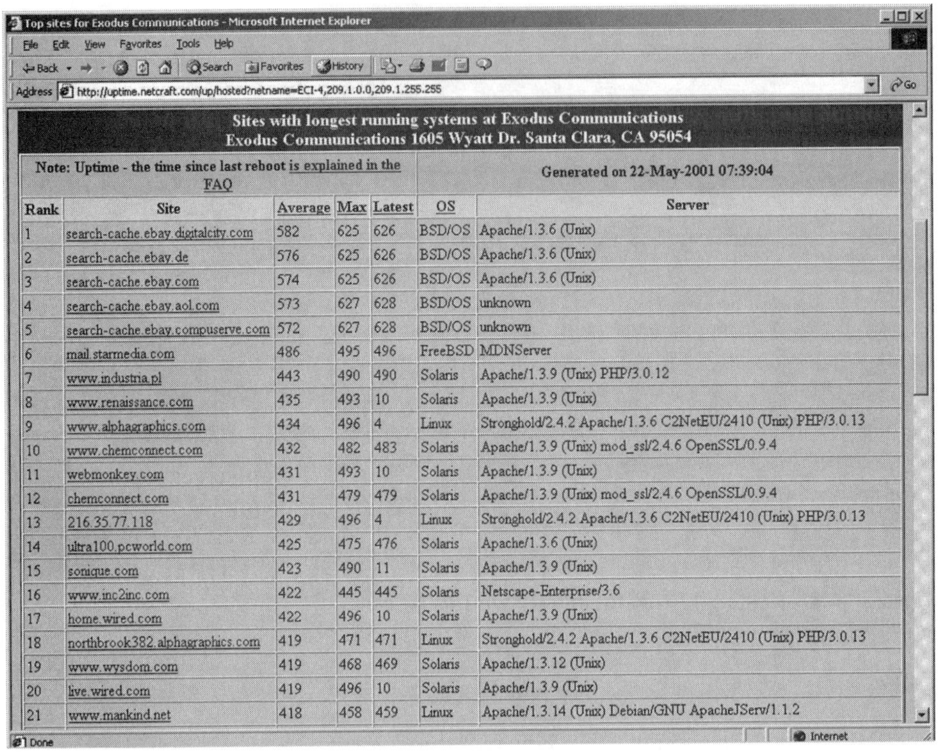

Top sites for Exodus Communications - Microsoft Internet Explorer

Address http://uptime.netcraft.com/up/hosted?netname=ECI-4,209.1.0.0,209.1.255.255

Sites with longest running systems at Exodus Communications
Exodus Communications 1605 Wyatt Dr. Santa Clara, CA 95054

Note: Uptime - the time since last reboot is explained in the FAQ

Generated on 22-May-2001 07:39:04

Rank	Site	Average	Max	Latest	OS	Server
1	search-cache.ebay.digitalcity.com	582	625	626	BSD/OS	Apache/1.3.6 (Unix)
2	search-cache.ebay.de	576	625	626	BSD/OS	Apache/1.3.6 (Unix)
3	search-cache.ebay.com	574	625	626	BSD/OS	Apache/1.3.6 (Unix)
4	search-cache.ebay.aol.com	573	627	628	BSD/OS	unknown
5	search-cache.ebay.compuserve.com	572	627	628	BSD/OS	unknown
6	mail.starmedia.com	486	495	496	FreeBSD	MDNServer
7	www.industria.pl	443	490	490	Solaris	Apache/1.3.9 (Unix) PHP/3.0.12
8	www.renaissance.com	435	493	10	Solaris	Apache/1.3.9 (Unix)
9	www.alphagraphics.com	434	496	4	Linux	Stronghold/2.4.2 Apache/1.3.6 C2NetEU/2410 (Unix) PHP/3.0.13
10	www.chemconnect.com	432	482	483	Solaris	Apache/1.3.9 (Unix) mod_ssl/2.4.6 OpenSSL/0.9.4
11	webmonkey.com	431	493	10	Solaris	Apache/1.3.9 (Unix)
12	chemconnect.com	431	479	479	Solaris	Apache/1.3.9 (Unix) mod_ssl/2.4.6 OpenSSL/0.9.4
13	216.35.77.118	429	496	4	Linux	Stronghold/2.4.2 Apache/1.3.6 C2NetEU/2410 (Unix) PHP/3.0.13
14	ultra100.pcworld.com	425	475	476	Solaris	Apache/1.3.6 (Unix)
15	sonique.com	423	490	11	Solaris	Apache/1.3.9 (Unix)
16	www.inc2inc.com	422	445	445	Solaris	Netscape-Enterprise/3.6
17	home.wired.com	422	496	10	Solaris	Apache/1.3.9 (Unix)
18	northbrook382.alphagraphics.com	419	471	471	Linux	Stronghold/2.4.2 Apache/1.3.6 C2NetEU/2410 (Unix) PHP/3.0.13
19	www.wysdom.com	419	468	469	Solaris	Apache/1.3.12 (Unix)
20	live.wired.com	419	496	10	Solaris	Apache/1.3.9 (Unix)
21	www.mankind.net	418	458	459	Linux	Apache/1.3.14 (Unix) Debian/GNU ApacheJServ/1.1.2

Figure 20.9 Other sites hosted at Exodus.

Source: Exodus Communications, Inc.

a 45,000-square-foot Exodus data center lost power. PG&E, the local utility company, had suffered an underground explosion, and the Exodus backup generators failed.)

The list in Figure 20.9 also tells us the types of web-site owners that have chosen Exodus to host their sites. We see many well-known names, like eBay, Star Media, PC World, and Wired. Some of the big boys live here. If your web site is as large and complex as some of these, Exodus could be a good vendor for you. At least you now know some of the web-site owners you can contact to find out how satisfied they've been with Exodus. On the other hand, if your web site is much smaller than eBay's and Wired's, you might want to consider a web-hosting service that has customers whose sites are more similar in size to yours.

TIP **Use Netcraft to learn the identities of some of a web-hosting service's customers, possibly some that aren't on the vendor's customer-reference list. Contacting these customers could provide valuable information about the vendor.**

Another interesting bit of information is that the Starbucks web site isn't among the 50 longest-running web sites at Exodus. You might conclude this has something to do with Starbucks' content or code, but there are other possible conclusions you should consider. If you look closely at Exodus' 50 longest-running web sites, you'll notice that they're all running on combinations of the Apache web-server software and variations of the Unix/Linux operating systems. None of the top 50 is using Microsoft's IIS, NT, or Windows 2000. Is there a correlation here? If so, what's causing it?

We don't have enough information to answer those questions, but we can speculate on possible causes that may, in turn, lead us to ask additional questions. We can't tell whether these customers' servers are managed by Exodus or whether they are pure colocation customers who manage the servers themselves or use third parties. If Exodus does manage these sites, it may not be as skilled at managing Windows-based web sites as it is at managing web sites based on Unix and its derivatives. If your site runs on Windows, you may want to find a web-hosting service whose top 50 sites include some that run on the Microsoft platform.

TIP The Netcraft report of a web-hosting service's 50 longest-running web sites may be an indication of the operating systems and web-server software packages with which a web-hosting vendor is most successful.

On the other hand, we could instead infer that it's not an issue of Exodus' skills at all, but rather that Microsoft's software isn't as reliable as Unix/Linux. Or perhaps it's because all of the NT-based sites were recently upgraded to Windows 2000.

Analyzing a Hosting Service

Not every web-hosting service is what it claims to be. Some are no more than marketing companies that depend on someone else to do the actual hosting. Some have state-of-the-art data centers, but have no idea how to manage a web server. There's a lot of "virtual reality" on the Internet, and hosting services are not immune to the syndrome.

Next let's research a web-hosting service picked at random from advertisements in one of the computer trade magazines, to see if it's really all that it claims to be. On its web site, Webhosting.com claims that it has, for example:

- High-speed redundant backbone
- Dual air conditioners
- Dual power grid
- Fire detection systems
- 24/7 monitoring

It sounds like Webhosting.com runs an impressive data center. Too bad we can't check out the air conditioning, power, fire detection, or monitoring from our desktops. Or can we?

We'll start by studying Webhosting.com's own web server, www.webhosting.com. We don't know whether Webhosting.com uses its own data center to host www.webhosting.com, but let's assume that it does. (If it turns out not to, it sure would be interesting to hear the vendor's explanation as to why not.)

Let's first see how much we can learn about www.webhosting.com using Netcraft's tools. The first thing we can see from the Netcraft report in Figure 20.10 is that

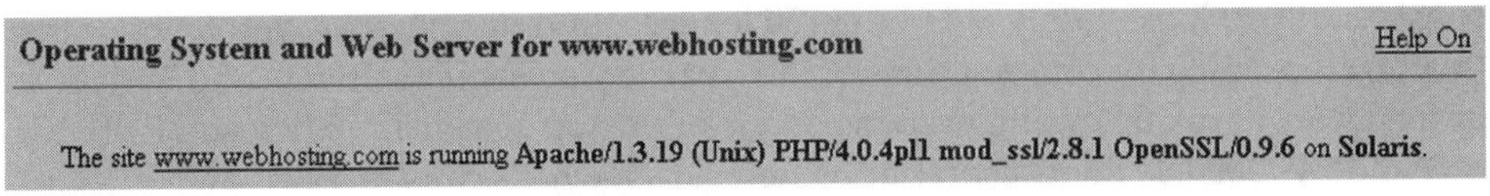

Figure 20.10 OS and web server analysis for www.webhosting.com.
Source: Netcraft

www.webhosting.com is running the Apache web server on the Solaris operating system. There's nothing to conclude yet; let's just file that fact away for future reference.

TIP Knowing the hardware and software platform a web-hosting service or MSP uses for its own site may provide insight into the vendor's skills and preferences.

Scrolling down, the Netcraft report continues in Figure 20.11.This part of the Netcraft report tells us that the www.webhosting.com web site has been up for the past 4.35 days and that the trend has been toward decreasing stability (i.e., the 90-day moving average of uptime has been going down). Again, we don't have enough information to know the cause of this trend. It could, for instance, be caused by intentional reboots, but it's something to make note of, and to perhaps follow up with the vendor.

Scrolling down still further, we see the table displayed in Figure 20.12. Here we see that www.webhosting.com upgraded from Apache 1.3.11 to 1.3.19 and from PHP 3.0.15 to 4.0.4 in March 2001. This upgrade corresponds with the reboot of the web server that occurred in early March, according to the graph in Figure 20.11; but it would still be interesting to ask Webhosting.com what happened in mid- and late-April to cause them to reboot the server again. It might also be interesting to find out who performed the Apache and PHP upgrades and why. The answer could provide further insight into Webhosting.com's skills and attitudes.

TIP Look for evidence of a web-hosting service or MSP's upgrades to its own web site to suggest directions for further research.

Who's Hosted There?

As we did for Exodus, we'd like to learn which web sites are hosted by Webhosting.com. Our hope is to learn a bit more about the vendor's skills, as well as to see who are its typical customers. This will help us determine the vendor's sweet spot, as described in Chapter 8, "Getting It Right."

By clicking on the links in the Netblock Owner column of the Netcraft report shown in Figure 20.12, Netcraft again returns a list of up to 50 other web sites hosted within the same netblock, as shown in Figure 20.13.

We can learn a lot from the report shown in this figure. For instance, Webhosting.com, Inc., is located in Toronto, at least according to its netblock registration. If you're not located in Canada, this may be significant. Perhaps there are issues of international commerce and taxation, or even copyright and trademark protection. (As we'll see shortly, however, this information can also be misleading. The data center and the business office aren't necessarily in the same location or even the same country.)

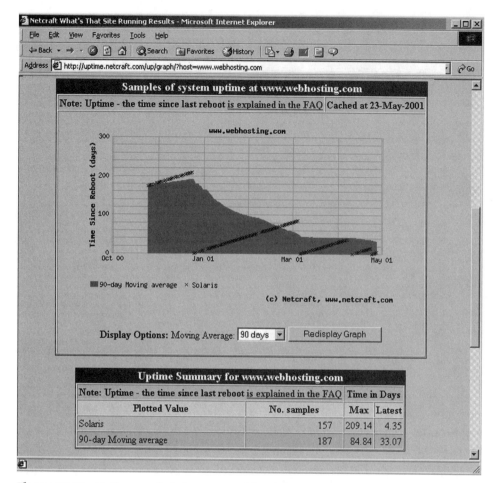

Figure 20.11   Uptime analysis for www.webhosting.com.
Source: Netcraft

| OS, Web Server and Hosting History for www.webhosting.com ||||||
OS	Server	Last changed	IP address	Netblock Owner
Solaris	Apache/1.3.19 (Unix) PHP/4.0.4pl1 mod_ssl/2.8.1 OpenSSL/0.9.6	21-Mar-2001	205.178.138.65	Webhosting.Com Inc.
Solaris	Apache/1.3.19 (Unix) PHP/4.0.4pl1 mod_ssl/2.8.1 OpenSSL/0.9.6	21-Mar-2001	205.178.138.65	Webhosting.Com Inc.
Solaris	Apache/1.3.11 (Unix) mod_perl/1.22 PHP/3.0.15	31-Oct-2000	205.178.138.65	Webhosting.Com Inc.

Figure 20.12   Hosting history for www.webhosting.com.
Source: Netcraft

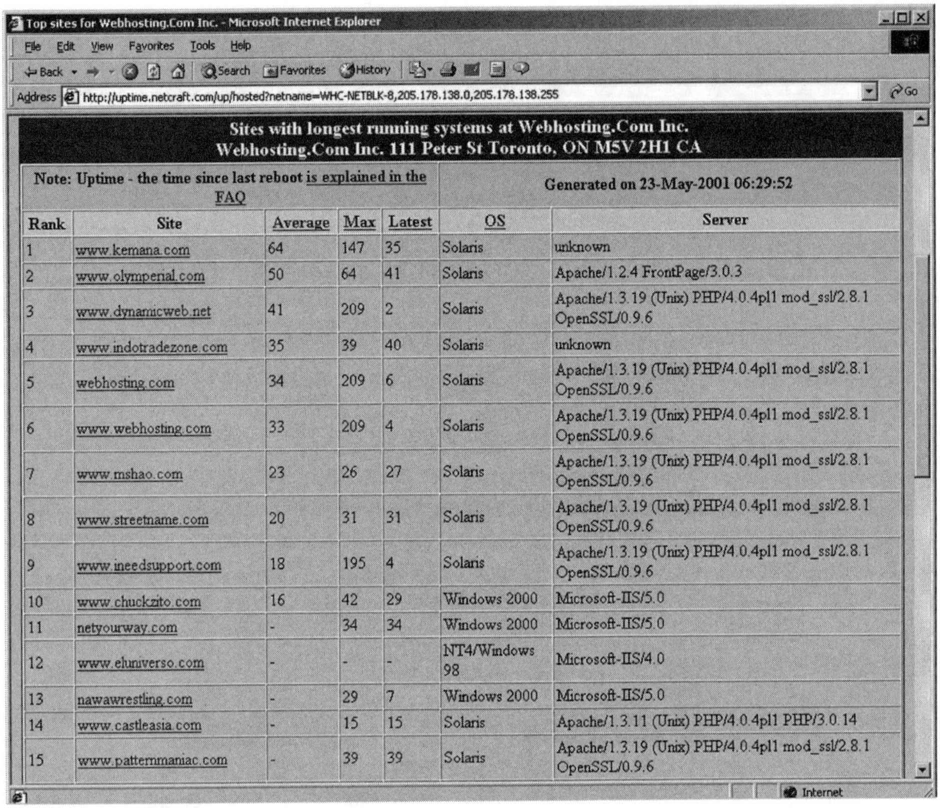

Figure 20.13 Other sites hosted at Webhosting.com.

Source: Netcraft

Webhosting.com hosts web sites running on both Microsoft Windows and Unix (Solaris). Its customers have a mix of operating system and web-server software revisions, which could mean a number of things. It could mean, for instance, that these are dedicated servers and that Webhosting.com is familiar with a fairly wide range of technologies. On the other hand, it could mean that these are colocated servers, and that Webhosting.com doesn't know a thing about them. It could also mean that Webhosting.com manages its customers' servers, but that it doesn't do a particularly good job of maintaining revision consistency across them. (There are five configuration variations within the first 15 servers listed.) There are many possible explanations for this, and we can't draw conclusions yet. But we're gathering data, and certainly adding to the list of follow-up questions to ask this vendor.

Of the web sites hosted at Webhosting.com and monitored by Netcraft, the site with the longest average continuous uptime comes in at only 64 days, as compared to nearly 10 times as long for the eBay servers at Exodus. Again, we've found an issue for further investigation.

It's time to put Netcraft back into our toolkit. We'll return to it one more time in this chapter.

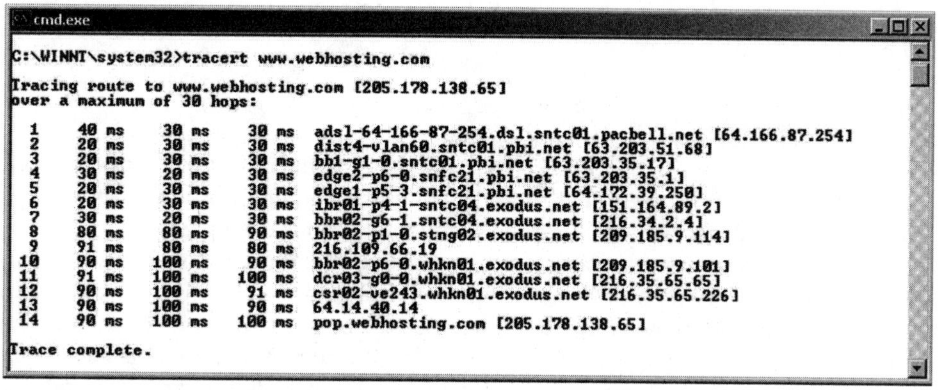

```
cmd.exe                                                              _ □ ×

C:\WINNT\system32>tracert www.webhosting.com

Tracing route to www.webhosting.com [205.178.138.65]
over a maximum of 30 hops:

  1    40 ms    30 ms    30 ms  ads1-64-166-87-254.dsl.sntc01.pacbell.net [64.166.87.254]
  2    20 ms    30 ms    30 ms  dist4-vlan60.sntc01.pbi.net [63.203.51.68]
  3    20 ms    30 ms    30 ms  bb1-g1-0.sntc01.pbi.net [63.203.35.17]
  4    30 ms    20 ms    30 ms  edge2-p6-0.snfc21.pbi.net [63.203.35.1]
  5    20 ms    30 ms    30 ms  edge1-p5-3.snfc21.pbi.net [64.172.39.250]
  6    20 ms    30 ms    30 ms  ibr01-p4-1-sntc04.exodus.net [151.164.89.2]
  7    30 ms    20 ms    30 ms  bbr02-g6-1.sntc04.exodus.net [216.34.2.4]
  8    80 ms    80 ms    90 ms  bbr02-p1-0.stng02.exodus.net [209.185.9.114]
  9    91 ms    80 ms    80 ms  216.109.66.19
 10    90 ms   100 ms    90 ms  bbr02-p6-0.whkn01.exodus.net [209.185.9.101]
 11    91 ms   100 ms   100 ms  dcr03-g0-0.whkn01.exodus.net [216.35.65.65]
 12    90 ms   100 ms    91 ms  csr02-ve243.whkn01.exodus.net [216.35.65.226]
 13    90 ms   100 ms    90 ms  64.14.40.14
 14    90 ms   100 ms   100 ms  pop.webhosting.com [205.178.138.65]

Trace complete.
```

Figure 20.14   Traceroute to www.webhosting.com.

Traceroute

The next tool you'll learn to use is *traceroute,* a utility that identifies each of the routers between the computer on which the utility runs and a remote host. We're going to use traceroute to see what we can discover about Webhosting.com's Internet connectivity.

On Windows computers, there's a traceroute-like program called *tracert* that can be run from the command prompt. We'll run it in a command window as we did earlier for telnet:

1. Click on the Windows Start button.

2. Click on Run.

3. Type "cmd" (or "command" in versions prior to NT and Windows 2000) in the Open box.

4. Click on OK. You'll see the Windows command prompt.

5. Type "tracert" followed by the name of the host to which you want to trace.

For instance:

```
tracert www.webhosting.com
```

Figure 20.14 illustrates tracert's command line and an example of its output for a route to www.webhosting.com.

Each line in the traceroute output represents one *hop* or router on the path between the computer running traceroute and the target web site, www.webhosting.com. In Figure 20.14 we can see that the computer running traceroute (tracert, in this instance) is connected to PacBell, and that the route switches from PacBell to Exodus at hop 6.

Exodus? Why Exodus? That's the same web-hosting service we just looked at when we were studying the Starbucks web site. Why would traffic from PacBell (an ISP) pass through the Exodus backbone on its way to Webhosting.com, another web-hosting service?

To uncover the relationship between Exodus and Webhosting.com, let's take a look at hop 13:

```
13    90 ms    100 ms    90 ms    64.14.40.14
```

The three times—90ms, 100ms, and 90ms in hop 13—are the round-trip times for each of three test packets that were sent from the computer running traceroute and the responding router. But we're not interested in the times in this example.

Notice that this is a hop that sits somewhere between Exodus and Webhosting.com, but there's no identifying host name string, just an IP address. Traceroute wasn't able to determine the host name of the router because the owner of the router hasn't made it public; but if we could figure out who owned that router, it might tell us a lot more about Webhosting.com. We do have the IP address of that router, so if we can find out who owns the block of IP addresses that includes this one, we'll have some idea of who controls the router. And that may explain why Exodus is in this picture at all.

> **TIP** Use traceroute to gather evidence of a web-hosting service's third-party relationships.

Whois

We've got a router's IP address, and we'd like to find out who owns that router. For this, we'll turn to our next tool, the *whois* utility. Whois allows us to look up a variety of information from the various databases that are used to manage the Internet. These databases include those that track the assignment of domain names (such as rds.com), and the assignment of the netblocks of IP addresses, such as we saw when using the Netcraft tool.

In this case we'll look up the IP address of our mystery router in the database of U.S. network numbers, to find out who owns that IP address. For this, let's point our web browser to a site called Geektools, operated by CenterGate Research Group, LLC, at www.geektools.com and shown in Figure 20.15. (You can find many other *whois gateways* on the web.)

To query the Internet databases, click on the Whois link on the Geektools web page, and enter the IP address (64.14.40.14 in this instance) into the form. Geektools runs the whois utility, then replies with the results shown in Figure 20.16.

The output shown in this figure includes far more information than we need to follow this clue, and we'll look at the rest of the whois output in the next chapter. But it tells us the most important thing: The mysterious router with the IP address of 64.14.40.14 is within a netblock 64.14.0.0 – 64.14.255.255 that's owned by Exodus.

> **TIP** Use the whois utility to discover who owns a network to which a router for which you only know the IP address is connected.

Looking back at the traceroute in Figure 20.14, we see that this is the next to the last hop (13), and, therefore, it must be the *last* router. This is because the very last hop (14) must be the www.webhosting.com web server itself.

Figure 20.15   Geektools whois search page.
Source: CenterGate Research Group

So the mystery hop is the last router, and it's on an Exodus network. Since Exodus is a hosting service, not an ISP that might provide connectivity to other web-hosting services, an important fact is becoming clear: Although Webhosting.com is a web-hosting service itself, the company apparently doesn't operate its own data center. Instead, its servers are probably located within an Exodus facility.

TIP Traceroute and whois, used together, can help you identify tenant and reseller web-hosting services—those that depend on the facilities of other vendors.

Is it good or bad that Webhosting.com depends on the facilities of others? That depends on your expectations. Certainly it's better than running your web site out of some guy's spare bedroom, but it implies that Webhosting.com runs a data center within a data center. It probably depends on Exodus staff for a variety of services. While it probably does have access to a "high-speed redundant backbone," dual air conditioners, and all the rest of the goodies it claims, is this misrepresentation? Does it make Webhosting.com sound like it has *skills* that it may not in fact have? These are issues for you to decide, hopefully with the help of additional research; but as your own Net detective work has shown you once again, things aren't always what they appear to be.

Yet another interesting clue comes from the traceroute output in Figure 20.14. Note that the router in hop 12 (the last Exodus router with a host name) includes "whkn01" in the host name string. Could this be an Exodus data center in Weehauken, New Jersey, right across the Hudson River from New York City? Does Webhosting.com have staff in

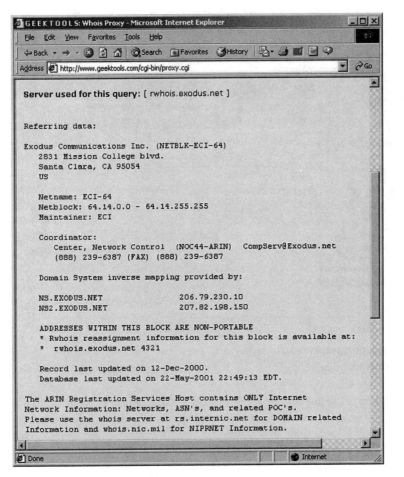

Figure 20.16 Geektools whois results.

Source: CenterGate Research Group

INTERNET NUMBER REGISTRIES

The American Registry of Internet Numbers (ARIN) manages IP addresses in North and South America. In some countries, such as Mexico and Brazil, they further delegate this responsibility to another agency. Here are the URLs for the most important registries' whois web pages:

American Registry of Internet Numbers (ARIN)   **www.arin.net**
Asia Pacific Network Information Center (APNIC)   **www.apnic.net**
RIPE Network Coordination Centre (RIPE, Europe)   **www.ripe.net**

The whois utility hosted by Geektools will either automatically select the best registry or allow you to select one manually.

OS, Web Server and Hosting History for www.brownies.com				
OS	Server	Last changed	IP address	Netblock Owner
Linux	Apache/1.3.9 (Unix) Red-Hat-Secure/3.1 mod_ssl/2.4.5 OpenSSL/0.9.4 PHP/4.0.2	21-Nov-2000	64.39.31.160	Rackspace.com

Figure 20.17   Netcraft report on www.brownies.com.

Source: Netcraft

Weehauken? Do they have to travel from Toronto to manage services in "their" data center? Again, these are only questions, not answers.

TIP The host name assigned to a router by a web-hosting service or ISPs often provides a clue as to the router's location. The location of the last few routers (as reported by traceroute) can, in turn, help you pinpoint the location of a web site or its web-hosting service.

Who's in Charge?

I was in the middle of writing this chapter when I received a promotional offering stating that "Sprint will help you build a professional web site for your business and host it for just $19.95/mo.*" (I never was able to figure out to what the asterisk referred.) The signup form also contained Earthlink's logo, and a promotion that read, "Your new site will be hosted by the highly acclaimed Earthlink." Way too tempting. I had to check it out.

First I went to the promotional web page at the URL they sent me, www.sprint.com/homeoffice. I navigated through there, found some success stories, and picked out one that sounded good to me: www.brownies.com.

Next I turned to Netcraft (as shown in Figure 20.17), and I learned that www.brownies.com was running on Apache/Linux and had an IP address within a block owned by Rackspace.com. Rackspace.com? What about Sprint and Earthlink?

By checking out Rackspace.com, I learned that it offers dedicated servers; yet at the $19.95-per-month price point, this Sprint offering clearly uses shared servers. The mystery deepened.

I chose another success story from the Sprint web site: www.carolinabenefits.com. I again went to Netcraft; the results are shown in Figure 20.18. Now what's going on? *This* success story appears to be hosted by Earthlink. When I sign up through Sprint, will I be hosted at Rackspace.com or Earthlink? That could make a huge difference, depending on what I learn about each of these companies' capabilities and reputations.

There's another important difference: www.brownies.com is running on a server with RedHat Unix and PHP, whereas www.carolinabenefits.com is on a server with the FrontPage extensions to Apache. This could be very important to you, as a customer. If your web site needs either PHP or the FrontPage extensions, it will run on one of these servers but not on the other. Does the vendor offer servers of both types?

Who's in charge here? Does Rackspace run the servers? Sprint? Is Earthlink running a bank of servers located within the Rackspace.com facility? If I host here (wherever "here" is) and I have a problem, will Sprint help me out, or will it just tell me to call

OS, Web Server and Hosting History for www.carolinabenefits.com				
OS	Server	Last changed	IP address	Netblock Owner
Compaq Tru64	Apache/1.3.6 (Unix) mod_frontpage/3.0.4.3	21-Nov-2000	209.86.240.149	EarthLink, Inc.

Figure 20.18   Netcraft report on www.carolinabenefits.com.

Source: Netcraft

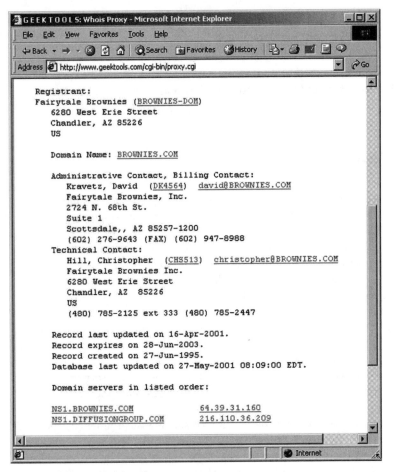

Figure 20.19   Whois output for brownies.com.

Source: CenterGate Research Group

Earthlink? Maybe it would be better if I just bypassed Sprint altogether and bought my service directly from Earthlink in the first place.

Still curious, I decided to use yet another powerful tool in the Net Detective's Toolkit: email! I first used *whois* on Geektools to get the domain registration information for brownies.com. I entered brownies.com on the same Geektools page we used earlier to track down the owner of an IP address, and got the response shown in Figure 20.19.

Using the information from the whois output in Figure 20.19, I sent a message to the nice folks at Fairytale Brownies, the owners of www.brownies.com, and learned their web site originally had been hosted at Mindspring/Earthlink, but they had outgrown their shared server there. They moved to dedicated servers at Rackspace.com but were still listed as a success story on Sprint's web site.

So in the end, there was a perfectly reasonable explanation for the discrepancies I'd discovered, but along the way I learned quite a bit about Earthlink, Sprint, and Rackspace.com. And although many of the clues and questions came from my on-line detective work, the best answers came from directly communicating with another web-hosting customer.

TIP Use the Net Detective Toolkit as a way to identify customers of your prospective web-hosting services, MSPs, and CDNs. Communicating with these customers will be your most valuable source of information.

Tracking Down a CDN

When you're evaluating the performance of a web site, such as one owned by a competitor, you should also check whether the site's images or other objects are, in fact, served by a CDN. Using a CDN *should* make a difference in the site's performance so its important to know whether you're comparing apples to apples. Also, since CDNs are still used by relatively few web-site owners, this information will tell you something about how important your competitor considers its web site to be. As an example, let's test the web page shown in Figure 20.20.

If you're viewing a web page using your web browser, you can discover the URLs of the images that make up the page by placing the cursor over an image and clicking the right mouse button. In this example, we've done this for the large oval image in the center of the page. From the pop-up menu that then appears, we select Properties, as shown in Figure 20.20. (On Netscape browsers under Windows, right-click on the image, then select View Image.)

The Properties box in Figure 20.21 shows us, among other things, that the image was retrieved from a host named "a116.g.akamai.net." Akamai is a commercial CDN, so we have, in fact, determined that this web site uses a CDN, and we even know which one.

Figure 20.22 illustrates another way to check this web page for the use of a CDN, and to evaluate the results. This is a Keynote Systems (www.keynote.com) diagnostic report for the same web page used in the previous example. Note in the chart in the upper half of the figure that it takes approximately 0.40 seconds to download the underlying web page from the site's primary server, but that it takes a total of less than 0.15 seconds to download the 15 images served by Akamai.

How much of a difference does the use of a CDN make in this one instance? The table in the lower half of Figure 20.22 provides additional information and more accurate timings. The underlying web page is a single file that's 23,632 bytes long. At a total download time of 0.41 seconds, that's an effective speed of 9,689 bytes per second, after accounting for the overhead of DNS requests, and so on.

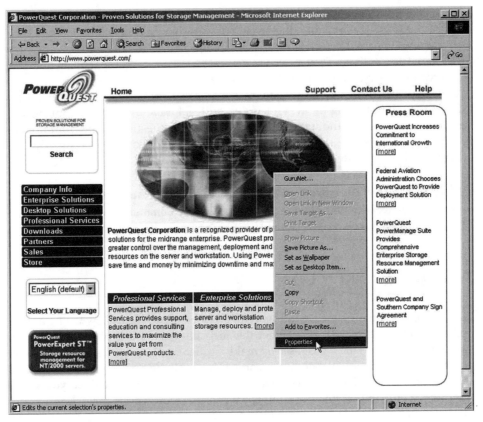

Figure 20.20 A web page suspected of being served by a CDN.

Source: PowerQuest Corporation

The 15 images combined total 18,864 bytes, and they were downloaded from Akamai in a total of 0.13 seconds. That's an effective speed of 145,108 bytes per second, or 15 times faster than the underlying page.

These numbers are only from a single sample, and there are other variables that need to be taken into consideration (such as the fact that the downloading of the images used four simultaneous TCP/IP connections), but clearly this web site is benefiting from its use of a CDN. (See Chapter 13, "Caching and Content Delivery Networks," for more information on CDNs and how to evaluate them.)

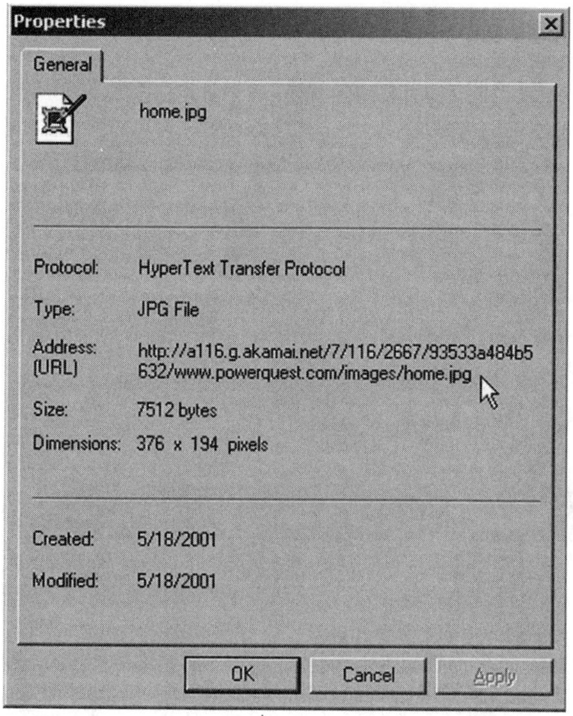

Figure 20.21 Properties of an image served by a CDN.

TIP Use third-party measurement and analysis tools as part of your
evaluation of the effectiveness of content delivery networks.

As we've seen throughout this chapter, things in web hosting are not always what
they appear to be. Hopefully the tools introduced here will encourage you to do your
own detective work as part of your due-diligence process when selecting a web-hosting
service, MSP, or CDN.

What you've seen here are only sample scenarios. The secret weapon in the Net Detective's Toolkit is your ability to use these and other tools creatively. By following your
own instincts to snoop and ask questions, you'll discover information that these tools
alone can't tell you. And you'll learn things that your prospective vendors may not
want to know.

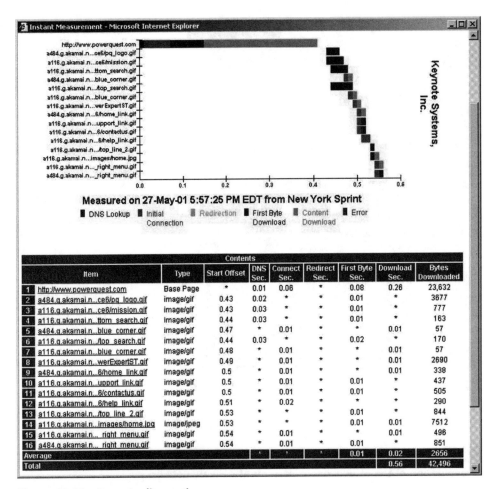

Figure 20.22 Keynote diagnostic.

Source: Keynote Systems, Inc.

Domain Names and DNS

As any long-time webmaster will tell you, a significant percentage of web-site failures can be traced to problems with the Domain Name Service (DNS). And most DNS problems are, in turn, caused by human error. It's remarkably easy (and common) to make a mistake when making a DNS change, and many people who are responsible for making DNS changes don't understand its subtleties. In this chapter we'll explore a number of issues surrounding DNS and domain names, including the threat from so-called domain pirates, who can steal your registered domain name if you're not careful.

In Chapter 20, "The Net Detective Toolkit," we looked at the whois utility in the context of researching someone else's web site or web-hosting service. In this chapter we'll discuss two important issues relating to *your* web site: the best way to configure your *nameservers*, and the proper way to register your domain names.

DNS is one of the most misunderstood components of the Internet infrastructure, so in order to build the foundation for our recommendations, we're going to start with a step-by-step explanation on some of the workings of DNS. Knowing how DNS operates is important for dealing with a variety of web-hosting issues, even if you don't have hands-on responsibility for your company's nameservers.

We'll begin with an explanation of the Internet's *name space*. We'll walk through the organization of DNS from two perspectives: We'll take the point of view of a visitor's browser trying to find a web site, and then we'll look at how you manage the DNS records and nameservers associated with your domain.

Once we've seen the way DNS is normally configured, we'll look at a better way to organize your domain, by *delegating subdomains* to your vendors. Finally, we'll take a look at the proper way to register and manage your domain name in order to maintain control and to protect yourself from domain-name piracy.

The DNS Infrastructure

All addressable devices on the Internet (e.g., computers, routers, etc.) are called *hosts,* and each host has one or more Internet Protocol (IP) addresses, such as 167.160.45.23. Hosts can also have alphanumeric names, such as www.rds.com.

The name www.rds.com consists of two parts: "www" is a *hostname,* and "rds.com" is a *domain name.* The combination of the hostname and the domain name (www.rds.com) is called a *fully qualified domain name,* or *FQDN.*

The Domain Name System is a distributed database that provides a mapping of domain names and hostnames to IP addresses, and vice versa. (DNS has a few other purposes, most notably the specification of email hosts, that we won't discuss here.)

The Name Space

The names we assign to our hosts and domains exist in a name space that's managed by DNS. The name space is hierarchical, as illustrated in Figure 21.1.

At the very top of the name space tree is the *root*—a hypothetical point from which all names originate. The nodes (or branches) in the next level of the tree are referred to as the *top-level domains* (or TLDs). There are two groups of TLDs. In one group are the *generic top-level domains* (or gTLDs), which are permanently designated and organized by type of organization (.com for business, .gov for government, .org for nonprofit, etc.). In the other group are the *country-code top-level domains* (ccTLDs) that are assigned to and controlled by geopolitical entities such as countries. This group includes, for example,

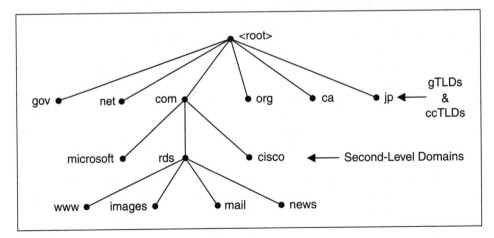

Figure 21.1 The DNS name space.

.ca for Canada, .jp for Japan, and so on. Except for the United Kingdom (.uk instead of .gb for Great Britain), the ccTLDs are assigned according to an international standard, ISO 3166 (see www.niso.org/3166.html).

The organizations responsible for the management of the gTLDs and ccTLDs may *delegate* responsibility for *subdomains*. For instance, the organization that controls .com has delegated control of the subdomain microsoft.com to Microsoft, and rds.com to RDS. These are referred to as *second-level domains*. (See *Registrars*, later in this chapter, for an in-depth discussion of the organizations that control the TLDs.)

As owners of second-level domains, we can create hostnames within our own domain name space such as "www" and "mail." But since nearly everyone who controls a second-level domain creates his or her own host named "www," we use fully qualified domain names such as www.rds.com and www.microsoft.com to keep them separated.

Nameservers

The DNS name-space database is stored in a distributed hierarchy of *nameservers*, as shown in Figure 21.2. Each nameserver in the hierarchy knows how to locate the *authoritative nameservers* for the next lower-level domains. In other words, the nameservers at one level know only one thing: where in the immediately lower level to refer the requests they receive.

To see how this works, let's follow the nameserver hierarchy for www.rds.com. The root nameservers (which can be found at a.root-servers.net) are authoritative for the root. In other words, they're the only guaranteed-accurate servers that can tell you where to find information about the next level: the gTLDs .com, .org, .gov, etc. But that's also all that they know. If you ask them where to find www.rds.com, the root nameservers won't answer you directly. Instead, they'll respond with NS (nameserver) DNS records that *refer* you to the gTLD nameservers that are authoritative for .com.

At the time of this writing, there are 12 gTLD nameservers that are authoritative for .com. They're named a.gtld-servers.net through l.gtld-servers.net. There are 12 of them because, as you might imagine, they receive many thousands of requests per second. The gTLD nameservers are operated by Network Solutions. Nine are located in the United States while the others, at this moment, are located in Japan, Hong Kong, and Great Britain.

The .com gTLD nameservers know where to find the authoritative nameserver for every second-level domain such as microsoft.com and rds.com. But as we saw with the root nameservers, the gTLD nameservers don't know anything else. So when a gTLD nameserver receives a request for the address of www.rds.com, it responds by referring the requester to the nameservers that are authoritative for the rds.com second-level domain. In this example (referring again to Figure 21.2), those are RDS' public nameservers, ns1.rds.com and ns2.rds.com.

Instead of an NS record, each of the RDS public nameservers includes an A (address) record that defines the www.rds.com host. The RDS public nameservers are the ones that finally and authoritatively can answer the question, "What's the IP address of www.rds.com?"

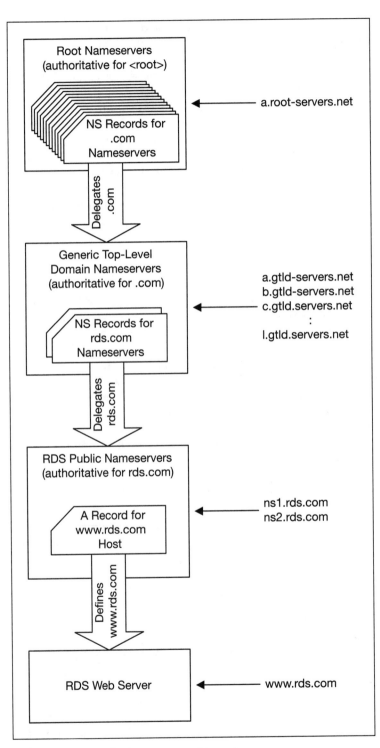

Figure 21.2 Standard nameserver hierarchy.

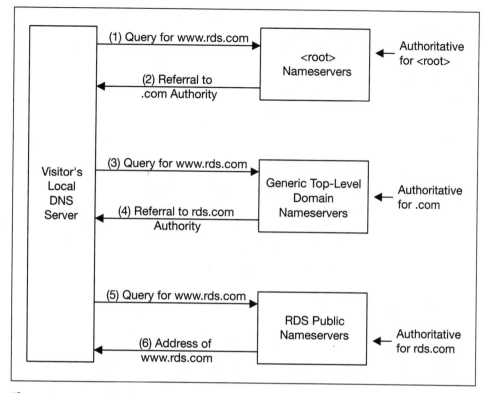

Figure 21.3 Standard DNS query flow.

DNS Queries

Now that we've seen the relationship of the multiple levels of nameservers in the DNS hierarchy, let's look at how a visitor's web browser locates a web site. We'll use www.rds.com as an example once again. Figure 21.3 illustrates the step-by-step process by which a visitor's local DNS server finds the IP address of www.rds.com when DNS is set up using the standard configuration we've been discussing. For the sake of this example, we'll assume that the visitor's local DNS server has just been rebooted and has no cached entries from previous lookups. (If a server has nonexpired cached entries for any hosts or domains, including the root and gTLD nameservers, it skips the steps of locating those nameservers.)

The visitor's browser (not shown in Figure 21.3) makes a *recursive* DNS query to its local DNS server to find www.rds.com. It's called a recursive query because the browser expects the local DNS server to do whatever's necessary to get the answer, even if it has to contact multiple other DNS servers, which, in fact, it does need to do in this example.

The purpose of the visitor's local DNS server is to convert the recursive request it receives from the browser into multiple simpler *iterative* requests. For instance, the visitor's local DNS server makes a single iterative DNS request to a root nameserver, and the root nameserver returns a referral rather than tracking down the complete answer on its own. This reduces the workload on the root nameservers and places more of the burden on the visitor's local DNS server. The Internet's root and gTLD nameservers are busy enough just making referrals and will refuse to handle recursive queries.

The visitor's local DNS server starts by asking the root nameservers for the address of www.rds.com, (1 in Figure 21.3). The root nameserver sits at the very top of the Internet's domain name infrastructure and doesn't know about www.rds.com or even rds.com, for that matter. But it does know which servers are authoritative for the .com gTLD, so it refers the visitor's local DNS server to those gTLD nameservers (2).

The visitor's local DNS server repeats its request for the address of www.rds.com to the .com gTLD nameservers (3). The gTLD nameservers know about rds.com, but they still can't provide an answer for www.rds.com. They therefore refer the visitor's local DNS server to the RDS public nameservers that are authoritative for rds.com (4).

The visitor's local DNS server then asks the RDS public nameservers for the address of www.rds.com (5). Finally, it's asking nameservers that know everything there is to know about the rds.com domain, and those nameservers reply with the IP address of host www.rds.com (6). The visitor's local DNS server then returns that address to the web browser, and the browser is able to contact the www.rds.com web site.

DNS Data Updates

The foregoing discussion explains how DNS nameservers respond to queries. But there's another important aspect to DNS: the methods by which the DNS nameservers' content is maintained. A number of processes exist in order for the right information to be available in each of the various nameservers. Figure 21.4 illustrates the two processes that involve you, the web-site owner.

The first process is the registration or modification of your second-level domain, such as rds.com. You perform these operations by submitting forms electronically (1 in Figure 21.4)—either through email or via the web—to one of the many *registrars*, such as register.com (www.register.com), as described in detail later in this chapter. The registrar, in turn, submits updates to the gTLD nameservers (2).

The gTLD nameservers only know where to find the public nameservers for your second-level domain. They have no knowledge of the hosts or other entities defined *within* your domain. So the other process you need to understand is the management of the DNS records on your public nameservers that define the entities within your domain. You can make changes directly to your public nameservers, but most medium and large-scale businesses operate additional private nameservers—typically behind their corporate firewalls—and use *zone transfers* to publish updated DNS records to their public nameservers (3). The private nameserver is referred to as a *master,* and the public nameserver as a *slave,* because of the direction of the flow of information. Although the public nameservers get their data via zone transfers from the private nameserver, it's the public nameservers that are registered and therefore known by the gTLD nameservers as the authorities for entities within rds.com.

You now understand the process by which a host (or web site) is found on the Internet. But before you get too comfortable, remember that what you've seen is the *standard* configuration—the one used by most web-site owners, web-hosting services, and MSPs. Next, we'll consider some of the disadvantages of this approach, and recommend a better one, based on the *delegation* of *subdomains.*

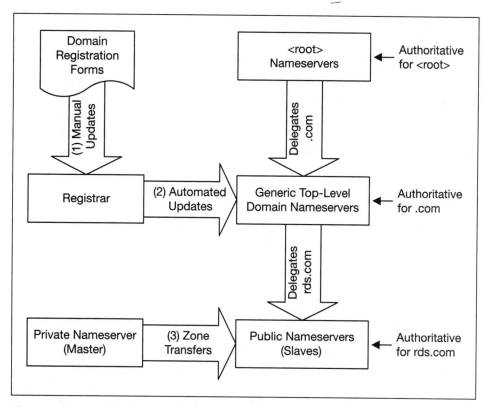

Figure 21.4 Standard DNS authority flow.

Delegating a Subdomain

Your nameservers include all of the DNS records for your domain. They include not only records for your web servers, but also the records for your internal hosts and the mail exchange (MX) records for your corporate email system. In Figure 21.4, we saw a configuration in which you use a private nameserver (e.g., behind your firewall) to manage the DNS records for your domain, and publish them to a publicly accessible nameserver, possibly managed by your web-hosting service or MSP. Therefore, all of your DNS records—both those that are public and those that are for internal use only—are managed together. If you hand over control of your DNS records to a third party, such as an MSP, that third party will then have control over *all* of your DNS records, even those that have nothing to do with your web site. If you want to make a change—even to your internal-only records—you'll need the cooperation and assistance of that vendor. Conversely, if you keep control of your DNS records in house, your web-hosting service or MSP won't be able to make changes without your assistance, in which case your vendor may refuse to take responsibility for the proper operation of DNS for your web site.

In this section we'll look at a better way to manage your domain, by giving control of a portion of your namespace to your vendor, while retaining control of the rest. DNS is a very complex and confusing system—some refer to it as a black art—so this won't be a definitive explanation. But it will give you an idea of what to do and why to do it. When it comes time for the "how," make sure you have help from someone who has a thorough knowledge of DNS.

This is confusing stuff, so we'll look at the updated diagrams and descriptions that illustrate and explain this process in more detail. Figure 21.5 shows how the CNAME, NS, and A records create www.msp.rds.com as an alias for www.rds.com, and delegate control of the msp.rds.com subdomain to our MSP's nameservers. (Because it hasn't changed—and in order to fit this all onto one page—we've left out the top two levels of nameservers in Figure 21.5.)

The example shown in Figure 21.5 differs from the earlier example, shown in Figure 21.2, in three ways. We:

Delegated a subdomain. We've created a domain named msp.rds.com. Although this looks like a hostname (similar to www.rds.com), it's actually a *third-level domain*—a *subdomain* of rds.com. We've used a nameserver (NS) record in DNS to tell the world that our MSP's nameserver—not our own—is to be considered authoritative for this new subdomain.

Created an alias. Next we've used a canonical name (CNAME) record to tell requesting DNS servers that when they're looking for our web site at www.rds.com, they should instead ask for www.msp.rds.com. Note that this will then refer all requests for our web site to the new subdomain that's under the control of our MSP. A CNAME is similar to a simple character-string substitution: an instruction to replace "www.rds.com" with "www.msp.rds.com." Using a CNAME does, however, require the requestor to reformulate its question and ask again.

Defined a host. When visitors' nameservers then ask for the IP address of www.msp.rds.com, the NS record will direct them to the MSP's nameserver, so that's where we'll use an address (A) record to define www.msp.rds.com. This, of course, is under the control of our MSP, which was our initial objective.

Next, let's again walk step by step through the process by which a visitor's local DNS server interacts with the various nameservers when subdomain delegation is used. This is shown in Figure 21.6. This time we'll also include sample DNS records for those who are interested in the gory details. These records were retrieved using the *dig* utility, which we'll explore later in this chapter.

We'll again assume someone wants to visit our web site at www.rds.com, so the visitor enters that string into his or her browser's Address: window. The browser then passes this request on to a local DNS server. The visitor's local DNS server then queries the root nameservers for www.rds.com (1 in Figure 21.6).

The root nameservers can't provide information regarding www.rds.com or even rds.com, but they do reply with information about the .com gTLD servers. They return the names and IP addresses of the 12 gTLD nameservers that are authoritative for the .com domain (2).

The visitor's local DNS server next queries one of the .com gTLD nameservers (3); but once again, this nameserver can't supply an address for www.rds.com. Instead, it refers the visitor's local DNS server to the nameservers that are authoritative for rds.com (4).

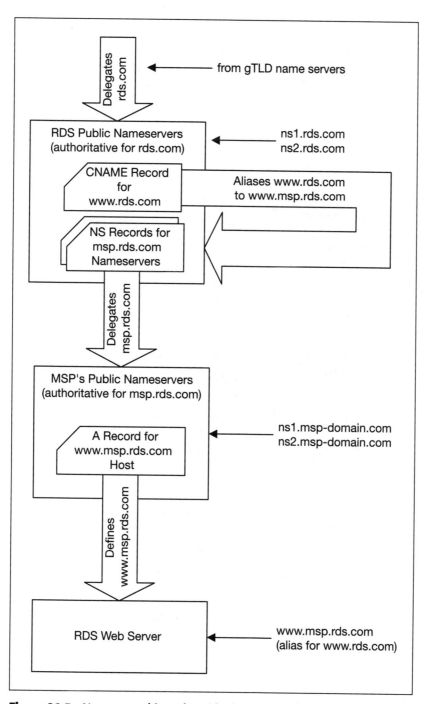

Figure 21.5 Nameserver hierarchy with alias and subdomain delegation.

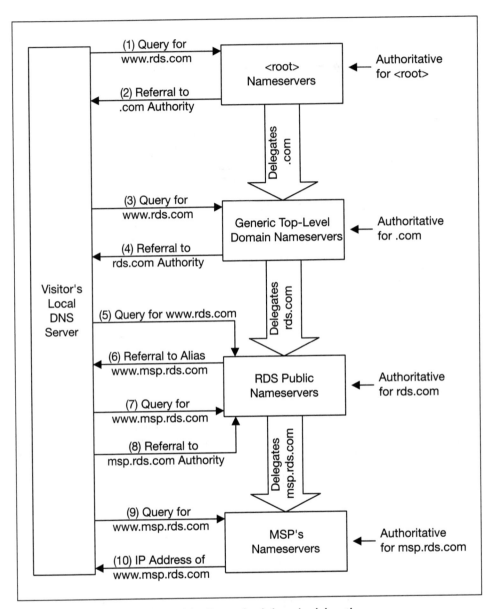

Figure 21.6 DNS query flow with alias and subdomain delegation.

```
rds.com.        2D IN NS    ns1.rds.com.
rds.com.        2D IN NS    ns2.rds.com.
ns1.rds.com.    2D IN A     198.81.209.2
ns2.rds.com.    2D IN A     167.160.23.2
```

This example shows the actual DNS records returned by the gTLD nameservers. The first records are NS records. They tell the visitor's local DNS server that there are two public nameservers for the rds.com domain: ns1.rds.com and ns2.rds.com. The other A records specify the IP addresses of these two nameservers.

The visitor's local DNS server then queries one of the RDS public nameservers, ns1.rds.com or ns2.rds.com (5). In the standard DNS configuration shown earlier, the RDS public nameservers returned the address of the host www.rds.com, and the search was over. In this case, however, the RDS public nameservers reply with an alias (6):

```
www.rds.com          2D IN CNAME      www.msp.rds.com
```

This response causes the visitor's local DNS server to query the RDS public nameserver again, this time asking for the address of www.msp.rds.com (7). But the RDS public nameserver still can't answer the question, so it responds by referring the visitor's local DNS server to the MSP's nameservers (8):

```
msp.rds.com          2D IN NS         ns.msp-domain.com
```

This reply from the RDS public nameserver is the record that delegates the subdomain msp.rds.com to the MSP. It does so by informing the visitor's local DNS server that its request for the address of www.msp.rds.com should be sent to the MSP's own nameserver.

Finally, the visitor's local DNS server queries the MSP's nameserver, ns.msp-domain.com, for the address of www.msp.rds.com (step 9 in Figure 21.6), and receives the record shown here (10):

```
www.msp.rds.com      6h IN A          216.136.180.150
```

The visitor's local DNS server now returns the IP address 216.136.180.150 in response to the browser's request for www.rds.com.

Here we've used the "www" servers, hosted by a web-hosting service, as examples. You would use a similar scheme for "images" servers (images.rds.com) if you were planning to outsource the delivery of your images to a CDN. See Chapter 13, "Caching and Content Delivery Networks," for more information on CDNs and the segregation of content in this manner.

DNS Tools: nslookup and dig

The *whois* utility we discussed in Chapter 20 is a tool for looking up records in the various Internet registration databases. Specifically, whois is the tool of choice for discovering the ownership of domains and networks and to locate the people who manage them. We'll use whois again later in this chapter when we study domain registrations, but it's important to realize that whois doesn't actually query the nameservers. It only queries the Internet administrative databases that, in turn, feed the nameservers.

There's an overlap between the data stored in the administrative databases (and reported by whois) and that found in the nameservers, but it's not unusual to find inconsistencies between them. When it comes to the actual operation of the Internet, it's DNS that counts. Creating or modifying a domain-registration record in the databases doesn't take effect until the change reaches all of the relevant nameservers.

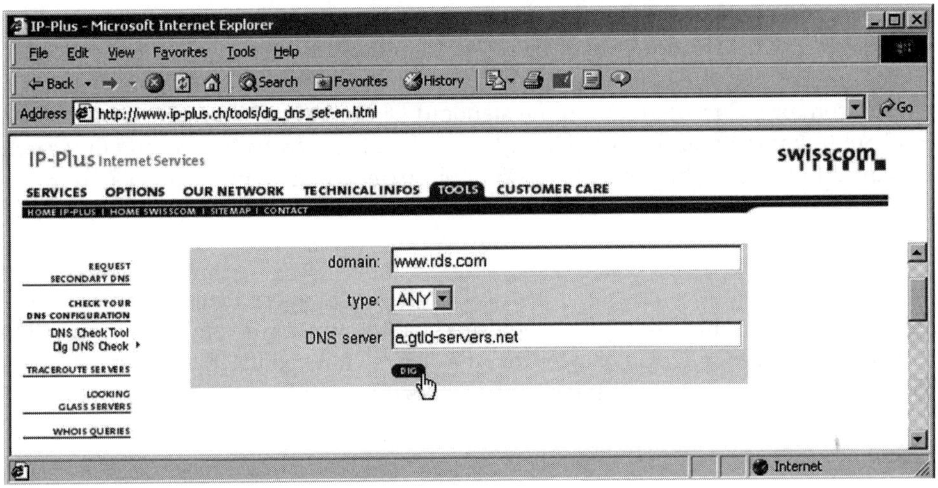

Figure 21.7 Online dig utility.

Source: IP-Plus Internet Services

There are two other utilities, *nslookup* and *dig,* that query DNS nameservers and re-port the results. If you have a Unix-derivative system, you have a copy of nslookup (Nameserver Lookup), and you may have a copy of dig (the Domain Internet Gopher) as well. In any case, there are many web-based implementations of each of these utili-ties. For our examples, we'll use a *dig gateway* hosted by IP-Plus Internet Services in Switzerland (www.ip-plus.ch).

Let's start by using dig to ask one of the .com gTLD nameservers about www.rds.com. The input form is shown in Figure 21.7. Note that we specify both the target domain (www.rds.com) and a specific DNS nameserver (a.gtld-servers.net). The output from the dig utility is shown in Figure 21.8.

The lines that don't begin with semicolons are the actual DNS records retrieved from the gTLD nameserver. The lines in the AUTHORITY SECTION are NS records stating that two hosts (ns1.rds.com and ns2.rds.com) are the authoritative nameservers for rds.com. In the ADDITIONAL SECTION, the A records provide the IP addresses for those nameservers.

You can use dig and nslookup interchangeably. We've used dig to generate many of the examples that appear later in this chapter. The output from nslookup is essentially the same.

Time to Live

Just as cache servers and web browsers cache web-page objects, DNS servers cache the DNS records they retrieve from nameservers. This caching is critically important to the performance of your web site. Imagine what would happen, for example, if every request for every object had to go through the laborious name-resolution process we described earlier. It would take longer to locate most objects than it would to download them.

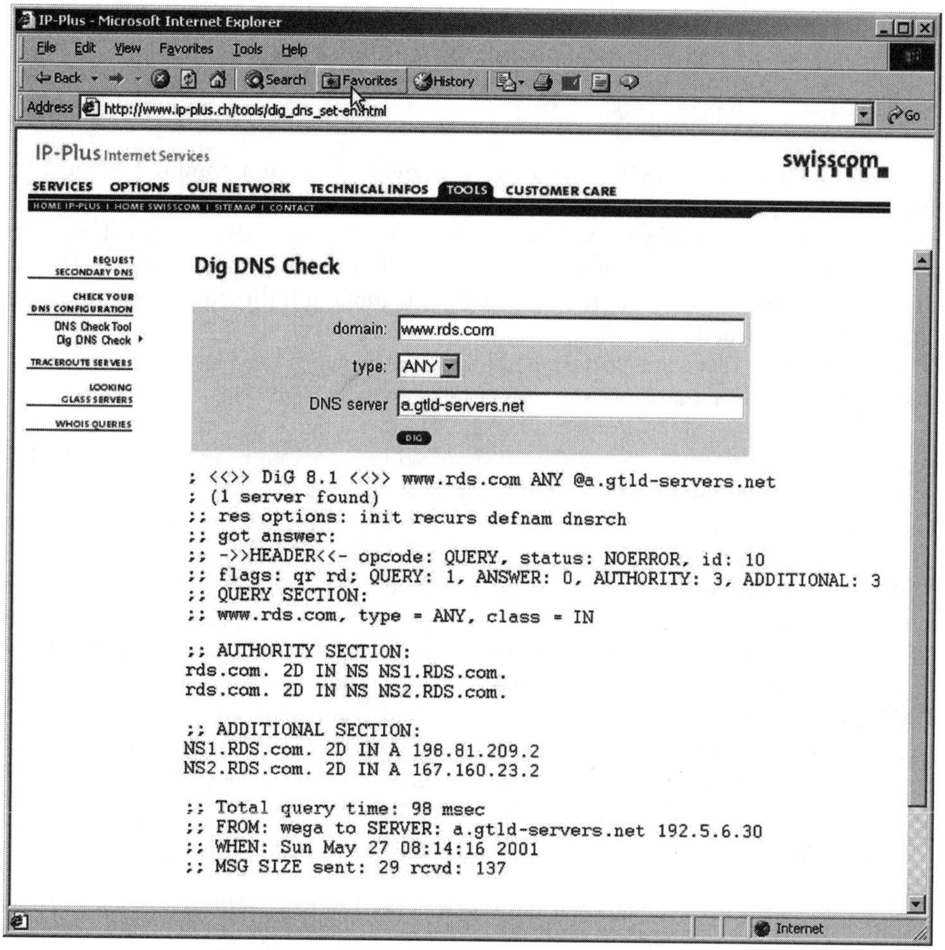

Figure 21.8 Output from dig.

Source: IP-Plus Internet Services

Thank goodness a visitor's web browser and local DNS server normally have to do this only once per session for each host, for example, www.rds.com or images.rds.com.

But because DNS data associated with your web site changes from time to time, a visitor's local DNS server can't cache your DNS records forever. If it did, you'd never be able to make any changes, since visitors' local DNS servers would forever use the old cached data.

Therefore, DNS includes the ability to specify the time to live (TTL) for each record. TTL is the amount of time that DNS servers are allowed to retain your DNS records in their caches. Once the TTL has expired, DNS servers are required to delete the cached record and request new data from an authoritative server using the processes we described earlier.

Notice in the dig output shown in Figure 21.8 that each line includes the characters "2D." For instance:

```
rds.com.        2D        IN        NS        NS1.RDS.COM
```

Here, "2D" (which stands for "two days") is the TTL for this record. The actual records are written using seconds, so the preceding example is the same as

```
rds.com.        172800      IN          NS          NS1.RDS.COM
```

Selecting the right values for TTL requires some thought and planning. Small TTL values allow you to make frequent changes within your namespace, but at a cost to the perceived performance of your web site since visitors' local DNS servers will have to resolve your hostnames more frequently. On the other hand, large values for TTL will maximize the performance of your web site while making it difficult for you to make changes due to cached data.

Although the TTL scheme is designed to help keep distributed DNS data current, it doesn't guarantee that all DNS servers will switch to updated data at the same time. Since the countdown timers associated with TTL start when a record is retrieved, DNS servers that retrieve a record at different times will expire that record at similarly different times. In other words, whenever you make a change to a DNS record, there's always a period of time during which some DNS servers out there on the Internet have the old data and some have the new data.

If your site is stable, a TTL of two days is reasonable. There's little advantage to using a TTL of anything longer than a week. At the other extreme, it's not a good idea to use TTLs shorter than 30 minutes except in special cases, such as when a CDN is deployed—CDNs often use TTLs of as short as 30 seconds—or when you're trying to propagate a DNS change, as described next.

If you're anticipating a change, start decreasing the TTL of the affected records according to a well thought-out plan. For instance, assuming that two days is your standard TTL, you might use a scheme such as the following:

72 hours (three days) before the change, reduce the TTL to one day (86400).

30 hours before the change, reduce the TTL to six hours (21600).

7 hours before the change, reduce the TTL to 30 minutes (1800).

45 minutes before the change, reduce the TTL to one minute (60).

After you make the change (and test it!), increase the TTL using the reverse of the sequence just given. That way you'll improve your ability to recover if you discover (even after your initial testing) that something's wrong.

> **TIP** Execute DNS changes by progressively reducing the TTL on the associated records. After making changes and testing them, increase the TTL progressively in order to reduce the impact of any uncaught errors.

How Many Nameservers?

"What's the optimum number of public nameservers, and where should they be located?" You'll hear many different answers to these questions. Theoretically, the correct answers are, "Just one, and anywhere, so long as it's always available and it's close to every visitor."

But because nameservers fail occasionally, like everything else, you need at least two of them. In fact, some registrars require that you specify at least two. In theory, you could have dozens of them, placed strategically at ISPs around the world, so that visitors in each country could resolve their DNS inquiries as quickly as possible, but that's rarely required.

Most successful web sites use between two and four nameservers. If your site isn't particularly performance-critical, two public nameservers should be sufficient. More important is that your two, three, or four nameservers be located on separate networks. One of them should be on the same network as each instance of your web site, so that in case of connectivity outages, a visitor who can reach one of your nameservers can also reach your web site, and vice versa. Visitors need to be able to reach both your web servers and your nameservers in order to see your web site.

TIP Use at least two public DNS nameservers. One of them should be operated by your web-hosting service or MSP, preferably on the same network as your web site. The other(s) should be on separate networks, and preferably operated by other business entities.

Registering Domain Names

As we explained earlier in this chapter, there are really two aspects to managing your domain. We've already covered the first: managing your nameservers. In this section we'll look at the second aspect: managing your domain name registration. We'll look at domain name registrars, the use of roles and email aliases, and the proper way to register your domain.

Your Own Domain

If you're the owner of a small web site, particularly one to be hosted on a shared server, you may be tempted by a low-cost offer from your web-hosting service to operate your site under the vendor's domain. In this case, your web site's *Uniform Resource Locator* (URL) would be something like this:

```
http://www.vendor.com/yourcompany
```

or

```
http://yourcompany.vendor.com
```

instead of the more typical:

```
http://www.yourcompany.com
```

Don't take the bait! You'll immediately become a victim of lock-in, as described in detail in Chapter 7, "The Dark Side of Outsourcing."

In the instance of http://www.yourcompany.com, your web address or URL is *portable*. As long as the domain was properly registered, you can move your site to another web-hosting service and take your address with you.

The first two instances, however, are *nonportable* URLs. If you want to move a web site with such URLs to another web-hosting service, you'll have to change your site's address, and if you want visitors to be *redirected* (automatically forwarded) to the new site, you'll have to continue to pay the old vendor for the service.

Realistically, if you find yourself in a situation in which you want to move your site, you'll most likely already be dissatisfied with your old vendor, and you may well discover that the vendor refuses to cooperate with your site relocation. Without your vendor's assistance, you can't create the redirection that will allow old visitors to find you. If this happens to you, there'll be no way to refer visitors from your old URL to the new one.

Ultimately, if your old vendor goes out of business, it'll be impossible to redirect visitors who try to reach you via the old address. Visitors will only receive an error message and assume your site has disappeared from the web.

> **TIP** Always register domain names yourself. *Never* create a web site under a domain controlled by someone else.

In the pages that follow, we'll explain how to properly register and manage your own domain name. It's easy to do and it costs only $35 per year per domain or less.

Registrars

A *registrar* is an organization that processes registrations and updates for domain names and other Internet-related records such as IP address netblocks, as seen in Chapter 20, "The Net Detective Toolkit." There used to be only one registrar, Network Solutions, Inc. (www.nsi.net), but now there are dozens. In fact there's a so-called registrar of registrars, named the Internet Corporation for Assigned Names and Numbers (ICANN). You can see ICANN's official list of accredited registrars at www.icann.org/registrars/accredited-list.html.

Not everyone posing as a registrar has honest intentions. Some are, in fact, domain pirates who steal domain names by offering to help you register and manage your domain, but retaining the right to modify your domain's registration at any time, including the right to sell it to someone else. Once a domain registration is stolen, it's extremely difficult to get it back.

> **TIP** Don't, under any circumstances, register or transfer a domain using an organization not on the ICANN-accredited list.

Whois Revisited

In Chapter 20, we used the whois utility to look up IP address (netblock) records in the Internet's databases. Let's use whois to show the registration record for rds.com, the site on which we've based our examples in this chapter.

The registration shown in Figure 21.9 is an example of a proper domain registration for a medium or large company, or, more specifically, one that's decided to delegate a subdomain in order to retain control of its second-level domain in house. We'll refer back to this example in the discussions to follow. Later in this section, we'll also look at a simplified registration for a small business.

```
Registrant:
RDS (RDS-DOM)
   11 Pimentel Court
   Novato, CA 94949


   Domain Name: RDS.COM

   Administrative Contact:
      RDS Hostmaster  (RH3757-ORG)  hostmaster@RDS.COM
      11 Pimentel Court
      Novato, CA 94949
      415-384-1400 (FAX) 415-384-1427

   Billing Contact:
      Accounts Payable  (AP1732-ORG)  accounting@RDS.COM
      RDS
      11 Pimentel Court
      Novato, CA 94949
      415-384-1476 (FAX) 415-384-1593

   Technical Contact:
      Network Operations  (NO412-ORG)  noc@RDS.COM
      RDS
      11 Pimentel Court
      Novato, CA 94949
      415-888-1722 (FAX) 415-384-1427

   Record last updated on 06-Dec-2000.
   Record expires on 30-Nov-2002.
   Record created on 29-Nov-1991.
   Database last updated on 24-May-2001 10:23:00 EDT.

   Domain servers in listed order:

   NS1.RDS.COM   198.81.209.2
   NS2.RDS.COM   167.160.23.2
```

Figure 21.9 Proper registration for a medium or large business.

When you register a domain name, you're actually creating information that's used in two ways. First, you're providing the addresses of your public nameservers to which you want the gTLD nameservers to refer requests when asked about your domain. For instance, when you ask one of the .com gTLD nameservers about rds.com, you'll be referred to the two RDS public nameservers:

```
NS1.RDS.COM   198.81.209.2
NS2.RDS.COM   167.160.23.2
```

The other reason you're creating a public database record is so that it can be used to get in touch with you or your organization regarding your domain. Reasons someone might want to reach you include:

- Spam—undesirable email—may be coming from a host within your domain.
- There may be a security attack originating from a host within your domain.
- Someone may want to purchase your domain name.

Contacts

As you can see in Figure 21.9 there may be as many as four different *contacts* associated with your domain registration: registrant, administrative, technical, and billing.

Registrant should always be your organization. This person or organization is the legal entity bound by the terms of the registrar's service agreement.

Administrative contact should be able to answer nontechnical questions about the domain's registration and the registrant. You'll probably want to keep this contact within your IT department, since a person who isn't familiar with domain names may be confused by some of the requests (and spam) that arrive at his or her email address. Many web-site owners assign the administrative contact to a *hostmaster* alias (see the next subsection—*Email Aliases*—in this chapter).

Technical contact is expected to be the person or organization that maintains the nameservers for the domain. Legitimate requests for this contact require that the recipient be able to answer technical questions about the nameservers and work with other technically oriented people to solve problems. This contact could be assigned to an alias such as "noc," or to the same "hostmaster" alias used for the administrative contact. In any case, you should include your vendors and anyone who can make DNS changes in the delivery list for this alias.

Billing contact is the person or department that should receive the invoices for domain name registration and renewal fees. We've used the alias *accounting* and the contact information for Accounts Payable for this contact in our example in Figure 21.9.

It's important to remember that although these four contacts sound very different from one another, in reality the distinctions are few. With some registrars, *any* named contact is allowed to make changes to the domain record. The only differences between the contacts are in how they're used by others to contact you. For instance, if there's a technical problem with your domain, someone will likely email the technical contact before contacting the accounts payable department. But when it comes to initiating any outbound actions (i.e., making domain-registration changes), any contact may do so.

TIP Investigate your registrar's policies regarding who's allowed to modify your domain name registration. Be aware that some registrars permit *any* named contact to make changes.

Email Aliases

You may have noticed in the example in Figure 21.9 that no *individuals* are specified. Instead, all of the contacts have been defined via email aliases such hostmaster@rds.com, accounting@rds.com, and noc@rds.com.

Email aliases (not to be confused with DNS CNAME aliases described earlier) should be used to prevent any communications regarding your domain from being tied to a particular individual. Consider what happens when someone leaves your organization or is on vacation and therefore doesn't receive an important email message or phone call. By using an alias, you can direct the email to more than one person, and thereby protect yourself from these problems.

It's important to use aliases no matter how small your organization may be. One reason is that since the domain registration databases are public, any email address associated with your domain registration will receive spam. If you use an alias, you can more easily filter messages sent to the alias using your email software.

TIP Always use email aliases for domain registration contacts.

Handles

To assign the same identity to multiple contacts, some registrars will allow you to use *handles*, shortcuts for a contact's name, address, phone and fax numbers, and so on. For instance, in Figure 21.9, the handle RH3757-ORG is a shortcut for RDS Hostmaster, and all of the other information specified for the administrative contact. You can reuse this identity by specifying only the handle instead of spelling out all of the contact information in detail.

Not only does using handles simplify the job of registering additional domains, it also means you can change the information for multiple contacts or multiple domains merely by editing the database record for the handle. For instance, if the RDS Hostmaster's phone number changes, it can be modified once, and all contacts that use the RH3757-ORG handle will be updated.

TIP Use handles to centralize the management of contact information.

Roles

The suffix -ORG on the RDS Hostmaster's handle, RH3757-ORG, identifies the contact as a *role*, not an individual. Some registrars support this distinction. For example, all of the contacts shown for the registration of rds.com in Figure 21.9 are roles, not individuals. The concept of a role is essentially the same as that of an email alias, except that the registrars don't allow you to attach multiple email addresses to roles within their systems. You still have to use an alias on your own email system to accomplish this.

There's no technical difference between roles and individual contacts. The only practical difference is that roles, by convention, make others more aware that they may be dealing with an alias, rather than an individual, although not too many people would confuse "accounting," for instance, with an individual.

There's one nasty aspect to roles that you need to watch out for. Many of the registrars don't explain that there may be both a role with the handle RH3757-ORG and an individual with the handle RH3757 (i.e., without the –ORG suffix). Many a webmaster has learned this the hard way, by creating a role handle, such as RH3757-ORG, then assigning *all* of his or her domain's contacts to RH3757. Once you make this mistake, it's too late. You'll have just given complete control of your domain to a stranger, and you'll no longer have the ability to change it back.

There are two ways to avoid making this mistake. First, be careful. Don't leave off the –ORG suffix if it's part of the handle. Second, change your contacts one at a time. For example, first change the administrative contact, but not the technical contact. That way, if you make a mistake and assign the administrative contact to the wrong person or role, you can still make modifications as the technical contact.

TIP Make domain name registration contact changes one at a time in order to preserve an escape route in case you make a mistake.

Authentication

Registrars offer a variety of methods for authenticating the people who are allowed to make changes to domain registrations. These include email authentication, password authentication, and the use of public/private keys, such as with *pretty good privacy* (PGP).

Email authentication is the most basic authentication scheme. The concept is that if you're able to receive messages sent to a particular email address, you're therefore assumed to be authorized to act on behalf of that addressee. Consider, for instance, the registration for rds.com in which hostmaster@rds.com is the email address for the domain's administrative contact. If someone fills out a form to change the registration of that domain, the registrar will send a verification message along with an authentication code to hostmaster@rds.com. In order to complete the transaction, the person receiving that verification message must return it to the registrar.

The problem with this method is that it's too weak. Unencrypted email is far too easy to intercept or spoof. Someone intent on stealing your domain would have little difficulty thwarting this type of authentication scheme.

Another problem with using email authentication is that if your web-hosting service, MSP, or CDN is named as one of the contacts or is added to one of your aliases, those vendors will receive authentication messages and hence have the power to modify your registration data.

Password authentication is the next most secure authentication scheme. Although far from perfect, it's substantially safer than simple email authentication.

PGP authentication is the most secure method of authenticating exchanges of information with a registrar. Using PGP, your transactions are digitally signed with a private key that, when combined with the associated public key, proves that the transaction author is authentic.

One advantage of both password and PGP authentication is that they allow you to separate authentication for the purpose of modifying your domain name registration from the identities of contacts. For example, if you decide to name your web-hosting service as the technical contact for your domain by not giving the password or PGP key for that contact to your vendor, you can prohibit your vendor from making changes while still allowing it to perform the technical contact function.

TIP Use password or PGP authentication to protect domain name registration transactions. Don't give your vendors the passwords or keys, and *never* depend on email authentication alone. Keep copies of your passwords or keys in a safe place. It's very difficult to make changes without them.

Your Web-Hosting Service

Most web-hosting services expect that they'll be identified as at least one of your domain registration contacts. They reason that since they're responsible for managing your DNS, they need to be named as, for instance, the technical contact.

Phooey! There's no need for them to be a named contact. In fact, it's a bad idea unless you're a small business that's chosen to outsource all of your Internet services, including email, to a single vendor. Even then, it's risky. Assuming you delegate subdomains, as discussed earlier in this chapter, you'll still be responsible for managing your second-level domain, so your organization should be the one that's contacted regarding any issues associated with your domain name.

It's important for third parties to be able to reach your vendors in case of a DNS problem within the delegated subdomain, but you can make that possible in a much less risky manner. For instance, you might take the following steps:

- Add your vendors to the distribution list for the technical contact email alias.
- Include the phone number of your vendors' network operations centers (NOCs) in the technical contact. Most DNS problems are resolved using email alone, but this will make sure your vendors can be reached in case email is down.

This way, your vendors will receive all urgent communications regarding DNS issues, and they can change DNS records as necessary. But they won't be involved in the process of managing your domain name registration. Keep that separate.

TIP Add your web-hosting service, MSP, and CDN to the email alias for your domain registration technical contact. You also may want to list their NOC phone numbers. But don't list them by name or give them passwords or keys that would allow them to change the registration.

Small Businesses

If yours is a small business, there's no need to have separate administration, billing, and technical contacts. In this case, simply assign the same handle to each of them. As opposed to the recommendations just given for larger businesses, if you've outsourced *all* of your Internet services including web hosting and email to a single vendor, you may, in fact, want to name your vendor as the technical contact. Be careful, however. Don't do this unless you first verify with your registrar that you can do so without also giving your vendor the right to make changes.

```
Registrant:
RDS (RDS-DOM)
   11 Pimentel Court
   Novato, CA 94949


   Domain Name: RDS.COM

   Administrative Contact, Billing Contact:
      RDS Hostmaster  (RH3757-ORG)  hostmaster@RDS.COM
      11 Pimentel Court
      Novato, CA 94949
      415-384-1400 (FAX) 415-384-1427

   Technical Contact:
      Really Good Internet Services
      123 Broadway
      Perfectville, CA 99999
      415-555-1212 (FAX) 415-555-1212

   Record last updated on 06-Dec-2000.
   Record expires on 30-Nov-2002.
   Record created on 29-Nov-1991.
   Database last updated on 24-May-2001 10:23:00 EDT.

   Domain servers in listed order:

   NS1.REALLY-GOOD-VENDOR.COM   195.102.216.1
   NS2.REALLY-GOOD-VENDOR.COM   161.119.204.76
```

Figure 21.10 Proper registration record for a small business.

Your registration will then look something like that shown in Figure 21.10 when reported by whois.

Using the concepts presented in this chapter, you should now be able to avoid some of the most common problems related to DNS and domain names. By properly registering your domain, and by delegating control of only subdomains to your vendors—rather than giving them complete control over your entire domain—you can create a buffer to insulate your site and your business from the DNS-related mistakes of your vendors and from malicious or unintentional domain registration problems.

APPENDIX

Resources

In this appendix I've pulled together a list of the most valuable on- and offline resources. The list is loosely organized according to the Table of Contents.

Because things are still very volatile in the web-hosting universe, we're also maintaining an updated resources list on the web site that accompanies this book, at www.wiley.com/compbooks/kaye and at my personal web site at *www.rds.com.* At these locations you'll also find downloadable copies of the Excel spreadsheets in Chapter 11, "Traffic Models," and a complete cross-referenced list of all of the tips presented throughout the book.

Strategies

Beware that many of the online directories of web-hosting services derive revenues from vendor fees. At the very least, most accept advertising. It's probably best to ignore any of their online ratings of web-hosting services, but many such directories have good articles and other tips.

If you have a brokerage account with a company that has an investment banking arm, ask your broker if the company publishes an analysis of this industry. Or, if you can afford it, consider purchasing a report from one of the major consultancies. They're not inexpensive.

And remember: Always check the financials of any prospective vendor.

Host Help (www.hosthelp.com/) hosted by FutureQuest, contains some good articles, particularly regarding shared- and dedicated-hosting services. Topics include the value of online host directories, resellers, and uptime guarantees. It's a bit out of date, but still valuable.

HostCompare.com (www.hostcompare.com/) is an advertising-sponsored site that compares web-hosting vendors. It also contains links to other comparisons and online articles.

Web Hosting Magazine (www.whmag.com) is published monthly by Infotonic. Intended as a magazine " . . . for Web Hosting Executives," it's of interest to anyone who wants to track the comings and goings, particularly in the middle and low end of the web-hosting market.

Gartner Group (www.gartner.com), a consulting and research firm, is very active in the analysis of web hosting and other areas of Internet infrastructure. In Chapter 9, "Risk Management," we quoted data and conclusions from *Making Smart Investments to Reduce Unplanned Downtime* (D. Scott, Gartner Group, 1999). Another Gartner publication, *Best Practices for Internet-based Business: Storage and Hosting Strategies* (Gartner Group, February 29, 2000), provided background material for our discussion of NAS and SAN technologies in Chapter 15, "Storage."

ActiveMedia Research (www.activmediaresearch.com) is another consulting and research company. In Chapter 1, "Web-Hosting Options," we used data from its report, *Real Numbers behind Web Hosting & Development 2000* (August 2000).

Tier 1 Research (www.tier1research.com), another consulting and research company, emphasizes hosting, storage, and CDNs. Its publications range from daily reports to geographically focused *Web Hosting Bibles*.

Robertson Stephens (www.robertsonstephens.com/), an investment banking firm, published an excellent analysis of many aspects of Internet infrastructure in *Virtual Bricks II: Virtual Econ 101 Update, A Comprehensive Guide for Understanding eCommerce Infrastructure Evolution and Convergence—CSPs, ASPs, IUPs and IPPs* (Richard A. Juarez et al., Robertson Stephens, May 2000). We used some of its data in Chapter 9, "Risk Management." Hopefully, the firm will follow up this with similar reports in the future.

Merrill Lynch (www.ml.com/), a financial services company, analyzes Internet infrastructure for its investment clients. We referred to *Internet Infrastructure 2000—IIS Launch: Survival of the Fittest* (Thomas W. Watts et al., Merrill Lynch Global Securities Research & Economics, July 25, 2000) for background material on CDNs in Chapter 13, "Caching and Content Delivery Networks."

ASP Research Center (www.cio.com/forums/asp/) hosted by *CIO Magazine*, is obviously focused on application service providers, but it includes valuable information on outsourcing in general.

The ASP Industry Consortium (www.aspindustry.com/) is an organization of application service providers. With that prejudice in mind, it's a good source for information about outsourcing and SLAs. One document, *Service Level Agreements* (Application Service Provider Industry Consortium, 2000), is an excellent introduction to the vendor's perspective on SLAs, and we used it as background material for Chapter 10, "Service Level Agreements."

FreeEdgar (www.freeedgar.com/) is a valuable resource for researching published financial data from publicly traded companies. Portals, such as Yahoo! (www.yahoo.com), and financial institutions, such as eTrade (www.etrade.com), provide additional data such as analysts reports.

The Art of War, by Sun Tzu, an ancient Chinese warrior/philosopher, is often quoted in business seminars and inspirational articles and books. One of the best translations (Lionel Giles, M.A., 1910) is available free online, at ftp://sailor.gutenberg.org/pub/gutenberg/etext94/suntx10.txt.

Architecture

There aren't too many resources that address web-site architecture, but these are helpful. The two Sun/Solaris books are excellent for that environment. Netcraft is a helpful site. And the RAID paper is just good reading.

RAID, first described in *A Case for Redundant Arrays of Inexpensive Disks (RAID),* available online at http://sunsite.berkeley.edu/Dienst/UI/2.0/Describe/ncstrl.ucb/CSD-87-391. Not only is RAID itself important to the web-hosting industry, but this 26-page paper, written in 1987, is a good example of pragmatic thinking about redundancy and cost.

Web Server Survey (www.netcraft.com/survey/), hosted by Netcraft, shows market share for Apache, IIS (Microsoft), iPlanet (Netscape), NCSA, and other web-server software.

Two books, although specific to the Solaris (Unix-derivative) operating system, will help anyone who wants to understand the quantitative aspects of server performance:

- *Sun Performance and Tuning: Java and the Internet,* second edition, by Adrian Cockroft and Richard Petit (Palo Alto, CA: Sun Microsystems Press, 1998).

- *Configuration and Capacity Planning for Solaris Servers,* by Brian L. Wong (Upper Saddle River, NJ: Prentice Hall PTR/Sun Microsystems Press, 1997).

Caching and CDNs

There are no good books on this topic. It's too new and things are changing too quickly, so the web sites listed below are the best source of information. Also check my web site at *www.rds.com* for updates to this list.

Web Caching (www.web-caching.com/), managed by Brian Davison, is a good centralized resource for information regarding caching and CDNs.

Caching.com (www.caching.com/), operated by Jupiter Media Metrix, contains CDN and caching news, white papers, and case studies.

Stardust.com (*www.stardust.com/*) publishes news and information about the CDN industry. They also produce tradeshows and "Stardust TalkRadio" in downloadable MP3 format.

Squid (www.squid-cache.org), is free caching software distributed under the GNU public license. The Squid FAQ (www.squid-cache.org/Doc/FAQ/FAQ.html) provides a good technical background on Internet caching.

Intel offers a number of free online courses, including one on caching (www.intel.com/training/olc/course/description/cache.htm). The course emphasizes Intel's own caching products, but it's still good for background information.

CacheFlow, a hardware cache vendor, hosts an online *cacheability tester* at www.cacheflow.com/technology/tools/friendly/cacheability/tool/index.cfm. If you enter a URL, this utility will analyze how the page is likely to be treated by the various Internet caches.

Content Alliance (www.contentalliance.org/) is one of two industry groups supporting initiatives for content peering, as discussed in Chapter 13, "Caching and Content Delivery Networks." This group was created by Cisco in August 2000.

Content Bridge (www.content-bridge.com/) is the other content peering industry group.

Edge Side Includes (www.edge-delivery.org/) is another industry-sponsored group promoting delivery of dynamic content from CDN edge servers. You can find the specifications for ESI on its web site.

Cisco (www.cisco.com) has published a number of excellent white papers. In some cases the most informative documents appear in support of particular products. One good tutorial on CDN technologies, *Cisco Distributed Director* (White Paper) by Kevin Delgadillo, 1999, can be found at www.cisco.com/warp/public/cc/pd/cxsr/dd/tech/dd_wp.htm. Vendor-specific, of course.

AOL (www.aol.com) has posted important information for webmasters who are developing a web site aimed at consumers, and hence AOL customers, at http://webmaster.info.aol.com. Particularly interesting is an article at webmaster.info.aol.com/index.cfm?article=12&expand=0&sitenum=2 all about AOL's access-side caching.

Connectivity

The first five resources below are online reports of the state of the Internet. You probably need to use them all in order to develop a reasonable picture of what's going on, particularly if you're trying to evaluate a specific vendor. The two books listed are the classics of computer networking.

Internet Ratings (www.matrix.net/research/ratings/), published by Matrix.net, compares the accessibility of rated ISPs and web-hosting services in terms of median latency, packet loss, and reachability for 24-hour, 7-day, and 28-day periods. We referred to this analysis in Chapter 18, "Connectivity Performance."

Internet Average (average.miq.net/index.html) is another report published by Matrix.net. This one shows graphs of rolling 24-hour, 7-day, and 28-day averages of overall Internet reachability, latency, and packet loss.

Internet Weather Report (www.matrix.net/research/weather/), a third report published by Matrix.net, includes geographical maps that show latency within the Internet. Its analogous to daily newspaper or television weather radar reports, except that it's about conditions within the Internet itself.

Internet Traffic Report (www.internettrafficreport.com/), published by Opnix (www.opnix.com/), monitors the flow of data worldwide every 15 minutes, and displays the results broken down by continent.

Internet Health Report (www.internethealthreport.com/), hosted by Keynote, shows the network performance (latency) between major United States Internet backbones.

UUNET/WorldCom (www.uu.net) has posted a document (www.uu.net/peering/) that describes its peering policies. It's a fascinating insight into the politics of peering between the major backbone ISPs.

Two excellent (but expensive) books on networking are:

Computer Networks and Internets, with Internet Applications, third edition, by Douglas E. Comer and Ralph E. Droms. (Upper Saddle River, NJ: Prentice Hall, 2001).

Computer Networks, second edition, by Andrew S. Tanenbaum (Upper Saddle River, NJ: Prentice Hall, 1996).

Security

The first two items are online services that report known security problems. Make certain you (or someone) monitor at least one of them regularly. Next, I've listed two specific software packages that are particularly helpful in maintaining secure systems.

There are probably more books on computer security than on any other topic I've discussed. Go to Amazon.com (*www.amazon.com*) or Barnes and Noble (*www.barnesandnoble.com*) and read the online reviews of the five books i've listed. Use those reviews to help you decide which are best for your needs and interests.

BugTraq, operated by SecurityFocus.com (www.securityfocus.com), is a full-disclosure moderated mailing list for the detailed discussion and announcement of computer security vulnerabilities. Someone responsible for your web site's security should subscribe to this list.

CERT (www.cert.org/), located at the Software Engineering Institute, is a federally funded research and development center operated by Carnegie Mellon University. The web site is an excellent source of security-related information.

Sudo (*superuser do*) is free Unix-only software maintained by Todd Miller (www.courtesan.com/sudo/) that allows a system administrator to give certain users (or groups of users) the ability to run some or all commands as root or another user while logging the commands and arguments.

AIDE (Advanced Intrusion Detection Environment), developed by Rami Lehti and Pablo Virolainen in Finland, monitors all file changes, verifies the integrity of data on network servers, and notifies you of any violations. It also identifies changes to other system attributes including file size and access permissions. AIDE is available from (www.cs.tut.fi/~rammer/aide.html). It's a Unix-only utility that's a free replacement for Tripwire (www.tripwire.com/), available for Windows as a commercial product.

Some of the better books on Internet security include the following:

Hack-Proofing Your Ecommerce Site, by Brent L. Huston (ed.), Ryan Russell, Teri Bidwell, Oliver Steudler, and Robin Walshaw (Rockland, MA: Syngress Media, 2001).

Web Security & Commerce, by Simson Garfinkel and Gene Spafford (Sebastopol, CA: O'Reilly & Associates, 1997).

Practical Unix and Internet Security, by Simson Garfinkel and Gene Spafford (Sebastopol, CA: O'Reilly & Associates, 1996).

Hacking Exposed, by Joel Scambray, Stuart McClure, and George Kurtz (New York: McGraw-Hill Professional Publishing, 2000).

Secrets and Lies: Digital Security in a Networked World, by Bruce Schneier (New York: John Wiley & Sons, Inc., 2000).

Monitoring

There are many free internal monitoring packages including MRTG and Big Brother, described below. If you want to buy a commercially supported package, at least use these two as a basis for comparison.

Keynote is the granddaddy of external monitoring on the web. The other services listed (or one of many others you may find) often do 80 percent of what Keynote does, but perhaps at 20 percent of the cost.

MRTG, the Multi-Router Traffic Grapher, was developed by Tobias Oetiker in Switzerland, and Dave Rand of AboveNet, in the United States. MRTG is free software that graphs any numeric values it can obtain using the Simple Network Management Protocol (SNMP) or other methods. The software is free and can be downloaded from http://people.ee.ethz.ch/~oetiker/webtools/mrtg/. Versions are available for Windows and Unix derivatives. Some of the graphs shown in Chapter 18, "Connectivity Performance," were generated using MRTG.

Big Brother (http://bb4.com/) is a free internal monitoring package that supports Windows NT/2000 and most of the Unix derivatives. We used Big Brother as our examples of internal monitoring and trend reporting in Chapter 19, "Monitoring."

Keynote Systems (www.keynote.com/) is a commercial external monitoring service that we used for many of the examples in Chapter 18, "Connectivity Performance," Chapter 19, "Monitoring," and Chapter 20, "The Net Detective Toolkit." Keynote's web site includes some good white papers on web-site performance and measurement at www.keynote.com/services/html/product_lib.html.

Alertsite (www.alertsite.com/) also offers an external site-monitoring service—one of many lower-cost alternatives to Keynote.

NetMechanic (www.netmechanic.com/) hosts a number of tools targeted at shared- and dedicated-server customers, including Server Check Pro, another low-cost site-monitoring service.

Appliant (www.appliant.com/) offers a combination of internal and external monitoring services. We used their external monitoring as an example in Chapter 19, "Monitoring."

Probester (www.solidspeed.com/) is an external monitoring service we looked at in Chapter 19, "Monitoring." Probester is one of a new breed of monitoring services that uses peer-to-peer (P2P) technology in order to measure performance from the desktops of a large number of web-site visitors.

Backup and Recovery

There's very little written specifically about backup and recovery. The Veritas papers are a good start. As with the free monitoring packages mentioned above, CVS is the standard by which you should judge any commercial version control system.

CVS (http://cvshome.org/), the Concurrent Versions System, is an open-source version control system for most flavors of Windows and Unix.

Veritas (www.veritas.com/) is a commercial vendor that supplies software for server cluster management and backup and recovery. Its white papers (www. veritas.com/us/products/whitepapers.html) are helpful for understanding some of the issues associated with backup and recovery, particularly of databases.

DNS and Domain Names

Everyone needs help with DNS, no matter how experienced they are. The Ask Mr. DNS web site and the *DNS and Bind* book go hand-in-hand. The references for ICANN, ARIN, RIPE, and APNIC are here for your convenience.

Ask Mr. DNS (www.acmebw.com/askmrdns/) is an archive of great information about DNS and BIND. Although its creators (Cricket Liu, Matt Larson, and Michael Milligan) are no longer enhancing the site (their company was bought by Network Solutions in June 2000), the archives continue to be valuable.

ICANN (www.icann.org) is the Internet Corporation for Assigned Names and Numbers. The nonprofit corporation was formed to assume responsibility for the IP address space allocation, protocol parameter assignment, domain name system management, and root server system management functions previously performed under U.S. Government contract by IANA and other entities. As recommended in Chapter 21, "Domain Names and DNS," *never* use a domain name registrar that isn't among those on the ICANN-accredited list at www.icann.org/registrars/accredited-list.html.

ARIN (www.arin.net/), the American Registry for Internet Numbers, is a nonprofit organization established for the purpose of administration and registration of Internet Protocol (IP) numbers for the following geographical areas: North America, South America, the Caribbean and sub-Saharan Africa.

RIPE NCC (www.ripe.net/) is the equivalent of ARIN for Europe, the Middle East, and parts of Africa.

APNIC (www.apnic.net) is another equivalent of ARIN, for Asia and the Pacific.

The standard text on DNS is:

DNS and BIND, 4th edition, by Paul Albitz and Cricket Liu. (Sebastopol, CA O'Reilly & Associates, 2001).

Tools

Finally, here are those resources that don't fall neatly into one of the earlier categories. It's an eclectic collection, but all quite valuable.

SamSpade.org (www.samspade.org), developed by Steve Atkins, is a portal to many of the other tools described in Chapter 20, "The Net Detective Toolkit," and listed here, as well as some unique ones. From the web site you can also download a copy of Steve's free Sam Spade utility that performs similar functions on Windows-based systems.

Netcraft (www.netcraft.com/) was used throughout Chapter 20, "The Net Detective Toolkit," as an excellent way to research an existing web site or web-hosting service.

Dr. Watson (http://watson.addy.com/), hosted by Addy & Associates, is a free service to analyze web pages, including features that verify links, generate word counts, spell-check non-HTML text, compute estimated download speeds, check search engine compatibility, and analyze HTML syntax.

traceroute.org (www.traceroute.org/), maintained by Thomas Kernen, is a list of international reverse traceroute and Looking Glass servers that can be used to track down various routing and performance problems.

Geektools (www.geektools.com/), hosted by CenterGate Research Group, provides gateways to traceroute and whois, and a searchable index to the RFCs. We used this site in some examples in Chapter 20, "The Net Detective Toolkit."

IP-Plus Internet Services (www.ip-plus.ch/tools/tools-en.html), also shown in some examples in Chapter 20, "The Net Detective Toolkit," provides gateways to dig, traceroute, and whois.

Stokeley Consulting runs an excellent site with Unix System Administrator's Resources (www.stokely.com/unix.sysadm.resources/). With topics ranging from firewalls to "Coffee and Caffeine," there's something here for everyone, even those running Windows 2000/NT.

Index